DREAM WORKS
Lovers and Families in Shakespeare's Plays

In a remarkable new reading of Shakespeare's plays, Kay Stockholder explores the dynamic between conscious goals and unconscious purposes. She begins with the premiss that the choices made by any artist, from the selection of a genre to the smallest detail of image and linguistic texture, are guided by the emotional associations that produce our dreams.

From this point of departure, Stockholder proceeds to the assumption that the protagonist is the dreamer of the work in which he or she appears, analogous to the figure we identify as ourselves in our own dreams when we awaken, who has unconsciously constructed the work that must be consciously confronted. This assumption allows an exploration of the interactions between the protagonist's expressed desires and unconscious impulses and ideas that create the configuration of figures and circumstances that impede their fulfilment.

Stockholder carefully traces the complex connections as plot and character become passionate images, as attributes that composed one character come apart and recombine to compose other figures, as configurations that formed the background of one play become the foreground of another and then retreat again to the shadows, and as action and character dissolve into images in the kaleidoscopically shifting configurations that compose the dreamscapes of the plays.

In the process of tracing the various ways in which the protagonists experience conflicts in their roles as lovers and as family members, Stockholder reveals a larger dynamic at work in the shaping of the Shakespearean canon, and suggests that Shakespeare's dramatic trajectory was shaped by an escalating tension between a transcendent ideal of love and a sense of dark passions at its core. Finally, one sees in this increasingly vicious cycle the emotional concomitants of the contending ideas and values in the particular historical milieu that produced Shakespeare and out of which he shaped his plays.

KAY STOCKHOLDER is associate professor of English, University of British Columbia.

KAY STOCKHOLDER

Dream Works:
Lovers and Families in
Shakespeare's Plays

UNIVERSITY OF TORONTO PRESS
Toronto Buffalo London

© University of Toronto Press 1987
Toronto Buffalo London
Printed in Canada
ISBN 0–8020–5743–8

Printed on acid-free paper

Canadian Cataloguing in Publication Data

Stockholder, Kay, 1928-
Dream works

Includes bibliographical references and index.
ISBN 0-8020-5743-8

1. Shakespeare, William, 1564-1616 — Criticism and
interpretation.
2. Love in literature.   3. Family in literature. I. Title.

PR3069.L6S76   1987   822.3'3   C87-093732-4

This book has been published with the help of a grant from the Canadian
Federation for the Humanities, using funds provided by the Social Sciences
and Humanities Research Council of Canada.

TO ROLF LOEHRICH

Contents

Preface

The argument of this book rests on a theory of the relation between dreaming and literature that permits one to assume that the protagonist of a literary work is analogous to the figures that we identify as ourselves when we awaken from dreaming. To approach literature in this way places it at the borderline between our dreaming and waking worlds. Literature shares with our dream experience the sense of total meaningfulness, rendered through its formal aspects as a feeling of aesthetic inevitability. At the same time, literary works include within a seemingly inevitable, and therefore meaningful, pattern of action, representations of and thought about external and historical circumstances of life. This book argues that artists, in the process of selecting from a range of options the means to carry out their conscious intentions, express as well unconscious projects that may or may not be at cross-purposes with their espoused intellectual and aesthetic goals. Whether he or she intends to propound a moral, communicate a philosophy of life or a conception of reality, write a work of a certain genre, or merely entertain, the selection from the options made available by the contemporary culture and institutions will be guided by the emotional associations that produce our dreams. These associations help to structure the largest components of a literary work, such as the genre, conventional motifs, and kinds of characters, as well as the smallest details of image and linguistic texture. In this way all components of a work, from the grand structures of thought and plot to the finest detail of rhetorical nuance, can be read as a grid of associations. Character and plot become images writ large, and each component of this grid, and its relative prominence, acquires meaning in terms of the others. The richness and formal structures then become available for psychoanalytic interpretation in a way that does not disregard its intellectual components nor reduce a complex literary form either to an author's symptoms or to a character's case history. The use of dream theory as a mode of literary interpretation links the nature of the creative process to rigorous and particular strategies of literary commentary. The story that emerges from close readings of individual plays in relation to one another in the light of this theory makes manifest the ways in which the most private human passions and struggles depicted in Shakespeare's figures are shaped by and expressed in the most public conventions and ideological conflicts.

I owe thanks to many people for their help in various direct and indirect ways during the time of writing this book. I am grateful to my friends and colleagues Ed Hundert and Roger Seamon for their sustaining friendship, their intellectual engagement with me, and for reading and criticizing various manuscript drafts of this book. I am grateful also to Ellen Tallman, whose knowledge as a therapist entered into our conversations through which I was able to enrich and deepen my understanding of the relations between dream theory and life experience. I am also indebted to Norman Epstein for his help in proofreading the manuscript, his suggestions, and his eminently sensible advice and steady spirit throughout the time this work was in preparation. My thanks are also due to my children, Jessica, Maia, and Peter, for being encouraging, understanding, and companionable. I owe thanks as well to the SSHRC leave grant that facilitated the writing of this book, to the English Department of the University of British Columbia for the facilities necessary for completing this project, to the Canadian Federation for the Humanities for their grant in aid of publication, and to the *Dalhousie Review* for permission to reprint the portion of the introductory chapter that appeared as an article entitled 'Worlds in Dream and Drama: A Theory of Literary Representation.' Finally I wish to thank Doreen Todhunter, secretary and specialist in word processing for the English Department of the University of British Columbia, whose care and precision in assisting with the preparation of the manuscript were invaluable.

DREAM WORKS

1

Introduction:
Dreaming Protagonists
and Problematic Love

A young man and woman chastely regard each other before their nuptials, after which they will return to Naples. Morally untainted and spiritually enlightened, this royal couple will form the centre of a perfect commonwealth, and will generate children like themselves. The laws and institutions emanating from their perfect love will reflect their moral rectitude so that all subjects, free of moral conflict, will have the option of lovingly embracing their duty. No person will have to choose painfully between two evils, or two opposing goods, for opposites will be reconciled within their orbit of perfect love and perfect authority.

However, these figures – Ferdinand and Miranda from Shakespeare's *The Tempest* – in their spiritualized loving are difficult to distinguish as individuals; their lineaments blur into the surrounding brightness. In other of Shakespeare's plays more realistically portrayed men and women, either at or close to the centre of power, are embroiled in mutual betrayal, suspicion, jealousy, hatred, and ruthless ambition. In turn, those corrupted family relations corrupt the commonwealth, eliminating a correct moral possibility and thereby muddying the mind and spirit of every subject. These figures, Macbeth and Lady Macbeth, Claudius, Edmund, Goneril, and Regan, and those figures who, though not themselves immersed in hate and violence, must negotiate through a foggy and tormented world, are so clearly individuated and carry such convincing depth that their names have entered our emotional lexicon.

The great divide between pure lovers and harmonious families of radiant symbolic significance and realistically depicted evil or greatly erring figures who comprise seemingly probable worlds obscures the relationship between them. Within the radical opposition between the late romances and the tragedies are multiple analogies, both in plot structures and in character types, though configurations that form the background in some plays emerge in others as the foreground. Figures that in the tragedies are fleshed out are reduced to line drawings in the romances, and the problematic situations that bring tragic protagonists to their demise are analogous to those in the comedies and romances from which the protagonists emerge into restored families. These deep analogies between plays of different periods and genres make it possible to see in the emotional, rather than circumstantial, conflicts articulated by the tragic characters, the implied significance of similar situations in the conventionalized plays that precede them and of the flattened characters and improbable worlds of the ideological plays that follow. The different formal devices that define different genre structures themselves signify different attitudes toward and strategies of dealing with the conflicts within the family and between lovers that form the framework of the plays. The bleak and the radiant visions of love and family form two sides of a single coin, each of which becomes significant in the light of the other.

From *The Comedy of Errors* to *The Tempest* different prominence is given to similar conflicts in love relations, to conflicts between young lovers and their elders and to those between fathers and their sons and daughters. These conflicts that in some plays are expressed in circumstance or among several figures become internalized in other plays to form the interior landscape of a single figure. The problematic nature of these pervasive variations on familial concerns and motifs comes into view in relation to the parts played by and the portrayals of women. Women are sometimes active and sometimes passive, but they are most often daughters; they are rarely wives, except in an image of the future that extends beyond their epilogues, and they are almost never both wives and mothers. Hamlet has a mother and a dead father, and Lady Macbeth and Macbeth, from whose marital intimacy radiate the widening circles of bloody crimes, constitute Shakespeare's closest approach to dramatizing a mature, married and childbearing, though significantly childless, couple. They have verisimilitude, as do Antony and Cleopatra, who are mature lovers, have children, but dramatically are not parents. Though their relationship declines into the Nile's ooze rather than closing into a family structure, they constitute Shakespeare's nearest approach to dramatically realized mature sexual lovers. Deprived of a wife, Lear makes his daughters his mothers, and Cymbeline, whose abuse of regal authority is, like Lear's, represented by his rejection of his virtuous daughter, has a wicked wife whose actions resemble those of Lear's two daughters. These fragmented families coalesce at the cost of psychological naturalism. Shakespeare achieves a vision of restoration only in the improbable worlds of the romances, where Posthumus has a vision of reconciliation with his brothers and both his deceased parents as a precondition to winning Imogen, Leontes regains his wife simultaneously with his daughter's marriage, and Prospero, who remains uncoupled, devotes his fully magical powers to ensure that the fairy-tale figures of Miranda and Ferdinand will become parents so that they can generate a line of ideal rulers who will, like their parents, preside over perfect polities.

The love and family relationships that structure almost all of Shakespeare's plays are often taken as conventional or peripheral devices in the service of other concerns. In the early comedies they are often ignored as merely conventional background to satiric, moral, or philosophic issues. In the problem plays and tragedies they are obscured by their protagonists' existential or political fates, and in the romances the family structures are often taken as metaphorical expressions of spiritual transcendence. However, the persistence of love and familial motifs suggests that more abstract concerns should not be seen apart from the frameworks in which they are articulated. Rather, as these frameworks become permeated with and representative of issues of commonwealth and cosmos, they enable a perception of the ways in which the conceptual systems draw their emotional power from the more immediate personal realm, and the way in which this augmentation of abstractions intensifies the import of the personal concerns that have been thus metaphorically extended.

The many generic variations of persistent themes and motifs that are extended into political and metaphysical significance suggest not only that relations between men and women were problematic to Shakespeare, but that these problems were centrally determining of the trajectory of his artistic enterprise. They suggest that Shakespeare, consciously or unconsciously, wrestled with the conflict between his sense of the necessity for romantic love integrated into a harmonious family to transform a world contaminated by hatred and violence, and his sense of the depth and intransigence of the dark forces embedded in the family. Once such a polarity has been generated, the struggle to resolve it, whether by denying or castigating the perceived reality, only deepens the conflict, for the evil perceived in the surrounding world becomes darker in contrast to the vision of what might and ought to be, and the ideology becomes more pressing, more seemingly crucial, in view of the perceived evil in human affairs. That Shakespeare was caught in such an escalating or intensifying cycle that conditioned his choice and handling of dramatic material is suggested by the movement of motifs and structural forms through different genres and modes throughout his writing career, the study of which constitutes one aspect of this work.[1]

The second concern of this book is to address these problems with a method of literary interpretation based on dream theory, which assumes the protagonist to be the dreamer of the work in which he or she appears. This device, which the remainder of this chapter will justify and explain, brings into relationship with one another underlying psychological forms, the overt ideas of moral, political, or cosmological import that relate works to their historical contexts, and the formal characteristics of literature.

To speak as I have of Shakespeare's imaginative trajectory being conditioned by underlying problems suggests that the creative process in some way fuses the conscious artistry and ideas that compose a work of art with less conscious aspects of the mind that are related to the dreaming process. This relationship between literature and dream has been suggested in various forms from early times. Artists regularly speak of feeling taken over by and made instrumental to forces external to themselves. This experience has been variously accounted for: the ancients called upon the Muses, or the gods, Milton attributed his sense of possession to God, and the Romantics to a spirit of Nature that plays upon the poet's imagination as does the wind on a harp. Novelists often feel that characters develop lives and wills of their own. The source of this sense of an independent life within a work of literature, or of an external force directing an author within and through consciously held purposes has in the course of our culture descended from the heavens, to the romantic intermediate zone of Nature, and then to the depths of a collective, or individual psyche. Coleridge, in his concept of a primary imagination that penetrated beyond the depths of an individual psyche to a subterranean stratum of being that binds life together, came fairly close in his topography to a Jungian conception of an unconscious. A Freudian viewpoint derives that feeling of inspiration from an unconscious that, though general in its components, is personal in its dynamic organization. Comparable to a part of the body that is numb but vulnerable to injury, the unconscious stores emotions that derive from past experiences and condition our reactions towards, and the ways we go about shaping, our present experience.

Though Plato suspected that divine inspiration was akin to madness, and therefore wanted artists honourably escorted to the city gates, theories in which the muses or gods or God inspired the artist endow the artist with authority, and confirm the importance of art for human culture. When the source of inspiration descended, along with the gods, to trans-personal depths of the human psyche, the artist remained secure, for if he no longer told us truths of the heavens, he told us instead the deepest truths of our own nature, as uncontaminated by the artist's particularity as before. But Freud, in eliminating a cosmology from his psychology, implicitly challenged the status of art and the artist. The challenge lay in his defining art by analogy to dreams as the imaginary gratification of unconscious wishes that, along with the ravings of madmen and lovers, derive not from an exalted source either heav-

enly or mysteriously subterranean, but from those infantile longings demeaning to the dignity of any reading and writing adult.

The implication of Freud's conception is akin to that of Plato, for it logically
implies that art, along with spiritual or religious experience, is a means to
evade or soften 'an honourable struggle with fate.'[2] The denigration implied
by the link between dream and art has ever since haunted literary criticism
based on the psychoanalytic model. Though the application of the Freudian
model to literary characters has raised questions that have sharpened perceptions of the text and have provided new ranges of significance, even the most
subtle of such perceptions carried the uneasy sense that something wrong or
reductive was being done to the literary work, that account was not being
taken of its mimetic, moral, or formal values. When Freudian criticism used
literary works to construct psychobiographical accounts of authors, this new
context of signification also led to new questions that sharpened perceptions
of patterns and detail and, for some, heightened the sense of meaningfulness.
But this strategy could not provide a rationale for throwing the weight of
inquiry onto an author's psyche, which could be of interest only because of
the work it produced, nor, having linked the work to the particularity of the
author, could it dispel the implied diminishing analogy between a symptom
and a literary work. Though both forms of psychoanalytic criticism created a
deep sense of complexity and asked new questions that created new frames
of reference for the generation of significance, by de-emphasizing intentional
and formal aspects they turned literature into a kind of veil to be penetrated,
analogous to the manifest content of a dream, the latent content of which was
to be sought elsewhere. They located meaning in the hidden, unconscious
drives, well beyond the flux of time and history, which appeared only on the
disparaged manifest level.

Norman Holland attempted a more inclusive mode of Freudian criticism in
The Dynamics of Literary Response,[3] for in conceiving of meaning, form, and
structure as strategies that both express and conceal the core fantasy, he
included more literary components within the psychoanalytical critical orbit.
Though Holland did not necessarily demean literature by regarding its cognitive and formal aspects as defense, or by referring to infantile fantasy as
constituting its core, the language tended in that direction. In response, Frederick Crews proposed a model of biographic criticism that, by linking an
author's personal and social conflicts to the cognitive and formal aspects of
the literary work, both avoided reductionism and maintained the significance
of authorial intention that Holland had avoided in the term 'core fantasy.'[4]
But the question remained of whether the fantasy resided in the author, the
work, or the reader, and Holland, building on the work of Simon Lesser but

lacking the humanistic consensus upon which Lesser relied unawares, turned his attention to studies of audience response.[5] Holland's study of identity themes in literary responses de-emphasizes the study of literature and raises a conceptual difficulty, for one's reading of a response to literature must be as subject to one's own style of responding as is one's reading of literature, and so the theory implies an infinite regress. Though some enhanced appreciation both of the complexity of literature and of the value of others' mode of reading ensue from Holland's practice, if one consistently avoids judgment of the responses, based on correctness, inclusiveness, or complexity, then the project logically becomes one of mutual self-exploration. And if a standard of judgment is invoked, then the work, and all the theoretical problems of criticism, remain in place.

Holland's and others' work on subjectivist criticism coalesced with the impact of structuralism and post-structuralist thought on literary theory. Within that world-view intentions and purposes along with the clear distinction Freud wanted to maintain between rational and 'primary process' or wish-fulfilling thought, are illusions generated by and perpetuating arbitrarily linked signifiers and signifieds, and are forever disintegrating through the gap into the pestilential vapours of absence. Literature that arises from and supports the illusion of the subject, once valued for its mimesis and moral vision of real worlds, now is valued as illustrative of the ways in which the discourse systems that constitute what the nineteenth century called reality throw up illusions of purposive characters in action. For the Freudian critic such a vision leaves neither characters nor authors to analyse, for they, along with distinctions of genre or distinctions between fiction and other forms of narrative, have dissolved into intertexuality and linguistic systems.

The psychoanalytic literary criticism generated by this intellectual movement derives from Lacan's version of Freud. His conceptual system, by reversing Freud's conception of the relation between the individual and the world, brought into psychoanalytical thought awareness of social and cultural forces, the neglect of which had been problematic for Freudian literary criticism. Whereas Freud sees us deviously seeking to satisfy innate drives in a repressive environment, Lacan sees those drives themselves created and shaped through that cultural nexus. The unobtainable immediate realm or register of the Real by definition forever eludes articulation, but creates at a remove the Imaginary and Symbolic orders that it permeates and by which it is in turn shaped. Our drives then, in any form they are knowable, and the social forms that produce them, become symbols, or signifiers of each other, rather than being symbolized in those social forms. The ego becomes a social, that is, a linguistic creation, or an illusion of unity forged (from an illusive Real) by the fluid social and cultural nexus constituted in language.

Lacan's conception of the self created within this flux creates a continuum rather than an opposition between conscious and unconscious levels of the mind, for the unconscious, 'structured like a language,' is constituted within signifiers that have been 'barred,' or excised from knowledge, but like the conscious is composed of the ideas, values, and conceptions of which the social framework is composed. The conscious sense of self and the unconscious are equally constructs, access to the latter revealing the architecture of the former. For Lacan, dreams do not so much fulfil a wish as speak it, revealing the structure of desire. Within his system it is difficult to say who is dreaming, since the self is constituted within the symbolic order, and dreams would presumably express a level of being that is prior to the formation of a self.

By using literature as illustrative of his theories, Lacan implies a mimetic conception, wherein literature presents the process by which the self tries to complete itself within and through the images of others that it generates. In the process he brings into play some aspects of the structural disposition of characters, relates the givens of the work to the central enterprise, and makes subtle uses of figurative language. In attempting to discern the gaps between the level of discontinuous images (roughly, the Imaginary) and the mimetic content (roughly, the Symbolic), the Lacanian approach softens the distinction between the manifest and latent content of literature by shifting the weight of emphasis from analysis of a figure to analysis of a text that is implicitly treated as mimetic of the ways in which consciousness and ego identity both constitute and are produced by the discourses that are the world.[6] This strategy avoids the reductionism implicit in a Freudian conception of literature as dream structures, the egocentricity of which has been disguised by elaboration in conformity to rational, aesthetic, and social norms, but it does so by devaluing those norms at all levels.

If Lacan absorbs what we normally call the rational into the irrational unconscious, the opposite route has been taken by Anglo-American work on dreams, primary process thought, and the relation of both to literature. Anton Ehrenzweig, drawing on the work of Object Relation theorists, describes the creative process as a means by which emotional levels that threaten the established structures of consciousness can be integrated into them in a way that produces higher, more complex, and richer cognitive structures. Art, therefore, by encouraging a fusion with the aesthetic object, allows the audience to enrich and revivify the adult and differentiated self with the emotional gain of that fusion.[7] Arthur F. Marotti extends Ehrenzweig's conception, based principally on visual art and music, to literature, arguing that formal properties of art derive from the ways the artist's 'personal identity and private vision' shape his perception of external and cultural reality.[8]

The conception of the unconscious as consisting of different layers of cognitive and emotional structures, rather than as an undifferentiated chaos underlying the structures of society, informs recent work on dreams, which attempt to integrate Freudian dream theory with that generated by cognitive psychology and by sleep research.[9] These studies soften Freud's radical separation of latent from manifest content by looking at dream structures as manifestations of the ways in which the dreamer organizes his or her waking experience. They de-emphasize Freud's conception of dreams as compromise fulfilments of infantile wishes in favor of an integrative model in which dreams are seen to reconcile present or ongoing experience or challenges to previous perceptual and emotional patterns of response. This account of dreaming, in emphasizing the manifest content of dreams, also places conscious, or present, and unconscious, or past, experience on a continuum rather than in opposition to each other.[10] This way of thinking about dreams, which tends to omit discussion of affect in favor of structures, and Freud's are not mutually exclusive. Joseph Sitterson draws on George Klein's conception that the order and form of infantile pleasure inform dreams, fantasy and art to argue that 'as long as "wish" is not defined reductively, then "wish-satisfying" and "meaning-generating" are not mutually exclusive.'[11] When they are conflated, one can think of dreaming as a process by which we forge the story, or narrative, of ourselves, making new and present challenges consistent with our sense of identity and our modes of pleasure, structured from the past, so that we can continue to wrest from the sometimes recalcitrant material of our daily lives gratifications of sometimes unlikely kinds.

All these approaches enrich the comparison of art to dream, but with the exception of Ehrenzweig's work on visual art and music, they do not provide a systematic way of analysing the interrelations between dreaming and waking mentation in a given work of art that does not look elsewhere for clues to what is hidden within it. Therefore they do not answer the old objection that art cannot be compared to dreams because dreams are interpreted through the associations of the dreamer, while literature cannot be so interpreted. There are, however, some approaches to dreams, deriving from non-Freudian conceptual systems, that attempt to systematize the manifest content of dreams, notably Calvin Hall and Robert L. Van de Castle's, *The Content Analysis of Dreams*, and David Foulkes', *The Grammar of Dreams*.[12] While their discussions of dreams offer ways to think systematically about formal patterns, they, like the discussions of primary process thinking, tend to bypass dramatic and emotional elements as well as their representational quality.

An approach to dreams that is systematically inclusive of their drama and intensity is to be found in the work of Rolf Loehrich.[13] His system of analysing, as distinct from interpreting, dreams relies on the associations made within a dream or sequences of dreams. But unlike Hall or Foulkes, he focuses on the role of the dreamer in relation to the configuration of the dream, taking into account such phenomena as the amount of control exercised by the dreamer, the degree of intensity of dream events, the different levels of awareness, the dynamics of changing configurations in the chronology of the dream, and the time markers within a dream that indicate different life stages. He also brings to dream analysis some common-sense relationships to waking life; for example, a dream in which one flies might be significant of several different emotional levels, but one thing that it signifies is an unrealistic sense of one's own abilities. Though his understanding of dreams is embedded in a far-reaching theory of needs that includes a study of psychosomatic illness and occult symbolism, his method of analysing the interrelations among dream figures, as well as interpreting the meaning of individual components from internal rather than external associations, allows an application to literature that attends to particulars and that comprehends both structural and dynamic aspects of literature. It allows one to make precise use of Breger's conception of the integrative function of dreams in connection with the wider range of representative material of realistic literature.

The advantages of Loehrich's system of dream analysis can be transferred to literary study by thinking of the relations among the figures in a literary work in analogy to the relations between the figure that represents us in our dreams, and the dream events that figure confronts, or, as I said, by assuming the protagonist dreams his or her fictional world. Before I discuss the systematic ways in which this conception, or thought strategy, can be used, I will give some rationale for it through a discussion of the process of artistic creation and of the role of the imagination.

An author may begin a work of fiction because an incident attracted his or her interest, because he or she wishes to convey a philosophical, political, or moral idea, to explore a character, or to ring changes on the inherited literary conventions. No matter which of these is primary in consciousness, a selection will already have been made from a field of possible incidents, characters, ideas or conventions, and literary forms. In that selection the author will have expressed both his or her conscious intention, and the range of discourse or the social and cultural institutions that make it possible for one in that time and place to have that intention. Further selections will be made from the various possible ways in which that intention could be executed, and the process of selection will continue from the largest structures that comprise the work to the smallest detail of language. Probably as the detail grows finer the artist will be less aware of the process of selection, but will rather be guided by intuitions of what is appropriate, or by a sense that the work generates its own inner dynamics. That feeling will be interpreted according to the ideas and concepts the world makes available, as inspiration of the gods, of muses, or of God, as the impersonal operation of archetypal forces, as moral and political imperatives, or as unconscious forces. Unlike life, no component of the work is given or accidental, including the portrayal of accident. Therefore all components are meaningful, whether or not an author is aware of the principle of selection that occurred. This account makes the work of art similar to a dream that has been touched off by an event of the previous day. The 'day's residue' cannot fully account for the dream because the person dreaming experienced a host of events out of which the sleeping self selected that one only. Therefore one expects the remainder of the dream, together with associations later brought to it, to reveal the significance of the initiating event or the ways in which the past gives significance to the present. Similarly, one looks to the detail of the work to surround with significance the initiating ideas or intentions. The difference is that in art the initiating idea or event is most often conscious, and consciously integrated into the author's world-view and value system, though the contents of consciousness, like language, will reflect the world in which the author's being is embedded. That means that the process of selectivity that guides the finer detail will reveal the unconscious ranges of significance attached to the much wider range of issues of more general and less exclusively personal initiating material than is the case in a dream.[14]

So far, that justifies the not unfamiliar analogy between the work of art and a dream, but does not give the rationale for thinking of the protagonist as dreamer. However, most people when they dream dream themselves. That is, when we awaken we refer to a figure in the dream as 'I,' even if the self we dreamt was of different age, appearance, or even sex than we are in life, and certainly that dream 'I,' whom I will call the dreamer, often behaves in ways that we don't regard as characteristic of ourselves. The dream, then, can be thought of as the story of what the dreamer does or experiences, and the stance – active, passive, observer, or participant – adopted by a dreaming person will be significant in view of what the dreamer in that stance encounters as external event. It may also reveal something characteristic of the dreaming person, but an author's conscious artistry widens the intervening gap. The author who constructs a work of fiction generally chooses, even if immediately concerned with event rather than character, persons to whom those events occur or who bring them about. If those characters are to generate an illusion of reality, depth, and multi-facetedness such as we associate with real people, their creation will entail a host of detail and nuance beyond what could be stated as conscious intention. It is my contention that in the process of that creation, the author generates a version of himself or herself, analogous to our dream selves within our dreams, and fashions that figure so intensely that it becomes the centre or vehicle of all the concerns, conscious and unconscious, that were involved in the artistic project. The work then becomes organized around the experience of that figure into whom the author's imagination has entered. Part of the author's conscious concerns becomes the consciousness of that figure, while the unconscious concerns are externalized into the events, setting, and other characters that are confronted. The action then is designed to unfold a consciousness experiencing and integrating, or failing to integrate, a nexus of event, values, and ideas from which it has itself emerged. In this way an art work expresses its author's social and historical determinants as well as the unknown quantity that constitutes his or her humanity within those determinants. But it does so through a depersonalized or fictive 'I' or speaking voice of a poem, which is a fictive person, whether or not the author intended it to be so, and whether or not the voice so created is espoused by its author.[15] In narrative fiction the primary voice might be the narrator's, or that of a character, but in drama, to which this discussion will be limited, that voice is embodied in a character. The depersonalized voice of the author becomes the figure of the protagonist who bears to his author the same relationship as do the figures and setting of our dreams to the dream figures whom we identify as ourselves. This relationship lends to the mimetic, intellectual, and formal components the intensity, organization, and force that derive from a dreamlike unfolding of the protagonist's central project or conflict. In the alchemical cauldron of the imagination, the author's moral and aesthetic intentions become the protagonist's 'secondary elaboration.' They constitute a kind of association, analogous to the way a bizarre dream component might remind a person of a real event, of an idea, or of a moral judgment. Therefore the conceptual, mimetic, and formal aspects of literature can be regarded as being on a continuum with, rather than as a disguise for, the protagonist's drives and desires manifested in language and images. In this mode of reading critical interest focuses on the movement of the protagonist's consciousness along that continuum.

The relationship, then, of the protagonist to the surrounding world becomes analogous, as I have said, to the relationship between the figure we identify as ourselves in any particular dream and the other components. In dreams that relationship represents the strategy by which we, at any given moment, are constructing our ongoing narrative of ourselves by symbolizing the material from our daily life in the modes by which our drives, desires, and self-conceptions have been constituted.[16] In looking at one's own dream in this way, one would comment on the stance taken towards the figures with whom the dreamer is in confrontation, whether active or passive, manipulative or combative, as well as the kinds of figures (from past or present, male or female, parental or contemporary) with which, since it is our dream, we have surrounded ourselves. Though without associations from a dreaming person one would not know how a particular dream related to events, present or past, that were not figured within it, one would know something of that person's vision of self in relation to other figures, as well as something of the ways in which components within the dream are associated with one another by the dreamer. The work of literature, which incorporates the fruits of the author's consciousness, vastly enlarges and renders more complex and multi-layered that network of associations, giving much greater significance to roles the protagonist adopts in relation to the configurations he or she is also seen to generate. Therefore, as I suggested earlier, this theory purports to analyse neither author, nor character, nor audience response. Rather it concerns itself with the ways in which configurations of characters, structure of action, language, conceptualization, genre and tone relate to each other as aspects of the protagonists' strategies to forge narratives which will permit them both to maintain their self-definitions and at the same time wrest from the worlds they have generated some manner of fulfilled desire.

An advantage of this approach is that, while the theory rests on a Freudian conception of consciousness as shaped by dynamic unconscious forces, and raises questions from Freudian expectations, the application of it does not rely on specific theoretical constructs outside of the work. For example, while images of daggers might in general be thought of as representing phallic desires, they would not be so considered in the absence of imagery that conjoined them to eroticism, and in its presence would signify the union of erotic and aggressive drives. The importance of such a union would depend on the place of the image in the work as a whole. Macbeth's approach to Duncan with a dagger tells us only that he has interpreted figures in the paternal realm as impediments to his desire, which he has defined as criminal. But he blends the aggressive with the erotic when he compares himself to Tarquin stealing through the dark to rape Lucrece. That link, in turn, can receive its significance only from other associations in the play, though it readies us to look for further understanding, from associations, of the link made between paternal and female figures. What can be said then is limited by the network of associations within the work, while associations brought by the reader either from theory or from personal inclination are irrelevant.[17] In this way one avoids the tendency to wrest detail out of its context into seemingly arbitrary theoretical frameworks, and the tendency to reduce dynamic experience to static conceptual statement. The approach provides some rules for analysing literature without dispersing the humane content of literary discourse; it weds a systemized understanding to a nuanced apprehension of action and language.

Considering the protagonist as dreamer in this way softens the polarity between deconstructionist and humanist criticism. It further softens that polarity by framing differently the question of a work's meaning. While it dissolves figures, plots, and ideas into networks of association and systematic polarities, it also conceives those networks and polarities as constituting an image of consciousness experiencing its own structures of meaning. The protagonist's emotional conflict then expresses the polarities of the work in which he exists in the same way that our conflicts remain ours even if we understand them and ourselves as expressing the social nexus in which we have our being. All aspects of the protagonist's world – other characters, events, genre, tone, and structural principles; mimetic fidelity or overtly dreamlike occurrences; moral judgments or philosophical abstractions; dramatic pacing and tone – express his drives and desires, his strategies of confronting or evading them, or his attitudes towards them. The work's meaning becomes the meaning for the protagonist of these various components, which is determined by the ways they are associated with one another. That network of associations becomes analogous to the associations, whether identified as memory or fantasy, that a person dreaming might make to his own remembered dream. The work of literature becomes a dream that contains within itself its own associations, collapsing the distinction between manifest and latent content.

In this way one preserves and accounts for a sense of intentionality pervading art and imbuing it with coherence, and one does justice to its multilayered meaningfulness, while side-stepping the question of authorial intentions; these intentions, even if known with reasonable certainty, are seen as aspects of the protagonist's strategies to create meaning and satisfy desire. Questions about a work's meaning are translated into questions about the protagonist's mode of creating meaning, and the work comes to represent the ways in which human beings signify their experience.

To sum up, this strategy brings all the 'givens' of a work, either its conventions or its basic circumstances, into the realm of signification. What the protagonists say, do, and see constitutes their consciousness; all that happens or that without their knowledge affects them, all that they, knowingly or unknowingly, confront as external circumstance, constitutes expressions of their unconscious. The plot, or structure of the action, renders their negotiation between the demands of unconscious drives and those of which they are aware, while the language, out of which all is composed, renders the ebb and flow of emotion, and the genre, whether comedy, tragedy, romance, or satire, expresses their stances towards themselves. The entire work becomes a moving image of the protagonists' approaches to and retreats from their desires and fears, the meaning of which resides in the relationship between the way characters experience their conflicts, and the way that conflict is expressed in their worlds. Shakespeare provides an unusually good subject for this exploration of the participation of dream process in literature because of the variety of genres in which he wrote; because of the span of time over which he wrote; because his rich language provides complex networks of associations in combination with large dramatic structures; and because the relatively naturalistic representation within a symbolized universe makes accessible the connections between the mimetic and the symbolic.[18]

Thinking about literature in this way changes the kinds of question one asks. For example, the question of why Hamlet delays fulfilling the ghost's command takes second place to the significance of Hamlet's defining himself as the son of the paternal ghost who confronts him with such a demand, and to the significance of his filling his dream-scape with paternal images or his splitting his image of the father into three distinct figures. The question of whether Claudius deserves to be killed dissolves into the value system within which Hamlet defines the attributes of Claudius as constituting those of a villainous person. The question of whether Hamlet is mad retreats into a discussion of the ideas and modes of behaviour he defines as madness, and of the relative distance he places between them and himself; the question of whether or not he is a coward takes second place to the figures and configurations of action in which he thinks himself cowardly, and to the values in terms of which he judges himself a coward, a conscious aspect of his unconscious struggle towards and away from the death he will finally espouse. The question of the degree of Gertrude's guilt takes second place to the emotions and ideas that Hamlet expresses in the vagueness in which her figure is articulated, and the question of his relation to Ophelia merges with an analysis of his approach to the heterosexuality he has defined through her, and leads to the question of why he has peopled his world only with younger and older versions of betraying women. The question of why he does not kill Claudius at prayer takes second place to the significance of his placing Claudius on his path to Gertrude, and the question of why he kills Polonius to why he places him behind the arras in Gertrude's bedroom. In general, rather than attempting to solve a text's irreducible puzzles, one finds significance in the protagonist's retreat from the issues that compose them. One steps back from the question in order to see it as an image.

This approach throws into primary significance the principle of selection, since it assumes that the artist's unconscious was involved in the particular choices he made from those available in his historical moment and by which he might have executed his conscious intention. His sense of what is appropriate or will 'work' to convey his artistic, moral, or political intentions will be infused with and shaped by the network of drives, desires, and fears that are associated with or symbolized within those conscious purposes. Shakespeare may have been concerned with the moral problems of revenge, with the intellectual problems deriving from a feudal concept of honour in an increasingly centralized power structure, and with the significance of life and death in the face of a world of shifting values. But these issues, out of which is created the figure of Hamlet, become for Hamlet a link in the chain of associations stretched between his conscious and his unconscious dilemma. That dilemma represents an internalized form of the problems of authority and the attitudes towards sexuality within which Shakespeare was himself created. We are brought, then, to the point where the sociological and the psychological join, to an apprehension of some particular ways in which, as Tolstoy says, fish are in seas and seas in fish.

So it is that the principle of association forms a chain of signifiers-signifieds that binds action, character, thought, and language into a hermeneutic circle that constitutes the protagonist's world. The work is self-referential in that each aspect of it refers to all others, and in that assertions about art found within art, such as those Hamlet makes, form part of the signifying chain, but that very self-referentiality becomes a mimesis of our own reflexive character.[19] Unlike other modes of semiology, however, this mode creates a topography of signification, for the relation of the protagonist's consciousness to the significations established by following that chain forms the largest part of the drama that we follow. Whether or not a relationship is Oedipal, for example, is less significant than the protagonist's movements between familial figures among whom sexuality is by definition guilty, and non-familial figures with whom it is permitted. Within this context it is mistaken to speak of Hamlet as having an Oedipus complex; rather we see him as moving towards and away from confrontations with the figures and emotions that would for a living person comprise an Oedipus complex, and experiencing those components at different levels. Hamlet, having evoked the sexually permitted, present- and future-oriented relationship with Ophelia, evades it by regressing into a parental drama. In the process he reveals the associations of sexuality with decay, betrayal, and death that necessitate his flight from Ophelia. Though that parental drama is defined among present figures, such figures more readily suggest past forms than do others, but a character can be said to have a past only in so far as the text provides images of pastness. Such images accumulate as Hamlet defines his father's murder as past, and suggest a deeper past that joins with the overarching revenge motif when Horatio imagines the Roman dead arising from their graves – an image that associates the past with public rather than private horror and disruption. That image attaches to women and becomes action when Yorick's skull emerges from the grave into which Ophelia will descend. That sense of pastness becomes personal and immediate when Hamlet associates the skull with his own birth and boyhood, and directs it to 'my lady's chamber.' Similarly, Lear approaches the infantile in envisioning himself within Cordelia's 'kind nursery.' He attempts to retreat from it by populating his world with nightmare images of foully sexual and cruel parental figures until he sends his imagination through the stench of women's genitals to see himself born wauling and crying into the smelly air. In the process he finds the 'ounce of civet' that will sufficiently sweeten his imagination to permit Cordelia to emerge, for a moment, from image into presence.[20] But he does not sweeten it enough to resolve the polarity between compassion, legitimacy, and relative sexlessness on the one hand, and ruthless cruelty, illegitimate individualist striving, and foul sexuality on the other between which all levels of the play stretch.

The main features of the inner landscape I have been describing are, in most works, other characters, which this approach may seem to be dissolving altogether into the network of images from which they arise. To resolve this difficulty I will pause to consider the relation, in dream, between the dreamer and other figures. Those figures fall into three categories.

Our dreams can include figures resembling people whom we know, either in the present or in the past, and we can, in our dreams, intermingle them. However realistic a dream figure might be, that figure is not the person, but rather a representation of our associations to and relations with that person, of the way he or she functions for us (though the representation may or may not correspond to the waking reality).

Some figures in dreams are realistic but not recognizable. These are most often thought of as composite figures, formed through the processes of dis-placement and splitting, representing a blend of attributes belonging to several persons who entered our lives at different times. They would suggest a dream-ing person whose emotions are less integrated to the reality of present life. This second category enters naturalistic literature through the convention of disguise, which provides a probable way in which one figure can transform into another. If Edgar is seen as dreamer, then the exuberance with which he adopts disguises makes particularly visible a sharply divided conscious sense of himself, though he espouses the sadistically moral Edgar rather than the devil-ridden Poor Tom. For Gloucester, the shifting appearances of his son show Gloucester's psyche infusing the present figure with images derived from other emotional dimensions; for Lear, past emotional forms have totally obliterated Edgar's present form from consciousness. Orlando's encounter with the male and female forms of Rosalind expresses his confusion about his sexual choice, a confusion that never becomes conscious because he, presumably, never learns the identity of Ganymede and Rosalind.

Finally there are fantastic figures, such as Hamlet's ghost or Macbeth's witches, who suggest emotions leading more immediately to past emotional levels that are not integrated into the present. Though folklore probably served to accommodate these figures convincingly within a primarily naturalistic convention, in general that convention demands that such figures be embedded in relatively probable circumstance. Edgar's disguise provides the needed cir- cumstance to allow the grotesque devils to enter the play, primarily as images, though the horned and thousand-eyed devil almost emerges from Edgar's language to become visible to Gloucester. When these grotesqueries coalesce from images into independent figures, they suggest dreamers whose ordinary sense of themselves is submerged by a sudden eruption of glaringly antithetic desires.[21] In tragedy they suggest dreamers who attempt to integrate emotional forms from the past into an emotionally depleted present. Either the dreamers partially succeed in ways that are too little, too late, and too disparate from ordinary creature pleasure, or they yield to the force of their unacknowledged desires, as Antony does when his sense of himself dissolves into the aura of magic with which he has surrounded both Cleopatra and Octavius. Comic or happy endings entail a vision of such integration or reclamation, but not its accomplishment, for the fantasy remains within the improbable means by which such endings are usually achieved. The ending that presents an im- possibly transcendent vision of harmony suggests that the redeeming vision cannot be integrated into ordinary causality, and the lower, or diffused, affect suggests a more hesitant approach to frightening emotion. Leontes' dream attempt to provide a probable account of Hermione's miraculous resurrection strains to bridge the gap.

So far I have discussed the significance of naturalism in the represented figures and events that constitute the topography of the dreamer's landscape. But the more naturalistic the other figures are, the more clamorous two questions become. The first is who shall be regarded as the protagonist, and the second is how to account for fully characterized secondary figures.

The answer to the first question is that *any* figure may be regarded as the protagonist. One may take Claudius as protagonist of *Hamlet*, though to do so makes the configurations more remote. Hamlet then becomes a distanced representation of Claudius' incomplete filial drama, through whom he expresses his fearful desire to be punished for the ambition that, without fully realizing, he has defined as evil, and Claudius' drama anticipates that of Macbeth. The play will then be analogous to a dream in which the 'I' is more spectator than participant, suggesting a dreaming person who experiences his own emotions through others' dramas, emptying himself of emotion too difficult to experience directly. Such a strategy allows us to see Claudius as the emotional alternative Hamlet rejects in favour of a version of an emotional love-death romance. It highlights the polarity, fundamental to the play, between bloodless, efficient machiavellianism and passionate life, a polarity the resolution of which Hamlet envisions in his praise of Horatio for 'co-meddling blood and judgement.' But it makes better sense to join rather than resist the affective force of the play by choosing the figure whose experience is most immediate and most strongly organizing. In works such as *Antony and Cleopatra* where the stories of two figures seem almost equally compelling, in order to see the depth at which each functions for the other one should pursue both. For example, Cleopatra's image of herself as a decaying womb in the mud of Nilus' banks betrays her self-hatred, which then throws light on why Antony interprets Cleopatra as 'poisoning' his enterprise. Finally, I believe, greater immediacy accrues from taking Antony as the protagonist, and subsuming Cleopatra's portrait to his, despite his earlier dream death. Generally, one figure will function most strongly to organize the configurations of a work.

In comedies this issue is more problematic, for often the most potent organizing principle seems to rest with a figure pervasively in the background rather than with the most prominent character. For example, *As You Like It* falls best into place if one takes as dreamer Duke Senior, the magical centre of the forest; *Twelfth Night* organizes itself nicely around Malvolio, and *A Midsummer Night's Dream* around Oberon. These plays then become analogous to dreams in which one experiences one's self primarily as an observing consciousness.

This strategy may seem arbitrary until we consider the second question, how to account for the full development of characters encountered by the dreamer. To do so I must return to the relation of dreaming to waking life. Though we regard our emotional lives as internal to us, and though as adults not all of our emotional capacities will be called into play by people with whom we have surrounded ourselves (and in whose dramas we unwillingly recognize our own supporting roles), all of those capacities were at one time shaped and made known to us in connection to other people. Therefore, while other figures in our dreams represent configurations of our own feelings, our dream relation to them represents the ways our feelings are known to us in relation to other people. If one dreams oneself rejected by a lover, the dream rejection still expresses a preference for the stance of the rejected rather than rejecting one, as well as covert rejection of the lover, even if the waking counterpart of the dream lover is rejecting. If there were a waking counterpart to the dream figure, then the dream might lead to some understanding of the emotions and ideas that were involved in the dreaming person's choice of partners. If there were not, then the dream might lead to an understanding of emotional dimensions involved but not overt in waking life. But in literature the waking counterparts of the other characters fall into the same empty space as the non-existent dreaming person. Reading in this way involves the assumption that the dreamer includes in his dream representations of figures who would play similar roles in the life of a dreaming person more or less like the dreamer. He is like a person who, upon awakening, says that he has been dreaming of his daughter. That statement constitutes an association – though a very immediate one – to the figure in his dream, and the analogy reinforces the principle that a work of art is like a dream that contains within itself its own associations.[22]

Most of this study will be concerned with individual plays, but as the survey of lovers and families earlier in this chapter suggested, the sequence of plays allows one to use related image patterns and similar characterizations and plot motifs, to interpret the implications of the more schematic comedies in the light of the fully affective tragedies. In so far as one follows a topography of the rise and fall in prominence of a motif or an emotion, or similar configurations shifting from background to foreground, one is assuming Shakespeare as the dreamer. For example, in *The Comedy of Errors* Shakespeare, in addition to doubling the twins, further complicated the plot by a frame story that includes a lost wife who emerges from a nunnery to resolve the plot. The tone suggests no symbolic significance, but some five years later, still doubling plots, Shakespeare created King Lear, who, because of stormy passions rather than a storm at sea, loses his daughter. Lear suffers an externalized manifestation of his inner storm instead of night-time Syracuse, before he can regain Cordelia, whose restorative return carries both emotion and symbolic resonance. Later still, we find in *The Winter's Tale* the quasi-magical return of Leontes' wife and daughter, the language of which absorbs emotion into the symbolic aura.

Another kind of topographical shift can be traced in the split between Portia's dead, magically controlling, and beneficent father, and the much more visible Shylock, his negative counterpart, who is central to the plot, fully emotional, and malignantly controlling. The balance alters in *As You Like It*, in which Rosalind's magical uncle coincides with her father in creating a quasi-magical beneficent presence in the centre of the restorative forest as opposed to the more conventional interfering paternal figures, Oliver and Frederick. The polarity takes on more centrality in Oberon, magical and casually good, and Egeus, arbitrarily controlling. The split between good and bad images of power becomes thematically central to *Measure for Measure*, while both sides of the polarity coalesce in the fully dimensional and central figure of Lear. The motif is finally stated in Prospero, who is central to and fully controls the action, and who, though beneficent, carries shades of the tyrannical father.[23]

As attributes that define several characters coalesce into one, or as those that constitute one figure unravel into several, as similar figures take different familial roles, or as love relationships of varying emotional intensity move between foreground and background, as women become daughters, wives, mothers, or witches, as naturalistic portrayal comes from and gives way to symbolic abstraction, and as landscapes and images change their colour and recombine, one can see in these kaleidoscopic configurations the dream dimension behind even the most realistically portrayed figures and situations.[24]

To return to individual plays, another aspect of dream topography is the narrative sequence, which also involves causality. Since events are here conceived as moving images in the process of completing themselves, an order of narration that violates chronology establishes a second-level story of the process by which a consciousness encounters its own ground. In *Hamlet* the ghost appears to the watch presumably at the same time as Hamlet hears Claudius' throne speech. But the sequence shows us the process by which Hamlet first remotely evokes the ghost, and then allows it to encroach on his consciousness at first as a tale, and then as a confrontation. Lear intersperses his approach to Dover and Cordelia with distanced evocations of her sisters' struggle for Edmund, the sequence expressing the flickering duality of his concerns, so that the formal structuring expresses the protagonist's enterprise.

Since time becomes an image, so does causality, the sense of which is generated by chronological sequence. When time and causality are seen as images, they then collapse into space. That is, the image completes itself only at the end of the work, and that end is then contained in the beginning, or consequence is contained in its cause, transforming a temporal, or diachronic, experience into a spatial, or synchronic entity. If in a dream one, having entered a house in search of cake, encounters a devouring monster, in dream logic one has entered the house in order to confront the monster. That is, the feeling represented by wanting cake presupposed the fearful desire to be devoured, indicating that the comfort of houses and cake signifies for the dreamer devouring monsters. Without associations from the dreamer, or from a sequence of dreams, that dream would not provide information about the particular emotional dynamics that might have generated fearful monsters. Since a literary work partakes of both waking and dreaming realms, its mimetic component provides what would be brought by a dreamer's associations to his life circumstances, filling out the picture of a life unfolding. In analogy, Hamlet's resolution of his conflicting drives in death is not the consequence but the cause of the action that eventuates in it.[25] This inverse relationship of consequence to cause generates the literary penumbra of aesthetic inevitability and of unity, for the end reveals what the beginning implied, creating a sense of a directed project, of a teleological vision of life, that contains its own meaningfulness.

Finally, this central difference between dream and literature leads to another dimension of similarity. Neither another person nor the dreamer can know what has been omitted, forgotten, or distorted in the retelling or remembering of a dream. Analysts rely on the assumption that the process of association outside of the dream will compensate for lies or omission in the dream report, and that even a direct lie, itself a kind of an association, will in an indirect process lead into the emotions central to the dream. They thread through a network of language clues, some of them thought of as dream language, and some not. The only dreams of which we have immediate experience are our own, and then only while dreaming, a remembered dream being only as reliable as any other memory. Therefore, we relate to fictional creations to which we are audience as we do to our own dreams while dreaming. Nothing can be omitted or misremembered because all is presently occurring. If while reading or watching a play, we disengage our intellectual capacities from our emotional involvment, we become like ourselves in those dreams in which we are aware of ourselves dreaming, or like our waking selves when we observe the behaviour in which we are presently engaged. Literature then provides us with an unusual combination of an experience at once unmediated and highly artificed.

The function of this unique phenomenon raises issues that go beyond the scope of this study. However, the approach taken here suggests an evaluative principle, for the more fully a work contains the materials that extend the significance and range of powerful passions toward large-scale historical and cultural issues, the richer the language in images that allow us to extend the associative resonance of plot, character, and concept, the more fully it reveals ways in which deeply personal struggles relate to historical and cultural struggles, then the more fully does it become a mimesis of the overdetermined complexity of the 'knot intrinsicate of life.' It is reasonable to speculate that we can tolerate numerous and deep formal flaws in literary works traditionally considered great because our evaluation depends on the degree to which these works function to enrich the narrative we spin out of the unmediated vagary of raw experience. Contemporary literature would then allow us to align such enriched inner narratives with the general values and sense of reality of the community in which we and the artefact exist, while literature of other times and places, in conjunction with knowledge from other sources, would deepen our sense of our own historicity, by providing an entrée into the different stresses involved in forging other stories within the conventions, constraints, and structures of those other times and places.

Though this study will not range beyond Shakespeare or touch upon the many recent studies of the family in his time, it will expose some ways in which fundamental emotions can be frozen into conventional forms, then break through those forms into full emotional immediacy and realism, and recombine with different conventional formulations. When an experience is rendered in an apparently conventional way, it should not be dismissed as without meaning, for the significance lies in what is taken for conventional. To consider the plays as dreams of their protagonists is also to see the significance that the conventional, whether literary or social, can acquire in the depths of individual struggles. Considering Shakespeare's plays as analogous to a sequence of dreams makes visible some complex ways in which their author participated in the ideas, institutions, and culture of his time.

It is to the study of that trajectory of private dreaming, structured within and playing itself out on the world's stages, using, breaking, and reconstituting conventions of thought, form, and language that we now turn. I will first briefly survey the configurations in the early plays of lovers and families that are suggestive of later developments. The first full analysis will be of *Hamlet*, followed by a briefer discussion of the problem plays that concentrates on the ways in which they relate to *Hamlet* and the later tragedies. *Othello*, *Macbeth*, *King Lear*, and *Antony and Cleopatra* each have a chapter to themselves, after which a brief discussion of *Pericles* and *Cymbeline* links the major tragedies to the fuller discussions of *The Winter's Tale* and *The Tempest* that follow.

Throughout these discussions of both groups of plays and of individual plays I have made use of comparisons and contrasts to define the different figures, to be precise about the ways in which their worlds are structured, and to trace the ways in which configurations of plot and event change over time. This level of the study necessarily implies the author, rather than his characters, as dreamer. Therefore in the concluding chapter, in order to integrate the scattered suggestions about Shakespeare's relation to his plays, I put the issues that have been central to the discussion of individual plays in a different frame of reference. This chapter relates the various means in different plays by which Shakespeare manifests his authorial control to the ideas about the authority within them, and speculates on what the sequence of plays suggests about Shakespeare's relation to his art.

2

The Paths of True Love

Because Shakespeare is unique among dramatists in that he excelled in comedy, tragedy, and middling genres, and because he allowed these different genres to interpenetrate, his works provide insights into the psychological import of genre structure. This necessarily sketchy survey of the early plays will show how emotions associated with similar motifs and characters are articulated in different ways in the different genres, thus making visible the ways in which genre forms represent strategies to express and contain the emotional forces that generate them. This overview of the plays will assume the dreaming mind to be Shakespeare's. However, it will also illustrate how each play provides clues to which figure is most immediate to the work's emotional sources. Thinking of those characters as dreamers, we shall trace, through the kaleidoscopic shifts in tone, image, and structure around portrayals of women, lovers, and families in the plays up to *Hamlet*, the forces that will eventually generate the great tragic protagonists and their worlds before Shakespeare inscribes his retreat from them in the late romances.

The Comedy of Errors, more coherently than any other of the plays of this early period, places figures who anticipate the good and bad women of later plays in dramatic structures that are parallel to those that shape the tragedies and the later romances. For this reason some of the gaps in the logic of plot development, in connection with motifs that find parallels in later plays, suggest the presence of some dream-level conflicts around women and their role in the family, conflicts that are not as yet allowed the shaping power that they will later acquire. One such gap occurs around the figure of first Antipholus' wife. Like Emilia in *Othello*, she complains to her sister that if their wives err, men should blame themselves because they both expect women to be perfect and disregard their feelings. She does not intend to act upon her words, but the confused comic action that follows inflicts upon her husband the experience he would have if she had done so: as a consequence of his long-lost twin, Antipholus II, being mistaken for him, he finds his door locked against him when he returns from his night-time revels. Though midnight Syracuse is not the wild heath, the circumstantial confusion of identity will later deepen to Lear's despairing quest for a secure ground of being.

The shaping force of this concealed anxiety about women's punitive power appears when the priestess, who will be revealed as Aegeon's long-lost wife, unjustly accuses Antipholus' wife of driving her husband mad. It is as though in the play's imaginative depths the priestess' passing thought had already transformed her into the punitive women of later plays. The other side of the split image of women that shapes the structure and expresses the ideology of later plays also appears in the priestess-cum-wife. Her fortuitous return from a shipwreck long past seems merely a device to resolve the confusion, but the combination of spiritual elevation and wifely devotion implicit in her story anticipates the symbolically radiant women of later plays, who in counteracting the destructiveness of their evil counterparts represent universal redemptive powers.

The play is like the dream of a person whose consciousness is remote from the emotional foundations of his life. Though absent from most of the action, Aegeon is the figure around whom the action turns and for whom it has most consequence. As his dream, the shipwreck that deprives him of his wife and children expresses his murderous feelings towards them, while his long search for them expresses his desire for the love and comforts of which his unconscious hatred has deprived him. The death sentence that hangs over him expresses his unacknowledged guilt, while the associations of reprisal and betrayal that accrue around Antipholus' wife suggest the crimes for which he is being punished. In the course of the action he substitutes his sons' comic despair and confusion for his own punishment, an arrangement that relieves him of enough guilt so that he can allow himself to be redeemed by an idealized female figure. Throughout the action he defines himself as acted upon rather than acting. Unlike future avatars of this figure, he assumes no control over the circumstances that affect him, and the distance he places between his own figure and the major action, as well as the plot's inconsistency and apparent comic triviality, express the dreamer's tentative approach to deep emotional issues and his efforts to minimize their import while finding a short-cut to a resolution.

The range of horrifying and lurid associations that will later colour the portrayals of lovers and families appears in random ways in other early plays. Lavinia's ruthless cruelty in *Titus Andronicus* and Queen Margaret's vengefulness and her vicious mockery of Warwick while murdering his son in

3 Henry VI, and her harpy-like choral function in *Richard III* are tragic versions of this figure, while her comic form is the shrew. The male struggle to subdue fierce women provides the comic matter of *The Taming of the Shrew* and of *Much Ado about Nothing*, and in distanced ways the association of women with disease and death colours the ending of *Love's Labour's Lost*. However, it is *The Comedy of Errors* with its night-time confusions, mistaken identities, and motif of loss and restoration of family that bears structural similarity to the comedies that pivot around love.

In these plays, the conflict between the dark associations with women and the efforts to imagine a benign romantic passion that in later plays will be equated with the powers of spiritual transformation and redemption, appears in the impediments to the consummation of love. In these romantic comedies, the task of overcoming the barriers erected by tyrannical fathers – or father figures – to the fulfilment of love that is at once romantic and socially appropriate falls mostly upon nubile, virtuous women.[1] However, the obstacles in the path of love do not remain safely in external circumstances or peripheral figures. On the one hand these young women, upon whose active virtue depend their plays' happy resolutions, often achieve their ends by acting in ways that outside the comic frame would seem cruel; on the other hand, by changing their minds, ardent young men jeopardize all that rests on socially sanctioned and loving marriages. As the impediments to love invade the lovers themselves they erode the power of heterosexual love to transform a world that can be transformed in no other way.

After the uncertain beginning in the *The Two Gentlemen of Verona*, the first full-scale romantic comedy, but one in which the hero's defects threaten to transform him into a stage villain, in both *A Midsummer Night's Dream* and *Romeo and Juliet* Shakespeare generates a vision of romantic love at once compelling and glowing. In different ways both plays counter romantic passion with dark inimical forces, but these forces, in most of the comedy and the whole of the tragedy, are envisioned as external social or cosmic powers.[2] Hermia and Lysander, Shakespeare's first delightfully poetic lovers, are joyfully impervious to the threats of Hermia's arbitrarily tyrannical father. Their social appropriateness and comic insouciance place Hermia's father and the Athenian law that authorizes him in opposition to social propriety. However, the internal source of the external opposition is suggested in several ways. It is suggested by Demetrius' protean loving, without benefit of magic, which recalls that of his prototype in *The Two Gentlemen*, and by Helena's abject doting, which causes her to betray her friend. It is suggested as well when the torment of unrequited love infects Hermia and Lysander, so that the four Athenians are thrown into the confused morass of betrayal and rejection. That midsummer nightmare is orchestrated by Puck, but its internal source is suggested by Hermia's dream of the serpent.[3] Finally, in the play's structure most of the lovers' torment derives from the discord between Oberon and Titania. Puck's apparently accidental errors that disrupt the love between Hermia and Lysander acquire symbolic resonance when Titania attributes the power to make a waste-land of the mortal realm to Oberon's jealousy over the changeling child. The disturbed love between these parental figures brings the 'contagious fogs' and consequent famine, sterility, and disease to mortals whose life is no longer 'with hymn or carol blest' (II.i.90,102), an amplified image of the four lovers' distress, which also, through Puck's agency, emanates from Oberon. These wasteland images, which will reverberate in language, characterization, and action of the tragedies as well as the romances, are dispersed by Titania's submission to Oberon. The renewed social harmony that flows from their accord anticipates *The Winter's Tale* and *The Tempest*, in which socially appropriate and loving couples become the centre from which radiate harmonious power relations within the polity.

The emotional and ideological significance of these parallels between the apparently arbitrary comic circumstances of these plays to the ideological control of the later plays emerges when one selects as dreaming protagonist Oberon, who is central to the power structure of *A Midsummer Night's Dream*. Titania's power over the child expresses Oberon's feelings of powerlessness in relation to her, and Titania's doting love for Bottom, which gives the play its most sexual scene, expresses Oberon's desire to debase and humiliate her. In distanced ways the power struggle at the heart of Oberon's relationship appears in the discord of the two couples, as well as in the images of warfare that initially define the love of Theseus and Hippolyta. Bottom functions to express Oberon's debased view of his sexuality and physicality, just as Caliban later expresses Prospero's, and Oberon's tendency to denigrate himself appears in the parodic parallels between Bottom's role as stage-manager and his own. Unlike Aegeon, who remains subject to others' power throughout his play, Oberon acquires power. His increasing mastery over his own passions is manifested in his capacity to control Puck, but it derives from his success in subduing Titania. His distance from his own passions determines the play's comic frame, but unease with the too easily achieved resolution, and his sense of himself as a clown, or an ass, appears in the tension between the tragic material of the Pyramus and Thisbe story, a version of *Romeo and Juliet*, and its comic enactment by Bottom. It appears as well in the long but apparently irrelevant exchange between Theseus and Hippolyta about their hunting hounds, which occurs as night gives way to morning amid the now correctly sorted sleeping couples. As Theseus invites Hippolyta to the mountain top to hear 'the musical confusion / Of hounds and echo in conjunction,' of his hounds, which are 'dewlapp'd like Thessalian bulls; / Slow in pursuit, but matched in mouth like bells, / Each under each' (IV.i.109–10, 121–3), the images of distanced baying suggest the temporary retreat of the grotesque violence, disordered passions, and misused authority that in *King Lear* will be represented by images of dogs and hounds. Oberon achieves a control that anticipates Prospero's power, and Shakespeare wrests from an incipient nightmare of love a romantic vision of contented lovers approaching their marriage bed. But unease about the project remains. Theseus' equation of lovers to poets and madmen points to the inherent dangers of loving, and leads to the potentially tragic parody of the play's comic plot. The main drama uses quasi-magic and the subsidiary drama uses farcical distancing, but these different devices are employed to solve the same problem, the containment of the destructive passions that for Shakespeare's protagonists are inherent in love.[4]

Romeo and Juliet, written either slightly before or after *A Midsummer Night's Dream*, does not restrain those forces, but it does externalize them. The romantic lovers create a radiant world apart by attributing all inimical forces to surrounding circumstance. The freer the lovers are from discordant emotions, the more violent is the world they encounter. 'Like a rich jewel set in an Ethiop's ear,' their love excludes all intuition of ambivalence, but the forces that draw them towards the tomb have been extracted from the heart of loving itself.

The integral connection between love and death appears in the prologue, which tells us that 'from out the fatal loins of these two foes' came a pair of star-crossed lovers. The image of 'fatal loins' suggests a kind of copulation in hatred between the feuding families. The intense enmity of the family feud does not cause the lovers' death, but rather generates the twin birth of love and death in the persons of the lovers. It suggests that they die not because they are children of warring families, but rather that their feuding parents are the circumstance of their meeting, their loving, and their death. The same magnetism that brings the two families together in order to fight also brings the two young people together in order to love and die. In the sequence of images the stars do not control the lovers' destinies, but are instruments of the family feud, which arranges their fatal conjunction even as it creates the lovers. The family tomb, emblematic of the feud, both gives birth to the lovers and calls them back.[5]

As Oberon's power determines the action of *A Midsummer Night's Dream* so Capulet's actions determine the lovers' fate. The hidden link between the cosmic forces and his figure is suggested both by his importance to the plot, and by his abrupt and unexplained change of character that occurs midway through the play. Early in the play his consideration for Juliet's feelings when Paris asks for her hand and his courtesy when he learns of Romeo's presence at his ball make him exemplary as a forbearing father and a reasonable host. However, after Juliet's marriage, Tybalt's death, and Romeo's banishment Capulet becomes a tyrannical father. It is as though the marriage of which he is ignorant has nonetheless stirred passions that he expresses in his otherwise unaccountable haste to marry Juliet to Paris and in his rage at her reluctance. The absence of a probable account of his outburst, together with its importance in determining the tragic conclusion, suggest that he is the figure closest to the play's emotional centre and can most readily be seen as the dreamer.

When Capulet is seen as the play's protagonist, the love that grows within the family feud expresses his association of love with family violence and death, and of life with coarse and loveless sexuality. He distances himself from that polarity, but approaches it more closely as Romeo and Juliet meet, love, and marry. In their love he expresses his denied desire, but distances himself from it by defining himself as Juliet's father, which both intensifies the guilt associated with sexuality by rendering it incestuous, and permits him to substitute power for pleasure. In their marriage he denies himself immediate pleasures, but in his furious haste to force her into a loveless marriage he achieves the alternate gratification of power. In the long term, however, his fury functions as part of a strategy to compromise between his desire and the evil he associates with it by simultaneously gratifying and punishing it in death.[6]

The conflicting pulls of the more ordinary pleasures of life, however denuded of love, create a counter-current. The nurse, whose earthy physicality anticipates Emilia's common sense, retards the rush towards the tomb, Friar Lawrence ineffectually tries to compromise with death, and Juliet's charnel-house vision of death, like Desdemona's plea for even a minute of life, opposes the romantic swoon into a dark embrace. But that impulse towards life is overwhelmed by the force of desire that has been fused with guilt and rage and can be realized only in the idealized, lifeless golden statues that emerge from the tomb.

Capulet marks a turning point in the development of father-daughter relationships. Unlike the conventionally articulated interfering fathers of the earlier comedies, he has emotional force, and more power than the potential manipulators – the prince and the friar. Unlike the fathers of the later plays, he is not the subject of his play, and his actions seem fortuitous rather than inevitable. However, these phenomena are a measure of the distance from which Shakespeare handles this figure, which will become central to his imagination when it transforms into King Lear and Prospero. The emotional currents that create those figures are dimly felt when Capulet, as an instrument of forces deeper in the play than he is, hastens Juliet to the tomb, just as Egeus and Shylock prefer to see their daughters dead than married to their beloveds.

Romeo and Juliet and *A Midsummer Night's Dream* form a pair. Though in one the characters wake from a nightmare to a happy life and in the other they die, both plays portray appealing lovers embattled against externalized powers. After those two different successes, Shakespeare complicates the balance of forces in *The Merchant of Venice*. By generating more intensity from the defeat of the tyrannical father than from the harmony that follows, the play tends to become Shylock's tragedy rather than Portia's comedy. Placing it in the context of the tragedies, as well as of other comedies, reveals some of the competing emotional forces that disturb the play's surface.

The play's structure resembles that of *A Midsummer Night's Dream* or *As You Like It*, except that the golden world of Belmont becomes background rather than foreground to the 'real' world of Venice. Like the forest in those comedies and like Prospero's island, Belmont is controlled by magical powers emanating from a paternal figure, though in this play a dead one. Like Rosalind or Helena in *All's Well*, but unlike the later Miranda, Portia carries this power into the contrasting world of Venice after she has proved her worthiness by submitting to her father's power. Like Cordelia, with whom she shares the aura of a fairy-tale heroine, she returns to a real world to rescue not her father but a father-like figure from the ravenous Shylock, whose relation to Antonio is like that of the pelican daughters to Lear. More successful than Cordelia, she restores both life and wealth to Antonio, but in relation to Shylock she resembles the evil sisters rather than Cordelia. From the very beginning she could have saved Antonio with the legal argument she later uses, but instead she manipulates Shylock into showing his worst side, just as Goneril does when she orders Oswald to provoke Lear so that 'it will come to question.' Though her male clothing and her pleasure in her own manipulative strategies keep her safely within the comic range, Portia's charm and wit have overtones of avenging and punitive women who enjoy humiliating men. She turns the sadistic edge of her pleasure towards Bassanio when in the last act she is to him as Maria is to Malvolio. Though bathed in the neo-Platonic glow of Belmont, Portia enjoys watching Bassanio suffer in the impossible moral dilemma she has created through the strategy of the exchanged rings.[7]

Though Portia saves Antonio and punishes Shylock, many aspects of the play relate these two paternal figures to each other, as well as to Portia's dead father. In different ways, both Portia's father and Shylock assert power over their daughters' marriage choice, and Antonio's ambivalence about Bassanio's marriage to Portia is reflected in the play's overarching structure. And all three figures in different ways conflate the spiritual values associated with romance with the material values associated with commerce.

The underlying connections are best revealed by taking Portia's father as dreamer, since his power initiates the plot configuration and is carried into the play through Portia's agency. Though this brief summary will not collect detailed evidence in the language to support the contention, one can take the clue from *Romeo and Juliet* to see Portia's father's desire to control her from beyond the grave as a sublimated expression of his denied desire for her. By dreaming himself dead he has removed himself from the immediate experience of conflicting desires and fears, and has idealized his own image. The idealization conceals but does not obliterate traces of the conflicts from which he withdrew into death. By interpreting his power as a magical force manifested in the casket device, he conceals his desire to control her marriage choice beneath the appearance of ensuring that she marry for love. The beneficence of his power will appear in the coincidence of her love for the one who fulfils her father's conditions. This sleight-of-hand reconciliation of competing value systems anticipates Prospero, who more openly contrives to give his daughter freedom to choose according to his will. By the same sleight of hand Portia's father also reconciles the play's otherwise irreconcilable opposition between material and spiritual value. He asserts an inverse relationship of money to love by associating Portia with the leaden rather than the golden casket, but she is at the same time the golden fleece, representative of spiritual value, which Bassanio wins in order to repay the debts he has incurred in his quest for a rich wife.

He accomplishes these magical tricks only by removing himself from the emotional forces that generate his dream, but he reveals in the two figures into which he splits himself, each of whom becomes the other's *alter ego*, his reasons for obliterating his own figure. In Shylock he expresses his most negative sense of himself. Shylock's desire to sequester his daughter represents the most extreme form of his possessiveness, while Shylock's equation of his daughter to ducats expresses his condemnation of his own incapacity to be true to the spiritual values he would like to espouse. Though the play focuses attention on the links between Shylock's usury and his hatred of Antonio, the plot is moved by Shylock's loss of his daughter to Lorenzo, for Shylock does not determine to turn his bond for a pound of flesh from play to earnest until after Jessica has fled. In Shylock Portia's father associates his desire for power and wealth with murderous hatred, greed, and, more generally, the reification of values represented by Venice in contrast to the neo-Platonic

Belmont. Both in his person and his role, Shylock reveals the impulses that are concealed in the idealized image of the dead father, but the underlying connections ruffle the play's surface in the disturbing illogic by which Portia both provides the necessary wealth to save Antonio and represents spiritual value in a play that opposes the one to the other.

In the melancholy Antonio Portia's father expresses his grief for the loss he incurs by his self-sacrificing withdrawal. In Antonio he substitutes a homo-erotic love choice for an incestuous one, but, as will appear more clearly in *Othello* and *The Tempest*, that strategy to avoid the frightening feelings associated with heterosexual love is equally impeded by clouds of fear and guilt.[8] The links between the father and Antonio appear in the devious ways in which they express their denied desires to possess both their loved ones and wealth, and in their equation of the two. Just as the casket scene reveals the desires it is intended to conceal, so do Antonio's answers to his fellow merchants. To their suggestion that he is melancholy because he cannot cool his soup or go to church without being reminded of the rocks upon which the winds might drive his ships, he responds that all his wealth is not at hazard, and he denies as well that he grieves for Bassanio's imminent departure. But the action denies his denials. Were all his wealth not at risk he could finance Bassanio without making the bond with Shylock. Were he not grieving for Bassanio he would not cast himself as competitor for Bassanio's love, as he does in the trial scene when he wishes for Bassanio to leave his wife only in order to witness his self-sacrifice, and as he does a second time when he urges Bassanio to prove his love for him by giving 'Balthazar' Portia's ring.

In Antonio's self-description as a 'tainted wether of the flock,' and in his otherwise unexplained drift towards death that anticipates Prospero's, Portia's father expresses a half-way point on the road he has travelled in his own figure. The split image of himself represents an attempt to find a compromise that will not end in death. In the enmity of Antonio for Shylock he expresses both his self-hatred and his pleasure in his gains from the aspects of himself he despises. In Shylock's hatred of Antonio, he expresses his sense of being victimized by his own evil desires as well as the substitute satisfactions of self-martyrdom. By separating these competing impulses into two figures, he is able to keep both of them alive, but the inadequacy of the compromise appears in the fact that finally both of them are comforted only by wealth, an odd conclusion to a play that thematically condemns reified value. Shylock has only enough money to survive in his bitter humiliation, and no fourth female appears to sweep Antonio into the happiness of multiple marriages. He remains to the end an isolated and melancholy figure. The uneasy compromise appears as well in the scattered emotional impact of the play as a whole, in the uneasy sympathy generated for Shylock and the shades of harshness and manipulative cruelty that tarnish Portia's image as advocate of mercy and agent of harmony. In the course of time the split images of the ravenous Shylock and the self-immolating Antonio will recombine as King Lear, both victim and victimizer, who also makes his daughters his mothers, while the merciful and cruel aspects of Portia will split into Goneril and Regan on the one hand, and Cordelia on the other.

While *A Midsummer Night's Dream* and *Romeo and Juliet* generate moving images of romantic love that overcome and, in different forms, integrate the negative perceptions of love between men and women, in *The Merchant of Venice* the dark or interfering forces, both Shylock and Antonio, have more power and impact than the romantic plot that surrounds them, and the whole of the last act lacks sufficient power decisively to sway the balance. In his last three romantic comedies, Shakespeare found new ways of manipulating the conflict into happy images before entering the deep waters of *Hamlet*.

In *Much Ado about Nothing* the loving and the negative elements are differently divided. Beatrice and Benedick, destined for marriage, are manipulated by third parties to recognize their mutual love, and until the very end neither exercises power over nor manipulates the other. Their mutually self-protective banter disarms the force of the anti-romantic so that it can be included in the romantic, and permits hostility between the lovers to be expressed and discharged amid the assurance of their ultimate love.[9] Within that assurance, they are vicious to each other, and sometimes not even wittily. Of the two, Beatrice is more cruel. Benedick's comment that 'She speaks poiniards, and every word stabs' (II.i.231–2) is confirmed when Beatrice wishes Benedick as much pleasure in her calling him to dinner 'as you may take upon a knife's point and choke a daw withal' (II.iii.245–6).

Her verbal power sometimes threatens to exceed the containing framework, the more so if her words are heard in context with her role in the final action. When she, believing that Claudio has slandered Hero, asks Benedick to prove his love and manly worthiness by murdering Claudio, she aligns herself with Lady Macbeth and earlier avenging females even though the moral context differs. The resounding starkness of her command that Benedick 'Kill Claudio' obtrudes momentarily into the surrounding comic reassurance.

So much do Benedick and Beatrice contain the vitality of both attraction and repulsion, of mutual love and mutual hostility, that they leave very little for the depiction of Hero and Claudio, both of whom are dramatically flat and formalized. The evils they suffer seem to arise from sources external to them, but Claudio betrays an inner source of the external trouble when he withholds his repudiation of Hero until their wedding, and maliciously enjoys her public humiliation.

However, as the play's most intense emotion lies in Leonato's reaction to

Hero's presumed shame, we may take the cue from that intense moment to consider him as dreamer. Like other fathers in the act of relinquishing their daughters he expresses his ambivalence about giving up Hero first by generating Don Pedro, who, for no reason that advances the plot, briefly appears to woo Hero for himself, having promised to do so for Claudio. As a prince Don Pedro shares with Leonato the realm of authority and can be identified with him. Leonato, then, allays his anxiety about forgoing Hero by generating a substitute for himself. That strategy would necessarily fail, since the figure so closely parallel to himself would soon generate the same anxiety and ambivalence. He further distances Hero when she is promised to Claudio, suitably younger, but Leonato's sense of loss and betrayal then generates Don John's plot to malign her. In this way Leonato expresses both his desire and fear that she be a sexual creature, and Claudio's repudiation of Hero allows Leonato fully to express his love for her, while simultaneously envisioning and condemning her sexuality.

Whereas *The Merchant of Venice* locates the negative forces in an explicitly evil father, and obscures his paternal significance by shifting the dramatic emphasis to a different father-daughter relationship, this play displaces the father's animosity onto Don John, a younger-brother figure similar to Antonio in *The Tempest*. Both plays show signs of the struggle to keep the romantic vision uncontaminated by the negative forces it generates. Those negative forms retreat for a while, making room for the two major romantic comedies, *As You Like It* and *Twelfth Night*. Each contains a negative figure, but a less threatening and more easily handled one, and each creates likeable lovers bathed in the happy glow of romantic love.

In Rosalind, Shakespeare achieved his happiest balance of passivity and assertiveness in a female figure. Rosalind's activity consists in manipulating circumstances so that four sets of lovers may finally unite. As she takes the self-dramatizing Orlando to task, her witty mockery of love is balanced by her tenderness and her admission of vulnerability. Whatever sadistic edge might be seen in her manipulation of Orlando and her harshness towards Phoebe is absorbed into general playfulness. Since she does not totally control events, but must herself also await time and circumstance for the resolution of her affairs, her capacity to control does not totally define her, as it does Portia once she is wed.

However, there lurks some mystery around both Rosalind's passivity to time and circumstance, and the active role she maintains in the play. Dramatically it is as though she cannot bring order to her affairs, nor resolve the other relationships in the play, until the evil father figures, Oliver and Duke Frederick, have been converted, though she does not in any direct way bring about their conversion. Furthermore, the play provides no explanation for her continued disguise. There is no apparent reason for her to conceal her identity from Orlando, except for her pleasure in the power she gains from superior knowledge. However, she associates that knowledge with a magical uncle who resides in the heart of the forest, first to justify her expertise in love to Orlando, and second to account for her capacity to sort out correctly and to arrange events for the loving or not so loving couples. The magical uncle exists only in Rosalind's words, but the resolution takes place in Duke Senior's forest glade, Hymen himself presiding over it. The action of the play, therefore, associates the image of the magical uncle to whom Rosalind attributes her power with the hidden father who in a pervasive way presides over the Forest of Arden which itself seems magically empowered to convert the evil to good. The action of the play is divided between the forest, secretly infused with the beneficent power of Duke Senior, and the court, which is controlled by the corrupt power of Oliver and Frederick. As the displaced elder brother, Duke Senior becomes an early and shadowy version of the commandingly magical Prospero.

If seen as the dreamer of the play, Duke Senior has had himself banished as a means of handling his ambivalent feelings towards his daughter and towards power. Frederick's sudden animosity towards Rosalind expresses his own need to reject her, as well as his desire for her. The ambivalence of that desire also appears when, having come to the Forest of Arden to seek him, she avoids him until she has arranged her marriage to Orlando. In *The Tempest*, Prospero clearly controls his island and arranges the circumstances that do not convert but do contain the power of the usurping younger brother. In this earlier play, the daughter is active rather than passive, and Duke Senior, somewhat like Portia's dead father, exercises his power through her.[10] As her father's dream agent, she keeps Orlando a dramatically flat character and arranges his mock punishment, for he cannot have her until he has forgiven Oliver – as though he must expiate his rebellion against even that debased authority. The idealized magical father, invisible in *The Merchant of Venice*, becomes barely visible in *As You Like It*, and after several tragic permutations takes centre stage in *The Tempest*, in which he explicitly manages conflicts that were not fully realized until the major tragedies.

These vagaries of motivation do not detract from the play's success. Better than any other of the comedies it manages the polarity between idealized romantic love and the sense of its danger, by putting in the foreground an active, intelligent, and loving daughter and leaving both the good and bad versions of the father well in the background. Though Oliver and Frederick initiate the plot, they have little stage time, and their negative energy drains away as Oliver is swept into marriage and Frederick is converted to a monastic life. From the play's beginning the most palpable counter-force to love is embodied in Jaques. Though he contributes little to the action and is mocked, his melancholy rejection of love provides a pervasive emotional refrain that is associated from the first with Duke Senior; in Jaques' melancholy is expressed the duke's reluctance to part from his daughter, since the process of her union with Orlando forms the major action. Jaques' presence at the final scene prevents the world of the play from closing around the four couples, when he announces his intention to seek out the monk's cell and declares himself 'not for dancing measures.' This strikes an emotional note similar to that of Prospero's declaration that once Miranda and Ferdinand are joined, his 'every third thought will be my grave.' Those mournful feelings that are an aspect of Prospero's character in this play create a second figure, in a way that parallels the development from Claudio-Don John through Iago-Othello and Posthumus-Iachimo to Leontes in *The Winter's Tale*.

The absence from *As You Like It* of any negative forces other than Jaques' humorous melancholy reflects its generosity towards so many aspects of loving. Though the union of Orlando and Rosalind comes closest to the ideally mutual loving associated with procreation and a renewed society (Rosalind tells Celia that she does not mourn for her father, but rather for her child's father), their joyous union embraces the earthy love of Touchstone and Audrey, as well as the initially imperfect and non-mutual love of Phoebe and Sylvius, with the cardboard romantic love of Celia and Oliver thrown in for good measure. This generous embrace of love in all its physicality and in all of its imperfect forms does not appear again until *Antony and Cleopatra*, a play that stands in relation to the tragedies as *As You Like It* does to the comedies.

Though not so joyously all-embracing as *As You Like It*, *Twelfth Night* also defends the imperfect real against Malvolio's ideal of purity. Parental figures have no overt presence; Malvolio as moral guardian and Sir Toby as Olivia's uncle can be seen as such figures, but are denied authority; comic coincidence, rather than unseen magical forces, controls the action. Olivia's dead brother and dead father exercise control from beyond the grave only over Olivia, who is criticized for attending to the dead rather than the living. In a minor way she, along with Malvolio, represents the anti-life forces, and is therefore a suitable object for Malvolio's unwanted attentions.

Malvolio is not a villain acting out of some inexplicable and gratuitous hatred. His envy of pleasures from which he feels excluded is easily exposed by Maria's plot, and it is a readily understandable human motivation, and though many critics feel that his crimes do not merit such harsh punishment as he receives, his voice compels no response, as does Shylock's, nor does it, like Jaques', suggest that a dimension of life has been excluded. The negative aspects of loving are in the lovers themselves, experienced by them as the pains of non-mutuality, but unlike in *The Two Gentlemen* and *A Midsummer Night's Dream* no blame attaches to their failure to return love, and unlike the lovers in *A Midsummer Night's Dream*, they are not coerced into loving. On the whole they are attractive people amid their difficulties, the resolution of which does not wait upon anyone's reformation, but only upon comic time and circumstance that will provide appropriate lovers for all parties. Viola has some of Rosalind's charm and ebullient spirit, but has neither her control nor her satiric edge. Rather, she is cheerfully passive as she runs Orsino's errands, finds Olivia inappropriately in love with her, and waits for time to 'untangle this, not I! / It is too hard a knot for me t'untie.' The satiric and manipulative aspects of Rosalind's character separate from her gentler aspects to compose the figure of Maria in *Twelfth Night*. That the romantic and the controlling aspects of the heroine are in this way separated, with Maria functioning towards Malvolio as Portia does towards Shylock, may indicate Shakespeare's unease with Rosalind's power, but if the fullness of Rosalind's characterization represents one kind of triumph, the freedom of this play from parental figures, and from symbolic extensions of them into magical powers, represents another.[11] The dark forces of previous plays have lost their mystery and power. The beneficent side of the parent figures retreats far into the background, becoming merely comic time and circumstance, and the darker side loses its compulsive and controlling power to become the ordinary envy of Malvolio for pleasures he lacks. That this happy disappearance of the parents, and their symbolic extensions, represents only a temporary resolution of conflict is perhaps indicated in the uneasy feelings that surround Malvolio. The 'madness' imposed upon him by Maria might be seen to prelude Hamlet's feigned madness, and his exit line, 'I'll be revenged on the whole pack of you,' as presaging Lear's impotent rage and the darker side of loving that re-emerges with full power in the tragedies to which we now turn.

3

'So Many Fathoms Deep':
Love and Death in *Hamlet*

Hamlet's dream hovers on the brink of nightmare; its structure, tone, and atmosphere reflect Hamlet's reluctant but steady movement towards fuller versions of the initial configuration until he finally succeeds in eliminating paternal figures that bar his way to both his mother and Ophelia. This process is expressed in the changing versions of his father's death, while the horrors he associates with his project are expressed in the discontinuity of the action, the obscurity of the story line behind the sequence of scenes that leaves questions about his motivations, and the relatively indistinct characterization of many of the other figures.

What the other characters and the sequence of action lack in full definition, Hamlet retains. While his solid or sullied flesh moves through a world of shadows, he dwells in his imagination on the emotions that in later plays create more substantial secondary characters and action. The result is a disparity between dominant emotions generated by his language and images, and the characters we see who don't quite correspond to his thoughts of them. He is Shakespeare's most thoughtful character, for by means of self-reflection he keeps himself on the brink of his own dream, only tentatively shaping the sea of troubles against which to take arms, or the rottenness in Denmark he is to remove. The task of cleansing the royal bed of Denmark by killing Claudius is joined to and expresses a more submerged but pervasive project, which is to achieve his own maturity – that is, to abandon his filial status for that of husband and father, both represented by becoming king. In his uncle's murder of his father Hamlet expresses both his desire to eliminate the father who bars his way to full manhood and his interpretation of that desire as treacherous and violent. Hamlet's fear of assuming his maturity has placed Claudius on the throne that represents it, and is expressed as well by the incestuous definition of love and sexuality.[1] He tries to retreat from the configuration he has engendered by asking to return to Wittenberg, but Claudius' refusal expresses a stronger drive to penetrate to the fears and desires that give rise to his conscious experience of mourning and melancholy, his 'suits of woe.' Those underlying desires will be revealed in the changing configurations he confronts as he struggles towards a resolution.

Hamlet expresses his inner state in the world he has generated around himself, peopled mostly by parental figures who, as argued in the introduction, express a retreat into past emotional forms from which he has distanced himself. In opposition to these parental figures he defines himself as studious and philosophical rather than martial, as world-weary, and sometimes as a coward. However, the conflict between his chosen stance and the rejected paternal value system appears in other characters with whom the action and language of the play identify him. In his relations to Laertes, Fortinbras, and Horatio he expresses his conflicting feelings towards the rejected alternatives.

Like Hamlet, Laertes is a son, but of a living father closely associated with Claudius. He is also identified with Hamlet in several other ways – through his similar desire to leave Elsinore, by being similarly spied upon, through his parallel project of avenging his father's death, and by his relation to Ophelia. His successful petition to Claudius expresses Hamlet's fleeting desire to escape his dilemma, and his repudiation of it. He, as it were, sends away his own desire to go. Laertes also expresses a trivialized version of Hamlet's sense of diseased sexuality, first in his image of the 'contageous blastments' that might sully the 'liquid dew' of Ophelia's youth, and later in the association implied by Polonius' assumption that Laertes might be discovered at a 'house of sale.' Polonius busies himself with ferreting out sexual secrets, indirectly those of Laertes, and directly those of Hamlet. Since he spies on Hamlet's talk with Ophelia and with Gertrude, the association of them with Laertes' brothels introduces Hamlet's equation of women with whores. More important, however, these parallel configurations generalize the extent to which Hamlet experiences himself as spied upon, by Polonius, Claudius, and Rosencrantz and Guildenstern, figures parallel to Reynaldo. The configuration shows Hamlet inviting and fearing the discovery of his secrets. But Hamlet also spies out the secrets of those who spy upon him. In being spied upon and in spying on others he expresses his own desire to discover the sexuality that he has surrounded with secrecy, evil, and betrayal.[2] The parallel revenge motif makes the contrast between Laertes' return with an army and Hamlet's return 'naked' to the kingdom, reveal the role that Hamlet rejects. Laertes' mistaken project against Claudius and his being manipulated by him express Hamlet's feeling that to act against Claudius is to be manipulated, to become a pipe upon which Fortune or others may 'sound what stop she please.'

Like Hamlet himself, Laertes combines a martial revenge project with his relation to women. The integral relation between the two is suggested by the contrast between Laertes and Fortinbras, who has no associations with women, but who, like Hamlet, is the son of a dead father. The parallel between Hamlet's and Fortinbras' situations is so strong that it generates an unexplained sick uncle, who for no apparent reason has succeeded to the Norwegian throne as Claudius has to Denmark's and who disappears at the same time as Claudius dies. Fortinbras, who acts without hesitation in his father's cause, is the kind of son Hamlet would like to be when he promises to 'sweep to his revenge.' In casting Fortinbras as his father's ideal son, Hamlet expresses both his self-rebuke for being otherwise, and his ambivalence about the martial ideal represented both by Fortinbras and by his father, who was 'our valiant Hamlet / (For so this side of our known world esteem'd him)' (I.i.87–8). His ambivalence structures the action when he encounters Fortinbras' army while on his journey towards England, from which he might, like Laertes, have returned with an army. That possibility never reaches the level of language, but its hovering presence appears in Hamlet's contradictory reflections on Fortinbras' enterprise, which is also a version of his father's.

Initially he rebukes his own inaction by admiring Fortinbras' courage in 'Exposing what is mortal and unsure / To all that fortune, death, and danger dare, / Even for an eggshell' (IV.iv.51–3). But the image of an eggshell expresses his doubts about these martial values when it leads him to an argument that is at cross purposes with the conclusion that he draws from it. Contrasting himself to Fortinbras, he reflects that one is merely bestial if 'his chief good and market of his time / Be but to sleep and feed,' and that we were not endowed with 'godlike reason / To fust in us unus'd' (IV.iv.34,38–9). However, though he purports to praise Fortinbras, it is he rather than Fortinbras who uses his reason and 'large discourse' to look 'before and after.' When he thinks about himself the thoughtfulness that was a virtue when associated with Fortinbras becomes 'bestial oblivion' that has 'but one part wisdom / And ever three parts coward' (IV.iv.40,42–3). These lines, however, contradict the previous ones, for having said that only our reason makes us more than beasts, he now claims that thinking 'too precisely on th' event' derives mostly from cowardice. He then emphasizes the triviality of the cause for which Fortinbras risks so much, and concludes in a syntactically confused and self-contradictory sentence that to be great is 'not to stir without great argument, / But greatly to find quarrel in a straw / When honour's at the stake' (IV.iv.53–6).

Though he has defined honour in opposition to the reason that distinguishes men from beasts, he still uses the concept to berate himself for his inaction while Fortinbras 'for a fantasy and trick of fame' commits twenty thousand men to fight for a plot 'which is not tomb enough and continent / To hide the slain' (IV.iv.64–5). Having defined Fortinbras' honour as thoughtless action taken in an unworthy cause does not, though he wants it to, undermine his own thoughtfulness. Rather the reverse; though the speech is self-berating, its logic shows Hamlet judging himself as more worthy than the martial Fortinbras in his eagerness to find 'quarrel in a straw.' Since Fortinbras' values represent those of the dead king, the speech, even while it attempts the opposite, reflects Hamlet's self-justification for being unlike his father, for rejecting his father's values and refusing fully to identify with him. The contrast between Hamlet and Fortinbras becomes something like the contrast between Prince Hal and Hotspur. Henry IV would rather have had Hotspur for a son, but Hal on his own terms proves himself superior to both. Though hidden, something of that impulse lies behind the logical confusion of Hamlet's speech.

If Hamlet secretly condemns in Fortinbras the heroic virtues he overtly admires in his father, in Horatio he secretly condones the aspects of himself that he overtly condemns. Like Hamlet, Horatio is a student, and duplicates Hamlet as observer rather than participant. His role as a kind of ego ideal appears in Hamlet's praise of him as one who has made himself invulnerable to being manipulated by Fortune by having his 'blood and judgment ... so well commeddled' (III.ii.69). When Rosencrantz and Guildenstern, most fully defined as manipulating and manipulated characters, declare themselves 'Fortune's privates,' Hamlet capitalizes on the traditional depiction of Fortune as a woman in punning 'In the secret parts of Fortune? O, most true, she is a strumpet' (II.ii.235–6).[3] That suggests that Hamlet fears women's manipulative strategies, and that his ideal of passions and emotions that are reasonable, incarnated in Horatio, can be maintained only by being isolated, like Horatio, from contaminating contact with women or with family. Horatio's detachment both expresses and alleviates the loneliness that follows upon Hamlet's ambivalence towards his father.

The emotional components that appear remotely and lightly sketched in the figures that extend from Hamlet's definition of himself, appear with greater force and immediacy in the array of parental figures he confronts, and lead deeper into the play's convolutions. As already suggested in discussing Fortinbras, Hamlet, in having disposed of King Hamlet, expressed both his idealization of and his rejection of the martial values he represents. By being confronted with a murdered father at the play's beginning he tries to disentangle the complex and conflicting emotions towards the paternal realm, for he has not so much disposed of his father as split him into four different forms.

The first of these is the idealized martial image of a dead father, which merges into the image of the ghost. Military values are emphasized by the armour the ghost wears despite having been killed while asleep in the garden, which throws into relief Hamlet's association of his father with military prowess. In the configuration he also undermines his father's prowess, for Horatio and the others discuss the renewed hostilities that now make 'the night joint labourer with the day.' That neither the ghost nor Hamlet says anything directly about these new wars, and that they appear only in peripheral action indicates Hamlet's inability to confront them directly, but their importance to him appears in the way they form the background of the entire play. The issue recurs when Claudius, having announced his marriage, instructs the ambassadors to his counterpart, Fortinbras' uncle. Claudius' diplomacy seems more successful than King Hamlet's wars, for the ambassadors return to announce that Fortinbras 'Makes vow before his uncle never more / To give th'assay of arms against your Majesty' (II.ii.70–1). The greater success of Claudius' diplomacy indicates Hamlet's strategy to undermine the military idealization of his father, and in a devious way to associate himself with Claudius, whose indirection is more like his own. Both sides of Hamlet's polarized feelings towards his father culminate when he gives his 'dying voice' to Fortinbras' election as king. This bizarre action in one stroke cancels both Claudius' diplomatic success and his father's military success. King Hamlet, known for his valour, won for Denmark a piece of land, and his thoughtful son, 'a glass of fashion and a mold of form' gives away the whole of Denmark to the son of his father's enemy. Even while Hamlet avenges himself on these paternal values that have so successfully undermined him, he also confirms them by giving the Danish crown to Fortinbras, who carries his father's values forward, and by endowing himself in death with the military honours he declined in life when Fortinbras orders that 'the soldier's music and the rite of war/ Speak loudly for him' (v.ii.404–5). Through Fortinbras' words Hamlet finally becomes in death the soldier he refused to be in life. He reinterprets the personal violence that has just filled the stage as military violence, uniting the public and personal levels that have not been in proximity since the beginning. It is as though Hamlet as he appears through Fortinbras has in fact, like Laertes, raised an army and won the kingdom from Claudius, rather than ironically announcing himself as 'Hamlet the Dane' come naked to his grave in Claudius' kingdom. In as witty a piece of unconscious over-determination as one could desire, Hamlet evokes in imagination a military triumph that his father would admire while in the process of repudiating all his father valued.[4]

Hamlet's idealization of his father's prowess conceals not only his ambivalence towards the manliness he also espouses; it also conceals his ambivalence about sexuality. He compares his father to Hyperion, a sun god, removed from sexuality and associated with the awareness and consciousness that Hamlet values in himself. He opposes to that ideal Claudius' satyrlike lust, and he stresses the polarity when he describes the grace of his father's 'Hyperion's curls,' his 'eye like Mars,' and his 'station like the herald Mercury / New-lighted on a heaven-kissing hill' (iii.iv.56–9). The ghost opposes his idealized martial image to sexuality in telling Hamlet that his own love 'Was of that dignity / That it went hand in hand even with the vow / I made to her in marriage' (i.v.48–50). The opposition between King Hamlet's dignified love and both Claudius' and Gertrude's 'shameful lust' sharpens when the ghost says that just as virtue is impervious to temptation even if lewdness, presumably Claudius, comes disguised in a 'shape of heaven,' so lust, presumably Gertrude, 'though to a radiant angel link'd, / Will sate itself in a celestial bed / And prey on garbage' (i.v.54–7).

Hamlet, then, has associated his father with a disembodied radiant angel, and the marriage bed with a celestial one opposed to 'incestuous sheets.' Male sexuality is associated with satyrlike lust and garbage, woman's with the diseased desire for it, and both with all that is rotten in Denmark. These frightening associations lead to the grotesque imagery in which the ghost describes the 'leperous distilment' that, when poured into the 'porches of [his] ears' caused 'a most instant tetter [to bark] about / Most lazar-like, with vile and loathsome crust / All [his] smooth body' (i.v.64,70–3). These images will echo in Hamlet's description of Claudius as a 'mildewed ear' and as a 'slave's offal.' The loathsome sexual Claudius represents King Hamlet's dead body, suggesting that in Hamlet's imagination sexuality equates with death – not death as a dissolution into vague blackness, the dominant image of *Romeo and Juliet*, but death as the corrupted body.

This equation of sex and death lies behind the images of death that first appear on the periphery of the main action and distant from Hamlet in Francisco's unexplained assertion that ''Tis bitter cold, / And I am sick at heart.' Horatio in equal mystery responds to the query of his identity with 'A piece of him' (i.i.8–9,22). Those unexplained expressions of deep unease are detached from but consonant with the description of the ghost as a 'dreaded sight' that 'usurp'st this time of night.' Horatio extends to a political realm the significance of this ambience of fear and depression when he tells how in the 'most high and palmy state of Rome,'

> The graves stood tenantless and the sheeted dead
> Did squeak and gibber in the Roman streets;
> As stars with trains of fire and dews of blood,

Disasters in the sun; and the moist star,
Upon whose influence Neptune's empire stands,
Was sick almost to doomsday with eclipse. (i.i.118–23)

These images of the moon 'sick almost to doomsday with eclipse' at the sight of the risen dead, which prelude the first mention of Hamlet's name, suggest a psychic past from which Hamlet's project arises.

Though Hamlet has generated the ghost from his own need to restore his idealized father-image, the feeling of awesome horror generated by that figure activates the very associations it is designed to repress, in a form that makes Hamlet uneasily aware of his participation in the experiences he confronts. Images of ghosts and of the risen dead are linked to inward emotional upheaval when Hamlet asks the ghost why he returns to make 'night hideous' and 'so horridly to shake our disposition / With thoughts beyond the reaches of our souls, (i.iv.55–6). Horatio emphasizes the inward dimension of the external-ized form when he warns that it may 'assume some other horrible form / Which might deprive your sovereignty of reason / And draw you into mad-ness' (i.iv.72–4). Hamlet extends Horatio's image when he reflects that the spirit might be a devil, who 'Out of my weakness and melancholy, / As he is very potent with such spirits, / Abuses me to damn me' (ii.ii.597–9). Hamlet here joins the idea of madness, that is, the possibility that the ghost arises from the dark recesses of his own mind, and the image of evil spirits – external forces that can make use of the mind's products. To succumb to weakness and melancholy that generate dark desires is to be damned. Hamlet tightens that connection between the mind's dark side and hell, when he says later that if the players do not trip Claudius into admitting his guilt, then 'It is a damned ghost that we have seen, / And my imaginations are as foul / As Vulcan's stithy' (iii.ii.82–4).

If Claudius is not guilty in the external world, then the ghost's accusation arises from his own hellish imagination. But the shift from a Christian hell to a classical 'Vulcan's stithy' suggests the source in his imagination from which such a 'damned ghost' might arise. Husband to Venus and cuckolded by Mars, Vulcan in his smithy prepares the device with which to entrap Venus and her paramour in the act of copulation. The image associates Hamlet with Vulcan, the outraged husband, suggesting that his imagination's foulness consists in its power to create and its desire to dwell on images of Claudius' and Gertrude's sexuality. It also reveals his secret claim to be Gertrude's rightful lover. By means of the ghost's call for revenge and his instruction not to taint his mind by letting his soul 'contrive / Against thy mother aught' (i.v.85–6) Hamlet temporarily shifts his attention from his conflicted feeling towards his mother to anger and rage at Claudius.

However, it is one thing to evoke a father who commands him to vengeance, and another thing to obey him. The reasons for Hamlet's reluctance to kill Claudius are the same reasons for which he generated him. After making the hesitant step towards Gertrude by eliminating his father, he had quickly to couple Gertrude with Claudius in order to keep himself away from her, both because of his association of sexuality with incest, disease, and death, and because the image of Claudius and Gertrude together allows him both to envision and to remain apart from their sexuality. He is not ready to dispense with Claudius, for the configuration he has so far generated has expressed and deepened the polarity between sex, death, and deviousness on the one hand, and martial values, manhood, and sexual abstinence on the other. It has provided Hamlet with no way other than secret voyeurism in which to placate desires so horrifying that their fulfillment entails his death.[5]

Between the polarity of the sexualized but corrupt body of the father and the idealized and dematerialized spirit, Hamlet inserts a third image of the father as a fool. One can see the ghost in the process of transforming into Polonius. While Hamlet swears Horatio and the others to secrecy, the ghost abandons its awesome dignity and, unaccountably and in a way difficult to stage, cavorts under the ground. Hamlet's mocking address, 'Well said, old mole. Canst work i'th'earth so fast?' (I.v.170), to the ghost who eavesdrops, as it were from the cellarage, parallels his ironic mockery of the spying and intrusive Polonius. Though the play's emotional tenor makes Polonius' antics seem peripheral, in fact he appears, until his death, in more scenes than any figure other than Hamlet himself; he arranges much of the circumstance Hamlet encounters, and, though not a person about whom Hamlet thinks, he is the target of most of Hamlet's verbal energy. Though the comic tone makes it appear that Polonius is an accidental object of Hamlet's revenge, in the configuration of action Polonius, a more fully dramatized personality than either Claudius or King Hamlet, emerges as the play's most emotionally prominent father-figure.

Claudius and King Hamlet function for Hamlet as symbolic images of diseased sexuality and idealized non-sexuality. He ruminates about these images that emerge from the past, but in the present he reveals deeper layers of his sexual imagination in his seemingly offhanded dealings with Polonius; in depriving Hamlet of Ophelia, Polonius functions as a debased version of Claudius, who deprives Hamlet of Gertrude. Hamlet appears to know that Polonius has caused Ophelia's change of heart, since his first words to him are, 'You are a fishmonger.' Hamlet reverses the slang meaning of 'fishmonger' to accuse Polonius of using Ophelia as a pawn in a political strategy. When Polonius denies being a fishmonger, presumably in its literal sense, Hamlet answers, 'Then I would you were so honest a man.' Still playing on the slang meaning, he implies that simple procuring is more honest than the political use Polonius makes of Ophelia. To Polonius' query about his meaning, Hamlet says, 'To be honest, as this world goes, is to be one man picked out of ten thousand,' and adds, 'For if the sun breed maggots in a dead dog, being a good kissing carrion – Have you a daughter?' The logic seems to be that there are few honest men because most men, being partially or potentially corrupt, walk in the sun, which hastens corruption. The focus sharpens in the last question, particularly when, after Polonius' affirmative response, Hamlet adds, 'Let her not walk i'th' sun. Conception is a blessing, but not as your daughter may conceive – friend, look to't' (ii.ii.174,176,178–9,181–3,185–6). Having referred to his dead father as the sun god, Hyperion, Hamlet in this passage implicitly equates himself with the sun, which will, if Ophelia should try to make good her denial of him, cause her to conceive in the way that carrion does. This is a stronger version of Laertes' image of the canker that 'galls the infants of the spring / Too oft before their buttons be disclosed.' With stark force Hamlet equates Ophelia's womb to a dead thing that can conceive only as dead things do, and himself to the sun that will so perversely impregnate her.[6]

He also associates Ophelia's corruption with her father's in images of physical decay; Hamlet tells Polonius he is reading a 'satirical rogue,' who says that 'old men have gray beards, that their faces are wrinkled, their eyes purging thick amber and plumtree gum, and that they have a plentiful lack of wit, together with most weak hams' (ii.ii.197–200). His disgust at Polonius' aging body joins the cluster of images already associated with his father's dead body, and with Claudius whom he calls a 'mildew'd ear,' with whom he would, were he himself not 'pigeon-liver'd,' have 'fatted all the region kites / With this slave's offal' (ii.ii.573–6). The carrion image in reference to Claudius harks back to the one referring to Polonius, and brings all three versions of the father within the aura of physical decay.

Hamlet's sexual competiveness with his father emerges in his mockery of Polonius. He taunts Polonius for his 'weak hams' and adds that he holds it 'not honesty to have it thus set down. For you yourself, sir, shall grow as old as I am – if like a crab you could go backward' (ii.ii.202–4). But he claims this competitive victory over the father only in the process of relinquishing the woman. Under the guise of blaming Polonius for Ophelia's corruption, implicitly blaming the father for the mother's corruption, Hamlet conceals from himself his own desire by projecting it onto both figures and rejecting them. This strategy allows him to claim victory in the Oepidal struggle with the father by translating his failure to win a woman into a triumph of moral superiority. But since that dynamic arises from his own sexual self-disgust, and his preoccupation with death and decay from his own association of sex with the deadly and death-dealing, he turns back against himself when he puns on Polonius' 'Will you walk out of the air, my lord?' with 'Into my grave?' (II.ii.206–7).

In the configuration of characters, Polonius' power, which elides with that of Laertes, to deny to Hamlet Ophelia's sexuality parallels Claudius' power over Gertrude. Gertrude and Ophelia are thereby associated with each other, and both are defined by the rank sexuality that leads to their betrayal of Hamlet. As merging mother-daughter images, they express controlling versus controllable versions of the same sexuality. Gertrude's sexual appetite, which 'grows by what it feeds on,' led her to betray Hamlet by having helped Claudius pop 'between th' election and [his] hopes,' and, as we will see, it is in indistinct ways associated with murder as well as with adultery. After the ghost's injunction that Hamlet should leave Gertrude to heaven, she temporarily becomes the background for Ophelia's relation to Hamlet.[7]

In Ophelia Hamlet creates a figure in the process of being drawn from the realm of springtime buds into the orbit of the 'contagious blastments' of his own sexuality.[8] The submerged love story between Hamlet and Ophelia expresses both nostalgia for a lost vision of pure love, and Hamlet's jaded view of his own and women's sexuality, which draws Ophelia into the whirlpool of incestuously defined sexuality. Both sides of his feeling can be seen in the disparity between the view of Hamlet as seen by Laertes and Polonius and Hamlet's view of himself. Laertes warns Ophelia to preserve her 'chaste treasure' from Hamlet's contagion, a warning that occasions Polonius to forbid her to see Hamlet on the grounds that his vows are 'Not of that dye which their investments show, / But mere implorators of unholy suits, / Breathing like sanctified and pious bawds / The better to beguile' (I.iii. 128–31). Laertes' and Polonius' image of Hamlet explicitly contrasts to Hamlet's declaration that his 'suits of woe' truly denote his inner state, a view of himself echoed by Ophelia's confidence that his intentions are honourable. In the contrast Hamlet expresses the gap between his self-definition and his unacknowledged association of his sexual passions with manipulation and betrayal.

Hamlet's association of Ophelia with female weakness and betrayal emerges in his mocking love letter to 'the celestial, and my soul's idol, the most beautified Ophelia.' Her painted face here represents her function as a decoy, but the same image will later incorporate associations between women and death. These associations are subtly suggested in the dramatic sequence, for in his first soliloquy Hamlet reflected that he had to live only because the Everlasting had 'fixed his canon 'gainst self-slaughter.' As he approaches the contrived meeting with Ophelia he again meditates on death, this time fearing not punishment from God, but rather from the bad dreams that may come 'when we have shuffled off this mortal coil.' Following the conventional association of sleep with death, to die is to be entrapped in a dream, or in his imagination, which may be 'as foul as Vulcan's stithy.' In this context he confronts an external image of his own imagination when he sees Ophelia at her 'orison.'

When Polonius poses Ophelia with the prayer-book he has given her, he generalizes the image he has thus created as representative of the way in which 'with devotion's visage / And pious action we do sugar o'er / The devil himself' (III.i.46–8). Claudius deepens the implied association of Ophelia's, or female, sexuality with duplicity when he feels his conscience stung by Polonius' reflection and takes Ophelia's pose as an image of his corrupt soul: 'The harlot's cheek, beautied with plast'ring art, / Is not more ugly to the thing that helps it / Than is my deed to my most painted word' (III.i.50–3). The painted harlot, an image of sexual corruption beneath womens' fair flesh, becomes an emblem of all human evil. That generalized image pervades Hamlet's renunciation of marriage when he tells Ophelia to 'Go thy ways to a nunnery.' Using both the literal and the colloquial meanings of the word, he creates a polarity wherein sexuality must be either corrupt, and breed sinners like himself, or absent. His anger at her merges with self-hatred when he says that he, being 'of woman born' could accuse himself 'of such things it were better my mother had not borne me.' He images himself and all men as insects when he asks, 'What should such fellows as I do crawling between earth and heaven?' (III.i.123,129). The image of the painted harlot comes to include all life, and extends more specifically to two images of the father, Polonius when Hamlet concludes his tirade with 'Where's your father?', and Claudius when he says, 'Those that are married already – all but one – shall live.' His mind has merged Ophelia with Gertrude in a way that makes this interview between Hamlet and Ophelia a rehearsal of Hamlet's more intense meeting with Gertrude, for which he is not yet ready.

Between the two encounters with betraying women Hamlet slowly recasts his vision of his father's death and of himself in ways that reveal what is obscured within the love-death equation. The first reenactment of the murder scene is indirect, contained in Aeneas' speech, recited by the player at Hamlet's request. Unconnected to the plot, this speech represents a freer play of fantasy than the other player scenes. In its lurid images, which equate Pyrrhus with himself, Hamlet expresses some of the passions that move below the surface of the other action. He recites the first part of the speech in which Pyrrhus' 'sable arms' that 'did the night resemble' equate with Hamlet's 'nighted colour,' and the midnight watch that opens the play, and Pyrrhus' concealment in 'the ominous horse' to Hamlet's concealment within his 'antic disposition.' The 'heraldry more dismal' with which Pyrrhus will soon be smeared, the 'blood of fathers, mothers, daughters, sons' (II.ii.454), suggests the coming blood-bath, and the free-floating rage that occasions it is suggested by the image of the hellish Pyrrhus who, as he seeks Priam, is 'Roasted in wrath and fire, / And thus o'ersized with coagulate gore, / With eyes like carbuncles' (II.ii.457–9). In the horrible images of Pyrrhus' rage, directed not at a Claudius figure but rather at 'grandsire Priam,' who more resembles King Hamlet, Hamlet expresses the hatred that lies concealed beneath his melancholy suits of woe. As the player takes over the remainder of the speech, Priam's murder is placed in a political context similar to that suggested between Denmark and Norway. Troy's defeat, which will follow upon Priam's death, anticipates the victory of Norway over Denmark implied when Hamlet's election of Fortinbras cancels his father's previous victory. The equations of Troy to Denmark and of Hamlet to Pyrrhus become more overt as the player describes the unequal battle in which,

> Pyrrhus at Priam drives, in rage strikes wide;
> But with the whiff and wind of his fell sword
> Th'unnerved father falls. Then senseless Ilium,
> Seeming to feel this blow, with flaming top
> Stoops to his base, and with a hideous crash
> Takes prisoner Pyrrhus' ear. For lo, his sword,
> Which was declining on the milky head
> Of reverend Priam, seem'd i'th' air to stick;
> So, as a painted tyrant, Pyrrhus stood,
> And like a neutral to his will and matter,
> Did nothing. (II.ii.468–78)

The trance into which Pyrrhus falls resembles the trance into which the ghost says Hamlet would fall if he were to see the purgatorial sufferings, as well as the trances into which Macbeth will fall when he first contemplates murdering Duncan, and sees the airborne dagger. These horrifying trances suggest the mind momentarily captured by a vision of what is at once fiercely desired and feared as antithetical to all conscious definition of self and espoused values. What transfixes Pyrrhus is not the murder of Priam, but is rather the 'hideous crash' of falling Ilium. In Pyrrhus' trance Hamlet portrays his terror of his own desire totally to eradicate all traces of his father's power, which he satisfies as though offhandedly in the process of envisioning his own death, while Hamlet's desire to have his 'malicious sport' witnessed by his mother generates the image of the half-naked and aging Hecuba's 'instant burst of clamor.'

The dumb show that prefaces the players' scene constitutes Hamlet's second reconstruction of the murder. Claudius' unaccountable patience with the dumb show, which is at least as pointed as the fuller presentation, calls attention to an emotional note that is contained neither in the original story nor in the enactment that follows. The stage direction reads, 'She kneels, and makes show of protestation unto him. He takes her up, and declines his head upon her neck.' That mute gesture remotely betokens a desire for women's maternal comfort that appears nowhere else. Reasons for its absence are suggested by details of the second presentation, in which the Player Queen protests, 'In second husband let me be accurst; / None wed the second but who kill'd the first,' and 'A second time I kill my husband dead, / When second husband kisses me in bed' (III.ii.174–5,179–80). Presumably Hamlet does not intend to accuse Gertrude of murdering her husband, but rather sees her infidelity as a kind of murder. However, in recasting the initial configuration he associates violence with women in a way that foreshadows Lady Macbeth and explains why he might hesitate to seek maternal comfort, except in the insultingly smutty way he rests his head on Ophelia's lap.[9]

In this episode Hamlet emphasizes the queen rather than Claudius, giving first an image of her as a murderer. When she wishes for an 'anchor's cheer in prison' should she remarry, her image of extreme self-denial anticipates Goneril and Regan's protestations of love that conceal sadistic cruelty. As though in response to images of violence and cruelty that extend from Gertrude's more ordinary humanity, Hamlet, urging the players on, uses images that later characterize Macbeth when he says, 'Come, the croaking raven doth bellow for revenge.' Hamlet becomes more closely identified with a Macbeth-like figure when the Player Nephew says,

Thoughts black, hands apt, drugs fit, and time agreeing,
Confederate season, else no creature seeing,
Thou mixture rank, of midnight weeds collected,
With Hecate's ban thrice blasted, thrice infected,
Thy natural magic and dire property
On wholesome life usurps immediately.   (III.ii.249–55)

That Lucianus is called the 'nephew to the king' identifies him with Hamlet, who is nephew to Claudius, and vaguely associates Hamlet with Hecate's dark realm. The poisonous 'mixture rank, of midnight weeds collected' merges with the generalized image of the world as an unweeded garden, possessed by 'things rank and gross.' These images are associated vaguely with Gertrude, who has posted 'with such dexterity to incestuous sheets.' Her sheets become the centre from which the surrounding rankness emanates when the ghost says, 'Let not the royal bed of Denmark be / A couch for luxury and damned incest' (I.v.82–3). At this point the sexualized images of weedy rankness fuse with the rank mixture that kills the king. In the logic of images, it is a corrupted sexuality administered by the nephew, representative of Hamlet, that poisons the player king, representative of the idealized father.

Together these three replays of the murder scene show Hamlet gradually making concrete the emotional currents that were incompletely expressed in the initial configuration. He gives externalized form to the eroticized violence towards Gertrude that previously was manifested only in vague images. In catching the conscience of the king, Hamlet for the moment frees himself from the murky emotions that impeded him. Along with his own guilt, he casts off the spies who now call him to his mother's bedroom. Exposing Rosencrantz and Guildenstern's venality in the recorder speech, and Polonius' time-serving by directing his interpretation of cloud shapes, he frees himself from the sense of being watched. He can dispense with those figures because he is about to approach more directly the guilty secrets that they tried to ferret out. Therefore the previously scattered images of violence, disease, and sexuality that first created the Macbeth-like Lucianus now characterize Hamlet's language as he approaches Gertrude:

> 'Tis now the very witching time of night,
> When churchyards yawn and hell itself breathes out
> Contagion to this world. Now could I drink hot blood,
> And do such bitter business as the day
> Would quake to look on. Soft, now to my mother.
> O heart, lose not thy nature. Let not ever
> The soul of Nero enter this firm bosom;
> Let me be cruel, not unnatural.
> I will speak daggers to her, but use none.
> My tongue and soul in this be hypocrites:
> How in my words somever she be shent,
> To give them seals, never, my soul, consent.   (III.ii.379–90)

The Macbeth-like image of the 'witching time of night' merges with images of yawning churchyards and the contagious breath of hell that earlier were associated with the Roman dead who rose from their graves to depict unsatisfied wrongs in a Roman past that Horatio likened to Denmark's. Hamlet's image of the churchyard as he approaches Gertrude places in the context of an unsatisfied family past the earlier image of the foul deeds that 'will rise /

Though all the earth o'erwhelm them, to men's eyes' (I.ii.257–8). Since he has already associated death with sexuality, that image suggests his own sexual arousal, which brings in its wake horrifying images of violence, as he comes near Gertrude's bedroom. Hamlet imagines himself as Nero killing his mother, but converts the image to one of verbal violence when he says that he will not use the daggers that he speaks.

Having at last envisioned the encounter with his mother towards which he has been moving, Hamlet's way to her is bedevilled by every variety of father image he has generated. In an effort to divert himself he encounters Claudius at prayer. The image of Claudius struggling with his conscience merges with that of his father suffering purgatorial pains, but finally having permitted himself to contrive in his soul something against Gertrude, he merely wishes that his father were in hell. But he will keep Claudius, the sexualized image of the father, on the scene until he has eliminated Gertrude and received his own death wound. The inhibiting impulses appear more powerfully, but not powerfully enough to check him, in the figures of Polonius and the ghost, who invade the bedroom itself. As Hamlet's progress towards Gertrude was checked momentarily by Claudius at prayer, his words are checked by the last appearance of the intruding and prurient image of the father eavesdropping behind the arras.

Only after having eliminated Polonius with a real dagger is Hamlet free to use his verbal one. In response to the queen's 'what a rash and bloody deed is this!' Hamlet says, 'A bloody deed. Almost as bad, good Mother, / As kill a king and marry with his brother' (III.iv.27–9). As though the language of the Player Queen – 'second time I kill my husband dead / When second husband kisses me in bed' – has altered the initiating fantasy, he accuses her, not Claudius, of killing the king.

This slide from one version of the murder to another relates to and casts light on the vague articulation of Gertrude's figure in this scene particularly, as well as in the play as a whole. Why does not Hamlet tell Gertrude directly that Claudius murdered the king? He only obliquely refers to the murder when in response to Gertrude's 'As kill a king?' he says 'Ay, lady, it was my word,' and later when he refers to Claudius as a 'murderer and a villain.' Why does he not directly tell Gertrude of what he accuses her? And why does Gertrude not ask, or respond when she is accused either of being or of being wed to a murderer? Later she seems to concur with Hamlet's description of her disgusting sexual relations with Claudius, but she seems unsurprised to discover herself wed to a murderer, nor is it clear whether Hamlet accuses her of adultery and of complicitous knowledge of the murder, or only of having incestuously married an unworthy man. These questions arise but no answers emerge, because Hamlet does not allow Gertrude's figure or, as we will see later, Ophelia's to take firm shape. Gertrude's sexuality is associated with corruption and disease, but what conscious intention is supposed to accompany that sexuality remains questionable. Earlier she had assumed that Hamlet was disturbed because of 'our o'er hasty marriage,' but she acts untouched by the player scene, and speaks with confidence in rebuking Hamlet's rudeness, saying, 'Have you forgot me?' If we are to assume that she defensively stands on queenly dignity, the absence of verbal cues remains significant. This dearth of information about how Gertrude sees herself and the vague articulation of her portrait suggest that concealed in the figure are associations that will emerge only later in *Macbeth* and *King Lear*. But her indistinct portrait also throws into relief Hamlet's preoccupation throughout the rest of the scene with images of sexuality in itself that collect and increase the force of those throughout the play.

Hamlet magnifies to mythical dimensions the power of Gertrude's sexual sin to pollute the entire created universe when he says that it

> blurs the grace and blush of modesty,
> Calls virtue hypocrite, takes off the rose
> From the fair forehead of an innocent love
> And sets a blister there, makes marriage vows
> As false as dicers' oaths – O, such a deed
> As from the body of contraction plucks
> The very soul, and sweet religion makes
> A rhapsody of words. Heaven's face does glow
> O'er this solidity and compound mass
> With tristful visage, as against the doom
> Is thought-sick at the act.   (III.iv.40–51)

Hamlet here makes sexuality in itself the source of pollution just as did Laertes' in his image of the canker that 'galls the infants of the spring.' The last four lines of those quoted recall the previous images of Judgment Day on which the dead will rise from their tombs. The line, 'as against the doom / Is thought-sick at the act,' in its obscurity conceals several references and associations. The 'act' can only be Gertrude's sexual act, which Hamlet will soon more fully describe. That act is associated with the day of judgment, on which, like a phallus, 'foul deeds will rise' and with them the foul-smelling 'blasts of Hell' and purgatorial fumes that accompanied the ghost. Though it is not clear whether the sun, the doom itself, or the universe as a whole is 'thought-sick,' the word recalls the mysterious unease of Francisco's, ''Tis bitter cold / And I am sick at heart,' and Hamlet's sinking heart when the ghost's appearance brings thoughts that extend 'beyond the reaches of our souls.'

The speech draws into a new context Hamlet's earlier and more philosophical description of his state of mind when he said to Rosencrantz and Guildenstern that 'This brave o'erhanging firmament, this majestical roof fretted with golden fire, why, it appeareth nothing to me but a foul and pestilent congregation of vapours. What a piece of work is a man, how noble in reason, how infinite in faculties, in form and moving how express and admirable, in action how like an angel, in apprehension how like a god: the beauty of the world, the paragon of animals – and yet, to me, what is this quintessence of dust? Man delights not me – nor woman neither, though your smiling you seem to say so' (II.ii.300–10). In this first of two references to the cosmos, 'foul and pestilent congregation of vapours' obscures the beauty of the created universe. The disease and foulness that spoil the otherwise magnificent cosmos fuse with the images that relate disease and crime to the stench of death that rises from the grave. At the end of this speech, Hamlet presumably responds to his interlocutors' smirk when he says, 'nor woman neither, though by your smiling you seem to say so,' but his experience of their smirk indicates a secret knowledge on his part that his jaded view of the universe might humiliatingly wind itself down to the sexual, that those pestilent vapours arise from women's genitals as they more clearly do in *King Lear*. In short, Hamlet's image of the 'solidity and compound mass' of the universe, which is 'thought-sick,' in its extreme condensation collects, and obscures, all the previous images of the frightful, diseased, and soul-chilling, the unthinkably horrible, in order to describe Gertrude's sexuality, which causes the dead to arise as it 'roars so loud and thunders in the index' (III.iv.53).

Hamlet contrasts the idealized to the sexualized versions of the father in order to berate Gertrude for choosing the latter, but in the process he conflates the two images he intends to polarize:

> See what a grace was seated on this brow,
> Hyperion's curls, the front of Jove himself,
> And eye like Mars to threaten and command,
> A station like the herald Mercury
> New-lighted on a heaven-kissing hill ...   (III.iv.55–9)

The father is first imaged as the herald Mercury, who is also associated with medicinal powers, landing on the 'heaven-kissing hill.' His image then descends to the hill itself when Hamlet continues:

> Look you now what follows.
> Here is your husband, like a mildew'd ear
> Blasting his wholesome brother. Have you eyes?
> Could you on this fair mountain leave to feed,
> And batten on this moor? (III.iv.63–7)

The contrasting images begin to merge as the mind moves from the god Mercury, to the hill on which he stands, to 'this moor.' The moor presumably refers primarily to a black man, or the evil Claudius, but in context it also suggests low-lying land or a valley, since Gertrude is imagined as feeding first on the hill, as though she were a grazing animal or 'a beast that wants discourse of reason.'

Hamlet next, in an oddly twisted passage, tries to deny altogether the sexuality he finds so abhorrent. He argues that Gertrude cannot be said to love Claudius because she is too old to have passions, and therefore must have used judgment in selecting him. But she could not have used judgment, or have any, because no judgment could 'step from this to this.' Lacking both passion and judgment, since she moves she must have sense, but no senses, even when distorted by madness, could have chosen Claudius, and therefore she must have been deprived of them by a devil's trick – deprived by sight, hearing, feeling, all except smell, but not even smell or 'a sickly part of one true sense' could delight in the foul smelling, sexual Claudius. At this point Hamlet has effectively imagined her dead, as he did his father, but out of that deadness bursts the image of 'rebellious hell,' the hell clearly being her sexuality, which this speech initially denied, and which, in context, as much rebels against his denial, against the 'deadness' he has imposed on her in his imagery, as it does against the constraints of judgment she ought, in his view, to have used. The movement of images that began in heaven with 'Hyperion's curls,' and descended to the heaven-kissing hill, to the fair mountain, to the moor finally comes to rest in the image that associates hell with Gertrude's sexuality. The deepest contrast of the passage, therefore, is not that between Claudius and Hamlet's father, but between Hamlet's father and Gertrude's hellish sexuality. The movement of the passage amplifies the significance of Hamlet's previous image of heaven, which 'With heated visage, as against the doom / Is thought-sick at the act.' 'Heaven's face' equates with the first image of the father in 'Hyperion's curls,' and 'the act' with the 'rebellious hell' of Gertrude's sexuality. The last lines of the speech return to the beginning of the 'index,' asserting the magnitude of pollution that extends from Gertrude's lapse.

The entire speech came in answer to Gertrude's question, 'What have I done that thou dar'st wag thy tongue / In noise so rude against me?' and Hamlet has essentially answered only that she has been sexually moved by an unattractive man. He has said nothing about what Claudius has done, and therefore the queen's vision in her soul of 'such black and grained spots / As will not leave their tinct,' in the overt logic of the sequence makes little sense. It does represent her agreement to Hamlet's proposition that her sexuality is in itself evil.[10] Having won that admission from her, Hamlet finally lets his imagination dwell on Claudius and Gertrude 'In the rank sweat of an enseamed bed, / Stew'd in corruption, honeying and making love / Over the nasty sty!' (III.iv. 92–5). The erotic violence implied when Hamlet said that he would 'speak daggers to her but use none,' is fulfilled when he hears Gertrude say that his words 'like daggers enter in my ears.' She here associates sexuality with violence in a way that substantiates the abstract argument that the ear, as an orifice, represents a 'displacement upwards.' The sexual suggestiveness of this image retrospectively colours the earlier images of Claudius and Lucianus pouring poison into the king's ear. The association between the two images shows the tendency of this eroticized violence to alternate between male and female objects, and for their images to fuse, as they do more startlingly in Lear's image of the centaur. That fusion is expressed in mockery when Hamlet, about to leave Denmark, justifies calling Claudius his mother by saying, 'My mother. Father and mother is man and wife, man and wife is one flesh; and so my mother' (IV.iii.53–5).

At Gertrude's pleading, Hamlet interrupts his anti-sexual tirade to fulminate against Claudius. One would think that at this point the ghost would have no need to disturb the scene by reappearing. Quite unjustly, he claims to have come to whet Hamlet's 'almost blunted purpose,' and even worse blames Hamlet for Gertrude's distress at her son's bizarre behavior. These gaps in ordinary logic emphasize the dream logic that drives Hamlet to evoke the third father image at the very moment that he vents his most violent passions against Gertrude. Hamlet's guilt at replacing his father in his mother's bedroom manifests itself momentarily in his father's reappearance, now suitably attired for the bedroom. But only after Hamlet has rid himself, finally, of his father's ghost does he give full expression to his vision of the 'ulcerous place,' which 'mining all within / Infects unseen.' The imagery of unweeded gardens comes to rest on Gertrude's sexuality when Hamlet cautions her not to 'spread the compost on the weeds / To make them ranker' (III.iv.154–5). With the excuse of warning Gertrude to abstain from sexuality, Hamlet allows his imagination to dwell on 'a pair of reechy kisses' or Claudius 'paddling in your neck with his damned fingers, / Make you to ravel all this matter out / That I essentially am not in madness, / But mad in craft' (III.iv.186–90).

Under cover of the negative injunction, Hamlet lets himself visualize the beginning of a sexual encounter. As his loathing attraction gains power the image threatens to break its containing negative form. His excuse for it, a warning to Gertrude not to tell Claudius that he is 'but mad in craft,' makes no sense, because by this time Hamlet knows that Claudius plans to send him to England, and, naturalistically, it could not have escaped him that the player scene that revealed Claudius's guilt also showed his own hand. By visualizing or imaginatively spying on a sexually active Claudius, Hamlet both denies and vicariously satisfies his desire for Gertrude. Having disposed of both the ghost and Polonius, it is only by keeping Claudius on the scene that he can achieve that compromise between desire and guilt. Having himself at least seen in his mind's eye the sexuality between Claudius and Gertrude, and having distantly satisfied the Oedipal project when Gertrude's ears received his verbal daggers, he drags the corpse of the play's arch-spy off the stage.

The previous images of the 'foul and pestilent congregation of vapours' that befoul Hamlet's world have come to rest and acquired substance in association with Gertrude's bedroom and her violent and diseased sexuality. In doing so, they bring Hamlet as close to sexual satisfaction in life as he will come. These images disappear from the remainder of the play as Hamlet begins his progress towards the grave in which he will reclaim his lost erotic passion. They are replaced by images of death that control the remaining action and that first collect in reference to Polonius, then to Ophelia, and finally to Hamlet himself. As though to punish himself for his approach to the Oedipal crime, Hamlet sends his imagination with Polonius through the cycle of decomposition to illustrate to Claudius how, with the help of a 'certain convocation of politic worms,' 'a king may go a progress through the guts of a beggar' (IV.iii.20,30–1). However, in the dialogue with Claudius, Hamlet not only forces upon him the lessons taught by death, the great leveler; he also moves towards his own death by enraging Claudius at the moment when he is most subject to Claudius' power.

The images of death that will culminate in the grave-digger scene flow through the Polonius episode, Ophelia's mad songs, and Gertrude's account of her death. These scenes advance the love-story between Hamlet and Ophelia that will be completed in her grave. Hamlet had first diverted his attention from Ophelia to Gertrude, and now expresses by his absence from the scene the distance between his passions and his consciousness. However, the depth at which Gertrude and Ophelia remain joined in his mind makes Gertrude audience to Ophelia's madness and, as though she were an eyewitness, narrator of her death. In this remote way, obscured in the circumstantial ambiguity of Ophelia's songs and intertwined with his feelings towards Gertrude, Hamlet most closely approaches the complex mixture of passions that constitute his erotic story. Ophelia outlines the obscured story in her Valentine's Day song, which tells of a maid who, having knocked at her lover's window, 'out a maid / Never departed more,' (IV.v.54–5). Here Hamlet brings closer to awareness the image of himself that he at a distance expressed and repudiated in Polonius' and Laertes' warnings to Ophelia. They imply a love-story in which she, having from weakness or confusion betrayed him by day, by night sought him to make reparation, for which he punished her by accepting her sexual advance and then despised her for being the betraying whore he had made her. In this implied story Hamlet has transformed imagistic associations into remote action, and transformed into her madness the antic disposition by which he mediated between his 'Vulcan's stithy' and an ordinary sense of reality.[11]

That is as close as Hamlet comes directly to implicating himself in sexuality. Despite the obscuring pastoral haze of Gertrude's narration, Ophelia is nonetheless absorbed into the rank weeds and mud of Hamlet's sexuality. Gertrude describes the dying Ophelia crowned with weeds, including the clearly phallic 'long purples,' for which the polite name is 'dead men's fingers.' Hamlet's equation of death and sexuality emerges as Ophelia goes to her muddy death for having raised from its grave Hamlet's dead man's finger on the night she knocked at his chamber door. With her 'weedy trophies' to which she is 'native and indued' she spreads 'the compost on the weeds to make them ranker.' In the images Ophelia is absorbed into the unweeded garden of the incestuous bed, and as she is pulled 'from her melodious lay' she is possessed by things rank and gross in nature. Since Hamlet can experience his own sexuality only in association with death, he cannot assert his love for Ophelia until she is in the grave that he encounters when, courting his own death, he comes without an army, 'naked,' to Claudius' kingdom.

As Hamlet's confrontation with Gertrude emerges from, encapsulates, and fuses the imagery of disease and sexuality that preceded it, so the graveyard scene, in fusing and translating into action the imagery of death, sex, and enterprise, emerges from and encapsulates the controlling forces of the play. In the clown, Hamlet confronts an externalized representation of his 'antic disposition,' or of himself as jester. In commenting on the clown's mode of speaking 'by the card,' Hamlet describes his own mode of pressing literal detail until it explodes into metaphorical significance, as he did in describing the progress of Polonius' corpse. The clown's song, which begins with 'In youth when I did love,' and ends with 'O a pit of clay for to be made / For such a guest is meet' (v.i.63,94–5), transforms the love-death equation into a jingle, and his jests on the stability of graves anticipate Hamlet's parallel reflections on the fate that awaits buyers of land and lawyers with their 'quips and quiddities.'[12]

Since in the clown Hamlet represents an aspect of himself, the juxtaposition of the clown's grim love-song with the reference to Hamlet's birth on the very day that the clown became a grave-digger and that King Hamlet overcame Fortinbras, renders Hamlet's conception of himself as born in order to undermine, or bury, his father's martial honours. When Yorick's skull arises like the Roman dead from the yawning grave of Hamlet's past, the conflation of his birth, his father's victory, and Ophelia's burial makes the grave beside which they stand both the source and the final resting place of the polarity between idealized martial manhood and sexualized decay and death that is expressed in Hamlet's figure.[13]

Hamlet presses his consciousness towards the implications of the configuration he has generated when he raises his gorge by examining the bones on which 'hung those lips that I have kissed I know not how oft' (v.i.182–3). When he directs the skull to tell his lady in her chamber that though she may 'paint an inch thick, to this favour she must come'(v.i.187–8), he extends the import of the emblem Claudius and Polonius generated from Ophelia's figure. Now woman's painting represents the duplicitous flesh that conceals the reality of the death's head, and the grave in which Ophelia's body will decay becomes emblematic of human mortality. Having narrowed his vision of death to Yorick's skull, Hamlet will widen it to encompass all of human history by imagining the dust of Caesar and Alexander 'stopping a bunghole,' or a hole to 'keep the wind away' (v.i.198,207). Both conquering heroes like his father and painted women will 'come to this.' This hidden yoking of male and female images in the grave, and images of holes plugged with the dust of dead conquerors leads subtly in the direction of the grim embrace suggested when Hamlet sends Yorick's skull 'to my lady's chamber.'

This necrophilic image hovers over the remainder of the scene as the funeral party enters and Gertrude reflects, 'I hop'd thou shouldst have been my Hamlet's wife: / I thought thy bride-bed to have deck'd, sweet maid, / And not have strew'd thy grave' (v.i.238–9). As though in response to her image of Hamlet and Ophelia together, Laertes, whose character seems to have swerved in response to the changes in Hamlet's dream configurations, initiates a contest in bombast that concludes with Hamlet's struggle with him in the grave to claim her body. The mock hysteria conceals the incestuous suggestions of Laertes' lover-like lines, which express Hamlet's desire as well as his revulsion from it. Within his mockery of Laertes Hamlet obscures an image of himself and Ophelia buried beneath a mountainous grave mound that, 'Singeing his pate against the burning zone' (v.i.278) will defy his Hyperion father.

This defiant consummation of love in death that occurs amid the grotesque comedy of the graveyard scene explains the curious image in which Gertrude describes Hamlet. Apologizing for his behavior as 'mere madness,' she adds that 'Anon, as patient as the female dove / When that her golden couplets are disclos'd, / His silence will sit drooping' (v.i.281–3). In her striking and apparently inappropriate image, the significance of which will emerge from its place among related images in this and other plays, Hamlet generates an alternate formulation of his ideas and passions that can survive his dream death.

At the end of *Romeo and Juliet*, the parents of the two lovers who, each thinking the other dead, have killed themselves inside the Capulet tomb, promise to construct outside the tomb two golden statues of the lovers. The image suggests a symbolic rebirth, an early version of the 'statue' of Hermione in *The Winter's Tale*, in a way that softens the actuality of their death, and that in some measure cancels the charnel imagery that competes with the sense of death as an engulfing darkness. Earlier in this play Ophelia in her madness said 'Fare you well, my dove' to someone in an imaginary grave. The image here of the 'golden couplets' symbolically suggests a fruitfulness or birth emerging out of the grave containing the bodies of Ophelia and Hamlet.

The shift from the suggested image of an almost necrophilic copulation to the palliative symbolic rebirth prepares for the appearance of Osric, around whom gather images that are associated with the 'golden couplets.' As Hamlet becomes more sombre, the verbal enthusiasm that first belonged to his antic disposition and then passed to the clown, now passes to Osric when he comes to announce the challenge that will bring the action to its bloody finale. Osric's verbosity parodies Hamlet's, and perhaps Shakespeare's. Looked at in sequence Osric happily emerges from the graveyard scene as a resurrected Yorick. But Osric's verbal pretentiousness is associated with his Frenchified dandyism and by implication with homosexuality. Most of the wit-play around Osric takes place in reference to his hat, which he flourishes instead of wearing. Hamlet says that he will hear the king's message if Osric will 'Put [his] bonnet to his right use: 'tis for the head' (v.ii.93) and the hat remains an issue until Osric dons it, and Horatio comments, 'This lapwing runs away with the shell on his head' (v.ii.183). This image of Osric as a newly hatched bird evolves from Gertrude's image of Hamlet brooding on the grave-born eggs, from which, imagistically speaking, Osric has been hatched. Out of the failure of love to find consummation elsewhere than in the grave has been born Osric's self-dramatizing verbal energy. Other images suggest the transformation that has taken place. He is called a 'chuff, but, as I say, spacious in the possession of dirt' (v.ii.88–9), and a 'waterfly,' an image that, given the belief in spontaneous generation, might have arisen from those waters in which Ophelia drowned and that, the clown tells us, is 'a sore decayer of your whoreson dead body.'

This delightfully comic fancy represents one possible resolution of the tensions in the play, a transformation of one side of Hamlet's entire disposition. The other side, without humour, takes Hamlet towards the death he has been seeking. The images of heartsickness that have coloured Hamlet's world return to their source when Hamlet says 'But thou wouldst not think how ill all's here about my heart.' He dismisses this foreboding of his own death as 'but foolery, of a kind that would perhaps trouble a woman.' In a way reminiscent of Gertrude's image of him as a female dove, brooding on her eggs, Hamlet's comparison of himself to a woman allows into the spiritualization of his death a dim suggestion that he solves the sexual problem by taking the female role unto himself, by becoming androgynous and therefore capable of himself giving birth, but 'not as [Ophelia] was like to conceive.' In this way he solves two problems. First, he rescues the powers of generation from the corrupting influence of women. Second, he repudiates his father's values in the contrast between this image and the sterile eggshell for which Fortinbras fights. The imagery of birds, which produce eggs but are at a safe remove from human sexuality or the process of human birth (only a man 'not of woman born' can kill Macbeth), pervades Hamlet's spiritual resignation when he converts the augury of his own foreboding, and the powerful but unloving gods the image implies, into the loving providence that, according to the Bible, has special concern for 'the fall of a sparrow'(v.ii.216). The newly hatched lively lapwing having briefly made its appearance, Hamlet opts for seeing himself as a sparrow falling gently into the arms of an embracing providence. Like Gertrude's image of the dove, this feminine or androgynous image of himself as a sparrow contains for Hamlet a kind of comfort that softens the aspect of death. Having internalized the previous fusion of Gertrude and Claudius, Hamlet can bypass the agonizing conflict he has been wrestling with, and envision dying as an easy breath into a maternal embrace.

Hamlet's association of himself with images of birds continues to the end. Having received his death wound from the poisoned rapier, he says, 'The potent poison quite o'ercrows my spirit' (v.ii.358). But as a defeated cock succumbing to death, he also defeats his father when he gives his election to Fortinbras, and his soul to 'flights of angels.'

Separated by many years from Shakespeare's other great tragedies, *Hamlet* marks the beginning of emotional engagement in the conflicts involved in heterosexual loving and sexuality. In confrontation with Ophelia, Hamlet experiences his ambivalent animosity towards his father and his ambivalent sexuality towards his mother. In the course of the play he does succeed in 'killing' his father – all versions of him – but he reclaims his own sexuality only in death. The later tragedies will abandon the more or less obvious Oedipal framework, but will penetrate more deeply into the emotions contained within it.

That penetration will also entail a kind of loss. Throughout this drama Hamlet's self-reflection gives one the sense of his mind moving over waters of his own dream life, of never fully engaging the images and action that he generates, of his holding, like a realized portrait of the psychic process involved in a comic protagonist, a sense of himself apart, first in intellectual and then in religious or spiritual detachment. This self-reflection accounts both for the sporadic quality of the play's action, and for the wealth and variety of psychic movements that can be discerned. It is as though the detachment that prevented a full exploration of any single psychic strand permitted instead a kind of low-flying overview of a terrain that in later tragedies will be explored more deeply, but less comprehensively. As the protagonists enter their dramas more deeply they will in the process become less complete themselves. As image passes into action, as the figure of the dreamer empties into the dream he confronts, no figure will be so multifaceted, so self-considering of his own complexity, as is Hamlet. Though we will find aspects of him in several protagonists, we will not find that self-considering mind that lends to the play its peculiar modernity. That will pass into the fools and tricksters who hover around the edges of their plays.

But before Shakespeare's imagination abandoned its hovercraft to negotiate, on foot, the various terrains of the later tragedies, he wrote a series of plays, his dark or 'problem' plays, of indeterminate form. These plays strain between comic distance and tragic immediacy, all of them marked by a feeling of jadedness and uncertainty. It is as though the problems opened in *Hamlet* let out a bad but compelling odour from which Shakespeare tried to, but could not, retreat.

4

'Pestilent Vapours'
in the Problem Plays

Evading the challenge of heterosexual love with Ophelia, Hamlet took flight
into the complex emotions of the family drama, to find there a stench of decay,
a world 'weary, stale, flat, and unprofitable,' in which love and sexuality could
be consummated only in death. It is as though in writing the three 'problem'
plays Shakespeare attempted to return to the more remote and controlled
world of the comedies, but found himself unable to contain the atmosphere
generated by *Hamlet*. Though figures in these plays do not experience their
worlds in the colours that Hamlet does his, the plays as a whole have for most
viewers the quality of feeling that characterizes Hamlet's vision. They have
the distance, control, and occasionally the wit of the early comedies but not
their *joie d'esprit*, and they lack as well any transcendent spiritual affirmation,
which in the late comedies surrounds similar plot sequences. The fact that
these three plays, and only these three of Shakespeare's plays, include overt
sexual episodes seems related to the jaded irony towards the issues of life,
love, and death that characterizes them.[1]

In two of the three, *Measure for Measure* and *All's Well*, the plot resolution
turns on a bed trick, and *Troilus and Cressida*, the only play in which the
overt sexual episode is not a trick, is also the only play except *Hamlet* that
includes an actually unfaithful woman rather than one falsely accused of
infidelity.[2] Also, each of these and only these three plays includes unpleasant
fool-like characters – Thersites, Lucio, and Parolles. All three characters function principally to cast sexual aspersions on others, with greater or less justice.
Thersites' excoriation of wars and lechery seems generally appropriate to the
actions of the central characters; Lucio's innuendoes about the 'Duke of dark
corners' are not literally confirmed, but correspond to the atmosphere generated by the Duke's proclivity to pry into others' private lives; and Parolles,
accused of sexual licence, in fact exposes Bertram and is himself exposed only

as a lying coward, somewhat like Falstaff though without that character's charm. These figures develop from Hamlet, Shakespeare's only tragic protagonist who, in his 'antic disposition,' plays the fool to other characters. Hamlet's jaded vision, articulated largely through his antic role, becomes separated from his fullness to form these single-dimensioned commentators on the sexual action that is overt and central to each of their plays.

The studies of these three plays will concentrate on the ways in which definitions of character and plot configurations, rather than verbal detail, relate to earlier and later plays. Shakespeare allowed the sexuality evident in *Hamlet* to envelop the world of *Troilus and Cressida*, and then used transformed versions of earlier motifs to contain the associations that come in its wake. In the process of introducing more strenuous controls he gave hints of emotional dramas that are not fully enacted until the later tragedies.

Troilus and Cressida reverses the relationship between parental and adult love relationships from that found in *Hamlet*. There the parental relations fill the foreground, while that between Hamlet and Ophelia hovers in the background. In this play parental figures appear only in the hierarchical structure of the two armies, and the lovers occupy the foreground. While Hamlet, who repudiates Ophelia and sexuality, moves in a world replete with an aura of meaningfulness even while he questions it, Troilus consummates his love for Cressida, but experiences a world in which all relationships, sexual, hierarchical, and those among peers, are drained of significance. The play's action is almost equally divided between that concerning authoritative figures and ideas, and that concerning the lovers. The two issues, love and authority, are so intertwined in both plot and language that the debasement of one necessarily implies the debasement of the other.

The jaded tone of the play emerges from Troilus' disparagement of himself. Having declared that his love of Cressida makes him unable to fight for Helen, who is 'too starved a subject' for his sword, he goes to the wars with Aeneas because 'womanish it is to be from thence.' He defines himself as a posturing lover in confrontation both with a war he renders unworthy by its object, and with a withholding woman whom he associates with Helen. He has drained of significance manly warlike activity by associating it with an unworthy woman, and undermined the worth of woman by rejecting her for an unworthy war when his actions negate his courtly stance.

Troilus' self-definition most sharply divides into contradictory roles as he approaches his night with Cressida. He defines himself to her as 'true as truth's simplicity,' and 'simpler than the infancy of truth,' but implies an opposite cynicism in the oxymoron of both claiming to be and being 'simple,' and in asserting simplicity to deny the knowledge of women's duplicity that he has just expressed in doubting Cressida's capacity to 'keep her constancy in plight and youth, / Outliving beauty's outward, with a mind / That doth renew swifter than the blood decays! (III.ii.159–61). He further denigrates the ideas by which he defines himself when he, Cressida, and Pandarus align themselves with their own literary predecessors. The implied parody of his role when he says he is as 'true as Troilus' while predicting the story's end before it begins, makes the cynical self-reflexivity of the play's tone emerge from the gap between Troilus' stances and his uses of them.

As Troilus empties himself of the complex feelings that will not conform to his self-definition, other figures with whom he is identified play a much larger role than do analogous figures in *Hamlet*. In the Greek council scene Ulysses expresses the wiliness that Troilus denies. Through him Troilus generates a vision of authority marred by petty skirmishing for status in which Ulysses reveals his implication even while he is in the process of exposing it. Under the guise of defending Agamemnon, Nestor, and Menelaus from Achilles' mockery, in imitating Achilles Ulysses covertly mocks them himself, and vents his own anger at Achilles and Patroclus for calling the 'still and mental parts' of war, on which he prides himself, 'bed-work, mapp'ry, closet war' (I.iii. 200,205). In the context of this defence of his wounded ego, and of his own violation of the degree he defends, he both voices and illustrates the consequences that occur when 'degree is shaked.' By calling on hierarchical ideas to undermine those who have authority over him, while pretending to defend them, he disqualifies his own stance in much the way Troilus does his. As well, Troilus' self-denigration and final sense of futility is expressed through the ineffectualness of Ulysses' strategems. His elaborate plot for mobilizing Achilles, which occupies a major part of the play's action, comes to naught, for only Patroclus' death moves Achilles to return to battle, and his plan to substitute Ajax for Achilles as combatant with Hector results only in the mockery of Ajax.

While Ulysses' function is primarily to disparage male authority, his later action also exposes Troilus' more hidden idea that authority is eroded by contact with women. When Cressida enters the Greek camp, Ulysses, after inciting his fellow Greeks to kiss her, refuses her his own kiss 'until Helen is a maid again.' His strategy humiliates both the Greek leaders and Cressida, and, by associating Cressida with Helen, exposes paternal triviality in fighting a war for a 'cuckold and a whore.' At the same time, in exalting himself Ulysses expresses Troilus' distance from his own stances. Troilus expresses through him his self-mockery when Ulysses in the exposure scene casts doubt on the authenticity of Troilus' railing against Cressida's infidelity.

In Diomedes Troilus expresses a crude view of sexuality that is only slightly suggested in his own figure, as well as scorn at those who spill their blood for Helen's 'contaminated carrion weight.' As Troilus dreams himself with Cressida, he more remotely generates Diomedes' vision of Paris breeding 'out his inheritors' from Helen's 'whorish loins,' and later he punishes Cressida for her related sexuality by giving her to that anything but courtly figure. His vision of Diomedes' impatient arrogance with Cressida as she hands him Troilus' sleeve exaggerates and stages what was previously implicit in Troilus' language, making this more subtle play within a play analogous in function to Hamlet's player scene.

While Troilus expresses through Diomedes the crude vision of love concealed in his mock-courtly stance, he expresses through Achilles his hostility towards Hector, who, as Troilus' older brother, carries paternal force. This appears indirectly when Achilles mocks the Greek leaders, and acquires deeper tones when Achilles scans Hector's body for a place to inflict a mortal blow. Achilles' womanish desire that he is 'sick withall' to see Hector's unarmed body suggests that a homosexually eroticized hostility similar to that between Coriolanus and Aufidius is the other side of the coin to Troilus' disgust with women.

Troilus' hostility to authority grows more subtle as it becomes more conscious, but its ties to his debased view of woman become more obvious. The links between the two are expressed in the same scene by Hector, who undermines his own authority by yielding to Troilus' argument for keeping Helen, as well as in the argument itself, which both assumes her worthlessness and is rendered spurious by the rest of the play. Troilus' argument reverses the standard hierarchy of faculty psychology, making senses act as 'two traded pilots 'twixt the dangerous shores / Of will and judgement' (II.ii.65–6). While substituting the senses for reason or traditional morality as the basis for action, he acknowledges the transience of sensuous pleasure, but accommodates his anticipated satiety by defining honour as fidelity to the senses' first choice. The images of the analogy debase Helen even as he deploys them in an argument to keep her:

> I take today a wife, and my election
> Is led on in the conduct of my will:
> My will enkindled by mine eyes and ears,
> Two traded pilots 'twixt the dangerous shores
> Of will and judgement – how may I avoid
> Although my will distaste what it elected,
> The wife I choose? There can be no evasion
> To blench from this and to stand firm by honour.

We turn not back the silks upon the merchant
When we have soil'd them, nor the remainder viands
We do not throw in unrespective sieve,
Because we now are full.   (II.ii.62–73)

This comparison of Helen to soiled merchandise and unwanted food colours even the images in which Troilus describes her transcendent beauty. He recounts the Trojans' pleasure when Paris brought 'a Grecian queen whose youth and freshness / Wrinkles Apollo's and makes stale the morning'(II.ii.79–80). Though in the syntax the image hyperbolically praises Helen, the sequence suggests the post-coital distaste, the staled morning, that will follow Troilus' night with Cressida. That distaste extends to Hector's authority when he equates honour with keeping a 'ransacked queen' and opposes it to 'these moral laws / Of nature and of nation [that] speak aloud / To have her back return'd' (II.ii.184–7). In Hector's betrayal of his own authority and that of the ideas and values on which it rests, Troilus indirectly enjoys his successful subversion of power, even while Hector's superior argument expresses his cynical self-reflection. The feeling generated by the continued war for Helen's 'whorish loins' suffuses the action that centres on Hector's challenge to the Greeks to defend their women's beauty. On one level Troilus evokes Hector as a paternal figure only in order to undermine him when he envisions him fighting for 'the lees and dregs of a flat tamed piece,' while on another he draws Cressida into the orbit of sexuality he has already associated with images of decay.

With the exception of Priam, the play's action contains no explicit parents; family configurations have all been distanced through parental figures who, remote from Troilus, form an Oedipal drama. The paternal function is divided between Agamemnon and Menelaus in the Greek camp and Hector in the Trojan, the actual father, Priam, being rendered for the most part an airy image. While Helen-Cressida can be seen as parallel to Gertrude-Ophelia, the female figures even less clearly than the male take on parental tones. No maternal quality is allowed to cling to the more explicitly corrupt Helen, but in that obscurity, the configuration is that of an accomplished rather than desired Oedipal crime, for Paris, who shares with Troilus a quasi-filial relation to Hector, has stolen Helen from the father-figure Menelaus.

The consequence of the fulfilled fantasy is to steep all the figures in the jaded aura that derives from Troilus' image of himself.[3] Ulysses touches most closely on the concealed parental drama when in his speech on degree he describes the disorder that would follow if 'the rude son should strike his father dead,'

Force would be right – or rather, right and wrong,
Between whose endless jar justice resides,
Should lose their names, and so should justice too.
Then everything includes itself in power,
Power into will, will into appetite,
And appetite, an universal wolf,
So doubly seconded with will and power,
Must make perforce a universal prey,
And last eat up himself.   (I.iii.114–24)

In aggrandizing himself by condemning hierarchical violation, Ulysses illustrates the process by which civilized values are drawn into the cesspool of
sexuality. By defining appetite as a 'universal wolf,' which will 'last eat up
himself,' Ulysses shows the underside of Troilus' elevation of the senses as
the guide to action. The vision that is obscured in Troilus' sophistry, revealed
in Ulysses' words, looks forward to Lear's experience of a world in which the
'bounded waters' very nearly do 'lift their bosoms higher than the shores,'
and in which humanity is seen to 'prey upon itself / Like monsters of the
deep.'

Ulysses' speech links the violation of paternal authority to the sexual in
the image of appetite that characterizes Troilus' relation to Cressida and that
associates her with Helen. Cressida is first mentioned when Pandarus likens
his seduction of her to baking bread, and is associated with Helen, who was
'too starved a subject' for Troilus' sword. Having surrounded both women
with imagery of food, Troilus also links them both with imagery of wounds
and battle. Troilus says that Pandarus plants 'in the open ulcer of my heart /
Her eyes, her hair, her cheek, her gait, her voice' (i.i.53–4) and says that he
'instead of oil and balm, / Thou lay'st in every gash that love hath given me /
The knife that made it' (i.i.61–3). The images of ulcers and knife wounds
show Troilus associating disease and violence with sexuality, and those images
link Cressida to Helen when Troilus, responding to Aeneas' news that Paris
had been wounded by Menelaus, says, 'Let Paris bleed,'tis but a scar to scorn: /
Paris is gor'd with Menelaus' horn' (i.i.111–12).

The imagistic association between Troilus' love wounds and Paris' wound
from Menelaus' horn shows Troilus in the process of generating Cressida's
infidelity, even before he has her. More explicit than Hamlet, he defines his
sexuality as an 'open ulcer,' so that to approach her sexually is to define her
as a diseased whore, the source of the 'bone ache.' Since Cressida, identified
with Helen, comes within the incestuous realm, in yielding to his desire she
debases herself, betrays the father, or the realm of authority, and confirms

Troilus' sexual self-loathing. A vision of sexual fulfilment simultaneously generates one of betrayal and debasement.

As Troilus approaches Cressida, the links to Helen become more evident. Helen and Paris, 'besotted with sweet delights,' joke with Pandarus about Cressida's possible love for Paris rather than Troilus. Through Paris, Troilus both remotely expresses his sense of women's betrayal and reveals his concealed cynicism. Paris says 'hot blood begets hot thoughts, and hot thoughts beget hot deeds, and hot deeds is love,' to which Pandarus responds that 'hot deeds ... are vipers! Is love a generation of vipers?' (III.i.124–9). The association of vipers with love's 'hot deeds' is also made by Lear when he describes Goneril and Regan, and by Othello about Desdemona when he believes her unfaithful. Immediately preceding Troilus' anticipation of his tryst, this image suggests what hovers within the sensual aestheticism of Troilus' comparison of himself to a soul waiting on the Stygian banks for 'swift transportation to those fields / Where I may wallow in the lily beds / Propos'd for the deserver!' (III.ii.10–12).[4]

The love-death equation that brought Hamlet to claim Ophelia in her grave here defines the illicit sexuality claimed in life. The image of the Stygian banks is equated with sex, and sensual delight with wallowing in lily fields. The image of wallowing absorbs the beautiful Elysian fields image into the darker image of the Stygian banks. It is easy to see, just under the surface, shades of Hamlet's images of rot and decay, and the potency of that rot and decay to generate serpents, asps, and vipers, as they do in *Antony and Cleopatra*. That range of association does not surface here; instead Troilus' overt connection of death to an excess of sensuous delight leads to an image of carnage, when he says that besides fearing the death that might ensue from a 'joy too fine, / Too subtle-potent, tun'd too sharp in sweetness / For the capacity of my ruder powers,' he fears as well that he will 'lose distinction in [his] joys, / As doth a battle, when they charge on heaps / The enemy flying' (III.ii.18–27). The battle image momentarily associates violence with sexuality, in much the same way as do the player's images of Hecate and the night in *Hamlet*, and brings that violence from the surrounding context of the war into the heart of Troilus' sexual desire for Cressida.

Concealing his sexual disgust beneath his anticipation of sensual delight, Troilus manages the sexual encounter with Cressida, but even then only by ritually defining it as the beginning of a story of betrayed love wherein he casts himself as innocent victim of women's corruption. The machinery for Cressida's exchange, set in motion even as he sleeps with her to provide the condition for her infidelity, reflects his incapacity to sustain the relationship. The deeper ranges of his sexual disgust colour his language, but never emerge in his consciousness. He first sees himself thwarted by time and circumstance, but his language betrays the sexual distaste from which the circumstance arises. The morning after their sexual encounter, Cressida, observing Troilus' haste to depart, says, 'I might have still held off, / And then you would have tarried' (IV.ii.17–18), and Troilus, when he learns of the exchange, comments only, 'How my achievements mock me!' (IV.ii.71). The speech in which he bids farewell to Cressida represents the passage from sexual excitement to post-coital jadedness:

> And suddenly; where injury of chance
> Puts back leave-taking, jostles roughly by
> All time of pause, rudely beguiles our lips
> Of all rejoindure, forcibly prevents
> Our lock'd embrasures, strangles our dear vows
> Even in the birth of our own labouring breath.
> We two, that with so many thousand sighs
> Did buy each other, must poorly sell ourselves
> With the rude brevity and discharge of one.
> Injurious Time now with a robber's haste
> Crams his rich thiev'ry up, he knows not how;
> As many farewells as be stars in heaven,
> With distinct breath and consign'd kisses to them,
> He fumbles up into a loose adieu,
> And scants us with a single famish'd kiss
> Distasted with the salt of broken tears.   (IV.iv.32–47)

Despite the syntax in which the 'injury of chance' is described as interrupting their love-making, the images build to a sexual climax, time jostling 'roughly by / All time of pause,' beguiling their lips, preventing their 'lock'd embrasures.' The climax is suggested in the image of vows, strangled 'in the birth of our own labouring breath.' The tension finds release with the 'rude brevity and discharge of one' sigh, and the rest of the passage suggests the decline of passion and affect after the love act; 'Time' is being held responsible for the ephemeral nature of sexual passion. It 'crams his rich thiev'ry up' and 'fumbles up [kisses] into a loose adieu.' The last image of the kiss, 'Distasted with the salt of broken tears,' recalls the images of unwanted food that define Helen, and will soon multiply around Cressida while Helen will disappear.

Within the role of the rejected lover, Troilus externalizes the sexual betrayal that Hamlet only imagined. Traces of Troilus' overt cynicism remain in the discovery scene, in which two opposing dramatic structures combine. On the one hand, the place in the action defines it as a moment of tragic discovery, and Troilus' words, although bordering on bombast, formally fulfil the requirements. On the other hand, the triple eavesdropping structure distances the emotion and drains the episode of the sense of meaningfulness that accompanies directly experienced emotion. At the centre of the scene a coyly hesitating Cressida gives Troilus' sleeve to the arrogant Diomedes. Troilus and Ulysses watch them, but Ulysses also watches Troilus, casting doubt on the authenticity of his emotion, and finally Thersites, watching all the others, floods the entire scene with his vituperation. In that configuration Troilus discredits not only Cressida but also his own reaction to her infidelity, through his disclaimed knowingness represented by Ulysses, and his disclaimed disgust represented by Thersites. In this context, Cressida's and Troilus' philosophical ruminations on the relation of senses to reason lose their impact, and the play's major concerns – the war, the debate on the nature of honour and worthy action – are overwhelmed by the central vision of Cressida:

Instance, O instance! strong as heaven itself:
The bonds of Heaven are slipp'd, dissolv'd and loos'd;
And with another knot, five-finger tied,
The fractions of her faith, orts of her love,
The fragments, scraps, the bits, and greasy relics
Of her o'er-eaten faith are given to Diomed.   (v.ii.154–9)

As though as a consequence of the corrupt and befouled woman at the heart of the matter, the play trails off into inconsequence – Troilus left alive on the field of battle, unsuccessfully pursuing Diomedes, and Hector killed while distracted by the 'goodly armour' that covered the 'most putrefied core' of a Greek soldier (v.viii.1–2), an image that encompasses the humanity portrayed in the play.

The entire play seems to emerge from the kind of sexual disgust that Hamlet feels when he approaches Gertrude or Ophelia. While Hamlet wrestles with his inner sense of foulness in an effort to keep his world meaningful, and does so at the price of denying his sexuality, Troilus claims the sexual, along with a world riddled with venereal disease. In the process he also becomes a thinner character, the components of Hamlet's complex character coming apart, as it were, to form several distinct persons in this play. Ulysses can be seen to develop from that side of Hamlet that strategizes, that is careful to avoid others' manipulation of him, and is adroit at manipulating others. Achilles has in common with Hamlet his refusal to fight, though his style is truculent, while Hamlet's is musing, and they both speculate on the basis for action and the nature of honour. Hamlet's antic disposition and the spying motif form the figure of Thersites, and his self-reflection appears in Troilus' ambiguous evocation of the story on which the play is based. As these threads disentangle into distinct characters, Hamlet's introspection and the intertwined complexity of his experience that make him so attractive a figure are lost. But there is a kind of gain as well, for though the romance of death may have more satisfying resonance, Troilus remains alive and claims sexuality, even clothed in images of garbage, at least for a moment.

The two plays that follow *Troilus and Cressida* carry forward the overt concentration on sexuality, but sharply reverse the generational relationships. In *Troilus* the parental figures are shadowy and remote, their authority disparaged and ignored. Agamemnon is subtly mocked, Menelaus broadly mocked for his cuckoldry and given very little role, and Hector, his leadership undermined, is killed without dignity. The sonlike figures – Paris, Troilus, Ulysses, Diomedes, Achilles – in the absence of a strong authority, win the day and have the women. As punishment for their victory Hamlet's aura of contagion contaminates their world with images of venereal disease in Thersites' steady stream of scurrility and Pandarus' epilogue. The denigration of the relatively remote parental figures allowed the fumes arising from the protagonist's vision of sexuality to poison his sense of enterprise. As though in order to push this genie back into the bottle, idealized parental figures emerge from their obscure places in the early comedies to trick or force the young men of *All's Well That Ends Well* and *Measure for Measure* into correct sexual behaviour.

In *All's Well* Bertram has some of Troilus' cynical sensualism, though it is more directly announced and less emotionally dramatized, but the configurations he generates around himself are more like those in *Hamlet*. Like Hamlet he has eliminated his father, and at the beginning of the play finds himself confronted with a mother who says, 'In delivering my son from me, I bury a second husband' (i.i.1–2). He gets himself away from so threatening a figure by having her send him to the king, a distanced paternal figure. Like Hamlet, Bertram makes a double motion, towards and away from the mother, though in more schematic fashion. The father's death appears to have been recent, since Bertram says that though he must weep for his father's death, he must answer 'his Majesty's command, to whom I am ... evermore in subjection' (i.i.4–6). Lafeu makes the link between the father and the king explicit when he says, 'You shall find of the king a husband, madam; you, sir, a father' (i.i.6–7). Having eliminated the father in an approach to incestuous sexuality, Bertram in fright reverses the motion, substituting for the father the more distanced but more powerful king, who is also desexualized and separate from the mother.

While he cannot continue his own approach to the mother, Bertram's ambivalence continues to shape his experience as he confronts not a ghost, but a mortally ill king and finds himself pursued by Helena. Her quasi-sibling role shows that Bertram defines her within the incestuous orbit, while in her refusal to be considered daughter to his mother he remotely attempts to detach her from that realm. Bertram externalizes his desire for Helena into her pursuit of him, and transforms his guilt into revulsion, so that the barrier to love is not external, as in *Romeo and Juliet*, but within psychological circumstance.

The countess and Helena, though dramatically problematic, are more virtuous versions of Gertrude-Ophelia and Helen-Cressida. As the mother-figure the countess moves to the background, leaving Helena some of the attributes of earlier comic heroines. Within a quasi-magical aura like those that surround Portia and Rosalind, Helena's knowledge of her own concealed identity empowers her to manipulate circumstance. Her powers that derive from a dead father are more comparable to those of Portia, but Helena's father was a doctor, from whom she has derived medicinal talents that equip her to cure in the king the diseases that have pervaded *Hamlet* and *Troilus and Cressida*. Though the waste-land motif is not specifically suggested in this play, the fact that his cure is the precondition for her wedding, which reconciles the older and younger generations to each other, aligns this play with *Pericles* specifically and with the late comedies in general, in which a restored commonwealth depends on a restored sexuality out of which can emerge a pure and fertile couple at its centre.

In Helena one can see Shakespeare's imagination struggling towards such a vision, since more than her predecessors she is associated with sexuality. With echoes of Cressida, Helena asks Parolles, a figure who expresses Bertram's sexuality as Thersites does Troilus', how virgins may 'barricado' their virginity against men. Parolles answers that 'Virginity breeds mites, much like a cheese; consumes itself to the very paring, and so dies with feeding his own stomach. Besides, virginity is peevish, proud, idle, made of self-love which is the most inhibited sin in the canon (i.i.139–43). The description of virginity in images that previously characterized corrupt sexuality shows Bertram as the first protagonist who assigns to the woman the task of providing a way for him to negotiate a path between the Scylla of sterility and the Charybdis of sexual corruption and diseased breeding. The struggle to wrest from that dichotomy an image of beneficent fertility creates the strained conclusion of this play and of *Measure for Measure*. The later tragedies plumb some of the sources of that painful dichotomy, and the late comedies attempt to transcend it. Only in *Antony and Cleopatra* does it soften sufficiently to allow an emotional middle ground to take dramatic form.

Bertram, having reversed the Oedipal configuration by experiencing a paternal figure forcing him into an incestuous sexuality, sends Helena back to the mother she came from, secretly assigning her the apparently impossible task of resolving his ambivalence towards her as expressed in his riddling challenge to show him his own ring and 'a child begotten of thy body that I am father to' (III.ii.63). But he actively participates in solving the seemingly impossible dilemma. Instead of projecting onto a Fortinbras the military prowess that would win paternal approval, Bertram takes on himself the quest for military honour. He distances into the figure of Parolles the images of cowardice and ebullient amoral survival. Second, he espouses his desire to sully the virginal woman when he tries to seduce Diana. His substitution of Diana for Helena suggests that his revulsion from Helena expressed a desire to preserve her purity, and by extension the purity of the maternal realm, from his own sexual desire. The identification between Helena and Diana appears in several ways. They both are lower in station than Bertram, both are in close connection with a mother – Diana with her own, Helena with Bertram's – and the substitution in bed merges the two figures into each other. Their names also suggest them to be two sides of a single coin. Helena is explicitly associated with Helen of Troy by the Clown who, when asked by the countess to fetch her, sings, 'Was this fair face the cause, quoth she, / Why the Grecians sacked Troy?' (I.iii.67–8): Diana, with all the references to her chastity, clearly suggests her goddess counterpart. Therefore, Bertram consciously wants to conquer the chaste Diana but his deeper feelings move towards sexualized Helena. Helena, substituting herself for Diana in bed, allows him to satisfy his desire to sully the pure, to accomplish his Oedipal desire to 'blow up' the representative of the mother, and saves him from the consequences. With the entire action supported by parental authority, Bertram in a nice strategy accomplishes his desire under the guise of being forced to do so by the very figures whom that desire violates.

The bed trick, having satisfied the conditions of the initial riddle, assures the correct resolution, but the process of making public and of bringing to Bertram's consciousness what has been accomplished in secret hints that Bertram, like Hamlet, associates more violent emotions with loving and sexuality than he allows fully to show. As a necessary condition for the play's resolution he must, like Posthumus and Ferdinand later, submit to paternal authority as a sign of his restored virtue and worthiness to have a woman. Bertram's submission preludes Helena's public solution to the riddle she has already resolved in secret. The change of heart that occurs when Bertram says 'If she, my liege, can make me know this clearly / I'll love her dearly, ever, ever dearly' (v.iii.309–10), violates psychological probability, but if the hidden emotional correlates of the improbable plot are taken into account, they suggest

Bertram's gratitude for having satisfied his appetites and evaded the guilt that he associates with them. As well, they express his pleasure at having negotiated a way through the difficult waters.[5]

That Bertram's language lacks images that suggest emotions appropriate to the depth of conflict schematized in the plot indicates that the action sidesteps rather than penetrates the intense emotions that generated the dilemma.[6] They betray their presence feelingly only in the pervasive tone of disenchantment and in Bertram's self-definition as a cad and liar. This tone also pervades *Measure for Measure*, which differs from *All's Well* mostly in its protagonist's consciousness of his desire to corrupt the pure and of his self-condemnation. Rather than being externalized into other figures, the polarized images of a corrupting sexual passion that entails death and of a life of sterile purity shape Angelo's emotional experience. Angelo defines himself as having a past in which he avoided mature sexuality by breaking his marriage contract to Mariana. Though more passive, Mariana parallels Helena, a sexualized and rejected woman, while the more active role passes to Isabella, who otherwise parallels the chaste Diana. The most significant difference between Bertram and Angelo is that Angelo overtly intertwines his sexual project with a bid like that Hamlet made to assume mature authority. He expresses directly his unease with the challenge he has generated when he asks that 'there be some more test made of my metal, / Before so noble and so great a figure / Be stamp'd upon it' (I.i.48–50). He assigns to the paternal duke the knowledge of his secret appetites that give rise to his self-doubt, when the duke describes him to the friar as one who 'scarce confesses / That his blood flows; or that his appetite / Is more to bread than stone. Hence shall we see / If power change purpose, what our seemers be' (I.iii.51–4).

In the configuration Angelo keeps a shadowy father image, rather than a quasi-maternal figure, on the fringes of his awareness in order to protect himself from the consequences of his now empowered corruption. The test that Angelo secretly knows himself bound to fail keeps him in a filial stance, playing with power that is not quite real. He gives himself a kind of playground of consequence-cancelling circumstance in which to have a trial run at transforming himself from filial to paternal status. Dressed in 'a little brief authority' he becomes a transitional figure between the young protagonists of the preceding plays and the paternal protagonists of those that follow, whose 'fantastic tricks before high Heaven,' whose unleashed desire, irrevocably devastate themselves and their worlds.

Angelo expresses his hatred and fear of sexuality when he attacks the fruitful union of Claudio and Juliet, a more realized, though more distanced, version of his desertion of Mariana. The two couples are linked by the parallel financial concerns in which Angelo deserted Mariana because a promised dowry failed to materialize, and Claudio and Juliet delayed their public nuptials in order to secure a dowry. Claudio then becomes that aspect of Angelo that has sought legitimated sexual union with Mariana and retreated from it. In condemning Claudio for 'groping for trouts in a peculiar river' (I.ii.83), he reveals his association of sexuality with the dirt and disease of bawdy-houses, as well as with the grave to which he almost brings Claudio.

Angelo generates Isabella, who as a novitiate represents chastity and purity, to force him to recognize his own sexual desires, and, together with the Duke, to protect him against the consequences of their illicit fulfillment. She resides vaguely in the maternal realm for Angelo, for she will be aligned with the Duke, clearly a paternal figure, and as Claudio's sister she rides between the maternal and the extension of that into the sisterly, as does Ophelia for Hamlet, Helena for Bertram, and later Imogen for Posthumus. By having the figure who represents chastity plead for leniency towards Claudio's sexuality, Angelo asks for and later receives more directly her indulgence of his own desires.[7] Her purity holds the promise of cleansing his sexuality, as Marina's purification of the brothel by her shining presence will allow Pericles to reclaim his. But he is conscious only of being aroused by the desire to befoul her purity. Though most of his psychological complexity is rendered through plot rather than language, his wonder and confusion at being tempted to 'sin in loving virtue' (II.ii.183) has emotional force. After he has told Isabella to return the next day for an answer, his first image, like those of Hamlet, joins his sexuality to physical corruption; 'But it is I / That, lying by the violet in the sun, / Do as the carrion does, not as the flowers / Corrupt with virtuous season' (II.ii.165–8). His fertility, like that of Hamlet's dead dog, can breed only rot and corruption.

In making Isabella choose between her chastity and her brother's life, Angelo remotely expresses his own choice between the living death of abstinence and a sexuality equated with murder. He puts himself in a double bind, for if she yields to him he will become a Troilus, disgusted with himself and with her, and if she refuses he is imprisoned in sterile self-loathing. Both sides of the dilemma are reflected in the action that follows. Isabella's unhesitating choice to let Claudio die reflects the force of Angelo's self-condemnation and desire to escape the dilemma in death. The bloody images in which Isabella sees Claudio putting twenty heads on 'twenty bloody blocks' before 'his sister should her body stoop / To such abhorr'd pollution' (II.iv. 180–2) reflects Angelo's fear of women who might punish him for his sexuality, for which he also condemns himself.[8] That complex of feeling comes into starkest opposition to the simple desire for life and fear of death in the encounter between Isabella and Claudio.

As Isabella tentatively prepares to tell Claudio her dilemma and assumes that he will choose death over her dishonour, Claudio, without as yet knowing the issue, proposes a love-death resolution when he says 'If I must die, / I will encounter darkness as a bride / And hug it in mine arms' (III.i.82–4). However, when Isabella dangles before him the possibility of life his feelings and views change. Illicit sex ceases to seem so grievous: 'Sure it is no sin; / Or of the deadly seven it is the least' (III.i.109–10). He then evokes Shakespeare's most chilling images of the 'cold obstruction' and 'rot' of death, and his most impassioned plea for the paradise, compared to the unknown horrors of death, of even 'the weariest and most loathed worldy life / That age, ache, penury, and imprisonment / Can lay on nature' (III.i.128–30). His passionate plea for the joys of life, despite the lure of love-death romance, despite the Duke's religious and stoic consolation, most resembles Edgar's sudden lyric effusion at the end of *King Lear*, 'O! our lives' sweetness / That we the pain of death would hourly die / Rather than die at once'(*King Lear* v.iii.183–5).

The absolute value of life that motivates Claudio lies behind Hamlet's meditations on his cowardice as well as behind characters like Juliet's nurse, Falstaff, Osric, Parolles, and even Thersites. Ultimately, the argument for life loses, for the plays succeeding *Measure for Measure* contain no similar amoralist, except perhaps Autolycus in *The Winter's Tale*, who is not tested in a situation that confronts him with death. The major tragedies contain villains but no amoral life-lovers, and the ideological resolutions of the late comedies have no place for such figures.

In Claudio's plea Angelo remotely rejects the tragic solution to his dream conflict, but Isabella's response makes clear that no other solution is available within the realm of the probable. Seeing Claudio's love of life as 'a kind of incest,' she reveal the hatred that Angelo associates with sexuality when she says that 'Heaven shield my mother play'd my father fair: / For such a warped slip of wilderness / Ne'er issued from his blood.' She would now 'pray a thousand prayers' for his death, but no word to save him (III.i.140–5).

If one considers Isabella as dreamer of the action, she has denied her sexuality in order to keep an image of an ideally desexualized father, when she assumes that Claudio's corruption must stem from his mother, rather than his father. To think her father ideally desexualized, so must she think herself, but her denied sexuality also appears in her behaviour. We encounter her first asking the nun, 'And have you nuns no farther privileges?' To the nun's 'Are not these large enough?' she responds, 'Yes, truly; I speak not as desiring more, / But rather wishing a more strict restraint / Upon the sisters stood, the votarists of Saint Clare' (I.iv.1–5), a stringency not suggested by her first question. There is the same inconsistency between her first reaction to news of Claudio's imprisonment, 'Let him marry her,' and the revulsion she expressed to Angelo, 'There is a vice that most I do abhor, / And most desire should meet the blow of justice; / For which I would not plead, but that I must; / For which I would not plead, but that I am / At war 'twixt will and will not' (II.ii.29–33). Her fear that Angelo will think her lax indicates that she takes him as a father-figure for whose approval she denies her sexuality. Claudio's impregnation of Juliet and Angelo's punishment of Claudio, therefore, express her desire as well as her guilt and rage at men whose desire sullies her. Her tendency to convert her rage to self-laceration appears when to Angelo's first hypothetical proposition she says that were she threatened with death, 'The impression of keen whips I'd wear as rubies, / And strip myself to death as to a bed / That longing have been sick for, ere I'd yield / My body up to shame' (II.iv.100–4). Her masochism is the other side of the coin to her violent rage at Claudio. Angelo's proposition to her, then, would represent her equation of sexuality with violence, incest, and shame, and her rage at Claudio, in which she anticipates Lady Macbeth and Lear's evil daughters, represents her rage at the man who will approach her with his passion, accuse her of cruelty if she refuses, and of corrupt carnality if she does not. When she is subsumed to Angelo's psyche, his self-punishing guilt creates her fierceness, and his rage at women creates her masochism.

The polarity between the desire to live, associated with corrupt sexuality, and the will to die, associated with love-death images that both punish and fulfil guilty desire, has been drawn as sharply as possible. It is prevented from further unfolding itself by the Duke's reappearance, which functions to protect Angelo from the consequences of his own unleashed passions, just as Hamlet generated his father's ghost to restrain his passions.

The images of violence and the association of sexuality with death remain in the ensuing action, but are drained of their force by the surrounding paternal protectiveness. The connection of sexuality with death remains visible in the link between Claudio and Barnardine, the murderer who refuses to be executed, in Angelo's failure to rescind the death sentence, in the substitution of the pirate's head for that of Claudio, and in Isabella's belief in Claudio's death. It also remains on a broader comic level in Pompey, the bawd, becoming executioner in order to shorten his prison term. The bed trick functions in much the same way as it does in *All's Well That Ends Well*. Consciously Angelo is aroused by Isabella's purity, while his yearning for a means by which to harmonize his passions with correct authority manifests itself in the substitution of his previously contracted wife, Mariana, for Isabella. He both eats his cake and has it; he both corrupts Isabella and leaves her pure, and finally returns her to the paternal Duke. However, the Duke' temporary confusion when Angelo breaks his promise to pardon Claudio, and Claudio's muteness in the final action, despite his central role in the plot, suggest that the violence associated with sexuality has been hidden, but not resolved.

The entire action can also be seen as the dream of the Duke, who then defines himself as controlling and manipulating, so that he may express and resolve through the figure of Angelo his remotely actualized sexual ambivalence which prevents him from having a wife. He expresses his unease about his sexuality in his ambivalence about enforcing Vienna's laws; he evades responsibility by empowering the 'son' version of himself to cleanse the city; and he has the pleasure of punishing in Angelo his own desires. The connection between the two figures surfaces when the Duke says, 'Shame to him whose cruel striking / Kills for faults of his own liking! / Twice treble shame on Angelo, / To weed my vice, and let his grow! (III.ii.260–3). His unease about himself as the image of idealized authority also generates Lucio, a development from Polonius, who for no clear reason, sticks to the Duke-cum-friar like a 'kind of burr' (IV.iii.178), taunting the Duke for sexual looseness, and saying that were the Duke present, Claudio would not be so severely punished by the 'old fantastical Duke of dark corners' (IV.iii.156). In the final action, Lucio both gains and loses credibility; he gains it since he always has inexplicable foreknowledge of events, but he acquires shades of villainy when without apparent reason he discredits Isabella's story by maligning the Friar. The Duke reveals his distance from his repressed desires by being unamused by Lucio and by threatening him with death. However, within the comic debasement of Lucio's punishment the Duke expresses his unacknowledged associations of sex with death and violence. Lucio, being forced to marry a prostitute, 'a rotten medlar' (IV.iii.173) whom he has impregnated, says, 'Marrying a punk, my lord, is pressing to death,/ Whipping and hanging' (V.i.520–1). The troublesome aspects of sexuality thus dispatched, the Duke-cum-friar can permit a dim vision of himself married to the nunlike Isabella onto the horizons of consciousness.

Like *As You Like It*, this play ends with multiple marriages on various levels of idealization and carnality – the Duke and Isabella, Angelo and Mariana, Lucio and his whore, Claudio and Juliet. But the unresolved issues at deeper levels appear in the unease and uncertainty that surround almost every aspect of the play. They taint Isabella's moral self-righteousness when Lucio subtly mocks her as 'a thing enskied and sainted,' and they appear in the comic notes Lucio's prompting inserts into her plea for Claudio.[9] Though her strenuous chastity is praised, it is also punished when the Duke forces her publicly to declare that she has slept with Angelo. The same uncertainty surrounds the Duke, whose desire to let Angelo clean up his mess may have machiavellian astuteness, but seems sufficiently shoddy morally to justify the odd light cast on him by Lucio. His identification with the friar, who ought not to exist apart from the Duke, seems odd when Mariana recognizes the friar from a previous meeting, and one wonders what the Duke was up to when he says that he knows Mariana virtuous because he has often confessed her.

The same uncertainty that surrounds the characters and the facts also pervades the issues. Angelo's attack on the bawdy-houses appears negatively when it is implied that the city houses will 'stand for seed' because of a rich burgher's bribe. It is undermined as well when Isabella asserts that begetting a child 'in coin that is forbid' is not as grievously sinful as murder, and by Escalus' leniency with Pompey when Angelo is uninterested in wasting his time on lowly persons, and by Pompey's convincing terseness when he says that if the authorities were to eliminate bawdy-houses, which finally they do, they would have 'to geld and splay all the youth of the city.' Even though Angelo is satirized for his snow-broth blood, by the time of *The Tempest*, Ferdinand needs 'white cold virgin snow' upon his heart in order to 'abate the ardor of [his] liver.' Also, there is uncertainty about the moral status of a marriage consummated after the engagement contract but prior to the church ceremony. The Duke assumes it is proper when he arranges for Angelo to sleep with Mariana, but Isabella does not make the same assumption when she argues with Angelo, nor does Claudio argue for his own innocence. Some vague unease about the need for ceremonial purification of the sexual can be seen again in the change that occurs in *The Tempest*, when Prospero warns Ferdinand that if they anticipate 'All sanctimonious ceremonies,' then 'Barren hate, sour-ey'd disdain and discord shall bestrew / The union of your bed with weeds so loathly / That you shall hate it both' (*Tempest*, IV.i.16,20–2). Only a magical ceremony can prevent the corrupt weeds of sexuality from sullying a beneficent fertility.[10]

The difficulty of positioning love relationships in a context that renders them legitimate appears also in connection with the play's overt thematic concern with the nature of the law. The Duke tells Angelo 'so to enforce or qualify the laws / as to your soul seems good,' implying that the law's beneficence depends upon the wisdom and virtue of the ruler. But given Angelo's obliviousness to his own desire, it does seem to his soul good to maintain the law's letter, and the Duke's leniency has let vices grow. Without law vice grows, but law without a virtuous ruler corrupts justice, and ordinary rulers are not virtuous. To resolve that dilemma, the Duke declares that judges ought not to condemn in others crimes of which they are guilty, but such a principle, in a less than ideal world, would eventuate in a lawless world. Shakespeare is burdened by his own relentless impulse to dredge the psychic depths that undermine both idealized paternal images, and the principles upon which the ideal rests. As long as those paternal images oppose sexuality, they intensify the guilt and rage they are generated to contain, and must become in turn still more repressive. In the major tragedies the idealized father steps aside to make room for the subject sons to become fathers, husbands, and kings, until hell breaks loose and he reappears as Prospero to force the lid on the cauldron.

5

Where Toads Knot and Gender: The Double Triangle of *Othello*

Hamlet makes a bid for mature authority and withdraws from the aura of corrupt sexuality he thereby generates. Troilus remains in his own eyes the virtuous son of discredited fathers while he enters Hamlet's sexual world. Bertram and Angelo each at a different level of consciousness espouse desires they think of as evil in worlds in which women remain pure under the protection of paternal figures, though Angelo tries on a 'little brief authority.'

Othello tries on a less brief authority by means of splitting and distancing the paternal image into the abstract authority of the Venetian State, and their enemies, the 'men of royal siege' from whom he claims derivation. In defining himself a stranger and warrior he permits himself fully to unfold the shape of his desires at the same time as he forgoes protection from the consequences. He also divides the same woman into the polarized images of redeeming purity and corrupting sexuality that in later plays will create separate figures. In doing so, he defines himself as 'simpler than the infancy of truth,' while he bequeaths to Iago Troilus' cynicism. The action slowly reverses the configuration, so that Othello espouses images of corruption in which he defines both himself and Desdemona, while his idealization of Desdemona retreats into a surrounding aura.

Unlike Romeo, Othello does not externalize his inner world into circumstance, and unlike Hamlet, he does not experience it as an engulfing environment of corruption and disease. Rather he casts himself as a kind of Everyman in a psychologically complex morality configuration. In other characters who represent extremities of good and evil, Othello expresses his divided image of himself, and in the gap between the way we see them and the way he sees them he expresses his confusion about which set of ideas and emotions to repudiate. Furthermore, each of the major figures with whom Othello surrounds himself functions in two competing love triangles, one heterosexual among Othello, Desdemona, and Cassio, and one implicitly homosexual among Iago, Othello, and Cassio.

By having married Desdemona, Othello has challenged the paternal voices that inhibited other protagonists. However, in the initial configuration he reveals that though he struggles with the fears and anxieties around heterosexuality that showed themselves in other plays, he has not overcome them. His underlying feeling that his sexuality renders him bestial appears when he and Desdemona try to consummate their marriage in an invisible bedroom while Iago shouts under Brabantio's window that he and his daughter are 'making the beast with two backs.' This sense of himself as 'an old black ram' tupping Brabantio's 'white ewe' lies behind his overt definition of himself as a black warrior who is alien to the domesticity and elegance of the Venetian society from which he has stolen Desdemona.

The internal sources of the external configuration appear when, warned by Iago that Brabantio will turn the senate against him, Othello prides himself on his freedom from fear or anxiety. Though he defines himself as a kind of war machine, the secrecy of his marriage betrays his intuition that the Venetians' admiration for his martial valour conceals their scorn for his manhood. His misgivings about himself as lover, implied by that secrecy, also appear in the way he idealizes the image of himself as warrior and in his exaggerated self-confidence when he says to Iago, 'My parts, my title, and my perfect soul, / Shall manifest me rightly' (I.ii.31–2), or, 'Keep up your bright swords, for the dew will rust them' (I.ii.59). His need to assert an absolute command corresponds to his secret uncertainty about his rights to his wife.

The two major figures with whom Othello is identified are Iago and Cassio. They each amplify different aspects implied in Othello's self-definition, but extend them into ranges that Othello's view of himself has been designed to conceal. Iago shares with Othello his exclusion from Venetian aristocracy. Defined as lower class, rather than foreign, he is as strange as is Othello to the 'curled darlings' whom Brabantio thinks suitable for his daughter, and like Othello, he declares himself 'little blest with the set phrase of peace' (I.iii.82). His self-definition as blunt soldier presents a cruder version of Othello's martial pride, and his overt sexual crudeness expresses Othello's concealed sense of himself. As well, Othello expresses his concealed resentment at the demeaning authority of the Venetian aristocrats in Iago's jealous hatred of the elegant Cassio for his courtly ease with women as well as for his place as Othello's lieutenant. Iago's overt reprisal at being demeaned by Othello extends from Othello's unconscious sense of having been demeaned by the Venetians in the service of whom he rests his pride. Iago's uncertainty about his reasons for hating Othello – whether because he thinks Othello has 'done

[his] office' or because he is attracted to Desdemona – surrounds with sexual associations his overt resentment at having been bypassed for promotion. In this way he joins the issues of sexual and social rejection in the same way that Othello does in relation to Desdemona. Finally, Iago reveals the most hidden component of Othello's self-recrimination when he describes himself in the diabolic images that he also associates with Othello's sexuality, saying that Desdemona will soon be unable to 'look on the devil' without beginning to 'heave the gorge, disrelish and abhor the Moor' (II.i.231–2). That image yokes together the sense of being sexually disgusting, in contrast to Cassio's 'daily beauty,' and Iago's envious hatred.

In rejecting Iago as his companion in authority, Othello has attempted to dissociate himself from his feelings of social inferiority and the related feelings of envy and anger. In choosing Cassio instead, he chooses the image with which he would like to be identified. Signs of a tenuous identification show in the parallel between Cassio's relation to Bianca and Othello's to Desdemona, for Bianca is to our vision what Desdemona is to Othello's, both a whore and not a whore, and Desdemona's handkerchief, which passes from Cassio's hands to Bianca, further links the two women. Cassio, whose elegance is as antithetical to Othello's self-image as it is to Iago's, is also associated with Othello when Iago fears that Cassio has had his 'night-cap too' (II.i.302). The relative vagueness of the relationship between Othello and Cassio expresses Othello's uncertainty and ambivalence about the image of himself represented in Cassio. Though intimacy between them is suggested by Cassio's role as go-between for Othello and Desdemona, by Othello's use of the given name when he says 'How came it, Michael, you are thus forgot' (II.iii.179), and by Cassio's 'Dear general, I did never give you cause' (v.ii.300), Cassio's importance to the action is disproportionate to the slight definition of their relationship. The something that seems concealed in that disproportion is suggested when the Venetian senate, for no reason connected to the events in Cyprus, of which they are ignorant, gives to Cassio Othello's place as governor. Since Cassio as the elegant Florentine is both more appropriate to Desdemona and more suitable to authority than is Othello, Othello in marrying Desdemona and becoming governor has attempted to identify himself with Cassio and to repudiate the identification of himself with Iago.[1]

All of the aspects of Othello's desire, visible in the play's architecture, are more subtly manifested in the initial configuration and the ensuing story of Othello's relation with Desdemona. Having generated in Iago the expression of his sexuality as bestial, and having defined himself as a stranger in order to distance authority figures in whose eyes he sees himself as such, he tries to consummate his marriage to the daughter he has stolen from the paternal

Venetian state. As he does so, he secures his military self-definition in the crisis brewing between Venice and Turkey. The two messengers, one from the senate and one from Brabantio, who simultaneously intrude on his awareness articulate the same polarity, so that he establishes his claim to Desdemona, and hopes to silence the voices from 'Hell and night,' on the basis of his value as a soldier to the senate. The opposing images come closer to his consciousness when Brabantio asserts that Desdemona could not of her free will 'run from her guardage to the sooty bosom / Of such a thing as thou? to fear, not to delight' (I.ii.70–1), and he defends himself against this assault only by asserting his importance to 'the present business of the state' (I.ii.90).

In winning Desdemona Othello both proves himself equal to or better than the Venetian 'curled darlings,' and places himself in a position to claim entrée into the Venetian society that has demeaned him. A crude version of this ambition appears in Iago's words, 'he to-night hath boarded a land carrack: / If it prove lawful prize, he's made for ever' (I.ii.50–1). Some consciousness of this repudiated motive appears when without provocation he asserts the contrary. As though in answer to an inner voice, he says that but for his love of Desdemona, he would not have his 'unhoused free condition / Put into circumscription and confine / For the sea's worth' (I.ii.25–7). In wedding Desdemona he can in a single act avenge himself on the Venetians for condescending to him, prove himself superior to Desdemona's Venetian suitors, and win the place among them that he denies wanting. [2]

Those feelings are far from his consciousness. Closer to it are the emotional consequences of living behind a public face that prevents him from expressing loneliness or pain. Desdemona's figure allows him to express and thereby remedy that inner isolation. In response to the first senator's question, 'Did you by indirect and forced courses / Subdue and poison this young maid's affections? / Or came it by request, and such fair question, / As soul to soul affordeth' (I.iii.111–14), Othello reveals the inner life of the estranged man. He has told to Brabantio the story of the 'battles, sieges, fortunes' that he had passed, but to Desdemona he tells of 'some distressed stroke / That my youth suffer'd.' The tears of which he beguiles her for the tender person beneath his image as a conquering hero water the parched desert of his inner being. Having opened himself to her pity, he includes her image in the definition of the inward self that has been invisible to himself and others. [3] She then becomes the 'fountain, from the which [his] current runs / Or else dries up' (IV.ii.60–1). But the enemy is now within the gates, for once he has 'garnered up [his] heart' in her, he grows dependent on her view of him, which in turn will reflect his vision of himself in her Venetian eyes.

Having assumed simultaneously the role of husband and that of governor in Cyprus, Othello is challenged to integrate the images of himself as lover and husband with his warrior self. He begins to do so when Desdemona appeals to the senate for permission to accompany him to Cyprus, but in supporting her plea he also reveals the feelings that will doom his enterprise. He denies his own sexuality and trivializes Desdemona when he says that he does not second her petition 'to please the palate of [his] appetite, / Nor to comply with heat, the young affects / In me defunct' (I.iii.262–4), and he renders her role in his life demeaning to rather than confirming of his manliness, in saying

> ... no, when light-wing'd toys,
> Of feather'd Cupid, foils with wanton dullness
> My speculative and active instruments,
> That my disports corrupt and taint my business,
> Let housewives make a skillet of my helm,
> An all indign and base adversities,
> Make head against my reputation! (I.iii.268–74)

By playing to the Venetian view he maintains the split between his self-image and his passions, thereby confirming Iago's image of his sexuality to which, in sending Desdemona under Iago's care to Cyprus, he commits her. Othello's dim awareness of the 'monstrous birth' inherent in their relationship appears when he greets Desdemona in Cyprus by saying that 'now to die, / 'Twere now to be most happy' (II.i.189–90).

The slow unfolding of the entwined emotions that contribute to his 'soul's joy' in Desdemona is rendered in the process by which Iago moves from the periphery of Othello's consciousness to its centre. Othello expresses remotely his feeling that he is inappropriate to Desdemona when Iago contrasts him, defective in 'sympathy in years, manners and beauties' (II.i.228–9) to Cassio, who is 'handsome, young, and hath all these requisites in him that folly and green minds look after' (II.i.243–5). Othello overlays his picture of Desdemona with his view of himself in contrasting Iago's 'And I'll warrant her full of games,' to Cassio's 'Indeed she is a most fresh and delicate creature' (II.iii.19–20). Othello shows his secret resentment of Cassio's appropriateness to Desdemona by casting him as Iago's first target.

In the night brawl that truncates Othello's second attempt to consummate his marriage, he admits the inextricable connections between authority and love that he denied to the senate. The threat Desdemona poses to his authority appears when Iago, after instructing Roderigo to 'cry a mutiny,' warns Iago that 'The town will rise, God's will, lieutenant, hold, / You will be sham'd for ever' (II.iii.153–4). Authority is also Othello's first concern when he wants the bell silenced that 'frights the isle / From her propriety.' He hints at the inner dimension of this threat to his external authority when he says, 'Are we turn'd Turks, and to ourselves do that / Which heaven has forbid the Ottomites? / For Christian shame, put by this barbarous brawl' (III.iii.166–7,161–3). The word 'barbarous' associates the brawl with his repudiated barbarian origins, while in demoting Cassio he moves a step closer to espousing that repudiated barbarian self. These shades of violence colour his relation to Desdemona when Iago describes the fight in images of violent love: 'friends all but now, even now / In quarter, and in terms, like bride and groom / Divesting them to bed, and then but now, / As if some planet had unwitted men, / Swords out, and tilting one at other's breast, / In opposition bloody' (II.iii.170–5). The eroticized violence that shapes the scene as a whole echoes in Othello's words to Desdemona, 'Come, Desdemona: 'tis the soldiers' life / To have their balmy slumbers wak'd with strife' (II.iii.249–50). The bright swords that were sheathed outside Othello's first trysting place with Desdemona are beginning to emerge.

The gradual process by which Othello relinquishes his delegated Venetian authority over his barbarian passions is presaged when he says, 'My blood begins my safer guides to rule, / And passion having my best judgement collied / Assays to lead the way' (II.iii.196–8). His passions lead him to recast Desdemona's image from that of a compassionate virgin distinct from her Venetian environment to that of a betraying whore who represents both the Venetians from whom she derives and their view of him as bestial barbarian. Out of his eroticized self-hatred and rage he generates the 'ocular proof' of Cassio and Desdemona copulating, which in turn leads him to release his violent passions. He therefore bids farewell to the 'plumed troop and the big wars, / That make ambition virtue' (III.iii.355–6), because the image of himself as cuckold opens to public ridicule the virtuous ambitions he gratified as Venice's warrior by exposing his vicious ambitions for social status and for revenge that he has denied were involved in his marriage. The image of Desdemona's corrupted sweet body being tasted by 'the general camp' sours the transport suggested by 'the neighing steed, and the shrill trump, / The spirit-stirring drum, the ear-piercing fife; / The royal banner, and all quality, / Pride, pomp, and circumstance of glorious war! (III.iii.357–60) Iago's comforting worldly wisdom only adds to Othello's gall, for his enterprise depended on proving himself superior to the Venetian elite. To think of himself instead as one among many Venetian cuckolds undermines the militaristic pride that served as his only defence against his self-denigration in their eyes. That pride now crumbles before his imagination of their scorn for and pleasure in his failure. In an ironic way he has fulfilled his desire to integrate his inner needs to his outward presentation of himself, for his emotional life has now totally intertwined with his sense of himself in the world. But his love-life has not added lustre to his image of himself in the world; rather his heroic image of himself has been coloured by his image of his inner self – 'my name, that was as fresh / As Dian's visage, is now begrim'd and black / As mine own face' (III.iii.392–4).[4]

As Othello's previously hidden self-hatred emerges, his language incorporates the images of foul sexuality that previously characterized Iago's. Comparing Desdemona to a falcon whose jesses 'were my dear heart-strings,' he says 'I had rather be a toad, / And live upon the vapour in a dungeon, / Than keep a corner in a thing I love, / For others' uses' (III.iii.274–7). A falcon, however, is a bird of prey, and he becomes its prey when he sees himself as a toad in the vapour of a dungeon. That image of the toad becomes an image of himself, which partakes of the foul quality he imputes to Desdemona. That identification appears later when he says,

> But there, where I have garner'd up my heart,
> Where either I must live, or bear no life,
> The fountain, from the which my current runs,
> Or else dries up, to be discarded thence,
> Or keep it as a cistern, for foul toads
> To knot and gender in! (IV.ii.58–63)

He replaces the image of himself and Desdemona as foul toads knotting and gendering in a cistern with that of the elegant Cassio and Desdemona coupling when Iago says, 'Would you, the supervisor, grossly gape on / Behold her topp'd.' That image in turn increases his self-disgust, at the same time as it gives him permission to vent upon Cassio and Desdemona his rage at the aristocracy they represent, whose gaze has rendered him ugly in his own eyes.

As the tentatively realistic figures whom he has generated to establish himself as husband and governor are swept into an emotional whirlpool, Othello escapes being totally engulfed by separating idealized images of Desdemona from her physical presence. His suspicions having taken shape, he rejects her suit for Cassio, but as she retreats from him he reflects, 'Excellent wretch, perdition catch my soul, / But I do love thee, and when I love thee not, / Chaos is come again' (III.iii.92–3). As his mind becomes further enmeshed in the images of vaporous dungeons that will cause him to reject the pity she offers with the handkerchief, he says when he sees her in the distance 'Desdemona comes, If she be false, O, then heaven mocks itself, / I'll not believe it' (III.iii.281–3). The idealized image, however, is opposed to living sexuality, so that as Othello contemplates her skin of 'monumental alabaster' he must quench the 'flaming minister' of life, because only dead is she safe from his corruption; 'I will kill thee, and love thee after' (v.ii.5,8,18–19). He separates the idealized image from her sexuality, but he becomes dark in proportion to the brightness of her image. That sharp polarity emerges in Emilia's words: 'O, the more angel she, / And you the blacker devil!' (v.ii.131–2). The images that she uses, 'most filthy bargain,' and 'as ignorant as dirt,' express his own 'begrimed and black' face, but as he fully espouses that vision of himself he uses language that cements the identification of himself with Iago: 'O cursed slave! / Whip me, you devils / From the possession of this heavenly sight' (v.ii.277–9). At the same time as the gentle Desdemona lies dead, the gentle Cassio replaces Othello as governor, and Othello has returned to the point from which he started, except that he has now identified with Iago's vision of his 'abhorred flesh,' and with the barbarian Turks who 'beat a Venetian and traduc'd the state.' Having internalized the split half of himself that had been externalized, he now becomes as well the defender of that state who, in killing himself, punishes the 'circumcised dog,' who presumed to aspire to an authority and a love that his possession could only degrade.

By punishing himself and in conferring on Cassio his delegated Venetian authority, Othello retains on the periphery of his dreamscape an ideal image of Desdemona that might save him from himself. In the coincidence of the Venetians' return just prior to the murder and suicide that consummates their love, Othello reveals the sources of the shouts and violence that initially seemed peripheral to the lovers' story. The previously invisible marriage bed, which has emerged onto centre stage laden with their dead bodies, is an image by which Othello at once punishes the authority that demeaned him, punishes himself for challenging it, and maintains his claim to Desdemona.

The love-death compromise that shapes the principal action opposes, as it does in *Romeo and Juliet*, a desire for life. That appears in one aspect of Desdemona's character that extends into the figure of Emilia. We see Desdemona almost exclusively in relation to Othello, and have little context to give depth to her figure. The imagery of idealization obscures her from our eyes, as it does from Othello's. The obscurity of her character is one way in which Othello makes confused efforts to separate her from his own impulses to turn flesh into alabaster. Another such effort appears in the way she resists being idealized when she says in response to Othello's preference for death over change, 'The heavens forbid / But that our loves and comforts should increase, / Even as our days do grow' (II.i.193–5). Later when Othello's mind oscillates between images of heavenly light and those of vileness and corruption, she pleads in terms of the ordinary: 'Send for the man and ask him,' she says, and finally pleads for time – 'Kill me to-morrow, let me live tonight,' 'But half an hour, but while I say one prayer!' (v.ii.50,81,83).

The contrast between this aspect of Desdemona's character and the idealizing images that obscure her from our eyes as well as Othello's makes her like a dream figure who hovers between expressing emotions integrated into a present reality and one that emerges from past less integrated emotions. That indeterminate place on the scale between realistic and distorted figures makes her a difficult character to enact, but enough detail is provided to allow a coherent portrait to emerge if one takes her, for the moment, as the play's dreamer. She then, having in the recent past held herself apart from love, sexuality, and marriage, generates in Othello a man who moves her sexually through her compassion for his heroic sufferings. His vulnerability links him to the gentleness by which she defines herself, while his strange and violent life compels her. As Othello is aware of his love for her gentleness, but is unaware of the significance he attributes to her Venetian identity, so she is aware of her admiring compassion, but is unaware of her own attraction to his potential violence. Her speech to the senate hints at her desire to identify herself with his martial image when, pleading for permission to go with Othello to Cyprus, she describes herself in military terms. Her 'downright violence, and scorn of fortunes, / May trumpet to the world' her intention, and, like Othello, she scorns to be a 'moth of peace' (I.iii.249–50,56). As Othello considers her his 'fair warrior' she also wants to share in his heroic violence. When she says that if she remains behind in Venice then 'the rites for why I love him are bereft me,' 'rites' carries a double meaning, referring in context both to the rites of war for which she loves him, but also to the rites of marriage. The two meanings being brought together in the single word associates them with each other, and suggests that his potential violence sexually excites her.

Desdemona's unconscious desire for Othello's potential violence generates his suspicion, which her behaviour at every point seems exactly calculated to fan. The conscious aspect of her behaviour derives from her stated desire to associate herself with Othello's soldierly life, but she also undermines his authority, first remotely in Iago's words, 'Our general's wife is now our general' (II.iii.305–6) and more directly when she asserts to Cassio that 'My lord shall never rest, / I'll watch him tame, and talk him out of patience; / His bed shall seem a school, his board a shrift' (III.iii.22–4). The pleasure she takes in identifying herself with Othello's professional life and the public pride she takes in their intimacy give the lie to his confidence that housewives could not make 'a skillet of his helm.'[5] But something more is implied by her consistently assertive behaviour in situations where she might accomplish

more by politic passivity, and her passivity in those situations in which assertive anger might have allayed Othello's suspicions. As though not content
until she excites his anger, she persists in urging Cassio's cause after Othello
has twice repeated 'I will deny thee nothing' (III.iii.77,84). When Othello
barely conceals his seething rage by referring to his aching, behorned head,
she courts his rage by offering him the handkerchief that he equates with
maternal pity. Having stirred his rage, she falls into passivity and confusion;
she loses the assertiveness with which she might have scolded Othello for
exaggerating the importance of a trifle, or have pressed him to explain himself.
In so far as she functions as an aspect of Othello's dreaming, her lost handkerchief signifies his denial of the maternal power with which he has endowed
her. After Othello publicly humiliates and abuses her in the presence of
Lodovico and the other Venetians who have come to Cyprus, she retreats
without demanding an explanation that might clarify or reveal the truth.
When in private he calls her a 'whore' and 'public commoner,' and accuses
her of doing things too foul to speak, she barely responds. She falls into a
kind of entranced passivity after Othello throws coins at her in leaving, saying
in response to Emilia's 'how do you?' 'Faith, half asleep'(IV.ii.98–9).

It is as though Desdemona has fallen into the sources of her own dreaming
when Emilia asks, 'what is the matter with my lord?' and she responds 'With
who?' 'Why, with my lord, madam,' says Emilia. 'Who is thy lord?' (IV.ii.100–
3). Out of that bemused or hypnotic state emerges, as though from the very
depth of her unconscious and without any explanation in ordinary reality, her
direction to Emilia, 'Prithee, to-night / Lay on my bed our wedding sheets'
(IV.ii.107).[6] It is as though she has already embraced the image of dying at
Othello's hands when she says to Iago, 'Unkindness may do much, / And his
unkindness may defeat my life, / But never taint my love' (IV.ii.161–3). She
expresses a more remote desire to live when, still entranced as she awaits her
enraged husband on her wedding sheets, she dreamily asks Emilia, 'Wouldst
thou do such a thing for all the world?' With an unromantic vigour worthy
of Juliet's nurse Emilia answers, 'The world is a huge thing, it is a great price, /
For a small vice' (IV.iii.67–9). As Emilia prepares the unresponsive Desdemona
for her deathbed, in unacknowledged response a more life-loving part of herself
speaks dreamily, 'This Lodovico is a proper man ... He speaks well' (IV.iii.35,
137). Though she cannot espouse Emilia's vision, her mind wanders to the
very kind of man that Iago maliciously predicted and Othello most feared it
would. But Iago was wrong, for her desire for life succumbs to the lure of
offering herself as willing sacrifice to the rage and violence she has attracted.
Her sexual swoon into the consummation of her marriage in death reveals
her in collusion with Othello even as she experiences herself as forgiving

victim.[7] Having generated in Othello's eyes an idealized image of herself, she holds it at a distance until she says that 'His unkindness may do much / But never taint my love,' and she fully identifies with it when in response to Emilia's question, 'Who has done this deed?' she miraculously revives to answer, in a sense truly, 'Nobody, I myself' (v.ii.124–5). She gives to Othello the remote satisfaction of her forgiveness, by which he becomes blacker.[8]

As an aspect of Othello's dream configuration, Desdemona's collusion in his project permits Othello to absorb her into perverse desires he cannot acknowledge, while in idealizing her as radiantly virtuous and mercifully forgiving he achieves some measure of relief from his self-loathing. Though the fuller emotional realization permits only the partial success of uniting their dead bodies on their bloody wedding sheets, Othello has generated a version of Angelo's and Bertram's bed trick, in which Desdemona is both the object of desires he regards as base, and the means by which he hopes to transform them. In those earlier plays morally positive figures arranged for the schematic resolutions of conflicting passions in the bed tricks. In this play Othello casts Iago as the power that weaves from Desdemona's goodness 'the net / That shall enmesh 'em all' (II.iii.353), thereby fusing homosexual drives into the heterosexual love-death drama.

Despite his sporadic attempts to dispel the mists generated by the polarity between idealized good and diabolic evil, Othello's attempt to purify the 'foul cistern' of his heterosexual loving by coupling himself with the exalted image of Desdemona's heavenly virtue creates in fact a polarity that further darkens him by contrast. That process is expressed in Iago, who turns Desdemona's virtue into pitch by insinuating himself between Othello and her with a sexual suggestiveness indicative of the homosexual component of Othello's passions. As a consequence, Othello inhabits a world in which his soul is at stake between the forces of heavenly virtue, which he associates with heterosexual love, Venetian authority, compassion, and his own estrangement, and the forces of hell, which he associates with greed, envy, intelligent manipulation, and the aura of homosexual passion. Initially, he introduced Desdemona to his dream-scape at the same time as he distanced his homosexual longings into images of the barbarian Turks and Iago's devious strategies. But as his closer approach turns her into an image of sexual betrayal and corruption, he slowly draws closer to Iago and the homosexual eroticism that he associates with damnation.

In order more conveniently to explore the subtle turns of that relationship, I will for the moment take Iago as dreamer, and then subsume the figure to Othello's dream configurations. Iago experiences himself rejected by Othello, who for Iago represents an exalted image of himself, military, excluded from Venetian society, and, in the play's suggested past, dissociated from women.

He experiences himself doubly rejected when Othello, in trying to storm the social barricade, has married Desdemona and has chosen Cassio as his most intimate professional associate. The configuration reveals Iago's self-hatred, and his embattled sexuality is expressed in his intensely prurient concentration on Othello's sexuality and his more remote interest in Desdemona's. Seeing himself as humbled in his professional, social, and erotic aspirations, his moment-by-moment improvisation expresses his uncertainty about the source of his own action, while defining himself as evil allows him to satisfy unacknowledged erotic desires that have fused with self-condemnation, hate, and envy.[9]

The dynamics of Iago's drama emerge when Iago speaks bitterly to Roderigo about Cassio, 'who in good time, must his lieutenant be' (I.i.32). When Roderigo sensibly suggests, 'I would not follow him then,' Iago describes himself as one who with 'shows of service ... have lin'd their coats' (I.i.52–3). But this rational, if not virtuous, desire accounts for little of the action. Iago has little hope either of materially harming Othello or of enriching himself when he reveals to Brabantio Othello's union with Desdemona so that he may 'poison his delight,' and 'plague him with flies' (I.i.68,71). With the ordinary, if illegitimate, desire for profit and status Iago screens his sadistic obsession with Othello's sexuality. He interprets his gratuitous pleasure in causing pain as diabolic when he espouses the 'Divinity of hell' (II.iii.341).

Iago's desire to poison Othello's delights does not take firm shape until he includes Cassio along with Desdemona on the periphery of his configuration. His preoccupation with Cassio as well as with Othello appears when Iago reflects, 'Cassio's a proper man, / Let me see now, / To get his place, and to make up my will, / A double knavery' (I.iii.391–2). The erotic component suggested in the 'proper man' also appears in the birth imagery he uses to describe his strategies: 'There are many events in the womb of time, which will be delivered,' and 'Hell and night / Must bring this monstrous birth to the world's light' (I.iii.369–70, 401–2). The sexual, and the sense of a corrupt fertility, in contrast to Othello and Desdemona's barren love, joins with Iago's professional resentments when he describes Cassio to Roderigo as 'a slippery knave,' who has 'salt and most hidden affections.' Iago's pleasure in manipulating Cassio is similar to that he takes with Othello, and he is similarly confused about his motivation, not knowing whether he wants to kill Cassio because 'He has a daily beauty in his life, / That makes me ugly,' or because he fears that 'The Moor / May unfold me to him; there stand I in peril' (V.i.20–1). With the same 'motive mongering' as before, he defines himself as merely self-seeking and self-protective to screen the sexual envy that emerges when, like Othello in relation to Desdemona, he sees himself as ugly in the light of Cassio's distant beauty. This sexual jealousy also shapes the action when Iago rather than Roderigo wounds Cassio in the leg.

Cassio is closer to Iago's homosexual orbit than he is to Othello's, but Iago draws his vaguely erotic resentment at Cassio's social distance into his concentration on Othello's sexuality. Iago's behaviour suggests eroticised aggression when, after reminding Othello that Desdemona deceived her father, Iago concludes, 'I humbly do beseech you of your pardon, / For too much loving you' (III.iii.216–17). The abstraction from which Othello answers with apparent offhandedness, 'I am bound to thee forever,' does not cancel the portentousness, which fuels the greater intensity that develops as Iago seeks to replace Desdemona in Othello's emotional intimacy.

When Iago approaches the anguished Othello after Desdemona's rejected handkerchief has been duly lost, found, and given to Iago, he conjures before Othello's eyes the image of Cassio with Desdemona, 'Would you, the supervisor, grossly gape on, / Behold her topp'd?' Having penetrated to the centre of Othello's privacy, he plays on Othello's fears when he describes them as 'prime as goats, as hot as monkeys, / As salt as wolves' (III.iii.409–10), and draws Othello's imagination into his own when Othello calls her a 'lewd minx.'

Iago then overlays this bestial vision of heterosexuality with a homosexual image. He substitutes an image of Cassio in his sleep mistaking Iago for Desdemona, and kissing him, 'As if he pluck'd up kisses by the roots, / That grew upon my lips, then laid his leg / Over my thigh, and sigh'd, and kiss'd, and then / Cried, "Cursed fate, that gave thee to the Moor!"'(III.iii,429–32). Imagistically he first appeals to Othello's disgust at heterosexuality, then shifts Othello's imagination from a heterosexual to a homosexual realm, and in that realm shows Cassio simultaneously engaged with Desdemona and with Iago, equating himself with her in the image. In the fantasy he has both won Cassio from Othello, and encouraged Othello to shift his homosexual attraction from Cassio to himself. In the 'thee' of the last line, which subsumes Desdemona's image to Iago's physical presence, he holds before Othello an image of Cassio mourning the loss of Iago to Othello. In this way Iago presents Othello with an image of himself as a love object made worthy by Cassio's love, and offers this homosexual union as an alternative to the heterosexual one.

This image leads to the mutual vow between Othello and Iago. In images that are associated with Desdemona, Othello swears vengeance by the 'marble heavens,' and Iago by the 'ever-burning lights above,' to do 'what bloody work so ever' in Othello's service. They complete their marriage ceremony, which will bring forth its 'monstrous birth,' when Othello swears to murder the 'fair devil' and replace her with Iago as his lieutenant, and Iago promises 'I am your own forever' (III.iii.486). The erotic intensity associated here with a choice of lieutenant can be read back into Othello's initial choice of Cassio, which would justify Iago's reading of that choice. Iago has achieved his purpose, has won Othello from Cassio and from Desdemona. Were his purpose merely to become lieutenant, he ought to have no further interest in pursuing his revenge. But it is clear when he promises himself to Othello that being lieutenant means more to him than professional success. His rage at being rejected, along with, presumably, his ignorance of his own motivation, drives him farther along the road he has already chosen. His final refusal to explain himself maintains the atmosphere of hell, which throughout expresses his self-judgment as well the mysteriousness in which his own behaviour appears to him.

To subsume Iago to Othello's dream configuration makes his figure represent Othello's fulfilment of the homosexual desires that he morally condemns. Within the overtones of hell and damnation, the passionate intensity of their mutual avowal suggests its central place in Othello's project. But were that the whole story one would expect, both from Freud's discussion of homosexual sources for obsessive jealousy and from the images already discussed, that Othello would identify with Desdemona and dream her together with Iago in order to envision himself with Iago. Hints of such a possibility appear in slight suggestions – his entrusting her to Iago's care on the trip to Cyprus, Iago's passing thought that he is attracted to her, and Iago's intense visualization of Desdemona's sexuality, as well as their limited contact with each other. But despite the intense relation to Iago, Othello's jealousy attaches to Desdemona with Cassio, which suggests him as the object of Othello's denied desire.[10]

The lack of exchange between Cassio and Othello, in combination with Cassio's crucial plot role suggest an Othello who evades something in relation to Cassio. Though most of the few lines that pass between them are gentle, no images indicate any sexualization of that friendly feeling. But Cassio's role in the plot looms larger than the contact with Othello would suggest. The key to the interrelation of the three figures lies in Iago's image of Cassio dreaming of Desdemona in bed with both himself and Iago. As Iago's dream it suggests his desire for Cassio, with remote implications of Desdemona, but the context in which he tells it focuses his primary desire on Othello. As Othello's more remote dream it suggests his desire – since he identifies with Cassio's aristocratic status – to embrace Iago, while Cassio's envisioned love of Desdemona substitutes Cassio for Iago as his love object. The total configuration suggests that Othello needs the aristocratic Cassio rather than the crude Iago as a figure on whom to project the homosexual desires he has repudiated in seeking entry into the Venetian world.

Cassio's appointment as governor signals the end of Othello's attempt to claim his sexuality and win authority. By killing Desdemona he has punished both Venetian patriarchs and women for his incapacity to sustain the enterprise. He espouses instead his identification with Iago, steeped as it is with hellish self-hatred, when he invokes images of Iago's devils to 'Blow me about in winds, roast me in sulfur, / Wash me in steep-down gulfs of liquid fire!'(v.ii.276–81). Within accompanying emotions of horror and remorse, he envisions himself 'ensnared body and soul' by Iago, whom he will join in 'Hell's pains' while he also sees his dead body joined with Desdemona's.

The impasse in which Othello ends is reflected by the double way in which the play's ideology functions. Some, but not all, of the imagery that idealizes Desdemona and vilifies Iago arises from Othello's language, appropriately reflecting his vision. Some of it comes from other sources, and so seems part of the play's ideology in which feminine chastity, weighted with the symbolic import of Christian compassion, self-sacrifice, long-suffering, must counterbalance the machiavellian self-seeking, manipulation, and deception associated with Iago, the devil, and hell. The play shows signs of Shakespeare's having tried to incorporate that ideology into a realistically drawn character, for Desdemona's character is filled out by her flirtatiousness with Cassio, her association with Emilia, and her bold assertion of her own desires. But the ideology competes with the naturalistic character portrayal, leaving her somewhat shadowy.[11] By the time he incarnated the compassion for which Othello loves Desdemona in Cordelia and Miranda, Shakespeare began to sacrifice naturalistic characterization to symbolic resonance. Perhaps intrigued by the source story, he only vaguely sensed that its cataclysm emerged from his lovers themselves, though he knew that well enough to include in muted ways all the relevant detail. In order to retain the romantic idealization of the chaste woman, he made Iago diabolical. But unless Iago were to be a comic stage villain, he needed a portrait with the force of probability, and in the process of providing that, he created the details that filled out the portrait of a homosexually jealous lover – a kind of machiavellian shadow of the idealistically heterosexual Othello.

Othello won Desdemona with the witchcraft of the idealized romance that both conceals and expresses the darker possibilities within love. *Othello* maintains the idealization of romantic love, but makes the feelings that destroy it integral to the protagonist even though externalizing the responsibility. And though the play creates the aura of a satisfying merger into darkness, it also contains the mixed stuff of which love can be made. In *The Winter's Tale*, where Leontes will play his own Iago, Shakespeare will attempt to take the story beyond its cataclysm, though in spiritualized rather than in psychological terms. But before attempting to cleanse the romantic vision of the sexuality from which it emerges he descended farther into the inferno.

6

'Blanket of the Dark':
Stealthy Lovers in *Macbeth*

Macbeth storms the barricade Othello attempted, seizes the woman with whose help he crowns himself king of the nightmare realm on the margins of which Hamlet delayed. By defining himself as husband, Macbeth becomes conscious of the emotions and associations that other protagonists avoided. In the process he creates a polarity between domestic and social harmony and sexual passion. Rather than being the source of procreation and love, Macbeth's relation to his wife is fulfilled in the murder of Duncan, who represents for Macbeth legitimate authority, gentle fathering, maternal nurturing, social accord, and childlike trust. His murder constitutes a psychological holocaust that is also the climax of Macbeth's erotic passions.

Macbeth is not only pervaded by dreamlike occurrences, but Macbeth experiences himself in a dreamlike state. As a consequence of the different levels of dreaming involved, this play more explicitly than others involves connections between internal and external experience. The introductory sequence of action parallels the full sequence of earlier plays in which the protagonist comes to experience as emotions what previously he confronted as external circumstance. But most of the action reverses that process to render a figure transforming his own dreamlike state into what he later confronts as external reality.[1]

The world Macbeth inhabits contains, besides himself, only three defined figures, two of whom he eliminates in short order. The remaining figures with whom he peoples his world, all in some degree shadowlike, fall into two categories. Those relatively realistic but thinly characterized figures who extend from Banquo and who slowly become inimical to Macbeth represent royal authority. The other more dreamlike figures extend from Lady Macbeth to seduce Macbeth into the depths of nightmare. They include the witches, Hecate, and, in the imagery, the country itself as well as the owls, rooks, ravens, and all the extensions of Lady Macbeth's language that compose almost the entire lurid landscape on which Macbeth moves, more real to him than the pallid remnants of the more present-oriented figures.

We encounter Macbeth in a state of transition, indicated by the male figures who acclaim him as 'Valour's minion' (I.ii.19) in images of violence and blood and those who couple his name with that of the traitor thane of Cawdor. Both Cawdor's treason and the blood of battle are associated with Macbeth's role as husband when he is called 'Bellona's bridegroom.' The drama of Macbeth's emerging redefinition of himself is enacted when Duncan gives Cawdor's title to Macbeth while he reflects that 'There's no art / To find the mind's construction in the face: / He was a gentleman on whom I built / An absolute trust' (I.iv.11–14). Macbeth momentarily resists donning the 'borrowed robes' of Cawdor's treachery, but his inner readiness generates the witches' prophecies. In the 'horrible imaginings' that appear to his inner eye instead of images of the 'imperial theme,' he reveals that his desire to kill Duncan, only vaguely suggested before, has suddenly coalesced into an identification of himself with Cawdor's treachery.[2] Cawdor's defection was as mysterious to him as is the image of Duncan murdered by his own hand that fills his inner vision and obscures what previously constituted both his external reality and his self-definition, so that now 'nothing is but what is not.'

Macbeth's previous and fading self-definition appears in his characterization of and relation to Duncan. Duncan as king occupies a paternal realm, which Macbeth emphasizes when he says, 'our duties / Are to your throne and state, children and servants;/ Which do but what they should, by doing everything / Safe toward your love and honour' (I.iv.24–7). Duncan's paternal role, which Lady Macbeth emphasizes when she says that the sleeping Duncan reminds her of her father, also appears in Duncan's praise of Macbeth's heroism: 'The sin of my ingratitude even now / Was heavy on me,' and 'More is thy due than more than all can pay' (I.iv.15–16,21). Duncan's lament that he cannot adequately reward Macbeth becomes ironic when Duncan in the next breath names Malcolm as successor to the throne. In a subtle way Macbeth casts himself as a slighted 'worthiest cousin' rather than eldest son. In doing so he expresses his feeling that he is unworthy of the mantle of authority, and he fuels a sense of grievance that derives from his having interpreted as betrayal his ambition for paternal authority and the maturity it represents. Hearing himself praised as his country's saviour is then a strategy by which he justifies the betrayal that is already taking shape.[3] Already hidden within the initial configuration is the image of himself as a 'dwarfish thief' in the process of acquiring a 'giant's robe' (v.ii.21–2).[4]

However, the paternal image that excites Macbeth's divided feelings carries distinctly maternal colouring, in a way that makes more explicit Hamlet's merger of maternal and paternal figures. In praising Macbeth, Duncan says, 'I have begun to plant thee, and will labour / To make thee full of growing,' and wishes to 'bind us further to you' (I.iv.28–9, 43). Even while Macbeth reflects on his 'black and deep desires,' Duncan associates himself with nurturing and food: 'he is full so valiant,/ And in his commendations I am fed;/ It is a banquet to me' (I.iv.51,54–6). The association of Duncan with nurturing fertility is elaborated when he approaches Macbeth's castle: 'This castle hath a pleasant seat; the air / Nimbly and sweetly recommends itself / Unto our gentle senses' (I.vi.1–3). While Macbeth plans to murder Duncan as king and father, he surrounds him with an aura of creaturely warmth.

The only figure with whom Macbeth identifies is Banquo. They are companions in battle, in encountering the witches, and in earning Duncan's praises. Macbeth completes the isolation of himself and Lady Macbeth when he moves Banquo into Duncan's orbit by associating him with the images of children from which he begins to remove himself. After the witches vanish Macbeth observes that Banquo's 'children shall be kings,' and immediately upon learning that he is thane of Cawdor he says, 'Do you not hope your children shall be kings' (I.iii.86,118). Macbeth's association of Banquo with children also associates him with Duncan, who, after having promised to make Macbeth 'grow,' has more intimate words for Banquo: 'let me enfold thee, / And hold thee to my heart' (I.iv.31–2). Banquo becomes for Macbeth a figure fused with Malcolm as a more legitimate successor than he to the mantle of authority, when Banquo adds to Duncan's praises of Macbeth's castle his observation that

> The temple-haunting martlet, does approve,
> By his loved mansionry, that the heaven's breath
> Smells wooingly here: no jutty, frieze,
> Buttress, nor coign of vantage, but this bird
> Hath made his pendent bed, and procreant cradle:
> Where they most breed and haunt, I have observ'd
> The air is delicate.   (I.vi.4–10)

His association of Macbeth's castle, within which Macbeth and Lady Macbeth plan a different kind of birth, with images of fertility and tender nurturing contrasts this external image of Lady Macbeth to her interior, which she describes in a different bird image when she says, 'The raven himself is hoarse / That croaks the fatal entrance of Duncan / Under my battlements' (I.v.38–40). Macbeth generates the two opposed images of femininity; he espouses the latter but distantly expresses in Banquo's words haunting regret for the realm of nurture, fidelity, affection, and procreation, which is for him in opposition to his marital intimacy with Lady Macbeth.

Having defined his desires for becoming father and king as illegitimate, Macbeth has reversed the classical Oedipal paradigm in which the son in order to marry the mother wishes to kill the father. Rather, he has married the mother, and included the implied sexuality in the project of killing the father. Becoming Bellona's bridegroom meant for him forgoing Banquo's 'bosom franchis'd, and allegiance clear' (II.1.28), and eating of the 'insane root, / That takes the reason prisoner' (1.iii.84–5), so that he may with her aid enter, as Hamlet did not, the Vulcan's stithy of his own imagination.

Macbeth's attitudes towards women appear first in the figures of the witches and Hecate. As non-realistic figures they represent emotions from past con-figurations that have not been integrated into present circumstances. The sense of depth in this play derives largely from these figures and the resonant imagery that surrounds them and spreads to other figures. Unlike most plays, *Macbeth* contains no reference to any circumstance or event prior to the action we witness, but the sense of pastness is suggested by the entranced or dreamlike state into which the witches draw Macbeth. In their first appearance, remote from himself, Macbeth reveals the feelings he has aroused in himself in the process of casting himself as husband. Their plan to waylay him expresses his fear of women's devious strategies, and the surrounding 'fog and filthy air' expresses his moral confusion in which 'fair is foul, and foul is fair.' He casts himself as the object of women's nefarious designs, and in interpreting these women, most unseductive in appearance, as preternatural, he reveals the gap between his self-conception and the seductive desires that have generated these fateful figures. In the image of the 'blasted heath' on which they appear Macbeth associates women with all that is the reverse of the gentle nurturing suggested in the images with which Banquo and Duncan describe the exterior of Macbeth's castle.[5] That the first and second appearances of the witches sandwich the voices that declare his martial heroism suggests that these bubbles of the earth are the opposite side of the coin on which is stamped his self-image as bloodily heroic.

The meaning of the witches for Macbeth unfolds later in the action as more associations cluster around them. Through their relation to Hecate they are associated with murder, but more important, despite his initial revulsion, Macbeth links them to the sensuous images with which he anticipates mur-dering Banquo when he says,

Ere the bat hath flown

His cloister'd flight; ere to black Hecate's summons
The shard-born beetle, with his drowsy hums,
Hath rung Night's yawning peal, there shall be done
A deed of dreadful note.   (III.ii.40–4)

These images of the night creatures that are radically opposed to legitimate daylight activities evoke a kind of dark ease that overwhelms and cancels the moral horror that is the overt content. Macbeth savours the theoretically horrifying deed when he continues, 'Light thickens; and the crow / Makes wing to th'rooky wood; / Good things of Day begin to droop and drowse, / Whiles Night's black agents to their preys do rouse' (III.ii.49–52). The language with which he invokes Hecate associates sensuous darkness with moral outrage ('Fair is foul and foul is fair') and adds a more specifically sexual note when 'Night's ... agents' rouse their prey. These lines that precede Banquo's murder show Macbeth swooning into an anticipation of erotic violence that he interprets as supernaturally induced.

In the witches and Hecate Macbeth evokes a distanced and diabolically defined version of an offended mother. Hecate scolds the witches like erring daughters, Macbeth's sisters rather than his mother, and sounds like a neglected and resentful parent when she rebukes them for having favoured 'a wayward son, / Spiteful, and wrathful; who, as others do, / Loves for his own ends, not for you' (III.v.11–15).[6] In Hecate's words Macbeth expresses his sense of himself using women for his own ends, and of them in reprisal manipulating him through an equivocal seduction that will 'palter with us in a double sense;/ That keep the word of promise to our ear, / And break it to our hope' (v.viii.20–2). All of the images that compose these remote actualizations of feminine figures are also associated with Lady Macbeth.[7] These unrealistic and dreamlike forms in their wavering reality and supernatural attributes depict emotional components from a past or infantile level out of which Macbeth assembles the more present figure that he espouses in his wife. Her figure merges with theirs when she awaits Duncan as the witches did Macbeth, and calls upon the spirits that 'tend on mortal thoughts' to

        unsex me here,
And fill me, from the crown to the toe, top-full
Of direst cruelty! make thick my blood,
Stop up th'access and passage to remorse;
That no compunctious visitings of Nature
Shake my fell purpose, nor keep peace between
Th'effect and it! Come to my woman's breasts,

And take my milk for gall, you murth'ring ministers,
Wherever in your sightless substances
You wait on Nature's mischief! Come, thick Night,
And pall thee in the dunnest smoke of Hell,
That my keen knife see not the wound it makes,
Nor Heaven peep through the blanket of the dark,
To cry, 'Hold, hold!   (I.v.39–53)

The images of 'thick night' and 'dunnest smoke of Hell' recall the earlier 'fog
and filthy air,' and the croaking raven is the first of the crows, owls, bats, and
rooks that reach deep into the later murky depths. Lady Macbeth's desire that
'direst cruelty' should fill her 'from the crown to the toe' recalls the figure
that Macbeth 'unseam'd ... from the nave to th'chops' (I.ii.22), and 'make
thick my blood' leads to the images of blood that flow through the play. More
explicitly than the witches, she opposes herself to the nurturing that defines
Duncan. Banquo will grow in Duncan's bosom, but no nourishment will flow
from her breasts, and in wanting freedom from any 'compunctious visitings
of Nature,' she relates herself to the barren infertility of the 'blasted heath.'[8]

Her scorn of the weak, milky-natured nurturing aspect of Macbeth, which
is associated with the benign and foolishly trusting Duncan, extends through
associated images to infants and mothers. She separates children from the
sexuality that generates them by relating sexuality to her murderous desire
that Duncan, who reminds her of her father, should pass beneath her battlements. The raven that will herald him, along with bats, beetles, rooks, is
associated with owls when Lady Macbeth says during the murder, 'It was the
owl that shriek'd, the fatal bellman, / Which gives the stern'st goodnight'
(II.ii.3–4). Lady Macduff, blaming Macduff for leaving his family unprotected,
says, 'for the poor wren / The most diminutive of birds, will fight / Her young
ones in her nest, against the owl' (IV.ii.9–11). Macbeth himself becomes the
child-killing owl when Macduff says, 'O Hell-kite! All? / What, all my pretty
chickens, and their dam, / At one fell swoop?' (IV.iii.219–21). Ross and the
Old Man include in the portents on the night of the murder 'A falcon, towering
in her pride of place, / Was by a mousing owl hawk'd at and kill'd' (II.iv.12–
13). Since a falcon image underlies Macbeth's invocation, 'Come, seeling
Night / Scarf up the tender eye of pitiful Day / And with thy bloody and
invisible hand / Cancel, and tear to pieces, that great bond / Which keeps me
pale!' (III.ii.47–50), the falcon killed by the mousing owl comes to represent
a fusion of regal pride with infantile tenderness and pity. Though a prideful
falcon may seem an unlikely image for an infant, it coheres with Macbeth's
image of Pity, like a new-born babe, riding the blasts. These clustering images,

which are implied in Lady Macbeth's croaking raven, fuse infanticide into the aura of erotic violence in which Duncan's murder is anticipated.

Lady Macbeth's denied maternity is associated with perverse sexuality through another cluster of images that relates her to the witches, and casts Macbeth as child to her. On the witches' second appearance, one says that she has been 'killing swine' (i.iii.2), and when Macbeth wishes to consult the witches' masters the witch says to pour in their cauldron 'sow's blood, that hath eaten / Her nine farrow' (iv.i.64–5). Lady Macbeth, when planning the murder with Macbeth, says that when Duncan's attendants are 'in swinish sleep / Their drenched natures lie, as in a death, / What cannot you and I perform upon / Th'unguarded Duncan?' She calls them 'spongy officers' (i.vii.68–71,73),and while she awaits Macbeth's return she says, 'The surfeited grooms / Do mock their charge with snores' (ii.i.5–6). Her scorn is a bit unjust, since it was she who 'drugged their possets,' but the image of swinish sleep merges with that of drunkenness. She associates swinishness with drink and sleep, and connects the grooms to her revulsion at Macbeth's softer nature when she rebukes him, 'Was the hope drunk, / Wherein you dress'd yourself? Hath it slept since' (i.vii.35–6). When she says that Duncan's resemblance to her father stopped her hand, she responds lovingly to that maternally tinged father image, but that image merges with those of the swinish grooms who arouse her murderous revulsion, so that she can without difficulty smear their faces with Duncan's blood. Through Lady Macbeth, Macbeth expresses his fear of woman's scorn for male passivity, seen as swinishly sodden.

A more specific form of the implied sexual impotence is evoked through the Porter, who is a version of Hamlet's grave-diggers. Though more remote from Macbeth's consciousness than is the grave-digger scene from Hamlet's, like the grave-diggers, the Porter's grotesque comedy makes explicit what is elsewhere vaguely implied when the Porter says, 'Much drink may be said to be an equivocator with lechery: it makes him, and it mars him; it sets him on, and it takes him off; it persuades him, and disheartens him; makes him stand to, and not stand to: in conclusion, equivocates him in a sleep, and, giving him the lie, leaves him' (ii.iii.30–5). The parallels between equivocating drink, the equivocating witches, and Lady Macbeth's equivocating femininity as expressed in the opposing images of her castle relate Macbeth's experience of feminine duplicity to male impotence, explicitly associated in the Porter's words with the drunken swinishness of the sleeping grooms. That image completes an emotional circle in which Macbeth defines women as cruel and mocking, fears them therefore, joins them in order to safeguard himself and to use them against paternal authority, in the process wedding aggression to eroticism and becoming impotent in ordinary ways. As a consequence, he fears even more the mocking voices of women.[9]

Lady Macbeth also shares her ambiguous sexual definition with the witches, whose beards cast doubt on their sex, and with Duncan, who carries feminine attributes. She asks to be unsexed, and she imagines herself in a sexually dominant role when she wants to 'pour my spirits in thine ear,/ And chastise with the valour of my tongue / All that impedes thee from the golden round' (I.v.26–8), and in her attribution to Macbeth of the 'milk of human kindness' that she denies in herself. Her language binds in a single cluster images of denied nurturing, barrenness, cruelty, and role reversal, and joins that cluster to an aura of sexualized violence when she desires that Heaven not 'peep through the blanket of the dark' to see the wound made by her 'keen knife.' Her words, ringing in the same register as Macbeth's, 'let that be, / Which the eye fears, when it is done, to see' (I.iv.52–3), gather and focus the implications that have already shadowed his figure.

In Lady Macbeth Macbeth has wedded himself to a figure on whom he projects his own eroticized violence, with all the related ideas that are suggested by the imagistic associations that condition the language of the entire play. But he also projects onto her the spurs 'to prick the sides of [his] intent' (I.vii.26), so that he may experience himself in part as passive to women's force ('he loves for his own ends / Not for you'). Despite the many images and structural forms that relate Lady Macbeth to the witches and Hecate, she is on a different dream level from the other feminine figures. Like a dream figure who appears identical to one in waking life, she carries a full sense of present reality. Macbeth, at whatever cost, has generated a female figure who complements his own, and has succeeded in envisioning a mutually loving relationship, though the nature of the shared enterprise that defines their love also carries back to the more dreamlike experiences from which these dark lovers and childless parents have arisen.[10] As their relationship takes shape it also brings to a more presently defined adult level the full implications of the surrounding suggestiveness. Therefore I will consider some of the passages already discussed in that more adult context in order to see how the associations from a deeper past, suggested by the more fantastic configurations, shape Macbeth's love for his wife.

The letter Macbeth writes to Lady Macbeth in its suggestive brevity reveals an intimacy that substantiates the lovingness expressed in its close: 'This have I thought good to deliver thee (my dearest partner of greatness) that thou might'st not lose the dues of rejoicing, by being ignorant of what greatness is promis'd thee' (I.v.10–14). Their loving intimacy is further suggested by her instant intuition of Macbeth's excited fear, and her similar assumption that circumstances alone will not fulfil the witches' prophecy. As Macbeth immediately envisioned Duncan's murder rather than himself enthroned, so she will 'catch the nearest way.' She surrounds the projected murder with perverse sexual intimacy, and associates her genitals with cruelty when she imagines Duncan entering her castle. She turns impulses of 'compunctious tenderness' to 'murthering ministers,' and evokes tender sexual feelings, associates them with mothering, and negates them even as they arise when she asks them to 'take my milk for gall.' She equates Duncan's murder with rejecting both her own normal sexuality and mothering. Macbeth expresses his desire to kill Duncan through the image of her cruelty, giving her the 'keen knife' that will make the death wound beneath the 'blanket of the dark' in the atmosphere of an intimate sexuality. A vague image of a sexual act begins to form, in which the hostility Macbeth feels for the paternal Duncan imbues his imagination of woman's violence. But he also associates himself with Duncan remotely when Lady Macbeth describes his nature as full of the 'milk of human kindness,' so that the anticipated murder includes an image of himself as passive victim of her sexualized violence.[11]

When Macbeth enters this aura of perverse sexuality she tells him that, having been transported by his letter beyond the ignorant present, she feels 'the future in the instant.' The previously denied procreative power now generates images of power in her allusion to his new title, which promises him the throne. Macbeth defines his love within his wife's unspoken thought when he responds, 'My dearest love, / Duncan comes here to-night' (I.v.57–8). The mutually intuitive understanding of their exchange drains the impact from Macbeth's vacillating demur 'We will speak further' (I.v.71). The accord of her mind to his shows that in writing to her he relied on her resolve to steady his, a naturalistic extension of what the images have suggested, and so in his passivity to her he can 'wrongly win' that which he would not 'play false' to attain.

Their relationship to each other provides a rhythm by which each excites the other to the point of action. The first movement occurred in Macbeth's sending the letter, in Lady Macbeth's response, and in his collusive reaction to her. The second begins when Macbeth for a moment enters a meditation, like that of Hamlet, on this 'bank and shoal of time' between life and death. Like Hamlet, he shrinks from the dreams that may arise in the 'undiscover'd country' (*Hamlet*, III.i.79) of the 'life to come' that he cannot jump. But Macbeth has defined himself as Claudius rather than Hamlet, and so envisions himself as victim rather than instrument of the 'even-handed Justice [that] / Commends th'ingredience of our poison'd chalice / To our own lips' (I.vii.10–12). That thought rouses his more filial feelings as Duncan's 'kinsman and his subject,' as well as his host. The image of himself as host arouses his protective feelings so that he envisions himself guarding the gentle Duncan, who has 'borne his faculties so meek.' From that double image of gentleness violated is born the image of 'Pity, like a naked new-born babe, / Striding the blast,' riding the winds in vengeance against him, before which he falls back from his 'vaulting ambition.' But even as he generates an image of a natural child, he turns it against himself, for he has already chosen his Gertrude and eliminated any Ophelia against whom to unpack his heart with words.

As previously Macbeth came, as though called, at the end of Lady Macbeth's soliloquy, now she comes, as though called, to do in fact what she and Macbeth had anticipated she would. By chastising 'with the valour of my tongue / All that impedes thee from the golden round' she draws his enraptured vision into his ordinary reality and daily life, where 'Time and the hour runs through the roughest day' (I.iii.148). He initiated the integration of the past to the present level of his reality in writing the letter. She overcomes the impeding pity by equating his murderous desire to his sense of manliness, and his pity, with all its accumulated associations, to cowardice, and by implication in view of the swinish grooms, to sexual impotence. In her Macbeth generates the voice he needs to join his desire, first experienced through the witches, to his 'own act and valour' (I.vii.40). He permits himself a fleeting resistance, looking for an alternative equation between manliness and seemliness, but her words carry his deeper impulses when she argues that Macbeth's pledge to her is more binding than a mother's love for her child. Given the strong metaphorical equation generated throughout the play of the kingdom to a family, in asserting that Macbeth's pledge to her supersedes his bonds to kind and country, she opposes the love between herself and Macbeth to the encompassing scale of creaturely accord that extends from sucking infants to social harmony. When she says 'From this time / Such I account thy love' (I.vii.38–9) she defines their love as a world apart from ordinary reality, like that between Romeo and Juliet. However, in the idyllic romance of the earlier play the violence appeared as external to the lovers. That violence, seeping into the love of Hamlet and Ophelia, Desdemona and Othello, kept them apart. Here it invades and defines love, rendering it inimical to familial and social harmony when Lady Macbeth confirms Macbeth's purpose by saying,

> I have given suck, and know
> How tender 'tis to love the babe that milks me:
> I would, while it was smiling in my face,
> Have pluck'd my nipple from his boneless gums,
> And dash'd the brains out, had I so sworn
> As you have done to this.   (I.vii.54–9)

In generating Bellona for his bride Macbeth has expressed his hatred and fear of his own child self – weak, vulnerable, in his eyes despised by woman as swinishly ineffectual. Therefore Lady Macbeth's image of destroying her child does not repel him, but rather persuades him to murder the gentle Duncan. He implicitly associates her image of the sucking babe with Duncan's murder when he responds, 'if we should fail?' He completes their secret collusion in acknowledging the role he has assigned her in saying, 'thy un-daunted mettle should compose / Nothing but males' (I.vii.74–5), and prepares to take her keen knife into his hands when he advises her as previously she had him: 'Away, and mock the time with fairest show / False face must hide what the false heart doth know' (I.vii.82–3).

As he approaches the murder the two levels of Macbeth's awareness draw together. Defining the airborne dagger as a 'false creation / Proceeding from a heat-oppressed brain' (II.i.38–9), he gives it a reality midway between the dagger Lady Macbeth imagines herself wielding, and the dagger with which he will kill Duncan. Pointing to Duncan's room, it preludes the murder, and then stained with 'dudgeon gouts of blood,' it marks a transition from the past to the future, and a stage in the process by which Macbeth congeals free-floating emotion into images of reality. As he follows the dagger to Duncan's bedroom the perverse sexuality that has been dimly associated with the murder comes closer to his awareness:

> Now o'er the one half-world
> Nature seems dead, and wicked dreams abuse
> The curtain'd sleep: Witchcraft celebrates
> Pale Hecate's off'rings; and wither'd Murther,
> Alarum'd by his sentinel, the wolf,
> Whose howl's his watch, thus with his stealthy pace,
> With Tarquin's ravishing strides, towards his design
> Moves like a ghost. (II.i.49–56)

Having stilled the compunctious visitings of nature, Macbeth with deep self-reflectiveness defines himself as a wicked dream that disturbs both Duncan's and his own 'curtain'd sleep.' The logic of the sentence then becomes discon-tinuous, but in the sequence he identifies with Hecate and offers the murder to the celebrating witches. Abandoning the female identification, he personifies himself as Murder, but that image elides with that of 'Tarquin's ravishing strides.' The passage moves from a negative female image of witchcraft and Hecate to a negative male image of Murder represented as a wolf's howl, a distant image that suddenly transforms into the more immediate one of Tarquin. But Tarquin was not pacing towards a murder, as is Macbeth, but rather towards the rape of Lucrece. Macbeth's sudden identification with Tarquin associates the dagger penetrating Duncan to sexual penetration of a woman.[12]

The total configuration is composed of two sets of fused images. Macbeth's image of himself as a wicked dream contains both female and male ranges, and the sleeping Duncan fuses beneficent paternal with feminine and maternal associations. With his self-image fused with the image of Hecate, Macbeth gets revenge on the unmanly, swinish paternal figure 'drenched in sleep,' who 'loves for his own ends, not for you,' while as Tarquin he interprets his dagger as a bloody phallus with which he violently penetrates the equivocating and seductive woman, and revenges himself on the passive paternal figure loved by the woman, as well as on this version of his own unmanly self. In a remote Oedipal configuration Macbeth's erotic drive towards the mother has blended both with his fear and horror of it and with rage at the interfering father, so that Macbeth in a single configuration expresses the active and passive ranges of his desire, since, identified with Duncan, he is also penetrated. But in espousing the active range he opens the wound in images of father, nurturing mother, and more remotely the children associated with her, the sexual woman, and those aspects of his own emotional capacities represented by those figures. 'Who would have thought the old man to have had so much blood in him?'

Neither our eyes nor Macbeth's peep through the blanketed dark to the invisible bedroom in which Macbeth and Lady Macbeth consummate their love. But what Macbeth does not wish to see or be seen, he wishes both to hear and to be heard. For having envisioned the sexuality implied in his association of women with malicious manipulation, illegitimate authority, and violence, he calls into action representatives of the legitimate authority he has violated. Through them he both maintains his self-definition as evil – for he can be evil only in terms of some concept of virtue – and generates the agents of his own punishment.

The punitive powers that will finally overwhelm him are first dimly heard in the knocking at the Porter's gate, the sound of which links the interior of Macbeth's castle where Macbeth hears it to the exterior where the Porter describes all equivocating professions being drawn into the interior hell. In this remote form Macbeth defines his castle as an underworld that draws into itself the surrounding social world. In a reverse movement he then envisions the devastation from the bedroom encompassing the cosmos when Macduff says, 'up, up, and see / The great doom's image! – Malcolm! Banquo! / As from your graves rise up, and walk like sprites / To countenance this horror!' (II.iii.76–9). That image of doomsday joins with Lady Macbeth's 'hideous trumpet [that] calls to parley / The sleepers of the house' (II.iii.80–1), both of which were implicit in Macbeth's earlier vision of Duncan's virtues pleading 'like angels, trumpet-tongu'd against him.'

Hamlet associated Gertrude's sexuality with doomsday in images of the risen dead and of heaven's face 'thought sick' at witnessing Gertrude's 'act.' In a complex image Macbeth calls for his own punishment in evoking the Judgement Day, but also associates it with images of birth when Ross describes the 'obscure bird' that 'prophesying with accents terrible / Of dire combustion and confus'd events, / New hatch'd to th'woeful time ... Clamour'd the live-long night' (II.iii.56–9). As well, he associates himself with a birth of another kind when he says that 'Augures, and understood relations, have / By magot-pies, and choughs, and rooks, brought forth / The secret'st man of blood' (III.iv.122–5). That combination turns the doomsday image into one of the death of himself as a swinish swiller in the milk of human kindness and the birth of himself first as a usurping tyrant and then as a fiend. He also generates the opposing forces by which he can so define himself, thereby preserving in his world a vision of the good, protective paternal force, figured first in the images of the avenging babe and later in the avenging paternal figures whose forces are gathering. As well, in a remote form he satisfies perverse desires by distancing them into images of a country deprived of food, sleep, and peace. Secretly colluding with the avenging forces of legitimate authority by the self-defeating ways in which he pursues those creature pleasures, he also gradually separates himself from Lady Macbeth, even as he is reborn as the man she wanted him to be.

In Macbeth's new state his barren sceptre and fruitless crown deny the childlike and creaturely feelings that he fears. In what he defines as a means to restore natural pleasures, he repeats in externalized and remote ways the infanticide that deprived him of them. Having failed to kill Fleance, and having Hecate's assurance that no man 'of woman born' can kill him, he murders Macduff's wife and children. Since their murder in no way secures the peace of mind for which he says he commits it, the action becomes an image of his perverse relation to domestic tenderness. At the same time children become messengers of reprisal, from the image of Pity as an avenging babe, to the bloody child who gives him false security, and the crowned child who shows him Banquo's progeny.[13] Consciously in search of relief from the 'affliction of these terrible dreams, / That shake us nightly' (III.ii.17–20), and the 'restless ecstasy' of his nights with Lady Macbeth, he generates images that simultaneously extend and punish his initial perverse act. In order to eat and sleep in safety he murders Banquo, but brings his ghost back to destroy the ceremonial banquet about which Lady Macbeth says, 'to feed were best at home; /

From thence, the sauce to meat is ceremony; / Meeting were bare without it' (III.iv.34–6), a punning image that merges the familial and the social realms. Under the guise of seeking peace Macbeth turns his country into an extended image of the original murder. The daggers that killed Duncan are recalled when Lennox says the country weeps and bleeds as 'each new day / A gash is added to her wounds (IV.iii.40–1), Ross says that it 'cannot / Be call'd our mother, but our grave' (IV.iii.164–66), and Macbeth's determination to eat and sleep in peace is echoed in Macduff's quest in England for succour that will 'Give to our tables meat, sleep to our nights, / Free from our feasts and banquets bloody knives' (III.vi.33–5).

As Macbeth transforms his inner turmoil into images of a waste-land kingdom he also gradually redefines himself in his relation to Lady Macbeth. The collusive intimacy between them fades almost immediately after Duncan's murder, for as Macbeth espouses her image of him as an unthinking man of action he redefines her in a more conventional feminine role. The altered relationship appears in Macbeth's secrecy about his plan to murder Banquo, and in her secrecy about her fears. He projects onto her figure the reflectiveness that previously defined him when she says that all has been for nought 'Where our desire is got without content; / 'Tis safer to be that which we destroy, / Than by destruction dwell in doubtful joy' (III.ii.5–7). But she denies her anxiety by dismissing his when he envies Duncan who 'After life's fitful fever' sleeps well, and he savours the secrecy of his planned murder when he tells her to 'Let your remembrance apply to Banquo' (III.ii.30). Both withdraw from their 'restless ecstasy' with each other to 'make our faces vizards to our hearts / Disguising what they are' (III.ii.34–5). He approaches his plan indirectly, saying 'O! full of scorpions is my mind, dear wife!/ Thou know'st that Banquo, and his Fleance, lives.' When she responds that 'in them Nature's copy's not eterne' (III.ii.36–9), he secretly obtains her validation of his unspoken plan. She addresses him as 'gentle, my lord,' and he her as 'love,' but in calling her 'dearest chuck' and withholding knowledge from her he reestablishes the conventional protectiveness of men towards women. The banquet scene depicts in association with each other Macbeth's separation from his wife, his isolation of himself from the realms of creaturely and social pleasures, and his redefinition of himself as a man of action when he says, 'Strange things I have in head that will to hand, / Which must be acted, ere they may be scann'd' (III.iv.138–9). In Banquo's ghost he experiences for the last time an emotionally laden image of his inner state, an image that occasions the last rebuke for lack of manliness he will hear from Lady Macbeth.[14] He dismisses the ghost as an 'unreal mock'ry,' and starts to empty himself of his resonant inwardness and deep desires, which will remain in his consciousness only remotely when he attributes them to Lady Macbeth, from whom he will have separated himself.

This is the last scene in which Macbeth and Lady Macbeth appear together. Thereafter he allows the presently oriented image of woman defined in Lady Macbeth to sink into the inward sea of blood as he leaves it behind. Simultaneously he revivifies the more distant images of women and families, sups 'full of horrors' at Hecate's cauldron rather than at the banquet table, and then, having made the 'firstlings of [his] heart ... the firstlings of [his] hand,' kills another image of the family in Macduff's wife and children.

Just as before the regicide he had anticipated the avenging forces that would pursue him, so after it he anticipated the emptiness that would follow from externalizing his emotions into images of a devastated mother country. Earlier, after Duncan's murder, he was the better able to dissimulate for being able to say truthfully that, 'There's nothing serious in mortality; / All is but toys: renown, and grace is dead; / The wine of life is drawn' (ii.iii.91–3). Later he says without dissimulation, 'I have liv'd long enough: my way of life / Is fall'n into the sere, the yellow leaf' (v.iii.22–3), and finds himself confronted simultaneously with the avenging armies and with news of his wife's 'thick-coming fancies / That keep her from her rest,' an image that attributes to her the 'thick night,' thickening blood, and light that previously they had shared. As he dons his manly armour he equates the disease that troubles his wife with the English who trouble his country when he asks, 'What rhubarb, cyme or what purgative drug, / Would scour these English hence? Hear'st thou of them?' (v,iii,55–6). In the conflicting images of Lady Macbeth and of the battle Macbeth expresses his now divided and disowned feelings. When Macbeth feels confidence that 'Our castle's strength / Will laugh a siege to scorn,' the cry of women, as though in mockery, is heard from within that castle – the centre now of disease and corruption. In response he asserts his dry indifference in an image that completes the motif of nourishing food, milk, and human warmth, when he says, 'I have supp'd full with horrors:/ Direness, familiar to my slaughterous thoughts, / Cannot once start me' (v.v.13–15). Macbeth associates his incapacity to feel with his separation from Lady Macbeth in the announcement of her death that immediately follows.

Her death signifies his final retreat from his nightmare of love:

She should have died hereafter:
There would have been a time for such a word. –
To-morrow, and to-morrow, and to-morrow,
Creeps in this petty pace from day to day,
To the last syllable of recorded time;

And all our yesterdays have lighted fools
The way to dusty death. Out, out, brief candle!
Life's but a walking shadow; a poor player,
That struts and frets his hour upon the stage,
And then is heard no more: it is a tale
Told by an idiot, full of sound and fury,
Signifying nothing.   (v.v.17–28)

Since he is preoccupied with reassuring himself of his imperviousness to death in battle, he rejects the knowledge of his own mortality already implied in his wife's death. As well, since she dies immersed in the inner world of fantasy that he has escaped, he tries to dismiss the news of her death with affectless dry weariness when he says, 'She should have died hereafter.' As a strategy to avoid the impact of her death in the present, his mind moves first to the future, and then to the past. But when he has emptied the present of significance, the future stretches ahead, 'To-morrow, and to-morrow, and to-morrow,' partaking of the present emptiness, the 'petty pace' that he presently feels. In that state of mind the prospect of escaping death in battle and living forever can give no joy when all recorded time is composed of the insignificant syllables of meaningless action. But the phrase 'creeps in this petty pace' suggests that infant state that he has violated first in himself and then in the world. With that suggestion his mind swings from the future to the past. He no longer responds to the horror of that past; only the sense of meaninglessness remains that he has already projected onto the future. All those 'yesterdays' from infancy to the present, at one time alight with desire, now appear illusory, leading to a 'dusty death' that is indistinguishable from his former vision of his future. Therefore he wants to extinguish the candle that, by illuminating the past, reveals the meaning of Lady Macbeth's death. He sees instead his inner condition writ large when he calls life 'but a walking shadow,' whereas he is now the walking shadow, the bloodless form of himself without the content of passion. The image of the moving shadow suggests one of the stage, but since the candle has been blown out, it is a darkened stage, a scene like Duncan's bedroom that Macbeth both wants and fears to see. Just as sound replaced sight earlier, so he now hears in the dusty darkness the player who 'struts and frets' upon the 'bloody stage' that he himself has generated, and which, Ross says, the heavens threaten. In turn, this suggests an image of Duncan's bloody bedroom, coloured by Macbeth's desires and revulsion, guilt and rage on which he does not wish to look again. So threatening is his projection of what he might see if he allowed himself to look that he takes a further and final means to distance himself from the vision. He transforms the image of the stage to the less immediate one of a tale; but a tale is told to a child. Despite himself, Macbeth evokes the image of a child, but denies what that child might reveal by attributing the tale to an enlarged and grotesque version of a child – an idiot. In this way he eradicates the meaning of his past, present, and future. But thereby hangs another tale of the process by which Macbeth, in fearing to see the images that reveal the emotional content of his actions, transforms life into a tale 'signifying nothing.'[15]

Before Macbeth encounters the witches, one of them says that, having been refused chestnuts, she will pursue through the ports of the world the 'rump-fed ronyon's' sailor husband in a sieve;

> I'll drain him dry as hay:
> Sleep shall neither night nor day
> Hang upon his penthouse lid;
> He shall live a man forbid.
> Weary sev'n-nights nine times nine,
> Shall he dwindle, peak and pine:
> Though his bark cannot be lost,
> Yet it shall be tempest-tost.   (I.iii.18–25)

Macbeth associates himself with that image when he conjures the witches and Hecate to foretell the future 'though the yesty waves / Confound and swallow navigation up; / Though bladed corn be lodg'd, and trees blown down' (IV.i.53–5), and the witches' images prefigure the feelings he later experiences. But the last two lines seem contrary to the play's end, since by any ordinary account Macbeth, called a fiend by Macduff, would seem as damned as man can be. But amid the increasing vilification in which he approaches his death, he also generates purified images of authority. Macduff is not of woman born, and children are referred to in images of wrens, eggs, and nestlings that remind one of those in *Hamlet*. They also are not of women born, and Malcolm evokes and dissociates himself from all of Macbeth's crimes, specifically declaring himself 'unknown to woman' (v.iii.126). Birnam wood, a disembodied female image detached from the 'rooky wood' in which Banquo dies, moves towards Macbeth's embattled tower in which Lady Macbeth lies dead. While on the one hand he claims his wife, though within the sense of evil that comes with the voices who couple them – 'this dead butcher and his fiend-like Queen' (v.ix.35) – on the other he sees his head, like Cawdor's earlier, on a stick, without blood, passion, or body. That final stage image seems to flow from Macbeth's earlier words, 'They have tied me to a stake; I cannot fly, / But bear-like I must fight the course' (v.vii.1–2). One might say that in these words he initiates a process by which he denies his body, merges it with the stake to which he feels bound, and completes the process in the image of his bodiless head on a pole. One might speculate further, though it is perhaps far-fetched, that Macbeth's last vision of himself foreshadows Prospero, who has detached himself from his bodily passions, which are contained in the figure of Caliban, and who exercises total control of his domain through his books. Such a speculation gains some credence from the witches' assurance that the sailor's bark cannot be lost, though it can be tempest-tossed.

7

King Lear's Quest for 'An Ounce of Civet'

Unlike any previous protagonist, King Lear defines himself as both legitimate king and father, and generates a world in which familial and social authority function as strong analogues for each other. That being so, each event on the social level participates in the emotional intensity of familial events, and each familial event resonates with the breadth of social consequence. Also, since Lear conceives his authority as sanctioned by a natural principle of the universe inscribed on the hearts of men, the significance of familial and social events is carried upward to an abstract cosmic order and inward to the psyche. This allegorical grid amplifies to cosmic proportions any flicker of desire contrary to Lear's conception of virtue. As a corollary, Lear also sees any failure of authority on the intermediate realms of family and society as giving licence to any psychic impulse or fantasy.

Within this system of strong analogies that symbolically amplify consequences of the most trivial event, Lear, more explicitly than previous protagonists, defines sex and authority as mutually exclusive. In this structural configuration, by casting himself as father to all women figures he renders all sexuality incestuous.[1] By defining himself as old, however, he has denied having the sexual desires that might destroy domestic affection, social order, and the cosmic principle of order itself.[2] In his intention to 'crawl unburdened toward death' he expresses his weariness from having long repressed desires that signified to him the destruction of universal order. In relinquishing his crown while keeping the privilege of kingship he unknowingly empowers the feared desires that his role as king had been designed to restrain.

In Cordelia alone Lear expresses his hope for a benign and comfortable virtue that can save him from himself, and his conscious project is to find with her the rest and maternal comfort of which he feels deprived. However, his fears of women and revulsion from sexuality that emerge with his abdication threaten to besmirch her image if he allows it to remain in proximity to his own. Therefore, to preserve an image of female purity he instead casts himself as a son and victim to images of evil mothers, while permitting himself to regress to more childlike stages of sexuality that he associates first with boyish boisterousness, then with humiliation and deprivation, and finally with disgust. His object in passing through these stages is to know himself as 'a man' rather than as king and father, and to reclaim Cordelia. For a moment he subtly recasts her as an appropriate object of his desire. But as the horrific images he has momentarily dispelled rush back upon him he, like his forbears, seeks the consummation of love in the grave.

Since Lear's strategy to claim Cordelia involves redefining himself, he also redefines the roles in which he has cast other figures. Those changes are further complicated because as Lear redefines his power relations to other figures he also changes emotional age levels. As Lear sees himself as a child to other figures, those figures change not only function, but dimension, for they assume the exaggerated size of parents in a child's vision, and, as Lear regresses in time, naturalistic figures acquire an aura of the fantastic, as though the witches and Lady Macbeth comprised a single figure. As these figures assume more than natural proportions they not only symbolize the family and common-wealth; their symbolic resonance acquires cosmological import, an amplifi-cation that in turn intensifies the significance of, and the difficulties inherent in, Lear's project to regain Cordelia, from which arose this symbolic amplification.

Lear becomes most clearly childlike in relation to the female figures, but he also surrounds himself with male figures who, in accord with Lear's own split and changing self-definition, also change their relation to him, sometimes functioning as paternal figures with whom he identifies, and sometimes in relation to whom he plays the child. Since Lear simultaneously casts himself in filial and paternal roles, the surrounding figures function for him simul-taneously in different ways. These changing configurations express the dy-namic in which Lear generates from the sexuality he fears a strongly repressive authority that in turn betrays the taint of its origin. Using that taint as justification for undermining the concept of authority, Lear allows himself fully to experience the fearful images he associates with sexual desires that have been intensified by the repressive authority. In confiming his need for that authority, they complete the circle. In the midst of those intertwining relationships, more than his predecessors in Shakespeare's plays, Lear merges male and female images, the female images blackened by the rage displaced from paternal images, which Lear wishes to protect from his own hatred. In order to disentangle these complex relations, we will first focus on Lear's definition of his authority, both in his own figure and in his relation to other male figures. These changing configurations among male figures show Lear distancing from himself some of the more horrendous emotions implicit in his conception of authority and his relation to Cordelia.

On the one hand, he defines as absolute his authority over the actions and feelings of others. To maintain himself as 'an image of Authority,' he limits his feelings to a dragonlike wrath that excludes tenderness, love, and sexuality.[3] On the other hand, the figures who oppose him render his sense of himself as in violation of an ideal of justice, and the combined love test and decision to abdicate indicate some vague stirrings of the realms of feeling that are lost to him. Some intuition of Lear's confused motives for abdicating appears in Kent's admonition that he 'see better,' and in Goneril's interpretation of Cordelia's and Kent's banishment as evidence that he 'hath ever but slenderly known himself' (I.i.292). The tormented sexual passions and fears that his role as king had been designed to suppress emerge in the action, but they do so in a partial form. As Hamlet retrieves the ghost of his father from the grave to which he consigned him, so Lear abdicates his kingship but wishes to retain the 'name and all th'addition' that attend it.

Lear's images of himself split between those of himself as powerful, and those of himself as victim. Each of these images further subdivides along moral lines, for he initially identifies himself with beneficent universal powers, but comes to see himself as a bad king. That image, however, merges with his victimized self, which he then defines in images of one deservedly punished, an abused and kindly father, and an abused child. These images are fluid, merging with one another and with other characters, but as the action unfolds they, along with the figures with whom he peoples his landscape, tend to become more radically polarized. In the most extreme form, Lear creates images that later become his reality, so that his language acquires the power to create or cause events. He then becomes victim to the events he has himself generated in a way that portrays his own dream process. This dynamic appears when, abused by his daughters outside of Gloucester's palace, he first sees himself as victim of the gods' collusion with his daughters, and then imaginatively aligns himself with them against the daughters, 'I will do such things, / What they are, yet I know not, but they shall be / The terrors of the earth' (II.iv.277–80). This double image becomes clearest on the heath, when Lear both 'bids the wind blow the earth into the sea' (III.i.5), and remains a 'poor, infirm, weak, and despis'd old man' (III.ii.20). As the split in his self-image widens it reveals his deepest feelings. Identifying his powerful self with Goneril and Regan, who are also the 'servile ministers' of the storm that has arisen from his whirling words, he associates with them the power to reveal hidden truth when he says that now the gods will discover the

>   undivulged crimes,
> Unwhipp'd of Justice; hide thee, thou bloody hand,
> Thou perjur'd, and thou simular of virtue
> That art incestuous; caitiff, to pieces shake,
> That under covert and convenient seeming
> Has practis'd on man's life; close pent-up guilts,
> Rive your concealing continents, and cry
> These dreadful summoners grace. I am a man
> More sinn'd against than sinning.   (III.ii.52–60)

Lear appeals to those imagined criminals to 'rive your concealing continents,' as he himself will on the heath when he tries to undress. His hidden identification with the criminals presses towards consciousness, and shows itself in the logical break that occurs when, having bid the criminals to 'cry / These dreadful summoners grace,' he denies his implied identification with the 'simular of virtue / That art incestuous' by declaring himself 'more sinn'd against than sinning.'

As Lear more fully identifies with the victimized, he parodies his own paternal image – 'When I do stare, see how the subject quakes' (IV.vi.109) – and describes it in canine images that join 'the great Image of Authority' to covert sexual desires when he says,

> Thou rascal beadle, hold thy bloody hand!
> Why dost thou lash that whore? Strip thine own back;
> Thou hotly lusts to use her in that kind
> For which thou whipp'st her. The usurer hangs the cozener.
> Thorough tatter'd clothes small vices do appear;
> Robes and furr'd gowns hide all.   (IV.vi.158–63)

Lear as king becomes the 'dog that is obey'd in office,' punishing in others his secret lusts, and deriving thereby sadistic pleasure, both of which deny his entitlement to the image of Authority. The dog images throughout the play carry associations of sadistic brutality. Goneril and Regan are Lear's 'dog-hearted' daughters, whom he acknowledges as extensions of himself when he says that it was 'this flesh' that begot them. The mad and ravening dogs that pervade the language are then associated both with the two sisters and with Lear as father and king.

The many ways in which Lear sees himself are reflected both in the polarized figures with whom he identifies, and in the partial splitting of single figures expressed through the dramatic device of disguise. Lear, while keeping the 'name and additions of a king,' defines himself as a truculent child in Goneril's castle, but he keeps the image of Kent in the background to represent the ideally faithful subject, a version of a good child and of the ideal authority Lear violates in his own person. However, Kent disguised as Caius functions to indulge Lear's childlike willfulness. The way in which both sides of Kent's persona reflect both sides of Lear's appears when Kent warns Cornwall that in stocking the king's messenger he will 'do small respect, show too bold malice / Against the grace and person of my master' (II.ii.127–8). The identification of the king with his messenger not only emphasizes Lear's sense of outraged majesty, but suggests a deeper identification in which Lear experiences in Kent's humiliation a distanced but more extreme version of his own. Through Kent he expresses his sense of himself as deserving to be punished like 'the basest and contemned'st wretches' (II.ii.139), or like his dog, at the same time as he desires to punish in Kent the ideal paternal authority that renders his desires guilty.

A similar dynamic structures Gloucester's role. As duped father Gloucester is a distanced image of Lear's own folly in subjecting himself to Goneril and Regan. But Gloucester is victimized for the 'good sport' he had at Edmund's begetting, suggesting that Lear associates the sexuality he denies with the suffering he incurs. The parallel stories imply that Lear expresses through Gloucester his own sense of having empowered Goneril and Regan in order simultaneously to satisfy and to be punished for the sexuality he denies. But the parallel plots also juxtapose Gloucester's abuse of sexuality to Lear's abuse of authority, thereby suggesting that Lear associates the two. The identification suggested by that parallel plot becomes more immediate when Gloucester appeals to Regan and Cornwall for help against the son who he thinks seeks his life, at the same time as Lear pleads for redress for the wrongs done him by Goneril.

However, just as Kent moves from a parallel to a paternal figure, so does Gloucester. When he tries to help Lear, he begins to function as the 'old kind father' that Lear likes to think himself, but Lear expresses his deeper sense of guilt by giving Gloucester as a substitute victim into the hands of his daughters and Cornwall. Through Gloucester, Lear both vicariously experiences his own punishment for unacknowledged sexual guilt, and punishes the ineffectual parent for failing to protect him. The degree to which Gloucester's blinding, like the stocking of Kent, represents Lear's punishment appears in the many references Lear makes to his own and others' eyes. Kent wants to remain the 'true blank' of Lear's eye; Lear doubts his own eyes when Goneril attacks him, wants to pluck them out for weeping at her unkindness, and invokes the 'nimble lightnings' to blind her 'scornful eyes' (II.iv.162–3). Lear's desire not to see and not to be seen by her 'fierce eyes' are strategies to avoid the shame of exposure, which he associates with Gloucester's sexuality. The central importance the image has for Lear gives the motif its climactic position in which Gloucester's role as Lear's surrogate and the imagery of eyes coalesce. After Regan has imagistically appropriated Gloucester's phallus by plucking the hairs from his beard, which will 'quicken and accuse' her, Gloucester in imagery of fierce animals that previously characterized Lear's speeches explains that he helped Lear, 'Because I would not see / Thy cruel nails pluck out his poor old eyes; / Nor thy fierce sister in his anointed flesh / Rash boarish fangs' (III.vii.54–7). Just as Lear had verbally anticipated action to which he later fell victim, so here Gloucester virtually directs his persecutors when, after describing Lear's suffering in the storm, he echoes Lear's previous impotent threats in saying, 'but I shall see / The winged vengeance overtake such children.' Cornwall renders Gloucester's words ironic when he says, 'See't shalt thou never,' and turns that vengeance against Gloucester. The figure of Lear here merges most fully with that of Gloucester, who is blinded because of the good sport at Edmund's making. This substitution of Gloucester for himself allows Lear simultaneously to punish himself for his guilty desires, and the father for rendering his desires guilty.

Lear expresses his wrath at both versions of himself through Cornwall, whose 'fiery quality' and implacable determination represent the Lear who warned Kent not to come between 'the dragon and his wrath.' Fully confident of his power, Cornwall puts into action the rage that Lear limits to words. He becomes for Lear a kind of ego ideal of absolute and ruthless authority. When Cornwall blinds Gloucester, saying, 'yet our power / Shall do a court'sy to our wrath, which men / May blame but not control' (III.vii.25–7), he exercises the kind of command that Lear wanted but failed to exercise in the abdication scene, and he accomplishes the revenge Lear in his own person only impotently threatens. Lear more fully repudiates this aspect of his power than that expressed in any other figure when the gods for once do send their avengers in the person of the nameless servant who mortally wounds Cornwall. In the distance provided by Lear's own absence, and in the social distance between Lear and the anonymous servant, this sequence provides the most polarized images of Lear's divided self. The nameless servant who in killing a major figure violates both genre and court decorum most fully expresses the child's retaliation on the most immediately articulated version of the tyrannical father.

The sexuality for which Lear sees Gloucester punished remains manifest in the figures of Edmund and Edgar. Lear gives Edmund a remote place in the initial configuration, for the abdication of authority by which Lear empowers his unknown desires occurs immediately after Gloucester tells Kent of the 'good sport' of Edmund's making. Gloucester's sexual pleasure and Edmund's illegitimacy in turn become one with Edmund's illegitimate desire for power and adulterous sexuality with Goneril and Regan. In Edmund's figure, then, Lear joins the ruthless pursuit of power, violation of family affection, as well as hierarchical obligation to sexual licence. Edmund defines himself by that cluster of associations when he claims that bastards like himself get from the 'lusty stealth of nature ... / More composition and fierce quality / Than doth, within a dull, stale, tired bed, / Go to th'creating a whole tribe of fops, / Got 'tween asleep and wake' (i.ii.11–15). He opposes the sexual passion that begot him to the customary society, predicated on an ideology of hierarchy that Lear, through Kent, Cordelia, and Edgar, maintains as the only viable means of restraining human depravity. The nature by which Edmund justifies the rights of the strong and clever represents the ideas that Lear denies but implicitly acts upon in empowering the sexual Goneril and Regan rather than the relatively desexualized Cordelia. In Edmund's figure Lear represents the love that he both fears and desires. He defines it as evil, but keeps him as much trickster as villain to separate him from Goneril's and Regan's ravaging violence.

Lear allows the identification between himself and Edmund to become more apparent when, at the end, Edmund's character wavers as does Lear's own. As it was Lear's mandate that banished Cordelia, it is Edmund's that kills her, and as Lear regretted his actions, so Edmund also tries to countermand his order. After being defeated by Edgar, Edmund with uncharacteristic resignation echoes Lear's image of the 'wheel of fire' when he says, 'Th'hast spoken right, 'tis true. / The wheel is come full circle; I am here' (v.iii.172–3). The bond underlying the opposition between his figure and Lear's emerges when Edmund, somewhat improbably, is moved to repentance by Edgar's story of Gloucester. But he does not countermand Cordelia's death until he hears of Goneril's and Regan's death. When all three are about to 'marry' in the instant of their death, Edmund's surprised satisfaction in having been loved, more in line with Lear's need for love than with his previously depicted character, finally moves him to interdict his orders to kill Cordelia and Lear. In these tenuous ways, his wavering figure reflects Lear's ambivalence about Cordelia, and his bad timing manifests Lear's continuing inability to live with Cordelia, even though he cannot live without her. Just before Edmund reveals that he had ordered their deaths, the bodies of Goneril and Regan are somewhat implausibly brought on stage, only to be carried out along with the dying Edmund. The tableau makes a kind of dark version of the love-death motif, their illicit sexuality being accomplished in their ugly death.[4] The contrast emphasizes the other love-death tableau consisting of Lear and Cordelia, for as Edmund, Goneril, and Regan are carried off, Lear enters carrying the dead Cordelia. It is as though the two images are two sides of one coin, the dark side revealing what the light side conceals.

Just as Cordelia's compassion forms a polar opposite to her sisters' cruelty, so Edgar's morality does to Edmund's sexuality. But both virtuous figures reveal their links with their evil counterparts. Edgar's paternal function parallels the benign maternal function assigned to Cordelia. He honours the 'natural' hierarchy even when it has dishonoured him, and like Cordelia he is kept apart from any sexual involvement. But Lear's distrust of that desexualized ideological purity appears in the punitive uses to which Edgar puts it, both in his own person and in his impersonations.

Though Edgar prefigures Prospero in therapeutically manipulating others in the name of spiritual transformation, his actions are disturbingly similar to those of Goneril and Regan. When he hears the newly blinded Gloucester lament that Edgar's touch would compensate for his lost eyes, rather than comfort his father by revealing himself, he remains disguised. He claims to feel compassion, but his tears do not endanger his disguise, under which he continues the torture initiated by Goneril and Regan. He says he trifles with Gloucester's despair only to cure it, but this is contradicted later when he laments that he 'Never – O fault – ' revealed himself until just prior to his father's death. Edgar seems at least as pleased with his dexterity in shifting roles as does his wicked brother. In his figure Lear links abstract moral principle to sadistic cruelty, for Edgar's assertion that Gloucester's blinding illustrates the justice of the gods, who 'of our pleasant vices / Make instruments to plague us' (v.ii.170–1), carries chilling echoes of Regan's 'to wilful men / The injuries that they themselves procure / Must be their schoolmasters' (ii.iv.301–2). The parallel aligns Edgar's righteousness with Cornwall's cold cruelty and Goneril and Regan's humiliating mockery, for Lear derives as much spiritual education from them as Gloucester does from Edgar.[5]

Just as Lear in Kent's disguise renders him a semi-split dream figure, one side a figure of moral authority while the other joins Lear in his wilfulness, so he also partially splits the moral Edgar. In his own person Edgar betrays an underlying association of moral authority with a cruelty that participates in Goneril and Regan's sexual sadism, while in the disguise as Poor Tom Lear associates moral authority with a sexualized masochism. The two images joined within a single figure show Lear associating sadism and masochism with each other as two sides of a coin, but they also together turn what is otherwise a single-dimensional figure into a plausible psychological portrait of a sanctimonious, self-righteous person.

Edgar, having been rejected by his father and driven from society, neither wonders at nor resents his father's behaviour. Even more long-suffering than Cordelia, who at least has angry words for her sisters, he turns his anger only against himself when he impersonates the Bedlam beggars who 'Strike in their numb'd and mortified bare arms / Pins, wooden pricks, nails, sprigs of rosemary' (II.iii.9–16). Edgar in the figure of Tom imagines himself punished by pettily sadistic devils for sexual sins when he accuses himself of having 'serv'd the lust of my mistress' heart, and did the act of darkness with her; swore as many oaths as I spake words, and broke them in the sweet face of Heaven; one that slept in the contriving of lust, and wak'd to do it. Wine lov'd I deeply, dice dearly, and in woman out-paramour'd the Turk' (III.iv.84–90). His self-laceration becomes associated with the dark place where Edmund was begotten. When Lear brings Edgar into the orbit of his awareness, the images of the punitive sadistic devils merge with sexually suggestive ones. Overtly Lear responds only to Edgar's appearance rather than to his words, so that the ignored sexual innuendoes seem a voice from his mind's deep recesses that cannot be silenced, but can be ignored. While Lear asks whether Edgar's daughters 'brought him to this pass,' the Fool points out the sexual implications of Edgar's nakedness: 'Nay, he reserv'd a blanket, else we had been all sham'd' (III.iv.65). The implicit reference to Edgar's genitals beneath the blanket reminds Lear that ''twas this flesh begot / Those pelican daughters' (III.iv.73–4). That image, reinforced by Edgar's phallic image in 'Pillicock sat on Pillicock hill' (III.iv.73), leads Lear to take Edgar as an emblem of 'unaccommodated man' and to join him in his nakedness. As Lear discovers himself as just 'such a poor, bare, forked animal' and calls oblique attention to his phallus, images of his daughter hover in his catalogue of luxurious clothing. In identifying with Edgar, Lear begins to espouse the desires that were hidden beneath the furred gowns of his social and hierarchical roles. As he identifies with the poor and the outcast of his kingdom, he also approaches his own outcast sexuality. Thus Poor Tom, inviting Lear into his inner landscape composed of frogs, tadpoles, newts, and the 'green mantle of the standing pool,' an image that Shakespeare often uses, particularly in *The Tempest*, for corrupt sexuality, becomes his 'philosopher,' and his justice-dispensing 'good Athenian.'

Lear's espousal of Edgar is as double-edged as the figure he has generated. His partial affirmation of his sexuality is concealed within and coupled with his idealization of Athenian Edgar's harshly repressive judgments, both those implicit in Poor Tom's masochistic attack on his flesh and those explicit in Edgar's words and actions. In Edgar Lear attempts to maintain a vision of ideal values, but his world becomes so bleak because the idealized character betrays the same sexual violence that he is intended to counteract and contain.

Though Edmund is overtly parallel to Goneril and Regan, his figure never becomes grotesque as theirs do. But Edgar is linked to them more closely than is his brother when he evokes devils and fiends who punish Poor Tom for sexual sins and who taunt him in the way Regan and Cornwall taunt Gloucester. There is some accuracy in his image of himself as the fiend that led Gloucester to the imaginary cliff, who had 'a thousand noses, / Horns whelk'd and wav'd like the enridged sea' (IV.vi.70–1). The devils that Edgar releases into Poor Tom's language become a grotesque comic version of the devil Albany sees when Goneril has, with shades of Lady Macbeth, called him a 'milk-liver'd man' and 'moral fool!' for showing compassion to Lear. He says, 'See thyself, devil! / Proper deformity shows not in the fiend / So horrid as in woman' (IV.ii.59–61). Edgar's monstrous devil, who obscures the image of Gloucester's loving son, and who plays cruel jokes on a suffering old man, is not far removed from Albany's image of Goneril and Regan as tigers who, if not controlled by some 'visible spirits' sent by the heavens, will produce a humanity that preys on itself like 'monsters of the deep' (IV.ii.46,50).

At his death Lear is survived only by Edgar and Albany, who have most condemned women's sexuality. But as Edgar suggests in his closing speech, 'The oldest hath borne most: we that are young / Shall never see so much, nor live so long' (V.iii.324–5), the survivors are relatively pallid figures. Though they suggest Lear's need to maintain in his world an expression of the traditional moral order still associated with anti-sexual figures, he allows no strong figure to replace him as a paternal authority, nor does he allow a single version of cosmically enlarged paternity to dominate his final vision. The gods for him may either be just, 'and of our pleasant vices make instruments to plague us,' or they may be 'wanton boys / Who kill us for their sport.'

Lear's manipulation of these shifting paternal images constitutes his strategy to placate, evade, and maintain paternal authority, both in its emotionally immediate personal forms and in its extension in ideas of cosmic order and justice, while he renegotiates his relationship with women. Since all women with whom he has populated his world are daughters, sexual love becomes incestuous, and since all the daughters are either married or about to be, for him love is associated as well with adulterous betrayal. These barriers in turn express the evil he associates with sexuality. In the simultaneous love test and abdication Lear expresses his need for love and his efforts to abandon the imperiousness by which he fends it off, while the intimate link between these events and Cordelia's impending marriage centres the entire emotional configuration upon his relation to her.[6] The images suggest some of the associations with sexuality from which emerge both the initial circumstances and the later action. Though he claims that he has decided to 'publish / Our daughters' several dowers, that future strife / May be prevented now' (1.i.42–4), the imagery shows the conflicting emotions that are involved with his project. In the vows he elicits from Goneril and Regan, Lear exposes his covert knowledge of the cruelty he associates with them. He addresses Goneril most coldly, saying only, 'Goneril, / Our eldest-born, speak first,' and the chilliness of hyperbolic response matches his when she claims that Lear is 'Dearer than eyesight, space and liberty' (1.i.55). In somewhat warmer tones Lear addresses Regan, 'What says our second daughter / Dearest Regan, Wife of Cornwall?' and in a more pallid version of her sister's self-immolating imagery she declares herself 'an enemy to all joys' other than her father's love (1.i.72). The order is significant, since after he has rejected Cordelia to whom he will speak most warmly, he will choose to sojourn first with Goneril, to whom is he coldest and of whose husband he makes no mention, next with Regan towards whom he is warmer and whose husband he mentions, before he finally can reclaim Cordelia whose impending marriage he stresses in his address to her.

He infuses sensuousness into the image of her marriage when he says that France and Burgundy 'Long in our court have made their amorous sojourn,' and surrounds it with an aura of nurturing when he says that 'The vines of France and milk of Burgundy / Strive' for her young love. In envisioning Cordelia's marriage Lear has both brought her sexuality into focus and separated himself from her.[7] By declaring himself ready to 'crawl toward death' while resting in 'her kind nursery,' he has in a reverse motion imagined himself as a child included in her marriage. The combination of the death image that precedes Lear's mention of Cordelia's suitors, and the image of himself as child to her after he has disowned her, suggests that Lear both yearns for and fears the sexuality which, implied in her marriage, he associates with death. The same ambivalence marks her responses; she distances herself from Lear by reminding him of her marriage – 'That lord whose hand must take my plight shall carry / Half my love with him, half my care and duty,' (1.i.100–1) – but she also echoes the marriage ceremony in declaring 'You have begot me, bred me, lov'd me; I / Return those duties back as are right fit, / Obey you, love you, and most honour you' (1.i.95–7).[8] On underlying levels, Lear's rage is as much a response to the physical immediacy and promise of her words as it is to her reminder of limits.

Until this point the figures of the three daughters are relatively naturalistic, reflecting Lear's present-oriented emotions. Cordelia's indignation at Lear's demand that she express her love in return for land might be expected of a favoured daughter, and Goneril and Regan react as might be expected of unloved and angry children. But the naturalistic base that softens Edmund's figure disappears from Lear's vision of women as he heightens them into mythological figures who fuse the two levels that remain distinct in the witches and Lady Macbeth.[9] As Lear renders himself childlike, women acquire the magnitude of mothers in a child's vision, and are configured into a fairy-tale split image of good and bad mothering. But this fairy-tale configuration merges with the analogical universe the adult Lear keeps in place. He amplifies his infantile split image of the mother into cosmic principles of good and evil when he swears by the 'sacred radiance of the sun, / The mysteries of Hecate and the night, / By all the operation of the orbs / From whom we do exist and cease to be' (I.i.109–11). Having elevated motherliness to a cosmic principle and split it into images of good and evil, Lear extends the nurturing and compassionate mother, Cordelia (now as seen by others only), into an image of universal order and harmony. He associates the bad mother, for the moment Cordelia as he now sees her but ultimately Goneril and Regan, with a pelicanlike, punitively sadistic sexuality, devouring rather than nurturing, which he cosmically amplifies into a vision that anticipates Darwin's nature, red in tooth and claw.

Lear's response to Cordelia reveals the terrifying desires that generate and are generated by these grandiose maternal images, and that determine his choice of the bad rather than the good mother. He says,

> The barbarous Scythian,
> Or he that makes his generation messes
> To gorge his appetite, shall to my bosom
> Be as well neighbour'd, pitied, and reliev'd,
> As thou my sometime daughter.   (I.i.114–19)

Though the word 'generation' can refer to either parents or children, in context the primary meaning should be children, since Lear compares himself to the 'barbarous Scythian,' but the ambiguity is appropriate. Since Lear sees himself as child, the image shows his fears of being devoured, as well as his desire to devour Cordelia. He has abdicated his power in order to regain the pleasures of the infant at the breast, but since his maternal image also contains aspects of Goneril and Regan, to approach the fantasy involves experiencing instead the fierce-eyed monstrous mother. Insofar as he identifies with the passive infant, Lear attributes his own rage to the mother, and experiences himself punished for his desire even as he deviously satisfies it by imagining being devoured by, and thereby made one with, the mother. Both his desire to merge with the mother, and the rage engendered by images of that desire are contained in Lear's response to Kent: 'Come not between the Dragon and his wrath. / I lov'd her most, and thought to set my rest / On her kind nursery' (I.i.121–3).

In more subdued form the same sequence of impulses repeats itself when

Lear says, 'So be my grave my peace,' as he tells Cornwall and Albany to 'with my two daughters' dowers digest the third' (1.i.124–7). Lear equates his desire to be absorbed into Cordelia's motherly comfort to the peace of the grave,[10] which he avoids by repudiating her, while giving her to be devoured by Goneril and Regan when he says that their dowers should 'digest the third.' These images both avoid and express the cruel devouring he more explicitly associates with his 'pelican daughters,' whose 'sharp-toothed unkindness' represents humanity preying on itself like 'monsters of the deep.'

As he heightens his own and his daughters' images Lear opens a cleavage between the probable human beings dramatized and their symbolic function. To Cordelia he attributes an inarticulateness that he associates with loving purity, while in her actual articulateness she functions as a protective mother. The contradiction appears when she most articulately contrasts her silence to her sisters' speech, while regretting that she cannot protect him from them. She equates their 'glib and oily art' to sexual seduction when she rejoices that she lacks the 'still-soliciting eye' that accompanies 'such a tongue' as they have (1.i.223, 230). In her speech Lear expresses his association of inarticulateness with a denial of sexuality, and women's verbal power with a tawdry sexuality. But since he needs an articulate Cordelia to defend him, he shunts her sexuality onto the threatening figures of Goneril and Regan.

Since Lear sees Cordelia's superior lovingness manifested as hostile competitiveness with her sisters, that hostility threatens to undermine her loving persona when she says that she, like a sister, is 'most loth to call / Your faults as they are named' (1.i.269–70). In her voice Lear commits himself to their 'professed bosoms' and the sexuality joined to their 'plighted cunning,' while Cordelia's hatred of them shows him dimly aware of the nature of his choice.

The sisters also assume a more than naturalistic aura of evil as Lear commits himself to them, which derives from Cordelia's description of them, and from their self-knowledge, which resembles that of Iago. If we think of them naturalistically as two older sisters jealous of the greater love and affection received by a younger sister, they would not concur in Lear's earlier opinion that Cordelia was more deserving than they, or that their father showed 'poor judgement' in rejecting her. Nor would they think Lear wrong to banish Kent, who clearly disliked them. They would instead feel vindicated, since ordinarily mean or jealous sisters do not think themselves evil, but rather mistreated. Goneril and Regan's self-declaration gives them a diabolical aura that places them between non-naturalistic figures like Macbeth's witches and fully individualized figures. The childlike role that Lear takes in relation to them magnifies their evil, for he attributes to them the omniscience that a child attributes to parents.[11]

By the end of the first act he has uneasily rejected the vision of tender comfort involved in Cordelia, and uneasily committed himself to the sadistic sexuality he confronts in Goneril and Regan. Having removed Cordelia from his orbit, Lear simultaneously experiences himself as diminished, and within the safety of his consequent powerlessness allows himself access to the network of the fears and desires he associates with women. Like Macbeth, he attributes to women the power to use their knowledge of his secret vices to entrap and humiliate him. Directing Oswald to provoke Lear's anger so that she will have an excuse to scold him, Goneril says, 'Now, by my life, / Old fools are babes again, and must be us'd / With checks as flatteries, when they are seen abus'd' (I.iii.19–21), and later asserts as the source of her power, 'I know his heart' (I.iv.329).

As Lear becomes increasingly infantile to his daughters' increasing power, Cordelia's voice remains present in the person of the Fool. Lear's identificaton of the Fool with Cordelia appears when he is told that his fool is pining for Cordelia, in the Fool's disappearance when Lear begins his journey to Dover and Cordelia, and in the fused image that Lear creates when, carrying the dead Cordelia in his arms, he says, 'And my poor Fool is dead.' The two figures constitute a fully split image that parallels the partial split observed in Edgar and Tom o' Bedlam, or Kent and Caius. Along with both Poor Tom and Caius, the Fool is an uncontrollable figure whose wild and whirling words combine multiple emotional ranges and give to the play its grotesque farcical overtones by which Lear challenges the same moral assertions that he uses to condemn himself. The Fool's barbed reminders to Lear of his folly express Lear's unacknowledged recognition of the anger he does not wish to attribute to Cordelia. When the Fool, comparing Lear's divided crown to the two crowns of an egg, says 'thou hadst little wit in thy bald crown when thou gav'st thy golden one away' (I.iv.159–60), he unites in a single image Lear's sense that his power, uninformed by an ideal, is sterile, and that his life is also sterile without Cordelia as his generative centre, or as the golden yolk of the egg. The image reveals Lear as one who has broken Hamlet's dove eggs in dissatisfaction with their sexlessness, even though having done so entails confronting the horrors that Hamlet avoided in that image of sexless fertility. In the Fool's sexual puns Lear exposes his passion for Cordelia, while he keeps her figure within a remote aura of purity.

With the Fool keeping Cordelia present to Lear's inner imagination, Lear makes claims on Goneril and Regan mainly through his one hundred knights, who become the central image of his humiliation. Appearing only in relation to Goneril and Regan, no mention having been made of them before Cordelia's banishment, they function like Ulysses' fellow sailors. By the end of his journey, Homer's Ulysses comes alone to Ithaca's shores, and by the end of the play, Lear must come alone to Cordelia, the retainers who represent his royal power having slowly dwindled and disappeared. Goneril attacks Lear by attributing Lear's unruliness to the knights, as though they are an extension of him, when she blames Lear both for his fool's behaviour, and for his 'insolent retinue,' who 'hourly carp and quarrel, breaking forth / In rank and not-to-be-endured riots' (I.iv.199–200).

The Fool translates her words into an image that fuses maternal devouring with castration when he says, 'For you know, Nuncle, / The hedge-sparrow fed the cuckoo so long, / That it's had it head bit off by it young' (I.iv.213–14). As well, when he sings 'So out went the candle, and we were left darkling' (I.iv.215) he relates the phallic image to the blindness Gloucester suffered on Lear's behalf.[12] Goneril associates the knights' rowdiness with the sexuality that the 'old and reverend' Lear ought not to have when she says that his men are 'so disorder'd, so debosh'd, and bold,' that their manners turn her court into 'a riotous inn; epicurism and lust/ Makes it more like a tavern or a brothel / Than a grac'd palace' (I.iv.239–43). Lear expresses his desires through the knights, and his guilt through Goneril's punitive words. He projects onto the mother figure his rage at her rejection of his incestuous wishes, and then finds himself her victim. In this way he satisfies his hostile sexuality by seeing her as a 'detested kite,' who both excites and punishes his guilty desires. Caught in that dynamic, he rejects both sexuality and generation when he invokes nature to denature her, to sterilize her 'derogate body' or 'turn all her mother's pains and benefits / To laughter and contempt, that she may feel / How sharper than a serpent's tooth it is / To have a thankless child!' (I.iv.284–7). The image of the thankless child as a 'serpent's tooth' stands for both Goneril as his child, and for himself as hers, since he has made his daughters his mothers. In that image of perverse sucking he expresses his desire to have, and to punish her for having, the forbidden sexuality that provokes it.

With almost dreamlike improbability, Lear is punished for his rebellion from maternal power. He exits and re-enters saying, 'What! Fifty of my followers at a clap' (I.iv.292). Their sudden and unexplained disappearance adds to the sense of Lear's participating in his own diminution, and bringing on himself the impotence he feels when his tears make him ashamed that Goneril has 'power to shake my manhood thus.' In his humiliation he looks for a protector, first in nature when he invokes the 'Blasts and fogs' to join with his father's curse to 'Pierce every sense about thee,' and then in his other daughter, who when 'she shall hear this of thee, with her nails / She'll flay thy wolvish visage' (I.iv.305–6). The very images in which Lear invokes kind and comfortable mothering deny it; even though he suffers the lack of gentle mothering, his imagination turns the mother's face into that of a wolf. In the same way he could not for long keep Cordelia within his consciousness, he cannot forgo the emasculating punishments he associates with the nurturing for which he longs. When Lear pleads ignominiously outside Gloucester's palace to see Regan and Cornwall, the Fool once again highlights the sexual implications by saying, 'Cry to it, Nuncle, as the cockney did to the eels when she put em i'th'paste alive; she knapp'd 'em o'th'coxcombs with a stick, and cried, "Down, wantons down!"' (II.iv.120–2). In his helplessness he invokes verbally a cosmic mother with her 'nimble lightnings' to redress his wrongs, even as he once again seeks maternal protection from Regan when he says,

> No, Regan, thou shalt never have my curse:
> Thy tender-hefted nature shall not give
> Thee o'er to harshness: her eyes are fierce, but thine
> Do comfort and not burn. (II.iv.168–72)

But as he casts himself as a nurtured infant looking into loving maternal eyes, the fierce ones he sees instead remind him of his humiliation and defeat as he glances at Kent and asks, 'Who put my man i'th'stocks?'

Lear reaches the nadir of infantile nightmare helplessness when Goneril reappears to co-operate with her sister in cutting him down to size. After Regan has told him to return to Goneril with half his knights, Lear envisions himself choosing instead 'To wage against the enmity o'th'air; / To be a comrade with the wolf and owl, / Necessity's sharp pinch!' (II.iv.207–9). He attributes now to the cosmos the images that also characterize his daughters, and imagines himself preferring to be victim of the cosmic version of their dark maternal power rather than suffer the humiliation of returning to Goneril. But the desire that drives Lear to humiliate himself is stronger than his fear, so that he does not choose the emnity of the air until he has offered to return to Goneril, who will let him have fifty rather than twenty-five knights. He stays the course until Regan says, 'What need one?' (II.iv.261) and the knights disappear with the words.

On the heath Lear completes the transformation of naturalistic figures into mythical images, and further polarizes the images of himself as victim and victimizer. Having enlarged his daughters onto a cosmic screen, he invokes the thunder to 'crack nature's moulds, all germens spill at once' (III.ii.8), and falls victim to the answering storm. From that extreme polarization, something begins to emerge in the middle. Denuded of the extensions of his ego in his knights, the infantile helplessness he had imagined acquires a kind of physical reality and begins, at first remotely, to merge with his self-image. In the

Fool's song he evokes his creature needs for food and shelter, and equates them in a simple way with straightforward sexuality:

> He that has a house to put's head in has a good head-piece.
>> The cod-piece that will house
>>> Before the head has any,
>> The head and he shall louse;
>>> So beggars marry many ...
> For there was never yet fair woman but she made mouths in a glass.   (III.ii.25–35)

The sexual suggestiveness of the Fool's song amplifies that of Poor Tom's ravings. As Lear brings the recognition of his physicality closer to him in Edgar's nakedness, and espouses an image of himself as a 'bare forked animal,' he begins to reintegrate the images of rage and sexuality he had projected onto other figures when he says that, 'twas this flesh begot / Those pelican daughters' (III.iv.73–4). In approaching his own physicality and sexuality he also realizes compassion for the suffering endured by the extensions of his childlike self in the 'Poor naked wretches' of his kingdom, thereby incorporating some of the maternal compassion he associates with Cordelia.

Thereafter the menacing maternal power associated with Goneril and Regan recedes, to be replaced by images of their corrupt sexuality. No longer in contact with them himself, Lear remotely experiences their sexuality as they vie with each other for Edmund. The images of monstrous female sexuality and the debasement of authority are fully orchestrated when Lear and Gloucester meet at Dover. Now in his own words Lear concentrates the two motifs that have conditioned the action throughout, misused authority and sinful sexuality. He makes his own contribution to the farcical forces of his world when he mocks himself both as one who has authority and as criminal victim of that authority: 'No, they cannot touch me for coining; I am the king himself' (IV.vi.84). When he sees Gloucester, he combines male and female images – 'Ha! Goneril, with a white beard!' – and associates that double image with the voices that deceived him into thinking that as king he was more than man, and he abandons for a time the 'old kind father' version of himself.[13] He connects these flattering voices to sexual crimes, vaguely at first, when he says in the storm that 'would not peace at my bidding, there I found'em, there I smelt'em out' (IV.vi.102–3). This begins a sequence of images that concentrates on the sense of smell, first introduced when Gloucester was told to 'smell his way to Dover.' These images lead Lear's consciousness into the centre of the sexual corruption that he felt was hidden beneath his royal robes when, in a speech that brings together the play's major image patterns, Lear says,

> Ay, every inch a king:
> When I do stare, see how the subject quakes.
> A pardon that man's life. What was thy cause?
> Adultery?
> Thou shalt not die: die for adultery! No:
> The wren goes to't, and the small gilded fly
> Does lecher in my sight.
> Let copulation thrive; for Gloucester's bastard son
> Was kinder to his father than my daughters
> Got'tween the lawful sheets. To't, Luxury, pellmell!
> For I lack soldiers. Behold yond simp'ring dame,
> Whose face between her forks presages snow;
> That minces virtue, and does shake the head
> To hear of pleasure's name;
> The fitchew nor the soiled horse goes to't
> With a more riotous appetite.
> Down from the waist they are Centaurs,
> Though women all above;
> But to the girdle do the Gods inherit,
> Beneath is all the fiend's: there's hell, there's darkness,
> There is the sulphurous pit – burning, scalding,
> Stench, consumption; fie, fie, fie! pah, pah!
> Give me an ounce of civet, good apothecary,
> To sweeten my imagination.
> There's money for thee.   (IV.vi.107–31)

Much as Hamlet did with Gertrude, Lear verbally indulges his fascinated disgust and fear under the cloak of ironic logic according to which it follows from the unkindness of his lawfully born daughters that all is permitted. When he imagines himself pardoning adultery, his irony towards the royal power that makes his subjects 'quake' shows him accepting for a moment his implication in the evils he castigates. But as his mind moves from a vision of nature pervaded with sexuality – wrens and flies – to Gloucester's bastard son and his own daughters, he shifts responsibility from himself to them – 'For I lack soldiers.' Within that reassurance of helplessness that renders him innocent, he imagines all women's chaste appearance concealing bestial appetites like those of 'the soiled horse.' He associates animal passions with those of prostitutes, 'fitchew,' and collects them into the image of the centaur – 'down from the waist they are Centaurs, / Though women all above.' But in mythology the centaur is predominantly associated with male, not female, sexuality, with rapine, murder, and bestiality. In adding these traditionally male attributes to women's sexuality, Lear heightens his horror of sexuality in the combined male and female image, which now expresses his feeling about himself.[14] That combined image strengthens the association first made by Albany between women and devils, but Lear makes it more specifically genital: 'But to the girdle do the Gods inherit, / Beneath is all the fiend's: there's hell, there's darkness, / There is the sulphurous pit – burning, scalding, / Stench, consumption.' The devils that represented human sadism combine with the violent animal images, and both contribute to the imaginative recreation of an infantile sense of smell that first appeared in the previous speech. In emphasizing smell, Lear imagines himself close to those hellish female genitals, for one does not smell at a distance, and identifies himself as one who smells things out, like those ravenous animals, and like the blinded Gloucester. He both acknowledges and resists the implications of his own images when he calls for 'an ounce of civet' to 'sweeten [his] imagination.'

These images of malodorous female genitalia, which Hamlet avoided in his images of birds, lead first to images of death and then of birth, the two fusing. To Gloucester's 'O! let me kiss that hand,' Lear responds, 'Let me wipe it first; it smells of mortality,' wiping from his hand the stench of woman's genitals that he has equated with mortality as well as with the 'sulphurous pit' that his imagination had made out of the 'dark and secret place' of his own begetting. In doing so he equates his discovery of his human and mortal body beneath his royal garments with his victimization by Goneril and Regan, and associates all with the recognition of his sexual nature.

He has recovered the sexual disgust and loathing that gave rise to the configuration shaped by Goneril and Regan and the rejected Cordelia, but now the experience of his own taintedness colours all authority:

And the creature run from the cur? There thou might'st behold
The great image of Authority:
A dog's obey'd in office.
Thou rascal beadle, hold thy bloody hand!
Why dost thou lash that whore? Strip thine own back;
Thou hotly lusts to use her in that kind
For which thou whipp'st her. The usurer hangs the cozener.
Thorough tatter'd clothes small vices do appear;
Robes and furr'd gowns hide all.   (IV.vi.154–63)

Having generated images of women who are tainted because they have genitals, and men who are tainted because they lust for them, and having associated Gloucester with the brothel in the phrase 'blind cupid,' Lear acknowledges his identification with him: 'If thou wilt weep my fortunes, take my eyes; / I know thee well enough; thy name is Gloucester.' In verbally returning to Gloucester the eyes that were lost on his behalf, Lear travels far along the road to the inner source of the world he experienced as external to him. Since that inner source is also the past, the birth image that has hovered beneath the surface becomes explicit when Lear says, 'we came crying hither: / Thou know'st the first time that we smell the air / We wawl and cry ... When we are born, we cry that we are come / To this great stage of fools' (IV.vi.176–8,180–1). The 'smell' that Lear earlier associated with women's genitals now becomes the atmosphere of the world into which the child is born. Verbally Lear has become the infant he envisioned himself with Cordelia, and his madness has been a process in which he he recovered lost feeling by imagining himself as a newly born infant. Having confronted the monsters of his own deep imagination, he finds the ounce of civet that can allow Cordelia back into his dream.[15]

When the gentleman sent by Cordelia finds him, Lear accepts the tears that previously humiliated him: 'Why this would make a man of salt, / To use his eyes for garden waterpots, / Ay, and laying autumn's dust' (IV.vi.193–5). His greater openness to gentle feelings now allows him to amplify, though still under cover of his madness, the marriage image of the first scene: 'I will die bravely, / Like a smug bridegroom' (IV.vi.195–6). The line both suggests the love-death drama that soon will be enacted, and relates that drama to the infantile images of monstrous women that he has just expressed.

Goneril and Regan have been associated with the violent forces of nature, cannibalistic monsters, and ravenous animals, all of those having given cosmic magnitude to Lear's images of mothers and of female sexuality. Though Cordelia has been kept apart from the aura of sexuality, she, unlike her sisters, did assert that when she married, she would love her husband. Lear rejected her in order to keep her image free from the smell of sexuality linked to mortality, which would blur her image with those of Goneril and Regan. As Lear sexualized his image of the two sisters and associated them with dark cosmic forces, the bodiless image of Cordelia became increasingly glowing. Albany's description of Goneril as a devil is followed by Kent's revelation that Cordelia has come without her husband to England. Though the usual explanation of Shakespeare's exclusion of the French king – that an English audience would not take kindly to a stage image of a French king leading a French army into England – is probably correct, that exclusion falls easily into the patterns of Lear's psyche, for neither Lear nor Cordelia refers to any aspect of her life that is not concentrated on him. This exclusion of even a mention of France, which might focus Cordelia's sexuality, coheres with the images in which

Cordelia is described. Othello's polarized images of Desdemona here become distinct figures as the sisters' characters accumulate overtones of devils and hell, and Cordelia starts to accumulate the opposite aura. The action that centres on Lear's slow movement from the realm of the two sisters towards Dover and Cordelia has its more hidden counterpart in the slow movement, expressed through passing references, of Cordelia towards Dover and Lear. Structuring the play's end, these two movements create a version of love-death romance between Lear and Cordelia. Her separation from France contributes to this motif, while the idealization and fragmentation of her character disguise it.

The gentleman's description of her that prepares for her return to the stage makes Cordelia a benign cosmic counterpart to the maleficent storm that extends from her sisters:

> You have seen
> Sunshine and rain at once; her smiles and tears
> Were like, a better way; those happy smilets
> That play'd on her ripe lip seem'd not to know
> What guests were in her eyes; which parted thence,
> As pearls from diamonds dropp'd. In brief,
> Sorrow would be a rarity most belov'd,
> If all could so become it.   (IV.iii.17–24)

The suggestion of a sensual and physical presence remains in the image of her 'ripe lip,' but is overshadowed by images suggesting the calm that follows the storm, of pearls and diamonds, imagery far removed from the burning and scalding stench of hell. The two feelings that characterize Cordelia are compassion for Lear and anger at her sisters,[16] but Lear places those reasonably ordinary human feelings in contexts that idealize and dehumanize them:

> Faith, once or twice she heav'd the name of 'father'
> Pantingly forth, as if it press'd her heart;
> Cried 'sisters! sisters! Shame of ladies! sisters!
> Kent! father! sisters! What? i'th'storm? i'th'night?
> Let pity not believe it!' There she shook
> The holy water from her heavenly eyes,
> And clamour moisten'd, then away she started
> To deal with grief alone.   (IV.iii.25–32)

Lear's conflict in envisioning Cordelia appears here. If she is to 'redeem Nature from the general curse / That twain have brought her to,' then her feelings must be sufficiently intense to counterbalance the energy generated by Goneril and Regan.[17] But intense feeling can go in unexpected directions. The intense emotion, as well as physicality, that is suggested in 'she heav'd the name of father,' and 'press'd her heart,' is superseded by more elevated images – the 'holy water' that she shook from 'her heavenly eyes.' When Cordelia appears, her language acquires some force as she describes Lear 'As mad as the vex'd sea,' but is again overlaid by ideological images when she says, 'All bless'd secrets, / All you unpublish'd virtues of the earth, / Spring with my tears! Be aidant and remediate / In the good man's distress!' (IV.iv.15–18). The first image, the 'unpublish'd virtues of the earth,' in association with her compassionate tears, forms an opposite to the vile aspects of the earth associated with Goneril and Regan. But as though uneasy with the physical proximity and intimacy contained in the image of her tears falling on Lear, she distances him from her by referring to him as 'the good man.' Lear further distances his vision of her tenderness into ideological hyperbole when she says,

> O dear father!
> It is thy business that I go about;
> Therefore great France
> My mourning and importun'd tears hath pitied.
> No blown ambition doth our arms incite,
> But love, dear love, and our ag'd father's right.
> Soon may I hear and see him! (IV.iv.23–9)

The last line has immediacy, but the others do not. When she says 'our ag'd father's right,' it is as though Cordelia is looking at her own action through a conventional formulation. Her use of the formal 'our' further distances and depersonalizes Lear. And if the line, 'It is thy business that I go about' is supposed to raise biblical echoes, so much the worse – that is, so much the more remote does she become from a possible human embodiment of the compassion that Lear needs to counterbalance Goneril and Regan's cruelty.

Lear's efforts to minimize and distance Cordelia's full humanity also appear in the succeeding scenes, even as he fulfils his fantasy of being nurtured by her.[18] These scenes in which Lear culminates his enterprise are probably the most difficult in the play, because the imagery keeps taking odd turns, and no single emotional current is allowed more than momentary expression before being cut off by another or channelled into an emotionally remote image or reference. Until now, the most hostile components of Lear's infantile desire found expression and spent most of their force in action that did not directly involve him. Meanwhile, in the process of approaching Cordelia, he also has been carried farther and farther back into the experience of archaic emotions that culminate with 'when we are born, we cry that we are come / To this great stage of fools.' Once having found Cordelia, Lear no longer fends off infantile sexuality, but rather the possibility of mature and loving sexuality. Lear first associates Cordelia's love with re-established cosmic harmony when she implores the gods to 'Cure this great breach in his abused nature! / Th'untuned and jarring senses, O! wind up / Of this child-changed father' (IV.vii.15–17). Lear, by symbolically equating a harmonious mind to music, distances and makes abstract the impact of Cordelia's presence. He becomes the instrument that the gods, through Cordelia's intercession, will mend, but the last line, 'O! wind up / Of this child-changed father,' veers in a different direction, and, like the earlier image of the Scythian who 'makes his generation messes to gorge his appetite,' is capable of two equally suitable readings that merge with each other. The sentence can be read to mean that Lear has been changed into a child, or that he has been changed, that is 'untuned' and jarred, by his children. When the two meanings merge, he has been changed into a child, untuned from his adulthood, by his children. The merged meaning dominates the speech, since Cordelia's blame of Goneril and Regan pervades almost all of her utterances, and shows that her idealization depends upon Lear's keeping her within the configuration of the vilified Goneril and Regan.

When the sleeping Lear is carried on stage, the imagery of changed clothing and music makes the nursery an emblem of spiritual rebirth, and Cordelia is transformed into a maternal physician when she says,

> O my dear father! Restoration hang
> Thy medicine on my lips, and let this kiss
> Repair those violent harms that my two sisters
> Have in thy reverence made! (IV.vii.26–9)

The first two lines have the emotional immediacy of her desire to be the agent of his cure, and the kiss in which she expresses her desire is fully sensual. But that sensuality is no sooner expressed than her mind veers once again to her sisters in a way that puts her now sensual loving in a comparative relationship to the 'violent harms' made by them, and in so doing yokes the one to the other. Her anger at her sisters deflects her sensual approach to Lear and absorbs whatever hostility a person in her situation would have good reason to feel towards him. When she compassionately imagines Lear on the heath, 'In the most terrible and nimble stroke / Of quick, cross lightning? to watch – poor *perdu*! – / With this thin helm?' her mind again moves to an implied comparison of her feeling to that of her sisters when she adds, 'Mine enemy's dog, / Though he had bit me, should have stood that night / Against my fire' (iv.vii.34–8). The image of the dog has been associated with Lear himself, both as the fawning dog that flatters, and the dog 'obeyed in office.' Therefore, Lear attributes to Cordelia his own recognition of his doglike quality, his desire both to fawn and bite, even as he basks in her compassion. The oral aggression that lingers here from earlier images suggests that the frightening components of Lear's feeling for her have been depleted but still hover in his imagination.

When Lear, upon awakening, says, 'Thou art a soul in bliss; but I am bound / Upon a wheel of fire, that mine own tears / Do scald like molten lead' (iv.vii.46–8), he reinforces the implications of Cordelia's image. The image of the wheel of fire, which derives from medieval renderings of hell, joins all the imagery of hell that has been associated with Goneril and Regan to reveal Lear still 'bound' to them. But the connection is more specific, for the language recalls Lear's description of the nether parts of women: 'Beneath is all the fiend's: there's hell, there's darkness, / There is the sulphurous pit – burning, scalding.' The split in the vision of the mother, 'a soul in bliss,' versus a hellish vision of female genitals, submerged but still present, finally will prevent Lear from remaining at rest within Cordelia's comforting embrace.

Evidence that the initial conflict still remains in place accumulates in the last scene between Lear and Cordelia. As the soldiers under Edmund's direction lead them to prison, Cordelia says,

> We are not the first
> Who, with best meaning, have incurr'd the worst.
> For thee, oppressed King, I am cast down;
> Myself could else out-frown false Fortune's frown.
> Shall we not see these daughters and these sisters? (v.iii.3–7)

Though one like Cordelia might indeed have 'best meaning,' not even such a one could claim that Lear did, though Cordelia includes him in the 'we' of the statement. If we take that 'we' not as a plural, but as an honorific, then it is a surprisingly distanced statement that sharply contrasts the elevation of that formal 'we,' to the 'for thee, oppressed King, I am cast down.' Of course the following lines change the meaning of that one, making clear her intention to reassure Lear that she is downcast for his fate rather than her own. But the literal truth, and the implied blame conveyed by the word order of the first statement still rings in the lines, and the second meaning is a subtler, though more morally elevated version of the first. Her implied blame of Lear gets shunted off to the sisters as Cordelia's undeviating concentration upon them expresses Lear's continuing movement of mind towards them and shows him, as he said, still bound to the 'wheel of fire.' Since he experiences her freely desiring to avenge the wrongs done him by her sisters, he does not need overtly to ask her help, as he did of Regan when he said, 'When she shall hear this of thee, with her nails / She'll flay thy wolfish visage.' To do so would attribute to Cordelia the qualities of Goneril and Regan. Having Cordelia volunteer such a statement spares him the need to know how much of his feeling is still involved in that negative realm, satisfies his own urge to punish them, and keeps him still in the posture of a small boy looking to Cordelia as a mother figure to take vengeance on his behalf.

Earlier in the play Lear experienced fear, rage, humiliation, and disgust; now in order to keep the idealized vision of Cordelia he pushes them from consciousness, but in attempting to dismiss them, he must isolate himself and Cordelia from all the world. Her speech and his denial mark a last and desperate attempt to wrestle with his own ambivalence, which prevents him from having the love for which he consciously longs:

> No, no, no, no! Come, let's away to prison;
> We two alone will sing like birds i'th'cage:
> When thou dost ask me blessing, I'll kneel down,
> And ask of thee forgiveness: so we'll live,
> And pray, and sing, and tell old tales, and laugh
> At gilded butterflies, and hear poor rogues
> Talk of court news; and we'll talk with them too,
> Who loses and who wins; who's in, who's out;
> And take upon's the mystery of things,
> As if we were God's spies: and we'll wear out,
> In a wall'd prison, packs and sects of great ones
> That ebb and flow by th'moon.   (v.vii.8–19)

In the midst of this envisioned intimacy Lear uses every kind of distancing device. He imagines himself and Cordelia safe from human sexuality in the image of them singing 'like birds i'th'cage.' When he says, 'When thou dost ask me blessing, I'll kneel down, / And ask of thee forgiveness,' the emotions envisaged are generous ones, but in alternately kneeling and rising Lear does not risk being face to face. Praying, singing, telling old tales, are all distanced activities; it is a vision of their being side by side, joined in activity, but not seeing each other. That sense of Lear straining for a remoteness from his own reality that will allow him to have Cordelia, becomes greatest with the image of them as 'God's spies,' apart from the flux of time and of the world. In the last image of the moon, the realm of passion, that controls the tides he tries to divorce himself from his own passions.

But his passions win a momentary victory as images of foxes crowd those of birds out of the language. After Edmund orders them away, Lear continues:

> Upon such sacrifices, my Cordelia,
> The Gods themselves throw incense. Have I caught thee?
> He that parts us shall bring a brand from heaven,
> And fire us hence like foxes. Wipe thine eyes;
> The good years shall devour them, flesh and fell,
> Ere they shall make us weep: we'll see'em starv'd first.
> Come.   (v.iii.20–6)

The quick shift of images, and the obscurity and oddness of phrase produced by the plethora of remote references make these lines turgid and conceal any single emotional thrust. If the sacrifice that he mentions refers to his and Cordelia's sacrifice of the world as envisioned in the previous speech, it makes little sense, since in that speech he does not think of their removal from the world as a sacrifice. But the image implies an answer to Cordelia's previous covert blame, for he here reassures himself, and attempts to convince her, that their being together will compensate, or more than compensate, her for having lost the world for his sake. With the image of their union in his mind, he says, 'Have I caught thee?' It is an odd line, since he has not literally 'caught' her. However, the phrase indicates Lear's fleeting recognition that he has been sexually pursuing her, since it refers to Sydney's poem in *Astrophel and Stella* in which the lover is prevented by fear of his mistress' rebuking eye from invading 'the fort' while she sleeps.[19] The image expresses Lear's loving and sexual desire for Cordelia, while the buried association with fear-inspiring eyes still links her to Goneril and Regan so that the single source of the three figures remains visible. The intrusion of that forbidden thought turns the images in the rest of the speech on their heads, so that what began with an image of Cordelia as sacrifice, suggesting the sacrificial lamb, concludes with an image of Lear and Cordelia as foxes. Previously in the play foxes have been associated twice with Goneril and Regan, once by the Fool, who says, 'A fox, when one has caught her, / And such a daughter, / Should sure to the slaughter' (i.iv.316–8), and once by Lear when in the mock trial he addresses his daughters as 'Now, you she-foxes' (iii.vi.23). Other references to the fox associate it with stealth; Edgar on the heath says, 'A fox in stealth' (iii.iv.91), and Regan associates it with ingratitude and treachery when she addresses the 'traitor' Gloucester as 'Ingrateful fox' (iii.vii.28).

Therefore, when Lear imagines himself and Cordelia together as foxes hiding from pursuit, he reveals that deep in his emotions he imagines their love as traitorous and stealthy, like the love of Edmund, Goneril, and Regan. For this moment the agonizing polarity between idealized good and sexualized evil wavers. The biblical references that come crowding into the lines function in the same way. Lear says, 'He that parts us shall bring a brand from heaven, / And fire us hence like foxes.' In the Bible, Sodom is destroyed by a brand from heaven, and if the lines also contain an echo of the story of Samson in *Judges* in which Samson sets afire the tails of foxes in order to destroy the enemy's corn, then the thought of himself and Cordelia as the guilty ones, Sodomites, being routed out by a brand from heaven has led Lear in turn to think of defying destruction, of rushing out to destroy the enemy. If we remember that Cordelia has referred to Lear as standing amid 'our sustaining corn,' a line that vaguely echoes Ruth amid the alien corn, then that image is also one of self-destruction – a single act that destroys themselves and the enemy. That the Samson reference does echo in the line is made more credible by the image that follows, for the unmentioned corn then links the fox image to the next image, 'The good years shall devour them, flesh and fell, / Ere they shall make us weep: we'll see'em starv'd first,' which refers to Pharaoh's dream in which seven good ears, or in Joseph's interpretation, years, are devoured by seven lean ones, and seven fat kine by seven lean ones. Lear reverses Pharaoh's images when he envisions 'them,' presumably Goneril and Regan, associated with lean years and blasted corn, devoured, blasted, 'flesh and fell.' That 'flesh and fell' seems to include a whiff of Pharaoh's first dream of the seven fat and seven lean kine. The line then reads that Goneril and Regan will be devoured by starvation: 'we'll see'em starv'd first'; that is, they will no longer devour others, before they will once again be able to humiliate Lear. In that image, along with the reference to Samson's use of the foxes to destroy the enemies' corn, Lear, coupled with Cordelia, espouses both guilt and sexuality. In the obscurity of these tangled references, Lear betrays the presence of emotions of which he never becomes fully aware, but that mark his farthest reach towards the realization of his desire, the fulfilment of which might reorganize his world.

That act of momentary and hidden defiance transforms Lear's deepest feeling. Could it be sustained, the figures of Goneril, Regan, and Cordelia would in actual dreaming merge into one figure, one neither grandly good nor evil, and who would be the kind of wife a figure like Rosalind in *As You Like It* might become in the course of years – sexual, smart, knowing, loving, sharp-witted, powerful.[20] Lear defiantly asserts his sexual claim to Cordelia only under the threat of death that will provide its punishment, but in the process, reflected, as suggested before, in Edmund's softened character, he loosens the equation between sexuality and ruthlessness. Lear no longer feels threatened with a sado-masochistic nightmare as he approaches Cordelia.[21] That threat gives way to the opposite fear, suggested earlier in relation to Cordelia, that allowing himself to love her will jeopardize his manly identity. In proximity to her he emphasizes his manliness when he says 'as I am a man, I think the lady be my child Cordelia,' the importance of which becomes clearer when, with the dead Cordelia in his arms, he brags, 'I kill'd the slave that was a-hanging thee.' After receiving the officer's confirmation, he adds, 'I have seen the day, with my good biting falchion / I would have made them skip. I am old now / And these same crosses spoil me' (v.iii.275–7). This evocation of past youthful prowess serves to protect his manliness from the 'gentle and low' sounds of Cordelia that threaten to engulf him. He generates the officer who hangs her so that he may assert his manliness in her defence, and thereby saves himself from the double threat his union with her poses.[22]

This fragmented action of the play's conclusion shows Lear divided between his desire to fulfil in death a sexual embrace with Cordelia and his conflicting desire for life, expressed most poignantly when Edgar says, 'O! our lives' sweetness, / That we the pain of death would hourly die / Rather than die at once!' (v.iii.183–6). That passion for life prevents the play from heading straight for its conclusion and throws up instead, as though to forestall and impede it, this flurry of unco-ordinated activity. This split between a drive towards the love-death sublimation of the infantile oral merger, and the desire for life at any cost conditions Lear's reaction to Cordelia's death. The love-death paradigm wins, but Lear's alternate rage at and disbelief in her death show him struggling for a vision of love in life.

Refusing to be compensated for her loss by a promise of ultimate justice or meaningfulness, he directs his rage first against the heavens, and then against those around him:

> Howl, howl, howl! O! you are men of stones:
> Had I your tongues and eyes, I'd use them so
> That heaven's vault should crack. She's gone for ever.
> I know when one is dead, and when one lives;
> She's dead as earth. Lend me a looking-glass;
> If that her breath will mist or stain the stone,
> Why, then she lives. (v.iii.256–62)

The image of cracking 'heaven's vault' with tongues and eyes at first seems strange, but it was Goneril's and Regan's tongues that wounded Lear, and their fierce eyes that he wanted struck by lightning. The line envisages hurling back at the heavens those weapons used against him. He repeats the movement, in his own action showing the heavens' injustice when he wishes a plague on the 'murderers, traitors all' who have been his succourers, and says, 'I might have saved her.' But there is a truth in his accusing Kent, Edgar, and Albany of being murderers and traitors, since as they represent the introjected voices that associate eroticism with hatred and cruelty that turned his world to nightmare, they have occasioned Cordelia's death, and Lear's desire might have saved her. Lear a third time asserts her death, and her life:

> And my poor fool is hang'd! No, no, no life!
> Why should a dog, a horse, a rat, have life,
> And thou no breath at all? Thou'lt come no more,
> Never, never, never, never, never!
> Pray you, undo this button: thank you, Sir.
> Do you see this? Look on her, look, her lips,
> Look there, look there! (v.iii.304–10)

In the sequence of the three speeches, Lear has incriminated first the heavens, then men, and finally those ravening animals which throughout the play have been associated with sadistic sexuality. Once again he asserts death's finality only to deny it. But there is a further element in this speech. When Lear says, 'Pray you, undo this button,'[23] he moves sensuously towards Cordelia's body, and the sensuousness is confirmed by his words, 'Look on her, look, her lips, / Look there, look there!' His concentrated attention on her lips recalls Cordelia's prayer that her kiss might be medicinal. The fantasy that she lives is also a fantasy of her sexuality, and that is Lear's triumph, momentary and partial as it is.

Hamlet has been discussed as a man struggling with his Oedipal strivings and trying to reconcile them with a present and real world. That play, which includes an actual mother, an actual father, albeit dead, and a stepfather, marked the first stage of Shakespeare's portrayal and penetration of those psychological depths, but Shakespeare distanced the emotions by keeping political issues in the foreground of the play. Written six years later, *King Lear*, even while it disguises the contents by eliminating an actual mother, suggests them by setting the play in the midst of England's mythic prehistory. It does not so much render a man struggling with Oedipal drives as the world of infantile strife itself. What Lear, and I believe Shakespeare with him, temporarily rescues from that realm of the monsters is some easing of struggle, some diminishment of monster-creating guilt, some greater capacity to join sexuality and loving.

Out of that achievement comes a play centred in and celebrating a relationship between a mature man and woman, *Antony and Cleopatra*. It is a partial victory only, for this play casts a benign light on a less committed relationship, but associates it with the decline and decay of kingdoms.

8

The Sweetened Imagination
of *Antony and Cleopatra*

Antony, like Hamlet and Macbeth, is distinguished by his self-awareness. Like Hamlet he inspects his inner state and consciously crafts the figure he cuts among those who populate his world, and like Macbeth he intuits the inner consequences of his actions as he performs them. In one respect he has more awareness than the earlier figures, for there is less of a gap than there is for Hamlet or for Macbeth between the elements that compose his figure and those he confronts. The views of him expressed by other figures and the images in which they render his conflicting drives more often than not resonate in Antony's own consciousness, and there are no figures who, by representing a repudiated set of values, function as *alter egos* to him. The protagonist of *Antony and Cleopatra* has at least partial awareness of the major conflicts that structure its action. Therefore in tracing Antony's relations to the various figures who compose his world we will be concerned with changing levels of emotional immediacy and degrees of awareness rather than with the sharp breaks that characterized the dreamscapes of previous protagonists. It is rather in the play's framework and structure of action that Antony confronts the unconscious dimensions of the ideas and fears that polarize the Roman martial honour and the Egyptian gratification by both of which he defines himself.

Antony's self-awareness is an aspect of the autonomy that initially defines his figure. Unlike Hamlet or Macbeth, he inhabits a world free of parents or parentally symbolized power relations. This freedom from overt parental forms frees him as well from moral ones. Unlike his predecessors, Antony asserts both mature authority and desire and does not surround his lover with an aura of either the demonic or angelic. The axis of conflict for Antony is not between good and evil but, as for Lear in his final state, it is between conflicting desires for self-assertion and for loss of selfhood. Consequently, in contrast to Hamlet or Macbeth, Antony is not in pursuit of furtive pleasures while dodging parental spying eyes or hiding beneath a blanket of the dark. Rather, openly coupling himself with Cleopatra, he confronts the equally unabashed gaze of an audience whom he challenges to witness his peerless love. However, his grasp on his freedom from the miasma that surrounds heterosexual love for other protagonists is tenuous, for, as in Othello's psychic economy, the martial valour that allows him to define himself as a lover is undermined by his doing so. The unease of the compromise he has made appears in Philo's opening lines:

> Nay, but this dotage of our general's
> O'erflows the measure: those his goodly eyes,
> That o'er the files and musters of the war
> Have glow'd like plated Mars, now bend, now turn
> The office and devotion of their view
> Upon a tawny front: his captain's heart,
> Which in the scuffles of great fights hath burst
> The buckles on his breast, reneges all temper,
> And is become the bellows and the fan
> To cool a gipsy's lust. (I.i.1–10)

Overtly the speech contrasts Antony's heroic military image with his debasement in love, but the hyperbolic images tend to spill their grandeur from the one realm to the other. The exaggerated size of Antony's 'goodly eyes' so elevates the 'tawny front' on which they gaze that it rises, as it were, to meet them. The second image, of Antony's heart becoming the 'bellows and the fan to cool a gipsy's lust,' makes little sense, since a heart hardly functions as a bellows. But the sequence contains a buried image, for the mind moves from Antony's heart, metaphorically his courage in battle, to an image of the physical manifestation of his courage, the massive lungs that burst 'the buckles on his breast' and that in turn become the 'bellows and the fan.' This heavy breathing, having already been associated with the odour of battle, when coupled with a 'gipsy's lust' generates an image of the sex act that competes in magnitude with the battle imagery from which it arose, even while it implies Antony's subjection to Cleopatra. When Philo says that Antony's heart 'reneges all temper,' the image reads as readily backwards to that of Antony in battle as it does forward to the sexual image, thereby spreading the grandeur to both. In this way the derogatory comments function doubly. Antony's 'dotage' which 'o'erflows the measure,' suggests the irresistible force of a swelling river that, like the Nile, brings fertility as well as destruction.

The same ambivalence colours Philo's fanfare as the couple grandly enters:

'Take but good note, and you shall see in him / The triple pillar of the world transform'd / Into a strumpet's fool: behold and see' (1.i.11–13). In the distance of Philo's voice Antony has emptied the Roman martial world of love and sexuality, and has made inimical to his self-esteem the Egyptian world of sensuality. Having defined each without the other as inadequate, Antony also defines the two as antithetical. Without Rome, Egypt threatens dissolution into slime, and without Egypt, Rome represents the calculating coldness of Octavius and a purposeless power struggle. Finding neither adequate alone, Antony attempts to reconcile them by translating his Roman martial stature to Egyptian heroic eroticism in order to rescue sexuality from the mire with which he associates it and neutralize the dangers it poses to his self-esteem.

Antony's defiance of Roman values thus reveals his complicity in them. The same dual impulse structures the sequence of action in which Antony and Cleopatra have their first exchange in the context of Antony's refusal to see the messenger from Rome. With the conditions for his withdrawal already provided by the presence of the Roman messenger in the wings, Antony dares to 'let Rome in Tiber melt.' In the juxtaposed images he makes his union with Cleopatra dependent upon the dissolution of the Roman self that makes them a peerless couple, so that he can commit himself to her only with the conditions for his betrayal of her already in place. As Cleopatra taunts him to see the messenger, he expresses in her figure the network of associations that produce the self-defeating polarity in which he is caught.

The associations that comprise that polarity become apparent in their exchange. She implies that his apparent pre-eminence in age and stature conceals a childlike relation to 'the scarce bearded Caesar' and the 'shrill-tongued' Fulvia. Her words reveal that he, to his shame, has empowered these Roman figures and Rome itself with parental force. His grandiloquent counter-assertion that he will force the world 'on pain of punishment' to acknowledge him with Cleopatra only confirms Cleopatra's implied accusation that Antony on her account feels diminished in Roman eyes, and thereby gives paternal force to Caesar and the militaristic honour he represents. A further dimension appears when Cleopatra in disbelief contrasts herself to the legitimate Fulvia and asks, 'Why did he marry Fulvia, and not love her?' His loveless but legal relation to Fulvia will be replaced by one with the 'holy, cold Octavia,' the 'married woman' who, unlike Cleopatra, can generate the 'lawful race' that alone insures his place and lineage in the Roman paternal arena.

With Rome, therefore, Antony associates full maturity, and parental powers that he can inherit only by forgoing love and sexuality, and to which he otherwise remains in childlike subjection. His associations with love and sexuality that oppose them to Roman honour appear in his definition of Cleopatra.

On the periphery of consciousness he first attributes to her the kind of knowledge of his secret duplicity that Lady Macbeth has of Macbeth or Goneril and Regan do of Lear. Having empowered her to undermine the stance he needs to keep her at a distance, he also associates her with resentful distrust and anger at the illegitimacy and consequent social barrenness within which he defines her figure. The shame that is correlative with this complex of associations prevents him from knowing himself as making a free choice in loving her. Instead he attributes to her charms a quasi-magical power, and feels his will compelled by them, thus simultaneously enhancing and evading his shame by defining his love as compulsive rather than as freely chosen. In this way he avoids knowing that her power derives from, rather than despite, her challenge to the Roman values by which he defines himself.

Feeling himself compelled by her charms further erodes Antony's confidence in his Roman autonomy and makes him feel that his 'soft hours' with her signify his dotage. Therefore when he silences Cleopatra's demands that he give audience to the messenger by saying, 'Fie, wrangling queen! / Whom every thing becomes, to chide, to laugh, / To weep: how every passion fully strives / To make itself, in thee, fair and admired!' (1.i.48–51), he also distantly expresses his sense of self-abasement in Demetrius's comment on their retreating figures, 'I am fully sorry / That he approves the common liar, who / Thus speaks of him at Rome' (1.i.59–61). Antony has generated the Roman world to protect him against a sexuality that he associates with a network of threatening emotions, but finding it loveless and cold, he seeks to regain love with Cleopatra. He can do so only in conjunction with a sense of illegitimacy, which in turn shames him before the Roman eyes that were designed to repress sexuality and that therefore threaten the image of himself as heroic lover that initially bound the two together.

In this first scene between himself and Cleopatra, Antony sketches the countervailing forces that will determine the ebb and flow of action between Rome and Egypt. The remainder of the first swing of action, which culminates in his departure for Rome, shows him internalizing the previously externalized image of himself as debased by his relation to Cleopatra, at the same time as he interprets his love and desire as the consequence of her preternatural powers.

Antony intensifies his shame by directing the messenger to 'name Cleopatra as she is called in Rome,' and identifies with the Roman view of himself when he says, 'These strong Egyptian fetters I must break, / Or lose myself in dotage' (1.ii.113–14). The news that Fulvia has died expresses both aspects of his desire. On the surface level it expresses his need to shore up the Roman aspect of his self-definition, for it is her death that calls him away from Egypt.

But on a deeper level the same news represents a deep stirring of his desire to be with Cleopatra and constitutes the counter-current, for he has eliminated with Fulvia's death the barrier to his union with Cleopatra. As a consequence he feels vague and nameless fear, regrets Fulvia's death, and concludes, 'I must from this enchanting queen break off, / Ten thousand harms, more than the ills I know, / My idleness doth hatch' (I.ii.125–7). His mind turns not to known, but to unknown dangers; moved not by the specific needs of Rome but by the vague fear associated with the enchanting queen, he announces to Enobarbus that 'I must with haste from hence.' Antony emphasizes not the Roman need of him, but his need to flee Egypt. While Enobarbus mockingly anticipates the love-death consummation with his comments on Cleopatra's 'celerity in dying,' Antony reacts not to the jest, but to that image of death with which he associates her now ominous power: 'She is cunning past man's thought.' He concludes, 'Would I had never seen her!' but shows an imagination already infected when he describes the Roman situation in images that throughout characterize Egypt: 'Much is breeding, / Which like the courser's hair, hath yet but life / And not a serpent's poison' (I.ii.190–2).

To prevent the serpent that 'hath yet but life' from becoming poisonous Antony flees to Rome, whose values overtly contrast to those of Egypt. But the series of broken promises and betrayals that characterize the fragmentary action in Rome suggest that he is in the process of undermining the power of the values by which he drew himself away from Cleopatra. Remote from Antony's consciousness, Caesar uses an image that expresses the hidden links between and shared source for Antony's two worlds:

> It hath been taught us from the primal state
> That he which is was wish'd, until he were;
> And the ebb'd man, ne'er lov'd till ne'er worth love,
> Comes dear'd, by being lack'd. This common body,
> Like to a vagabond flag upon the stream,
> Goes to, and back, lackeying the varying tide,
> To rot itself with motion. (I.iv.41–7)

The process by which Antony rots himself with motion accelerates as he draws closer to Caesar. Two strands intertwine in this second movement of the play, which concludes with his return to Egypt. On the one hand he empties the Roman world of value through the duplicitous relations depicted, first at a distance from himself, between Pompey, Lepidus, and Caesar, and more immediately as he involves himself in their power struggle after he betrays Cleopatra. On the other hand, as he approaches Caesar he generates, again first at the periphery of his consciousness but coming closer to the centre, a series of images that show him pulled back towards Egypt even as he moves away from it.

These images reveal that Antony associates Cleopatra, as magical enchantress, with images of food that later are joined to those of garbage, poison, whorishness, serpentine retaliation, and corrupting dead bodies. The food images represent a threat to Antony's martial stance when Pompey reassures Menas that 'Mark Antony / In Egypt sits at dinner, and will make / No wars without doors' (ii.i.11–12). When told that Caesar and Lepidus arm against him, Pompey invokes as his ally Cleopatra's 'charms of love' in images of erotic eating:

> Let witchcraft join with beauty, lust with both,
> Tie up the libertine in a field of feasts,
> Keep his brain fuming; Epicurean cooks
> Sharpen with cloyless sauce his appetite,
> That sleep and feeding may prorogue his honour,
> Even till a Lethe'd dullness.   (ii.i.22–7)

When Pompey hears that Antony approaches Rome, in a double image similar to those Philo used he wonders that 'this amorous surfeiter,' 'the 'ne'er-lust-wearied Antony' drew himself 'from the lap of Egypt's widow' (ii.i.32–7). The images that emphasize Antony's lustful feasting carry a suggestion of his decline into or merger with a distanced maternal figure who feeds him and on whom he feeds. However, they also contribute to Antony's heroic stature, both because of Pompey's fear that he will come to Rome, and because his image as warrior unites with the sexual stamina implied in 'the ne'er-lust-wearied Antony.' Though Antony has fled Egypt for fear of losing his Roman self and status, he in part secretly bases his claim for status in Rome on the very aspects of himself from which he fled and that shame him.

However, when Antony confronts the paternal values represented by Caesar, these double images begin to rot him with their motion. He defensively challenges Caesar's privilege as host to offer him a seat, loses that minor status struggle when Caesar, saying 'Nay, then,' proves his superiority by magnanimously acceding his right as host to Antony. Throughout the encounter Antony allows his Egyptian life, which hovers in the background, to diminish his status relative to Caesar's. After Antony has exonerated himself of implication in Fulvia's wars, Caesar accuses him of having denied the 'arms and aid' that he had promised. Finally forced to the wall, Antony uses Cleopatra as an excuse when he says that he neglected his duty only 'when poisoned hours had bound me up / From mine own knowledge' (II.ii.90–1). Confronted with an externalized form of his inner dilemma, Antony completes his betrayal of Cleopatra when he crumbles before Caesar's mockery of his Egyptian life with Cleopatra. When Caesar says that if Cleopatra heard Agrippa's proposal of a marriage between Antony and Octavia, 'your reproof / Were well deserv'd of rashness,' Antony responds 'I am not married, Caesar: let me hear / Agrippa further speak' (II.ii.121–4)

In using Cleopatra to protect himself from his own sense of guilt, and then in disclaiming her when he agrees to marry Octavia, Antony capitulates to judgment according to Roman standards and renders his love for Cleopatra shameful and destructive. As a consequence, he confirms her in the wantonness for which he blames her, and defines their union as illegitimate. Empowering Caesar to judge him, he intensifies this conflict between his sense of manliness and his desire for love and pleasure. As Cleopatra earlier implied, Caesar functions for Antony as a paternal authority empowered to judge, and to render shameful, his passions. Antony's increasing rage and humiliation at Caesar's youth as Caesar approaches Egypt derives from his failed attempt to trivialize, through Caesar's scarcely-bearded figure, Roman authority, and his incapacity to escape that authority, or to don it himself. The unconscious dimensions of this dilemma will appear when Caesar begins to share in Cleopatra's quasi-magical powers as he pursues Antony into Egypt where Cleopatra gathers to herself archetypal images of the eternal mother.[1] Gathering shadows of parental powers will overwhelm the relatively equal and sexual loving Antony had attempted.

Just as Caesar's paternal function is separated from his person, so that he functions as father to Antony only as a representative of Roman authority, so also are maternal images of Cleopatra as the goddess Isis separated from Cleopatra's present figure. Antony experiences the parental force of both figures as magical powers that emanate from Cleopatra's erotic nurturing. After describing the magic of Cleopatra's powers to compel the air itself to 'make a gap in nature'[2] as it follows her barge, Enobarbus says that Antony, 'Being barber'd ten times o'er, goes to the feast; / And for his ordinary, pays his heart, / For what his eyes eat only' (II.ii.224–6). The image moves from Antony's eyes that eat Cleopatra, to a more general image of food that is more directly sexual when she is described as being fruitful, like an earth mother, after being 'plough'd.' Enobarbus locates her magic in her nurturing powers when he assures Menas that, married or not, Antony will never leave Cleopatra because 'Age cannot wither her, nor custom stale / Her infinite variety: other women cloy / The appetites they feed, but she makes hungry / Where most she satisfies' (II.ii.235–8). In associating her magical appeal with gustatory delights, he indirectly translates Agrippa's denigrating insinuation into the amoral force of her 'infinite variety' of oral delight. Later he says less flatteringly that Antony will not stay with the 'holy, cold' Octavia, but 'will to his Egyptian dish again' (II.vi.123). These images show Antony experiencing Cleopatra as a kind of magically compelling food that draws him into a frightening subterranean realm foreign to the standards by which he customarily defines himself.

The nature of the menace he associates with that realm appears at a remove and obscurely as Cleopatra in Egypt at approximately the same time imagines Antony,

> murmuring, 'Where's my serpent of old Nile?'
> For so he calls me. Now I feed myself
> With most delicious poison. Think on me,
> That am with Phoebus' amorous pinches black,
> And wrinkled deep in time. Broad-fronted Caesar,
> When thou wast here above the ground, I was
> A morsel for a monarch: and great Pompey
> Would stand and make his eyes grow in my brow,
> There would he anchor his aspect, and die
> With looking on his life. (I.vi.25–34)

Her mind moves from the image of herself as serpent of the Nile to two images whose curious resonance joins to indeterminate meaning. The serpent image both here and later associates her with the archetypal force and fertility of the Nile's ooze and slime. In the sequence, that thought is 'most delicious poison' to her, because Antony regards her here not as an individual but as a cosmic force of generation, and it is 'delicious' because in the image she bends Antony to her will even though or because she poisons his hours. She embraces her archetypal shadow when she says, 'Think on me, / That am with Phoebus' amorous pinches black, / And wrinkled deep in time.' The overt references to her Egyptian complexion and her age are incommensurate with the image's resonance and tenor. Seeing herself as 'black, and wrinkled deep in time,' she becomes almost co-eternal with Phoebus. Rather than suggesting her beauty, the image merges her individuality into a kind of female principle deep in the reaches of the past, which then becomes associated with serpentine power.[3] But the cosmic female principle being by definition a whore, her mind leaps from her archetypal femininity to her various lovers of the more immediate past and equates the great Pompey's love of her with his death. In that connection she sees herself as 'a morsel for a monarch.' In her speech,

Antony joins her magical power to compel him to a sphere beyond his individual identity and to his death to the already established equation between her sexuality and irresistible food. In turn completing a circle, that compulsive power becomes associated with the serpent, with the Nile's slime that breeds serpents, and, as we shall see later, to the more distant images of the cycle of fertility.

The menacing aspects of these associations that extend the implications of Antony's description of Cleopatra as 'cunning past men's thought' prepare for Antony's betrayal, which increases her power over him by fixing her in the posture of a whore. She draws on that power when, learning of Antony's marriage, she rages at the innocent messenger: 'Some innocents 'scape not the thunderbolt: / Melt Egypt into Nile! and kindly creatures / Turn all to serpents! (II.v.77–9). She adds, when persuading herself that he has lied, 'O, I would thou didst, / So half my Egypt were submerg'd and made / A cistern for scal'd snakes!' (II.v.93–5). In this way serpents are linked to the previous images of melting that multiply as Antony's powers decline before Caesar's onslaught – 'My authority melts from me.' Cleopatra first calls upon the thunderbolt as an instrument of revenge for Antony's betrayal, but quickly abandons it for a serpentine power in a way that obscures how those serpents are to punish Antony. Other images illuminate the connection. Antony fears that Cleopatra's serpentine cunning will cause him to 'lose himself in dotage.' He also associates the serpent with poisonous fertility when he sees in Roman troubles the danger of 'a serpent's poison,' already associated with her cunning. Later Cleopatra, saying that she is safe 'if knife, drugs, serpents, have / Edge, sting or operation' (IV.xv.25–6), associates with serpents an easy slide into death. The negative range of the serpent imagery suggests a decadent breeding that poisons the well-springs of self-assertion. That image of poison becomes more explicitly deadly in association with the serpent when Cleopatra yokes this serpentine power to her wish for revenge, and joins it to the image of Egypt becoming a cistern – an image that Othello associates with a corrupt sexuality that breeds foul toads – as it melts into the Nile. The imagery suggests that Cleopatra will avenge herself on man's infidelity, poison his enterprise, and erode his assertiveness by her capacity to compel and betray him.

Antony had momentarily seen himself peerless and free, having supplanted the paternal Julius Caesar in both Rome and Egypt. Therefore, in betraying Cleopatra he has forgone the uneasy compromise by which he rescued his imagination of her from the Nile's slime. Since he expresses his sexuality only through her figure, his denial of her by keeping her a whore only deepens his ambivalence, so that he feels more disadvantaged before Caesar and more victimized by incomprehensible forces that both hound him from Rome and draw him to Egypt. Consequently he experiences her sexual power as punitive; he now generates images of the eternal mother who, 'wrinkled deep in time,' uses her deadly serpentine power to suck men back into the oozy slime of the Nile, whose eternal ebb and flow rots the foundation of their enterprise.[4] Antony experiences these tides as a mysterious force that weakens him in relation to Caesar, and at the same time draws him back to Cleopatra and her revenge. Just after Antony has promised Octavia to 'keep my square,' the Soothsayer warns him against proximity to Caesar. He tells Antony that his angel 'becomes afeard; as being o'erpowered' (III.ii.21), when Caesar's angel is by, reminding him of his losses at games. Confirming the Soothsayer's truthfulness from his remembered losses to Caesar in sports and gambling, Antony with self-deceiving casualness concludes that he 'will to Egypt; / And though I make this marriage for my peace, / I' the east my pleasure lies' (II.ii.37–9). The casual tone of his decision belies the force he attributes to Caesar's power, expressed in the Soothsayer's and his own description of their relations. This denial, in combination with the impotence of Antony's demon before Caesar's, shows Antony in the process of increasing his shame by detaching himself from, externalizing, and as a consequence further empowering, the paternal power of Caesar and Rome.

As a consequence of externalizing the passions that he previously acknowledged, on his return to Egypt Antony falls into a dreamlike world in which he is pursued by incomprehensible powers. The sense of a magical component in the action is rendered in the scenic structure, which, unlike that in Plutarch's narrative, leaps from Caesar's decision in Rome to attack Antony, to Antony's opening lines in Egypt in which he marvels that Caesar 'from Tarentum and Brundusium / ... could so quickly cut the Ionian sea, / And take in Toryne?' (III.vii.21–3). A little later, when told that Caesar has taken Toryne, Antony muses, 'Can he be there in person? 'tis impossible; / Strange, that his power should be' (III.vii.56–7). Antony's sense of Caesar's magic outweighs Cleopatra's skeptical 'Celerity is never more admir'd / Than by the negligent' (III.vii.24–5), when it is confirmed by the more impartial Canidius, who comments that 'This speed of Caesar's / Carries beyond belief' (III.vii.74–5). In this preternatural speed Antony attributes to Caesar the martial superiority that he himself once claimed. Together with the Soothsayer episode and the strange music that signifies Hercules' departure, this scene shows Antony divesting himself of his martial powers and translating them into a supernaturally punitive paternal force to which he, like Lear to the storm, becomes victim. In doing so he manages to defy a paternal witness while he claims a maternal Cleopatra, and simultaneously punishes himself for this Oedipal crime.

Just as in *Macbeth* both naturalistic and supernatural components bring

Birnam wood to Dunsinane, so Antony's self-victimizing impulses manifest themselves as well on a more naturalistic level when he courts defeat by irrationally insisting on fighting by sea. His flight from that battle is the decisive moment in which his previously interior world explodes and reshapes itself as external circumstance. Following Cleopatra out of battle 'like a doting mallard,' Antony becomes the child who seeks his mother's protection from the wrath of his father to whom she has betrayed him, and by blaming her for his defeat he renders her an image of the mother who seduces the son and then betrays him to an avenging father. That configuration remains below the surface, for having externalized his emotional forms, Antony can only observe and wonder at himself for violating 'experience, manhood, honour' and becoming a 'noble ruin of her magic.' He must now 'to the young man send humble treaties, dodge / And palter in the shifts of lowness' (III.ix.63–4) in a way that represents the collapse of his attempt to assume a maturity that is free of Oedipal mystification. Anticipating Coriolanus, Antony becomes a boy in relation to reinstated parental figures. Only amid this shame and humiliation can he allow himself an unqualified love. For a moment he rises, dolphinlike, above the cataclysm to assert his heroic love: 'Fall not a tear, I say, one of them rates / All that is won and lost: Give me a kiss, / Even this repays me' (III.xi.69–71), giving substance to what previously was hypocritical hyperbole: 'Let Rome in Tiber melt.'

As Antony commits himself to Cleopatra three major developments control the remaining action until his death. First, the sense of betrayal previously generated by images, though remaining suspended in ambiguity, becomes Cleopatra's action. Her intentions with Thidias and in the treasury scene remain obscure, and she neither confirms nor denies her betrayal of Antony to Caesar. That obscurity shows Antony avoiding the full impact of the feelings for her that emerge remotely in her images of herself. Second, and linked to the first, the Oedipal configuration comes into sharper focus, but, since it is entirely outside of Antony's consciousness he experiences it as a magical force. Third, as it does so Antony confirms his love for Cleopatra, yields himself to the punitive forces he has generated, and loses his self-definition.

These motifs are collected into Cleopatra's ambiguous response to Antony's accusation that she has betrayed him when she says,

> Ah, dear, if I be so,
> From my cold heart let heaven engender hail,
> And poison it in the source, and the first stone
> Drop in my neck: as it determines, so
> Dissolve my life; the next Caesarion smite

> Till by degrees the memory of my womb,
> Together with my brave Egyptians all,
> By the discandying of this pelleted storm,
> Lie graveless, till the flies and gnats of Nile
> Have buried them for prey!   (III.xiii.158–67)

The images of self-disgust in which she couches her reassurance challenge the overt intention, suggesting the betrayal she denies. She imagines the coldness of her heart generating poisoned hail that, on touching her warm body, will melt and kill her. The contrast of her heart's coldness to her body's warmth generates the second major image of the 'next Caesarion' smiting her womb. Literally, the next Caesarion would smite Egypt, but in associating Egypt with her womb she imagistically becomes the mother of 'my brave Egyptians all.' This image expresses remotely Antony's association of incestuous sexuality with violation, death, and decay. Hidden in the confused syntax is an image that recalls Hamlet's image of the dead dog that breeds carrion, for the 'memory of [Cleopatra's] womb,' which, along with the 'brave Egyptians' it has produced who 'lie graveless,' as prey for the flies and gnats of the Nile, produces an image that is only slightly removed from one of the womb itself rotting on the banks of the Nile. In the sequence, the image of the next Caesarion smiting her womb is superseded as the cause of the devastation by the hail image in 'the discandying of this pelleted storm.' The thought of her warm body brings to Cleopatra's mind her succession of lovers, and then an image of herself as a whore whose cold heart has rendered her generative powers disgustingly corrupt. Not yet ready to deal with that feeling, her mind deflects to the image with which it started, but she now contrasts the 'pelleted storm' to the warmth of decaying bodies covered in gnats and flies. The cold deadliness of her loving expressed here reveals the depths of Antony's fears. Since the brave Egyptians rotting on Nilus' banks include Antony as her 'soldier / making peace or war as [she] affects,' as well as his children by her, her image creates a stark opposition between the conception with Octavia that might have been a blessing and the way Cleopatra is likely to conceive. Antony's sexuality is bound up in images of corruption and self-loathing that arise from his imagination of an earth mother who as whore generates rotting bodies.

The images within Cleopatra's 'as if' framework correspond to Antony's self-description when he says it is easy for Caesar to anger him 'When my good stars, that were my former guides, / Have empty left their orbs, and shot their fires / Into the abysm of hell' (III.xiii.145–7). The image associates Antony's erratic emotion with the failure of his 'good stars,' the empty orbs of which vaguely suggest the paternal authority that Antony has violated by returning to Egypt. The sweep in the three lines from the heavens to hell recalls Philo's description of Antony: 'His goodly eyes, / That o'er the files and musters of the war / Have glow'd like plated Mars,' have fallen from their high place, their fires now not cooling 'a gipsy's lust.' The hellish abysm into which the stars have shot their fire is associated with Cleopatra because in the 'abysm of hell' the fires of Antony's eyes have merged with his lust.[5] Antony's answering confidence that he can 'fight maliciously' is denied by the context in which he has already empowered his enemy, and moves towards the love-death consummation Cleopatra's images have previously suggested when he says, 'The next time I do fight / I'll make death love me; for I will contend / Even with his pestilent scythe' (III.xiii.192–4).

Antony's dedication to death is expressed as well in diffuse ways. The loyal, plain-spoken, and hard-headed Enobarbus has functioned up to this time as a sort of Kent to Antony's Lear, representing Antony's subliminal feeling that it is folly to yield to his passions. Enobarbus' defection after Antony's reconciliation to Cleopatra shows Antony, worn away by the tides of emotion, loosening his grip on life. Enobarbus' terse and appropriately oral statement of that process is, 'A diminution in our captain's brain / Restores his heart; when valour preys on reason / It eats the sword it fights with' (III.xiii.198–200). Antony's dedication to death is expressed remotely through Enobarbus' spontaneous death, and less remotely through the dreamlike music that signifies the departure of 'the god Hercules, whom Antony loved.'

Once having ceased to struggle Antony rescues a moment of the equal love he envisioned. Earlier his sensuality and Cleopatra's have been expressed indirectly by others in images of food and feasting, but when the lovers have been together they have sparred or have been estranged from each other. Only within the aura of death do they display sensuous affection and intimacy, as Cleopatra first fumblingly and then deftly buckles Antony's armour, and he feels rejuvenated – 'This morning, like the spirit of a youth / That means to be of note, begins betimes' (IV.iv.26–7). He gives her a 'soldier's kiss,' and boyishly wants her to witness his prowess in 'the royal occupation.' Like Othello and later protagonists in the romances, Antony can afford to indulge erotic love only when he feels his identity protected by martial honour. The armour he dons as he prepares to challenge Caesar both permits and restrains intimacy. Coming triumphant from the battlefield in a short-lived victory, he declares a fully sexualized love for Cleopatra when he exclaims, 'O thou day o' the world, / Chain mine arm'd neck, leap thou, attire and all, / Through proof of harness to my heart, and there / Ride on the pants triumphing!' (IV.viii.12–16). She responds, 'Lord of lords, / O infinite virtue, com'st thou smiling from / The world's great snare uncaught?' (IV.viii.16–18). Though a battlefield might not be thought of as a snare, the image is apt for the emotional snare that has been pulling tighter around him, the strands consisting on the one hand of his weakness in relation to Caesar because of his love of Cleopatra, and on the other his incapacity to love Cleopatra fully because of his shame before Caesar. But for this moment he has escaped the snare, and openly declares his love. He does not return to her as to a mother, but as a loving partner when he says,

> My nightingale,
> We have beat them to their beds. What, girl, though gray
> Do something mingle with our younger brown, yet ha' we
> A brain that nourishes our nerves, and can
> Get goal for goal of youth. (IV.viii.18–22)

Momentarily free from guilt and shame, he invokes an admiring audience to blast the city's ear with trumpets and 'brazen din ... That heaven and earth may strike their sounds together, / Applauding our approach' (IV.viii.36–8). But he quickly succumbs to the psychic snare that made that achievement so difficult as Cleopatra becomes the 'triple-turn'd whore' who 'beguil'd [him] to the very heart of loss'(IV.xii.19,29). As her image darkens he, like Lear before him, generates polarized images of the 'good' but sexless woman punishing the evil and sexual one:

> Let him take thee,
> And hoist thee up to the shouting plebeians,
> Follow his chariot, like the greatest spot
> Of all thy sex. Most monster-like be shown
> For poor'st diminutives, for dolts, and let
> Patient Octavia plough thy visage up
> With her prepared nails. (IV.xii.33–9)

In an accelerating vacillation between giving Cleopatra to Caesar and taking her back he, like Hamlet, sees himself as Hercules in the 'snare of Nessus.' Antony escapes that intolerable and intractable polarity only by fully experiencing the dissolution that he had sought and feared from the beginning. He feels himself melting like the clouds, like 'black vesper's pageants' in which,

> That which is now a horse, even with a thought
> The rack dislimns, and makes it indistinct
> As water is in water ....

My good knave Eros, now thy captain is
Even such a body: here I am Antony,
Yet cannot hold this visible shape, my knave.   (IV.xiv.9–14)

Out of his desire Antony has generated the image of the archetypal mother;
out of his fear and guilt he has turned that image to a whore, and struggled
to escape its power by an unsuccessful effort to align himself with the paternal
Caesar. Having returned to Cleopatra, for a brief moment he has mastered
his fear of sexuality and transformed her into a sexual and loving companion
in enterprise, only to fall prey more fully to his image of her as poisonously
destructive. Finally he escapes the snare only by losing his 'visible shape.'[6]

Earlier Antony has said that the 'poisoned hours' he spent with Cleopatra
'bound him up from [his] own knowledge'; as though to fulfil a prediction,
as he asserts his love he loses his sense of identity. When he thinks Cleopatra
dead, the opposition between Roman virtues and Egyptian sexuality disappears,
for he attributes to her those virtues that, living, she undermined. He can
fully embrace both her and death, since in losing his 'visible shape' he has
foregone his body's lusts that had poisoned his imagination. When he is about
to give himself his death wound, he finally imagines legitimizing his union
with Cleopatra in marriage: 'but I will be / A bridegroom in my death, and
run into't / As to a lover's bed' (IV.xiv. 99–101). But the marriage bed remains
associated with the twin fears of violence and dissolution of the self.

Antony interprets his death as a punishment, one that substitutes for, as
well as evades, punishment by Caesar. He says, 'Not Caesar's valour hath
o'erthrown Antony, but Antony's hath triumph'd on itself' (IV.xv.14–15), and
'Bid that welcome / Which comes to punish us, and we punish it / Seeming
to bear it lightly' (IV.xiv.136–8). In the act of suicidal self-punishment Antony
defeats Caesar by becoming his own father, and claims a disembodied Cleopatra: 'Where souls do couch on flowers, we'll hand in hand, / And with our
sprightly port make the ghosts gaze: / Dido and her Aeneas, shall want troops, /
And all the haunt be ours' (IV.xiv.51–4). If Lear penetrates the infantile Oedipal
dream implied by but not realized in Hamlet's story, Antony and Cleopatra
partially fulfil what is potential in the relation between Hamlet and Ophelia.
Like Hamlet in his charisma and self-reflection, though without his thoughtfulness, Antony falls back into the filial self-definition from which he has tried
to free himself. But more explicitly than Hamlet at the moment of his suicide
he defies the paternal ghost and accepts the slime of sexuality as the price of
the visionary fulfilment of his love for Cleopatra in death. He embraces the
loss of self that his predecessors avoided, and disappears into Cleopatra's
language. He dissolves out of his own dream, and passes on to Cleopatra the
task of rescuing romance from images of betrayal and corporeal decay.[7]

In order to summarize the configurations Antony has generated in Cleo-patra, I will take her as protagonist-dreamer, and discuss the significance of the last act for her, before considering it as Antony's dream.[8] The uncertainty with which Antony surrounds her figure becomes her uncertainty about her-self. Within that vagueness, she emerges as an older and wiser Ophelia, or as one who plays the nurse to her own Juliet or Emilia to her own Desdemona. She is as deeply divided as Antony when her love for him conflicts with keeping her eye on the main chance. In that confusion, she rests her sense of herself on her capacity to charm and captivate men, which she in subliminal ways identifies with an archetypal image of herself as the eternal mother, giving birth and destroying, necessarily unfaithful, and always surviving. The infidelity of the earth mother defines her as a whore, which in turn makes her fear men's betrayal. Her serpentine charm become her means of reprisal. Associating her generative capacity with death, she fears the destructiveness of her own loving. Therefore she generates in Antony a lover whose Roman discipline will put distance between him and her inner sense of her corrupting sexuality. She wants Antony when she sees him as a Roman father whom she can seduce from the corresponding Roman mother figure, Fulvia or Oc-tavia. But if she succeeds, then he becomes a weak father, and a betrayer of the legitimate mother figure whom she despises, but with whom she identifies. Therefore, she is outraged by Antony's callousness when Fulvia dies, at the same time as she blames him for not making her, Cleopatra, the 'married woman.' She seduces Antony into sensuous pleasures, but cannot fully succeed because his image would then be besmirched by her own inner life. She needs him at a heroic distance to keep him worthy of her love, safe from its dangers, and to lift her self-image from the mire that threatens it. But that distance increases the danger by intensifying her image of herself as whore. In that dilemma she, like Antony, vacillates between rejecting him and drawing him back. But the more she wins him, the more she must betray him in punishment for the crime of loving her. Her decision, like Antony's, appears when she sees his heart tied to her rudder, and she almost immediately generates Thidias with whom to dally. She now sees herself through Antony's eyes no longer a morsel for a monarch, but as garbage, 'A morsel, cold upon / Dead Caesar's trencher,' and in her quasi-denial of having betrayed Antony reveals that she associates her sexuality with death and decay. She keeps Antony apart from those images by envisioning their loving moment in conjunction with An-tony's warlike and Roman self, as he arms for battle and comes victorious from it, but that distance threatens her hold on him. Therefore, to draw him closer she betrays him, and finally evades her fear of her own deadly sexuality by having him die into her language.

With that Cleopatra has accomplished her revenge, has taken Antony from the Roman realm, has allowed him to escape her snare long enough to envision herself elevated by his heroic love, before his proximity to her threatens to transform him into one of the rotting products of her womb. His death frees her from the terrors of her own destructiveness. Having dismissed from her horizon the possibility of corporeally fulfilled love, she realizes and distances herself from the 'baser elements,' earth and water that together make mud, slime, and rotting things. In the 'air and fire' of an imagination that has dismissed living bodies, she achieves a vision of herself merging into her own archetype and joining a bodiless Antony as both wife and mother.

She transforms the images of dissolution into the means of Antony's ex-altation when she says, 'The crown o'the earth doth melt. My Lord? / O, wither'd is the garland of the war, / The soldier's pole is fall'n' (IV.xv.63–5), and becomes a fair warrior, one with her Roman lover in resolving to die 'after the high Roman fashion.'

However, she can generate sufficient hatred of her betraying body to over-come the will to live only through the vicissitudes of the last act. Like Hamlet pressing his nose to Yorick's skull, or like Lear envisioning himself born from foul-smelling genitals before his reunion with Cordelia, or like Antony in asking to hear himself named in Rome, in slow stages Cleopatra disgusts herself with the vilest images of her living self in order to generate the vision of them united in death. Only after Dolabella has finally assured her that Caesar will not only lead her in triumph, but will do so 'within three days,' does she assert her determination to die rather than be chastised by Octavia's 'sober eye,' or mocked by censuring Rome's 'shouting varletry.' In these images she gives parental power to both Octavia and the generalized image of the Roman crowd, but first she avoids the imagination of their censure by repeating the image of her womb and dead Egyptians being buried by the 'flies and gnats' of the Nile when she says, 'Rather on Nilus' mud / Lay me stark-nak'd, and let the water-flies / Blow me into abhorring;' before giving herself more visibility in changing the image to one in which she will hang in chains on her 'country's high pyramides' (v.ii.58–62). Her next speech brings her imagination a stage closer to seeing herself through Roman eyes when she tells Iras that puppets will represent them in Rome where 'mechanic slaves / With greasy aprons, rules, and hammers shall / Uplift us to the view.' The general humiliation focuses on the word 'greasy,' which brings in its wake images of food when she adds that 'In their thick breaths, / Rank of gross diet, shall we be enclouded, / And forc'd to drink their vapour' (v.ii.206–12). Though still thinking of the puppets, she incorporates the images of rotten food that at a remove previously defined her, like Cressida, as a whore, before finally seeing herself as a whore when she says that saucy lictors

Will catch at us like strumpets, and scald rhymers
Ballad us out o' tune. The quick comedians
Extemporally will stage us, and present
Our Alexandrian revels: Antony
Shall be brought drunken forth, and I shall see
Some squeaking Cleopatra boy my greatness
I' the posture of a whore.   (v.ii.214–19)

She makes immediate to her imagination, though not to her body, the mocking audience that Antony feared, defied, and evaded, and in that process finally gives her voice to the names 'whore' and 'strumpet' that have throughout hovered around her.

Having fully associated her body with the most corrupt version of sexuality and generation, she becomes 'absolute for death,' but wants a death cleansed of the odours of corruption. As Hamlet expressed his divided imagination of death by opposing the charnel-house images of the body's corruption to his own glorification through the bird imagery in the words of both Horatio and Fortinbras, so Cleopatra opposes the Clown's description of the asp to the use she will make of it. The Clown imagistically emerges from and embodies the slime of the Nile, while his jokes, of two kinds, express ironic distrust of the transcendence she later imagines.

First, he plays on the polarity between immortality and the finality of death; 'for his biting is immortal: those that die of it, do seldom or never recover' (v.ii.245–6). Like those of Hamlet's grave-digger, his jests about death merge with jests about women when he tells of the very honest woman who 'died of the biting of it,' and gave a 'very good report o' the worm.' He refocuses the imagistic link between women and food when he warns that the deadly worm 'is not worth the feeding.' Cleopatra asks, 'Will it eat me?' and he responds, 'I know that the devil himself will not eat a woman: I know that a woman is a dish for the gods, if the devil dress her not' (v.ii.269–73). In his jests, which give some of Lear's cannibalistic grotesqueness to this play's otherwise softer oral images, Cleopatra remains food for monarchs, but only after passing through the guts of a beggar.

The Clown embodies in the asp the images of Nilus' slime from which Cleopatra escapes into visions of air and fire. He also calls attention to the missing middle term, the ordinary fertility she forgoes in death. After the Clown exits, Cleopatra says, 'Give me my robe, put on my crown; I have / Immortal longings in me. Now no more / The juice of Egypt's grape shall moist this lip' (v.ii.279–81). Her lines stand in ironic juxtaposition to the Clown's story of the 'very honest woman' who told of her own death, and his warning that the worm's 'biting is immortal; those that die of it seldom or never recover.' As he repeatedly wishes Cleopatra the 'joy o'the worm,' these ironic plays on death's finality call into question and cast doubt on the status of the love-death fantasy that so deliciously permits erotic fulfilment without taint from the world, the flesh, or sexuality.

That actualization in the clown scene of what previously was vague pushes Cleopatra's mind over the hurdle posed by the fear of death and its associated images of decay. Now envisioning death as a realm of purity and reunion with Antony, she dons her robe and crown and takes leave of the Nile's shifting tides to become, like Othello's heavens, 'marble constant.' She identifies now with the beneficent aspect of the archetypal Isis, and finally claims Antony as her 'husband.' Like Antony earlier, she associates her imagined marriage with death, both in Iras' spontaneous death, which parallels Enobarbus', and when she says 'the stroke of death is as a lover's pinch, / Which hurts, and is desired' (v.ii.294–5). The image reduces to erotic play the violence Antony associated with his death, and adds a familial dimension absent from Antony's language. In a detail not to be found in Plutarch's account, she puts the asp to her breast. As she says, 'Peace, peace! / Dost thou not see my baby at my breast, / That sucks the nurse asleep' (v.ii.307–9), she restores to their innocent source the images of monstrous devouring, and substitutes for an image of archetypal maternity one of ordinary maternal tenderness unique in Shakespeare's plays.[9] When she murmurs, 'As sweet as balm, soft as air, as gentle. / O Antony!' (v.ii.310–11), she transforms Nilus' slime into an image of Antony that she embraces within that tenderness. She becomes, indeed, 'a morsel for a monarch,' even though doing so simultaneously kills her.[10]

The episode suggests that Shakespeare's imagination of mothering grew more benign between the time he imagined the infant at Lady Macbeth's breast and writing this play. Though outraged by the sexual smells of the world, King Lear manages to imagine himself as an infant, and Antony, after dying into Cleopatra and being born through her words to more than his former glory, allows himself at a distance, like a dreamer absent from his dream, and at the price of becoming a slime-born asp, the last luxury of these gentle maternal words.

This excursion into Cleopatra's psychic structure necessarily duplicates Antony's own, but emphasizes the ways in which he has embodied in her figure both his association of sexual desire with shame, and has endowed her with maternal power to draw him into corruption and death that will fulfil his desire in its punishment. Once he ceases to struggle against that tide and merges himself into Cleopatra he gains everything and nothing. In her vacillation he, on the one hand, joins the offended paternal Caesar to satisfy his desire that she be humiliated and punished for her betrayal. On the other hand, by submitting totally to her he has bought a vision of himself resurrected as heroic lover, lifted dolphinlike by a disembodied eternal Isis out of the watery element. In Cleopatra's image of him, 'past the size of dreaming,' with legs bestriding the ocean that divides Rome from Egypt, he achieves an imagined resolution to his conflict even while he defines it as irresolvable.[11] He can claim her as lover, as wife, and more secretly retain a diminished corporality in the slimy asp in order to suck his nurse asleep.[12] In a strategy worthy of Hamlet, Antony can enjoy Caesar's tribute to and blessing on their union, while his escape into the grave acknowledges and defeats Caesar's paternal power.

But in the Clown's words Antony has also expressed the limitations of the disembodied imagination – those who have the joy of the worm 'do seldom or never recover.' Antony's fullest achievement, and in my view Shakespeare's, lies in his victorious invocation to Cleopatra to ride on the triumphant pants of his heart, even though that victory remains subject to the ebb and flow of life and time.

In *Romeo and Juliet* the hatred and betrayal that characterize later protagonists are externalized into the surrounding figures who, along with fortuitous time and circumstance, bear responsibility for the young lovers' death. All negative components are present, but in a form that obscures their relevance to the lovers. Juliet, as an early Cleopatra, gives her self-preservative impulses and capacity for betrayal to the Nurse, and insofar as Romeo stands behind Antony, his struggle away from love and sexuality are expressed through Mercutio, the fortuitous plague, and accidental mistiming. More deeply than *Othello, Antony and Cleopatra* invites us into the psychological morass that underlies the seduction of love-death romance, but in the process more fully engages, and momentarily overcomes the conflicted sexuality that underlies the form. In the protagonists' capacity to love each other despite their betrayals, the play's generous embrace of the imperfect makes it the tragic counterpart to *As You Like It*.

Like Antony's moment of triumph, Shakespeare's vision of loving sexuality between a man and woman quickly fades, the love theme disappearing from the remaining tragedies. In *Timon of Athens* there are no major women characters, and *Coriolanus* focuses on the relationship between Aufidius and Coriolanus, which is opposed to the paternal Roman values and the maternal Volumnia. In *Antony and Cleopatra* the homoerotic suggestions that appeared in previous plays remain only in Eros' sword. They re-emerge in *Coriolanus*, where the hostility between Coriolanus and Aufidius is articulated in images of homoerotic violence. In his passion Coriolanus betrays home, mother, wife, and son to embrace Aufidius in the comradeship of arms. The women remain naturalistic, but the polarity between the emasculating Volumnia and the compassionate Virgilia remains. Like Cordelia and later Miranda, Virgilia is defined by the single quality of compassion, and is finally as silent as Cordelia claims to be. Like Hamlet, Coriolanus has retreated from his appropriate mate, but has generated a mother who, in representing the patrician values of Rome, carries paternal associations. At the same time as her dominance intimidates Coriolanus, he experiences squeamish pleasure at the physical intimacy implied by her interest in his wounds. Equating that pleasure to schoolboy tears and to virgin voices, he vacillates between an approach to her, interpreted by him as destructive to his manhood, and an approach to Aufidius, or the homosexual, interpreted by him as betrayal of family and country. He evades that conflict by defining himself as a machinelike war god, but chooses Aufidius over country and family.[13] And though reduced to a 'boy of tears' by the familial ties he consciously repudiated, he has his moment of homoerotic violent passion with Aufidius, as Antony had his moment of passion with Cleopatra.[14] It is as though Shakespeare, in making the heterosexual assertion in *Antony and Cleopatra*, followed it with the more covert homosexual assertion of *Coriolanus*, thus extricating strands that in *Othello* were intertwined.

The last plays lose the drive to follow to their source in the human psyche and to their end in human fate the compulsions of sexuality and the tribulations of loving. Truncated signs of the conflicts remain, but the direct exploration of character diminishes, and the tragic sense of insoluble conflict disappears into improbable or magical reunions of lovers and of families. The imagination is released from the decaying flesh, but at the cost of the sexual and the sensual.

9

The 'Insubstantial Pageant' of the Last Plays: *Pericles* and *Cymbeline*

Tragedy, Bradley said, generates a feeling of irretrievable loss, and Shakespeare's tragedies in their various ways depict men and women carried on the currents of their passions into their graves. The possibility of love in life exists only in effervescent shadows, the golden statues, Gertrude's golden couplets, Desdemona's momentary revival from death, and Cleopatra's vision of herself and Antony, transcendently united beyond the grave. However, comedy, or at least romantic comedy, involves recovering what was or appeared to be lost. Accordingly, the four last plays reverse the tragic relationship in that they depict the happy consummation of love while hinting at tragic possibilities. In distanced and symbolic approaches to love-death situations – Imogen and Cloten's burial, and Pericles' visit to Marina's 'tomb' – and in sequences of action similar to those in the tragedies, these plays retain some tragic aura. But that aura is obscured by action that moves towards revival and restoration. Each of the four plays concludes with a couple or couples united, their union central to a correctly ordered polity, and each contains a protagonist who, as a precondition of wedded bliss, passes through a period of trial, suffering, or isolation, sometimes explicitly defined as punishment for wrongdoing, sometimes not.

But these plays that precede *The Tempest* seem to wrestle uneasily to their conclusions, to be struggling to find strategies for regaining some lost ideal that has taken on the depth, resonance, and import that was appropriate in the tragedies where the loss was irrevocable. To arrive at their conclusions the plays generate quasi-magical happenings that sit uneasily with their aura of depth and import. As a consequence they are characterized by sharp shifts of tone and focus, and uneven characterization. The occasional outbreaks of emotionally laden language are quickly restrained, and though some action flows from this language of emotion, most such language is superseded by action arising from other sources – benign accident, providence, or magic.

Pericles and *Cymbeline* are both quasi-magical; major plot events are brought about by fortuitousness so improbable as to suggest a hidden hand, or by visionary appearances – Diana in *Pericles*, and Jupiter in *Cymbeline*. The hidden hand becomes partially visible in *The Winter's Tale*, assuming the shape of Paulina, though benign coincidence still controls much of the action. Only in *The Tempest* did Shakespeare abandon the remnants of a naturalistic causality to give to Prospero unambiguous magical control over events almost all of which he arranges. It as though in these plays Shakespeare struggled towards a form that would give the illusion of probability to a vision of a transcendently pure love fulfilled in life. In *The Tempest* he abandoned that attempt; the scattered energy of the previous plays is there gathered to create the figure of Prospero, whose complete control brings about a vision of harmony, but in a world fully defined by rules other than those that obtain in our own.

The price paid for wresting the tragic emotional currents out of their course towards different versions of the love-death sea was the sacrifice of emotionally resonant language and of naturalistic character portrayal. In these plays the language is often flat and theoretical, the suggestion of strong feeling giving way to moral statement or to the aura of spirituality, and character portrayal is often shallow. Like daydream rather than dream, the happy conclusions, brought about by improbable action, clearly express a wish, but they lack the language suggestive of the associated fears that made them realizable only in fantasy forms. Therefore, their benign resolutions suggest the repression rather than dissolution of the conflicts that shape them. Because that is so, much of the argument here for the resonance of the action arises from parallels between the structure and characters of these plays and earlier ones. That is, it will be assumed that such parallels indicate that the emotions suggested by the language in earlier plays in a more remote way still lurk beneath the surface of these plays, and that these emotions can, if resorted to, fill in levels of ordinary motivation that these more ideological and emotionally sketchy works obscure. The reverse is also true; since images from previous plays often expand into the action and characters of these, they make more visible what was previously obscured. Therefore, I will pay more attention to ways in which these plays are linked to those that precede and follow them, and give fuller attention to *The Winter's Tale* and *The Tempest*, each of which in a different way more fully joins the theoretical structure to emotional depth.

Though no view of the authorship of *Pericles* is unchallenged, the most widely held is that Shakespeare took an old play by another author, made a few changes in the beginning, which did not interest him, and rewrote the last three acts, his imagination stirred by Marina's story. However, whether

Shakespeare about the time of *Titus Andronicus* found the sources of *Pericles* and began a play that he left unfinished until near the end of his career, or whether later in his career he found and only partially reworked a play by someone else that confusedly appealed to him, or whether he came upon the source stories and put them together badly because his intention to find a mode other than the tragic was not quite formulated, the play as a whole shows enough thematic and formal relation to those that went before and those that come after to make the work significant for the issues here discussed.[1]

Pericles' most obvious overt thematic link is to *King Lear*, which portrays anguished men asking whether they inhabit a just or meaningful universe. If there is an answer in the tragedy, it is only that if men fail, as they probably will, to 'show the heavens more just,' it will not make much difference to those on earth whether or not the heavens are just. In *Pericles* the heavens without human assistance manifest their justice by making visible previously hidden corruption. In the midst of their pride and pomp the incestuous Antiochus and his daughter are stricken by a fire from heaven that 'shrivell'd up / Their bodies, even to loathing; for they so stunk, / That all those eyes ador'd them ere their fall / Scorn now their hand should give them burial' (II.iv.9–12), and with only slightly more probability Cleon's subjects burn him and his wife for trying to kill Marina.

King Lear couples the overt theme of heaven's justice with Lear's covert desire for Cordelia. By challenging the barriers to sexuality represented by incest, Lear earns his death with Cordelia, and Antony and Cleopatra escape the murky depths long enough for an equal and mutual love to flower before that love and the world in which it grew decline into the ooze. Like a dragon lurking underground and sending out fumes of guilt and rage to distort all love relationships, incest has been worming its way through all the plays. The heavens can finally prove themselves just by punishing the incest that finally breaks out into the open at the beginning of *Pericles*.

This pattern suggests that the play's inadequacies reflect neither Shakespeare's indifference nor a different author's hand, but rather derive from his first attempt at a new way to handle old problems. Through his tragic protagonists he had explored as deeply as he was going to the dark recesses of the incestuous imagination. In the improbable world of moral certainties and guaranteed justice in *Pericles* Shakespeare for the first time overtly portrays incest. He distances and flattens the theme's emotional force by such devices as the dumb shows and Gower choruses, which both in their form and their content remind the audience of the stage on which an old tale is enacted. In *The Winter's Tale* the characters themselves comment that the staged events are like an old tale, or like a play, generating a thematic statement about the transforming power of art. The crude devices in *Pericles* seem ineptly to grope towards that later and more subtle artistry.

Pericles, having identified with his ego ideal and defined himself as idealized prince of an idealized country, confronts all other components of his psyche as externalized figures and events. As a consequence his own figure remains dramatically thin, but the kinds of emotions that generate the world he confronts are suggested as well by the fact that though he, unlike Hamlet, has eliminated his parents, he remains a prince rather than a king. Like Hamlet, though without overt reason, he seems not to have achieved his full maturity, towards which he ventures by seeking a wife. More obviously than Hamlet, he finds his way impeded by shades of incest and death that cling to sexuality. Antiochus and his daughter function for him as do Claudius and Gertrude for Hamlet. However, where Hamlet experiences himself punished by offended paternal figures for sexual claims he is unaware of having made, Pericles more statically confronts his desires in the clearly incestuous father and daughter, surrounded with skeletons of dead suitors that express both his equation of sexuality and death and his fear of a father-figure whom he has offended by his overtly competitive sexual claim. Defining himself as heroic agent of their exposure, he guesses their obvious riddle, some inappropriate details of which reveal Pericles' involvement in the dilemmas of earlier protagonists:

> I am no viper, yet I feed
> On mother's flesh which did me breed.
> I sought a husband, in which labour
> I found that kindness in a father.
> He's father, son, and husband mild;
> I mother, wife, and yet his child:
> How they may be, and yet in two.
> As you will live, resolve it you.   (1.i.65–7)

The image of a viper feeding on its parents' flesh recalls Lear's pelican daughters, or the cuckoo who 'bit off' its hedge-sparrow mother's head. The context here overtly equates incestuous sexuality with feeding on the mother, an image that for Antiochus' daughter could only mean that she equates her father-husband with her mother in oral sex. The image expresses Pericles' equation of incestuous sexuality with infantile cannibalism. Also, the lines, 'he's father, son, and husband mild, / I mother, wife, and yet his child' go unexplained, since presumably the daughter has not given birth, but the suggestion that Antiochus, while father to his daughter, is also son to his mother sketches a generational reversal, similar to that in *King Lear*, which then hints at the hidden fears that will be manifested in Marina's story.[2]

While Pericles keeps his own figure clear of Hamlet's pestilent vapours, when he has returned to Tyre he experiences an unaccountable melancholy that he only later attributes to his fear of Antiochus' tyrannical wrath. He then casts himself as victim to a paternal figure whose wrongs he has exposed. He remains heroic by undertaking a voluntary exile to protect his subjects, but the pattern resembles that of Hamlet, whose removal from Denmark finally cleanses it.

Still in the posture of helpful hero, Pericles externalizes his previous 'dull-eyed melancholy' into the waste-land kingdom of Cleon and Dionyza, the realization of the one described by Titania in *A Midsummer Night's Dream*. The absence of an explanation for the blight on a once flourishing kingdom emphasizes its symbolic importance, and its description shows Pericles associating with his previous melancholy images of familial cannibalism that resemble those in *Lear*:

> Those palates who, not yet two summers younger,
> Must have inventions to delight the taste,
> Would now be glad of bread, and beg for it;
> Those mothers who, to nuzzle up their babes
> Thought nought too curious, are ready now
> To eat those little darlings whom they lov'd.
> So sharp are hunger's teeth, that man and wife
> Draw lot who first shall die to lengthen life. (1.iv.39–46)

By casting himself as benefactor, Pericles distances himself from these expressions of the infantile dangers he fears in family life. His self-deception generates the action that follows, when on the shores of Pentapolis he makes a second bid for a wife. As Hamlet encountered the grave-diggers as a prelude to his consummation of love in death, Pericles encounters the fishermen as a prelude to his attempt to find love in life. As the grave-digger's resurrection of Yorick's skull marked a stage in Hamlet's approach to his grave, so the fisherman's retrieval of his father's armour signifies a stage in Pericles' approach to marriage. A trace of an otherwise concealed rift between Pericles and his father appears in the rust that needs to be cleaned from the armour despite its having been only recently lost. His reconciliation to paternal martial values is symbolized in the recovered armour, which enables him to emerge victorious from the tourney, with Thaisa as his bride. The parallels between Pericles' courtship of Thaisa and his earlier courtship of Antiochus' daughter show the later episode to be a version of the earlier. In the first he has to prove his virtue by solving a riddle; in the second by competing in a tourney. As a consequence of the first he encounters paternal enmity, and after the second Thaisa's father in jest accuses him of treachery. The image of the father as tyrant remains even though Pericles seems to have overcome the guilt associated with women by adopting the martial values that Hamlet rejected.

By seeing himself as heroically worthy he can permit himself to win a bride, but not to keep her. The strategy fails to disperse his dark view of sexuality that would emerge in close contact, and so in his characteristic way he becomes victim to forces that sever him from Thaisa, and takes in her stead the more controllable, but now potentially incestuous, version of the female, a baby daughter. Caught in the conflict between his desire for a woman and his fear that his underlying animosity will distort her image, he arranges for Thaisa's seeming death while, remote from consciousness, he keeps her alive and insures her purity by committing her to an ascetic religious life.

Having left himself alone with Marina, Pericles is in a situation that threatens to resemble that of Antiochus. While the infant female poses little immediate sexual temptation, any sexual arousal involves the threat of an incestuous violation of infantile innocence. Therefore, while he does not eliminate Marina from his consciousness as he does Thaisa, he leaves her to be raised by Cleon and Dionyza. His ambivalence is expressed in the improbable action as well as in indecision as to whether to proceed to his home, or to stop at Tarsus. Having decided that the infant cannot 'hold out for Tyre,' he reveals the emotion represented by that circumstance when he assumes that she will remain in Tarsus until her marriage. He turns himself from a Hamlet into a Lear figure when he vows that 'Till she be married, madam, / By bright Diana, whom we honour, all / Unscissor'd shall this hair of mine remain, / Though I show ill in't (III.iii.27–30). Though there are no images that suggest the self-punitive nature of his decision, the plot sufficiently parallels Lear's punishment for having banished Cordelia, and Leontes' for having exposed Perdita, to suggest that Pericles here punishes himself for unacknowledged crimes. That the term of his punishment should extend until Marina's marriage suggests that only when she is safely unavailable to him can he allow himself the freedom of his good looks and, by implication, his sexuality.

The emotionally remote reasons for which Pericles punishes himself appear in Marina's fate. In Dionyza he represents what Thaisa and Marina would become if he did not distance them from himself. Dionyza takes on shades of Lady Macbeth when, in her jealousy for her own child, she manipulates Cleon to agree to her plan to murder Marina. Cleon and Dionyza are the last images of murderous parents to appear in the play; their power is negated when pirates, reminiscent of those in *Hamlet*, save Marina from Leonine, who like Oswald in *King Lear*, represents the self-seeking servant. The two images involved in Hamlet's charge to Ophelia, 'Get thee to a nunnery,' develop separately, with Thaisa becoming, anachronistically, a 'nun,' while Marina is taken to a whore-house. In Marina's sojourn in the brothel Pericles expresses two related emotional strategies. First, he expresses his image of woman as whore, and his desire to debase her to the level of his own debased sexuality. In Dionyza's action he conceals from himself his base desire to besmirch the pure, which, if brought to consciousness, would turn him into an Angelo lusting after Isabella. Second, Marina's power to convert the brothel's clients to the paths of virtue expresses Pericles' desire for a female purity so radiant that it can cleanse his diseased imagination. The episode is a spiritualized version of the bed trick.

Pericles' underlying equation of sexuality with death appears in his thinking Marina dead, and being shown her 'tomb' by Dionyza, at the same time as she enters the brothel. Her 'resurrection' occurs after Pericles has suffered a long and stormy travail, similar to Lear's, which leaves him with a fourteen-years' growth of beard that makes him appear to be as old as Lear, and after Marina has proven the transcendent power of her virtue by converting the governor of Mitylene. Imagery of foulness, corruption, and disease surrounds the bawdy-house, recalling the plague imagery that precedes the entombment of Romeo and Juliet, but Marina proves her purity when, in imagery reminiscent of that in *Hamlet* and *Lear*, she wishes that 'the gods / Would set me free from this unhallow'd place, / That they did change me to the meanest bird / That flies i'th'purer air! (IV.vi.98–101). Having persuaded Lysimachus of her purity, she uses his gold to purchase Boult's help, and so escapes the brothel. In sequence, Pericles dreams her in her grave, then empowers her risen figure to cleanse the fetid stench of the brothel, equated with the grave, and finally allows her to surface to consciousness and to restore him to life and youth. The reconciliation scene has a curious edge, for when Marina revives the catatonic Pericles, they have no way of knowing each other to be father and daughter. Her miraculous effect upon him and their prolonged exchange suggest the possibility, one that occurs in the source story of *The Winter's Tale*, that they will fall into an incestuous love. However, the incest theme is submerged when the two discover their true relationship; it remains only in Pericles' insistence that Marina's spiritualized beauty resembles her mother's.

The identification implied by the resemblance also resonates when Pericles, again like Lear, clothed in fresh garments and sleeping to the sounds of healing music, sees in a dream-vision Diana, who directs him to Thaisa. It is, therefore, Marina's power to purify sexuality that releases Thaisa from the living death of sterile virtue, and that enables Pericles to eliminate from his imagination of sexuality the blight and violence of Cleon and Dionyza's kingdom so that he can claim Thaisa as his wife. He cleanses his imagination, however, only by generating polarized images of women who lose their full humanity, becoming either single-dimensional images of symbolic purity or of corruption and cruelty. While the re-united lovers of *Pericles* can be seen as a revived version of the golden statues that emerge from Romeo and Juliet's tomb, or as an embodiment of Antony's imagined afterlife, the emotional thinness and distance provided by the frame of Gower's tale show a protagonist removing himself from, rather than resolving, the conflicts that remain visible in remote configurations. In the improbability of the events that lead to the resolution the protagonist reveals his disbelief in the resolution he engenders.[3]

For the quasi-magical situations of *Pericles, Cymbeline* substitutes highly fortuitous ones, through which Shakespeare tries once again to resolve the conflicts of love, this time by explicitly joining them to the problems of authority. Where Pericles combines in his definition of himself components of both Hamlet and King Lear, Cymbeline divides the *Hamlet* and *Lear* motifs into several figures – his own, to which the issues of authority are most immediate, and Posthumus, Cloten, and Iachimo, to whom the issues of love and family are most immediate. Though the play most obviously concerns Posthumus' jealousy, so like Othello's, the surrounding and somewhat fragmented action concerning the relations of fathers and sons, paternal and filial figures, and political alignments upon which the love relation depends, comes into clearer focus around the figure of the title character. Therefore I shall read the play as Cymbeline's dream, rather than that of Posthumus. Unlike Pericles, who keeps his own figure in the foreground while flattening and idealizing it, Cymbeline retreats to the background, thereby suggesting his retreat from the various aspects of his conflicting emotions, for each of which he generates a separate figure. This multiple splitting results in simple and static figures embedded in complex action, which then, functioning as a complex image, bears most of the weight of significance.[4]

Cymbeline defines himself as an old man who dismisses from his present consciousness the effects of a past crime that still haunts him. In the play's present he justifies his opposition to Roman authority, but slowly brings to consciousness his sense of himself as a usurper. He associates his guilt with and blames it on his queen, in whom he expresses his imagination of female duplicity, illicit ambition, and murderous treachery. In this respect he corresponds to Lear, who violates a more amorphous cosmic authority in abdicating his role as king and as father. Where Lear expresses his sense of wrongdoing by becoming victim to Goneril and Regan and distances sonlike versions of himself to the sons of another father, Cymbeline distances himself emotionally from the female figures, while more directly experiencing the

loss of his sons to Belarius. Belarius becomes a Kent-like figure whose align-
ment with correct authority entitles him to the paternity Cymbeline feels
himself to have jeopardized.

Whereas Lear gives his own figure emotional priority, subordinating to it
the stories of the other figures, Cymbeline, who like Lear casts himself as
passive to others' actions, enacts most of his emotional project through younger
versions of himself. He works out his project with women through the three
major son figures, Posthumus, Cloten, and Iachimo – who might be seen to
correspond to Hamlet's three father figures, Posthumus replacing King Hamlet, Cloten replacing Claudius, and Iachimo functioning as a more malevolent
version of the prying Polonius who also sneaks into bedrooms where he does
not belong. However, Cymbeline keeps his most idealized 'real' sons uncontaminated by women, and by the end of the play forgoes them himself.

In Posthumus Cymbeline tries for an idealized or exonerated version of his
own sense of violated authority, but the younger figure betrays the same
unease about authority as the elder. Defined as a 'poor but worthy gentleman'
who has exceeded his station in wedding the king's daughter, Posthumus is
something like a successful Othello. His uneasy relation to authority appears
in his having eliminated from his horizon his parents and two brothers in
order to be fostered in the king's household. The configuration expresses his
ambivalence about himself. His sense of unworthiness for high status is expressed in his only quasi-filial relation to the king, which he balances by
asserting his personal worth. He is, in short, a social climber, but more like
Othello than Edmund, he remains virtuous in his own eyes while he unconsciously eliminates rather than consciously kills parents and elder brothers.
He challenges traditional hierarchical judgments with his personal virtues,
while expressing doubts about his worthiness through his dubious place in
the hierarchy. His unacknowledged culpability for unwarranted ambition appears in Cymbeline's and the Queen's hostility, which he interprets as an
unjust consequence of the Queen's wickedness and the king's foolishness. In
these strategies Cymbeline expresses his sense of unfitness for his authority,
while he opposes his self-condemnation by obscuring Posthumus' faults beneath the virtues attributed to him by others. He gives Posthumus shades of
Prince Hal's grandeur when he is described as being like an eagle or 'like a
descended god; / He hath a kind of honour sets him off / More than a mortal
seeming' (I.vi.169–71).

By Posthumus' devious challenge to hierarchical status, Cymbeline deviously exonerates his own violation. His challenge to hierarchical with personal entitlement appears more directly when Cymbeline tells Caius Lucius
that Britain's new strength justifies her casting off the Roman yoke. The issue

of authority blends with that of sexuality, since before the reappearance of the lost sons, Posthumus' route to the throne was through his relation to Imogen. The significance of the action appears in Imogen's implied denial of it when she deplores the 'desire that's glorious' and envies those of mean estate who 'have their honest wills, / Which seasons comfort' (i.vii.8–9).

But the illicit ambition Cymbeline subtly expresses through Posthumus he makes blatant through Posthumus' *alter ego*, Cloten. As braggart, coward, and clown, Cloten plays an unattractive Falstaff to Posthumus' Prince Hal. He has the hierarchical status Posthumus lacks, but where Posthumus counters his hierarchical unworthiness for Imogen with his personal virtue, Cloten's personal vices cancel his hierarchical appropriateness. The challenge to the hierarchy becomes overt when the naturally worthy Guiderius, still ignorant of his birth, is subject to punishment for having killed the doltish but princely Cloten. The two characters taken together show Cymbeline's unease with his entitlement to his kingship, based on conflicting ideas about authority that, as we will see, become more pressing in *The Tempest*.

Cloten, in himself and in relation to Posthumus, makes most visible the links between authority and sexuality that earlier characters reveal only in image patterns and plot configurations. The apparent opposition between Cloten and Posthumus is rendered significant by the underlying similarities that make them split images of a single figure. Posthumus as the son of a military hero, and Cloten as the son of a wicked queen taken together recall Hamlet, who is the son of a military hero and a wicked queen. The initial circumstances link the two figures: both have been raised in Cymbeline's court, and both bear a quasi-fraternal relation to Imogen. A body-mind relation between them is established when Imogen says to Cloten that Posthumus' 'mean'st garment, / That ever hath but clipp'd his body, is dearer / In my respect, than all the hairs above thee' (ii.iii.132–4), and when the second lord says of him that he is 'a wooer / More hateful than the foul expulsion is / Of thy dear husband' (ii.i.58–60). In this image Cymbeline makes Cloten's figure represent the foulness of an unruly body divorced from Posthumus' virtuous ideals, an association emphasized by Cloten's appropriation of Posthumus' clothing. He then associates Cloten's violent eroticism with death in the plot configuration in which Imogen and Cloten, having arrived simultaneously at Belarius' pastoral cottage, imagistically die together. Imogen appears dead, Cloten is beheaded, and together they are strewn with burial flowers by the king's lost sons. When Imogen awakens to mistake Cloten's headless body for that of Posthumus, in her subsequent swoon upon the corpse she is once again taken for dead by the Roman soldiers who discover them. Obscured only by comic reduction, the scene renders overt the hate and rage that carried other lovers to their graves.

The identity from which arise the split images of Cloten and Posthumus is further suggested when Posthumus appears on the battlefield with the bloody handkerchief, which was sent by Pisanio as a false token of Imogen's death, around his neck – as though he has been decapitated along with his double. The handkerchief, a concretized image, joins the two figures in a way that equates Posthumus' desire to kill Imogen because of Iachimo's lies with Cloten's desire to rape, humiliate, and debase her. This equation suggests that Posthumus' murderous jealousy is so easily aroused because for him, as for Othello before him and Leontes after, it screens a disposition in which erotic arousal accompanies rage at women.[5] Thus Cymbeline's violent misogyny appears most vividly in the Posthumus-Cloten polarity. Through Posthumus' and others' vision of Imogen he keeps present in his landscape an idealized female figure. But in the safety provided by the comic reduction of Cloten's impotent rage, Cymbeline expresses his brutal sexuality towards women's cold chastity, and through Cloten he siphons off the impulses that led other protagonists to consummate their love in death.

Just as the underside of Cymbeline's image of male sexuality is concealed within the trivialized figure of Cloten, so also is his dark view of women's sexuality and its power to undermine male authority concealed within the flattened and minimized figure of the Queen. Though she lacks a name and has little stage time, she stands in relation to Imogen as Goneril and Regan do to Cordelia. Her role as wife and mother rather than daughter makes explicit what was implicit in the earlier play. Like Lear's evil daughters, she hates her virtuous female counterpart, and strives for illegitimate political power. Her evil plotting is exposed at the play's resolution simultaneously with Imogen's restoration, just as Goneril's and Regan's deaths are linked to Cordelia's return. Parallels with other plays fill out the obscured associations with the Queen's sexuality. The poisons she prepares link her with Gertrude, who is through Hamlet's accusations imagistically linked to the poison that killed her husband; and like Gertrude, the Queen 'battens' on a Moor, that is, on her son. Her implied sexual corruption and betrayal are linked to a cruel disposition, like that of Goneril and Regan, when Cornelius says that her experiments with animals will render her insensitive to human pain.[6] Though she lacks the emotional force of earlier characters, through her Cymbeline expresses his association of women's sexual charms with poisonous corruption, cruelty, and betrayal.

Cymbeline represents an emotional regression, for where Lear in a spiritual cataclysm acknowledges his daughters as his own flesh, Cymbeline obscures the Queen's emotional importance when he increases rather than closes the gap between his own figure and the feelings he expresses in his wife. Upon hearing her reported deathbed confession of murderous plots, he denies responsibility for having been deceived by her beauty, flattery, and apparent virtue. Rather, 'It had been vicious / To have mistrusted her: yet, O my daughter, / That it was folly in me, thou mayst say' (v.v. 65–7). Cymbeline reduces Lear's agonized self-recognition to a minor error, excusable in a faulty cosmos that allows deceptive appearances. Even though Posthumus later admits his own fault, his comment that 'there's no motion / That tends to vice in man, but I affirm / It is the woman's part' (II.iv.172–4), expresses Cymbeline's emotional strategy in shaping the action. The combination of the Queen's flattened figure on its way to becoming the fairy-tale witch, Sycorax, and of her importance to the plot shows Cymbeline concealing rather than resolving the conflicting emotions suggested by her links with the more resonant figures in other plays.

In Imogen Cymbeline generates his image of a redeeming woman, while her status as daughter expresses his association of sexuality with incest. Her relation to figures in earlier plays highlights the way in which Cymbeline attempts to preserve in her an image of female purity that will not exclude sexuality, and the way in which that attempt threatens to blur the distinction between Imogen and the Queen. Imogen's function in the play is analogous to Cordelia's function in King Lear. Like Cordelia, she is surrounded by images that idealize her – diamonds, temples, and chapels – and also like Cordelia, she suffers paternal banishment in connection with her marriage, fears the power of an evil maternal figure, and aligns herself with a foreign power. As Cordelia's return heals Lear's spirit, so Imogen's is instrumental in restoring Cymbeline to a correct understanding of his obligations. However, Cymbeline endows her with stage-managing capacity similar to that of Rosalind, generating a powerful female figure to rescue him from his dilemma. By having Imogen married to, but rejected by Posthumus, pursued by Cloten, maligned by Iachimo, and hated by the Queen, Cymbeline both calls attention to her sexuality and endows her with a chastity as strong as castles and fortresses so that it can, by withstanding the assault of his embattled sexual desires, redeem him. But the combination gives her a hard edge, verging on the cruel, that colours Isabella's character in Measure for Measure. His uneasiness with her, his desire for a kind of desensualized or prophylactic sexuality, appears in the images of Diana, Cleopatra, and Philomela that Iachimo sees in her bedchamber, and in Posthumus' complaint that she deprived him of his 'lawful pleasure' and urged forbearance with 'A pudency so rosy, the sweet view on't / Might well have warm'd old Saturn; that I thought her / As chaste as unsunn'd snow' (II.iv.161–5). In context the word 'chaste' refers not only to fidelity, but to sexual disinclination, and the passage struggles between the 'unsunn'd snow' of her sexual coldness and the attribution of 'a pudency so rosy' that might warm 'old Saturn,' or Cymbeline himself.

The uneasy fusion of attributes that constitute Imogen's figure appears in some clinging images that reveal her secret kinship with the Queen, and that align her with Goneril and Regan rather than Cordelia. When Posthumus thinks her false, he gives her diamond ring to Iachimo, saying, 'Here, take this too / It is a basilisk unto mine eye, / Kills me to look on't' (II.iv.106–8). A similarly uneasy image appears when Imogen says that she wishes her father and Cloten together in Africa, 'myself by with a needle, that I might prick / The goer-back' (I.ii.99–100). The needle image is associated with her eye when she says that she looked at the departing Posthumus until 'The diminution / Of space had pointed him sharp as my needle' (I.iv.18–19). Later, when Imogen and Posthumus have been reunited, he calls attention to the way 'Posthumus anchors upon Imogen; / And she (like harmless lightning) throws her eye / On him: her brothers, me: her master hitting / Each object with a joy' (v.v.394–7). The second image attempts to soften the impact of the lightning image, but the line still recalls the 'fierce eyes' of Goneril and Regan, and the unease of the 'unsunn'd snow' image.

Despite the implied criticism of too rigidly denying sexual desire, there are in the play remnants of the jaded vision of *Troilus and Cressida* that show themselves in that part of the plot that parallels *Othello*. When maligning Posthumus, Iachimo says, 'The cloyed will – / That satiate yet unsatisfied desire, that tub / Both fill'd and running – ravening first the lamb, / Longs after for the garbage' (I.vi.47–50). The image suggests Hamlet's vision of Gertrude's desire for Claudius, as well as the images surrounding Helen and Cressida. Cymbeline's court becomes like the one that Goneril says that Lear has made of hers, when Imogen tells Iachimo that if her father approves of Iachimo's advances his court will become a 'Romish stew.'

These discordant notes around the issue of woman's sexuality seem part of an effort to maintain an idealized female image, and at the same time to blame men for denying woman's sexuality by insisting on too absolute an ideal. Imogen's belief in Posthumus' virtue despite Iachimo's lies, clearly contrasts to his failure to believe in her. But Posthumus repents, not so much for that as for his excessive rage, when he says, 'You married ones, / If each of you should take this course, how many / Must murder wives much better than themselves / For wrying but a little? (v.i.2–5). By implication he takes responsibility for and identifies with Cloten when, accepting the handkerchief that Othello rejected, he puts it around his neck, thinking it stained with Imogen's blood. Since Cloten has carried into his grave the fullest expression of sexual hatred, Posthumus' punishment is lighter. But before he can win Imogen he, like Leontes and Ferdinand, must submit willingly to a therapeutic punishment. Having been praised by Cymbeline for his heroic deeds in the battle against Rome, he seeks imprisonment by disguising himself as a Roman soldier. In casting himself as a traitor he interprets his murder of Imogen as a crime against Cymbeline's paternal authority.

Posthumus' restorative vision in prison most clearly articulates the ideology based on correct familial relations. In a scene reminiscent of the ritualized end of *Richard III*, Posthumus in a dream vision resurrects the parents and brothers disposed of by previous protagonists. Circling his figure, they praise his heroic virtue, lament his 'needless jealousy' that tainted his 'nobler heart,' and call on Jupiter for help. Jupiter himself then promises full restoration, happiness, and health for Posthumus and for Britain, saying, '"When as a lion's whelp shall, to himself unknown, without seeking find, and be embrac'd by a piece of tender air: and when from a stately cedar shall be lopp'd branches, which, being dead many years, shall after revive, be jointed to the old stock, and freshly grow, then shall Posthumus end his miseries, Britain be fortunate, and flourish in peace and plenty'" (v.iv.137–45). As we are told later, the lion's whelp is Posthumus, also called Leonatus, Imogen is the tender air, and the stately cedar is Cymbeline, who will flourish with the return of his lost sons.

Jupiter's prophecy, which also sanctifies Posthumus' union with Imogen, makes explicit the links that are implicit in the whole of the concluding action. Posthumus' union with Imogen depends upon his being reconciled to his lowly family. Only through that reconciliation can he obtain Jupiter's blessing, which in turn associates the health of Posthumus' family with that of the imperial throne Jupiter represents.[7] This interdependence of family, hierarchical commonwealth, and love, reveals the conceptual context of the enormous symbolic freighting of female figures throughout the plays. When Shakespeare's protagonists in any way tarnish their imagination of radiantly perfect women, all aspects of their lives fall into disarray and the monsters of the deep threaten to emerge. To batten down the hatches, Cymbeline generates in Posthumus' dream an idealized vision of correct hierarchical order as prelude to the restoration of his lost sons, which is coincident with the confession and death of the queen, and with Imogen's return.

The connection between the two issues is also made through the debate between Cymbeline's lost sons and their supposed father, Belarius, on whether it is right to fight for Cymbeline in his war against Rome, that uncertainty being a ramification of Cymbeline's defection from Roman paternal authority. The whole question is handled with uneasy tact; much is made of British military glory when the sons along with Posthumus are victorious in battle, but the play's resolution rests on Cymbeline's willing submission to Rome. In this confusion Imogen appears free from the taint of treachery that might have accompanied her service of a Roman master in a way that dimly recalls the French army Cordelia brought to rescue Lear, and Fortinbras establishing Norway's claim to Denmark while praising Hamlet. It is difficult to know the political significance of these elements, but the unease with which the motif is handled suggests that Shakespeare was aware that Cymbeline's submission to Rome, important for the moral themes of his play, had potentially disturbing implications.

The deeper range of feelings that inform similar situations and characters in earlier plays are submerged, as in *Pericles*, by the static symbolism and improbability of the action, which shows Cymbeline repressing rather than resolving the conflicts that have shaped his story. Having distanced his sexual project in Posthumus' story, he had made some compromise with sexuality by allowing Posthumus to have his Imogen, but only after Posthumus had submitted to punishment, overtly for having doubted Imogen, but implicitly for having aspired above his rank. By the time they are united the social distance between them is reduced by the return of Cymbeline's sons. But as Posthumus submits to punishment by Cymbeline to win his dream of renewal, so Cymbeline correspondingly submits to Roman authority, the most height-ened version of paternal authority rendered in the symbol of the imperial eagle and the god Jupiter, but he also now defines himself as alone, and to be succeeded by a son who is also wifeless. He still cannot merge a vision of mature authority with one of sexuality. A sexual possibility remains remote from him in Posthumus' very distanced dream family and in that last image of Imogen as a fruit hanging on Posthumus' branches, which allows consid-erably more sensuousness than images of temples and diamonds, but at the price of imaginative power and resonance. The plays that follow *Cymbeline* are also shaped primarily by the urgent need for a harmonious vision, but in them Shakespeare found different ways to tap emotional depth, in *The Win-ter's Tale* by keeping emotional realism separate from idealized possibilities, and in *The Tempest* by passionately embracing the controlling impulse itself.[8]

The Winter's Tale starts where Cymbeline leaves off. Cymbeline and the Queen are the first mature, married couple since *Macbeth*, and represent an advance in dealing with the problem of the family, since they both have children. This approach to a family is distanced by the Queen's being Cymbe-line's second wife, and their lacking children in common. *The Winter's Tale* is the first of Shakespeare's plays in which a mature couple has children, and it places the outbreak of jealousy within an already established family. It also portrays that jealousy as totally within Leontes' character, doing away alto-gether with the projected vice figure – Iago, or Iachimo.

10

From Matter to Magic:
The Winter's Tale

In *Macbeth* Shakespeare expressed the psychic and sexual dynamic of a mature and fully heterosexual relationship through public action that expressed metaphorically the protagonist's private state. In that play Macbeth associates the sexual centre of his mature relationship with a vision of evil and corruption that destroys the relationship and the harmony of the familial state that contains it.

The Winter's Tale more directly than *Macbeth* explicitly concerns itself with family relations and with distorted sexual passions that warp them. In this play, however, the consequent political disorder does not overshadow the family relations. As though in compensation for this greater directness, like the earlier romances it is more emotionally distant. The whole play is not permeated by the force of the protagonist's fantasy; rather the course of Leontes' passion for the most part is sketched rather than fully elaborated, so that we, like the figures with which he populates his world, observe him from a distance. And while his compulsive passions shape the lives of the other characters, they do not permeate the language of those characters with multiplying ironies that radiate from a dark centre. Leontes isolates himself in the dark world of his mind, and keeps others as observers outside his orbit rather than drawing them into it, as do Othello or Macbeth. As dreamer, therefore, Leontes has isolated his own figure as a strategy to preserve idealized surroundings that can rescue him from the passions to which he gives licence.

Within that safety Leontes boldly defines himself as king, husband, and father. In Hermione he has generated a stronger version of the good woman than have other protagonists. He allows her to be mother as well as wife, endows her with adult dignity and articulateness rather than virginal virtues, and he refrains from generating an Iago on whom to project his self-hatred and self-blame. At the same time, remote from himself initially, he generates an alternate self-image, clothed in nostalgia, of a presexual innocence that suggests the conflict shortly to become overt. Camillo and Archidamus surround the early affection between Leontes and Polixenes with idyllic romance that is opposed to and invulnerable to any 'matter or malice' of the present. Archidamus links that golden past with the present by juxtaposing it to Leontes' son, Mamillius, when after confirming the abiding love between Leontes and Polixenes he adds, 'You have an unspeakable comfort of your young prince Mamillius' (1.i.34–5). The configuration suggests that Polixenes represents Leontes' effort to retreat from mature sexuality into nostalgia for a simpler past, an attempt that later, ironically, revives the infantile roots of the sexual conflict it was intended to suppress.[1]

The erotic colouring of the two kings' early relationship appears when Archidamus describes how through the years they have exchanged gifts, sent 'loving embassies,' and 'though absent; shook hands, as over a vast; and embraced, as it were, from the ends of opposed winds' (1.i.28–32). Polixenes adds a sensuous note in saying, 'We were as twinn'd lambs that did frisk i' th' sun, / And bleat the one at th' other' (1.ii.67–8). Leontes clothes his homoerotic impulses in the vision of childhood purity, and opposes that prelapsarian purity to the world of women. He equates heterosexuality with the Fall, and by implication with all consequent evil and corruption, when Polixenes says that had they remained in their childhood world they 'should have answer'd heaven / Boldly "not guilty," the imposition clear'd / Hereditary ours' (1.ii.69–74). To Hermione's surmise that they must have 'tripped since,' he responds by associating prelapsarian innocence with ignorance of women, particularly of wives, when he says 'In those unfledg'd days was my wife a girl; / Your precious self had then not cross'd the eyes / Of my young playfellow' (1.ii.78–80). Hermione's objection spells out the implication: 'Of this make no conclusion, lest you say / Your queen and I are devils' (1.ii.81–2), especially since even as she says those words Leontes is already in the process of transforming her into a devil. Leontes sees even sexuality legitimized within marriage as the source of sin and corruption in contrast to a vaguely erotic male childhood companionship.[2]

Leontes compensates for his hidden association of women with evil by idealizing Hermione. This psychological strategy makes him like a person whose marriage appears to others ideal, but whose perfect-seeming wife makes him feel rebuked for his unacknowledged dark imagination of women, isolated, unloved, and empty within the image of familial bliss. Leontes expresses such dissatisfaction in calling into his present, 'over a vast,' feelings that he associates with past happiness, only to find, once he materializes Polixenes, that he has opened the hornets' nest from which his feeling of emptiness and nostalgia was designed to protect him.

The relation between the sexual conflict hidden in Leontes' nostalgia and his mature sexuality appears in the strained urgency with which he persuades his friend to stay, and Polixenes' equally unexplained urgency to depart. It appears as well in the fusion of Polixenes' visit with the onset of Leontes' jealousy. When Leontes ignores Polixenes' protest that to hinder his return home 'were (in your love) a whip to me' (I.ii.25), he seems jealous of his friend's obligations that take him away; at the same time his desire to be rid of him appears in Polixenes' determination to leave. The lack of naturalistic explanation for the urgency of either figure emphasizes the psychological significance for Leontes of his almost equal desires to keep Polixenes, and the associated idyllic childhood, present, and to avoid the revival of infantile conflicts hidden beneath and expressed in the nostalgic aura. Though not explicitly sexual, the intense love between the two men, placed in the past but carried to the present by association with Mamillius, functions as an alternative to Leontes' relationship to Hermione.

In Hermione's successful petition Leontes expresses his desire to keep Polixenes at hand, while he handles the implicit dangers by imagining the two together. Leontes' unease with his wife's sexuality appears when he casts himself in the role of a rejected lover while his wife flirts with his friend. Leontes says that she has for the second time 'said well,' the first time being when 'three crabbed months had sour'd themselves to death, / Ere I could make thee open thy white hand / And clap thyself my love' (I.ii.102–4). When Hermione gives that white hand to Polixenes and engages him in talk of their past, Leontes achieves the configuration from which can emerge all in his emotional life that violates his self-image. The intensity acquires the quality of a dream within a dream, as Leontes observes their retreating figures and murmurs 'too hot, too hot.'

During the trial scene Hermione says, 'You speak a language that I understand not: / My life stands in the level of your dreams, / Which I'll lay down' (III.ii.80–2). A distanced level of Leontes' awareness, externalized in the plot, maintains an innocent Hermione, while most of his consciousness succumbs to the explosion of feeling expressed in his sudden jealousy. Like Othello, he maintains the split image of the woman, the good and the bad, in two levels of consciousness rather than in two figures. In the plot configuration he keeps Hermione ideally innocent, while his own figure is overwhelmed by a vision of women as besmirched and betraying. Though less naturalistic, this event is comparable to the decisive psychic moments of other plays. The content of Leontes' experience is most like Othello's, but the quality of it is like Macbeth's, except that Macbeth experiences an altered state of consciousness, whereas Leontes denies, even while he betrays knowledge of, his state of mind when he says, 'Your actions are my dreams. / You had a bastard by Polixenes, / And I but dream'd it!' (III.ii.82–4). In another very convoluted passage, Leontes reflects on the relationship between dream and reality, seeming in the process to attribute greater reality to dream:

Affection! thy intention stabs the centre:
Thou dost make possible things not so held,
Communicat'st with dreams; – how can this be? –
With what's unreal thou coactive art,
And fellow'st nothing: then, 'tis very credent
Thou may'st co-join with something; and thou dost,
(And that beyond commission) and I find it,
(And that to the infection of my brains
And hard'ning of my brows). (I.ii.138–46)

Whether Leontes refers to Hermione's dream of affection, which then finds a real object, or to his own affection for her that has generated his dream of her infidelity, the passage indicates a brief moment of struggle before he detaches himself from his sense of ordinary reality and allows his compulsive passion to overwhelm his consciousness.

Leontes has been flirting on the edges of his inner dream from the moment he asked Hermione to persuade Polixenes to stay, as though wanting an opportunity to bring to the surface, to 'co-join with something' what his unknown passions were already generating. Before committing himself totally to his compulsions he, like Othello, makes one effort to keep his dream from becoming nightmare: 'This entertainment / May a free face put on, derive a liberty / From heartiness, from bounty, fertile bosom, / And well become the agent: 't may, I grant'(I.ii.111–114). Like Macbeth, he foresees the loss entailed in satisfying his darker desires when he counters Camillo's efforts to dissuade him by opposing to uncommon desires an inadequate common sense. Leontes thinks he could not be so 'muddy' as to sully

The purity and whiteness of my sheets,
(Which to preserve is sleep, which being spotted
Is goads, thorns, nettles, tails of wasps)
Give scandal to the blood o' th' prince, my son,
(Who I do think is mine and love as mine)
Without ripe moving to't? (I.ii.321–32)

Leontes cannot forgo his new image of Hermione for two reasons. First, even though he says that Hermione's actions are his dreams, he cannot conceive how he might desire what he fears. Second, the image of a sullied Hermione and betraying friend frees him from the painful contrast between himself and a radiant Hermione. His fantasy allows him to externalize in her the self-hatred that previously festered inside him. Hermione must be guilty, because if she is not, then he is.

Having substituted Polixenes for his own figure, Leontes vents his image of sexuality in language like Iago's when he sees Polixenes and Hermione 'paddling palms and pinching fingers,' and reflects that there is many a man 'That little thinks she has been sluiced in's absence / And his pond fished by his next neighbor' (1.ii.192–5). Women, as false 'as o'er-dy'd blacks, as wind, as waters' bring disease – 'were my wife's liver / Infected as her life' (1.ii.304–5) – that both infects men's sexuality and turns them into objects of ridicule.

While Lear expressed the process of his diseased imagination by casting himself in progressively more infantile roles, Leontes in a more detached way undergoes a similar process signified by his changing views of his own children. His already established identification with Mamillius becomes firmer when he sees him, and by implication himself, as a product of the foul adult sexuality he imagines between Hermione and Polixenes. As he and his son talk of childhood innocence, Leontes seeks detachment from the image of himself as child when, with pretended playfulness, he questions his paternity, asking Mamillius, 'Art thou my boy?' and observing that he has 'smutch'd [his] nose.' As Lear uses the smells of hell to describe women's genitals when he says 'there is the sulphurous pit: burning, scalding, stench, consumption,' so Leontes sees in the dirt on his son's nose traces of sexuality needful for conception. It brings to his mind images of bestiality, which he translates into images of cuckoldry by concentrating on horned animals, 'the steer, the heifer and the calf,' when he punningly tells Mamillius that he must be 'neat.' While he sees Hermione 'still virginalling / Upon his palm!' Mamillius, as a 'wanton calf,' becomes a metaphor for and sign of Leontes' belief that his wanton wife has given him cuckold's horns. The previously innocent-seeming animal imagery that described himself and Polixenes as 'twinn'd lambs that did frisk i' th' sun' now clearly is tarnished by sexuality, and he attempts to repudiate this now disturbing image by breaking his identification with the child, discounting the physical resemblance that, he says, women affirm.

Leontes' retreat from and advance towards his son reproduce the ambivalent movements he made towards Polixenes. Each time he draws Mamillius to him, the proximity intensifies his repulsion and turns his endearments into rejections. He calls Mamillius 'sweet villain! / Most dear'st! my collop!' then reflects, 'Can thy dam?' The image of Hermione as a 'dam' joins Hermione and his son, both male and female sexuality, within animal-like lowness. But being identified with his son, Leontes expresses his own sexuality in his images of Mamillius, and gives the lie to the prelapsarian innocence he had wanted as an alternative to mature heterosexuality. This process becomes clearer when he explains his distraction to Hermione by saying that 'this kernel, this squash, this gentleman' reminded him of himself as a child 'unbreech'd, / In my green velvet coat; my dagger muzzled / Lest it should bite its master, and so prove, / As ornaments oft do, too dangerous' (i.ii.155–8). In the process of repudiating it, he deepens his identification with his son within a recollection of childhood that has changed colour. The muzzled dagger suggests the erotically violent passions that were hidden in the idyllic memories, which now, having been unmuzzled, are biting their master. He makes a last effort to keep the image of childhood innocence uncontaminated when he says 'Give me this boy: / I am glad you did not nurse him: / Though he does bear some signs of me, yet you / Have too much blood in him' (ii.i.55–7). But he is unsuccessful, and at his command Mamillius disappears and, unlike his sister, is not resurrected, suggesting that Leontes decisively has repressed the homosexuality he associates with his childhood.[3]

Like Lear, he moves from an image of himself as a boy to one of himself as an infant, when Paulina brings his baby daughter, whom he with less obvious ambivalence but also less finality, obliterates. Enraged at the child for representing her mother's unreliable sexuality, he enacts Lady Macbeth's image when he says, 'The bastard brains with these my proper hands / Shall I dash out. Go, take it to the fire' (ii.iii.139–40). Along with the child, he repudiates his wife's sexuality, which generates children, and himself as a trusting infant at a maternal breast.

But eliminating with these figures his childlike feelings from his consciousness increases rather than diminishes their power to colour his perception of his entire world. Within the overriding safety of his fairy-tale world in which an ideally good Hermione is empowered to punish and cancel the consequences of his attemped crimes, he indulges what now becomes a fully paranoid vision that justifies his rage. Seeing all his court in a conspiracy of silent mockery, he associates Polixenes' and Hermione's supposed sexual betrayal with political conspiracy. He enters a self-enclosed and self-confirming system which uses all contrary evidence as grist for its mill.

The distance between Leontes' passion and the idealized world kept present by other figures appears in the unique way in which this play's most powerful image lacks resonance elsewhere in this text, but in other plays epitomizes both male and female sexuality with betrayal, cruelty, cannibalism, and death. Leontes, caught in his paranoid vortex and reflecting on the pain he incurs from his 'true opinion,' says,

> There may be in the cup
> A spider steep'd, and one may drink, depart,
> And yet partake no venom, (for his knowledge
> Is not infected); but if one present
> Th' abhorr'd ingredient to his eye, make known
> How he hath drunk, he cracks his gorge, his sides,
> With violent hefts. I have drunk, and seen the spider. (II.i.36–45)

The spider in the cup is an image of the way in which Leontes' conception of sexuality poisons his imagination of social and creature pleasures. The immediate context associates the spider with Hermione's supposed infidelity, and by extension to her sexuality, which Leontes has already described in images of disease and bestiality. He now adds to these an image of women, like spiders, deceitfully luring men into beautiful-seeming nets, like the snare from which Antony momentarily escapes, in order to poison and devour them. But the implicit net image is also suitable for Leontes' entanglement in his paranoid fantasy spun out of his own imagination. He both places himself outside of the image, and implies a secret recognition of his own complicity by attributing to his own knowledge the power to render the spider poisonous. He experiences with sharply focused intensity the nausea that has been suggested by previous images. If one sees Leontes' experience of the spider in relation to the nausea Hamlet felt before he directed Yorick's skull into 'my lady's chamber,' then Leontes confronts in the spider an image of the snare-producing womb that transforms men to insects and becomes their tomb as they are devoured.[4]

While on one level of consciousness Leontes allows his imagination full licence to project itself onto the figures with which he populates his world, on another level, as said before, he keeps at a distance from himself a reversed image in which a good world can release him from his evil impulses. This split consciousness is expressed most dramatically in the trial scene. His own figure expresses his impregnable fantasy system and the impossibility of a solution to the polarity in which it has entangled him, while in the other figures he clings to a vision of a world that will save him from himself. Both sides of his desire, and the self-confirming mechanism of his fantasy, appear in his deafness to Hermione's clarion assertion of her innocence. When the oracle most uncharacteristically and unambiguously affirms Hermione's guiltlessness he says, 'There is no truth at all i' th' Oracle; / The sessions shall proceed: this is mere falsehood' (III.ii.140–1). It is as though Leontes says of himself that even if the gods themselves should speak, which they never do, their intervention could not release him from the snare of his passions. As was the case with Macbeth, only by being enacted can the power of those passions be depleted. Therefore it is not the oracle but news of Mamillius' and Hermione's deaths that dissipate his compulsive desires. Having obliterated from consciousness both child and adult versions of male and female figures, he experiences himself as awakening from dreamlike compulsions. He defines himself now as in isolation and remorse, but on the periphery of his consciousness he has already set in motion the figures who, by punishing him, will revoke the seemingly irrevocable consequences of his action to provide a dream of a love consummated otherwise than in death.[5]

However, the process by which Leontes tries to persuade himself of the reality of fairy-tales reveals the same network of fears and desires from which he seeks rescue. Leontes' split consciousness generates two worlds. In Sicilia he replaces Hermione with Paulina, to whom he in his own figure becomes a submissive and punished child. In the overtly fairy-tale realm of Bohemia Perdita replaces Hermione as idealized female. There, the storm that destroys the ship and drowns the men, and the bear that devours Antigonus are the displaced and removed remnants of Leontes' rage and jealous passion. Like Lear's, his storm, which wears itself out on Bohemia's shores, functions as an externalized image of his inner upheaval, and the bear, humorous in the stage direction, retains its force when the clown relates how it devours Antigonus' shoulder bone and is about to consume the rest of him.[6] The bear is a distanced image of Leontes' fears, but also frees Paulina of a husband so that she can become a quasi-maternal figure for him.

In opposition to those forces represented by the storm and the bear, Leontes generates and excludes his own contaminating figure from a quasi-magical world in which a providentially benign nature and beneficent coincidence cancel ordinary causality amid elements of realism that remain oddly juxtaposed to images of the transcendently improbable. In this way Leontes refuses to admit the impossibility of the event he needs to effect his cure. Signs of his uneasy attempt to join the fairy-tale vision, in which impediments to love are external to the lovers, to a probable world appear in several ways, but are first notable in Autolycus, whose single plot function, one that could have been accomplished in other ways, is to expedite the process which proves Perdita's true parentage. Dramatically, however, his comic debasement of the otherwise golden world prevents a full polarization of Sicilia and Bohemia that would completely divorce from each other the realms of tragic consequence and comic resolution. Autolycus' presence in Bohemia asserts the possibility of lives being brought to redeeming resolution through accidental and unlikely but real instruments. Autolycus himself comments on the irony of his having unwittingly brought about the reconciliation between children and parents, when only the thought of profit can console him for the loss of his trickster pleasures. He is a kind of Puck without a master, or one whose master is concealed in the force of benign accident that, when it assumes the lineaments of Prospero, will turn him into Ariel. As well, as the comic rogue, Autolycus further links the pastoral Bohemia to the more probable Sicilia, which contains in Paulina another quasi-trickster figure.

The other element in Bohemia by which Leontes reveals his disbelief in the restoration he generates appears in the logical problems that are involved in the portrayal of Polixenes' anger at Florizel for wanting to marry a peasant girl, an episode that echoes his own anger at Hermione. The incompatability of probable causality with idealized fantasy appears when Polixenes, despite previously having observed of Perdita that 'nothing she does or seems / But smacks of something greater than herself, / Too noble for this place' (IV.iv.157–9), threatens Perdita with death and Florizel with disinheritance should they persist in their love. Though Perdita's beauty, which makes her the 'queen of curds and cream' (IV.iv.161), and her charming boldness in asserting that 'The selfsame sun that shines upon his court / Hides not his visage from our cottage' (IV.iv.475–6), cast Polixenes in an unsympathetic light, the social appropriateness of his anger is confirmed by Florizel's secrecy. He is illogically blamed for his unavoidable ignorance that Perdita is an appropriate choice for his son.

This disparity of levels produces a false analogy that shows Leontes' dream of restoration to be at cross-purposes to his own unacknowledged conception of reality. Our knowledge that Polixenes' anger is inappropriate to the 'true' circumstances creates a parallel between him and Leontes, for both figures discern evil where there is none. The overt point of the parallel is that true value or virtue is hidden beneath appearances, its perception requiring, as Paulina tells Leontes, an awakening of faith. The implied argument is that as Leontes should have known Hermione's worth, so Polixenes should have known Perdita's. But Leontes undermines the argument, for as we have seen, he gives himself no excuse to suspect Hermione other than the normal flirtatiousness of men and women. But he gives Polixenes good reason to object to his son's behaviour and so deviously expresses his unbelief in the resolution he generates through the distanced images of himself and of Hermione in the figures of Florizel and Perdita.

In this way the play indulges the romantic fantasy that true love can transcend all social obstacles and heal all spiritual wounds, while at the same time guaranteeing that this particular true love violates no social propriety. The romantic vision of an ideally loving couple as the source of transcendent spiritual value gains an easy, not to say false, victory over an illusory opposition in the magical world of Bohemia. Polixenes' socially justified outrage is made to seem inappropriate to the magical spirit that can save baby princesses on the seashore.

While Leontes tries to realize in distant Bohemia his idealized images of lovers free from destructive emotions, in Sicilia he submits himself to the punitive parental figure he has generated in Paulina.[7] His unease appears in the discrepancy between her depiction as a comic shrew, by which he restrains the frightening dimensions associated with similarly powerful female figures in other plays, and the gravity of the context. This mixed tone surrounding Paulina's portrayal is significant in relation to Hermione. Having allowed within his horizon a powerful woman, Leontes has tried to disperse her power over him by thinking her sullied, and to obliterate her maternal force by depriving her of children. He then avoids the love-death paradigm by collapsing into a passive and childlike submission to an alternate and semi-comic maternal figure, taming in the comically tinged Paulina the more awesome dimensions he has attributed to Hermione, and replacing in his own person the child-figures he has eliminated. Within the protected magical aura at the periphery of his consciousness represented by Bohemia, he allows himself, on condition of thinking it punishment, the passive gratification of becoming a version of Lear. In Paulina's not-so-kind nursery he finds a comic compromise between those nurseries that Cordelia and Goneril and Regan might provide on which to lay his head.[8]

Under the guise of submission to the process of spiritual regeneration, Leontes satisfies his desire for maternal nurturing. That nurturing, however, retains sexual overtones, and thereby betrays his association of sexuality with incest, because of the concealed identification of the now maternal Paulina with Hermione, and it acquires masochistic dimensions from being placed in a context that fuses it with punishment. Paulina's identification with Hermione appears most strongly in relation to the punitive force of both figures. In order to keep Leontes in constant self-castigation, Paulina accuses him of Hermione's murder while reminding him of her unparalleled virtues. With painful pleasure he co-operates by acknowledging his guilt and adding, 'but thou strik'st me / Sorely, to say I did: it is as bitter / Upon thy tongue as in my thought. Now, good now, / Say so but seldom' (v.i.17-20). Paulina's figure merges with an image of Hermione as a punishing ghost when, after having timidly suggested that he might remarry, Leontes agrees with Paulina that if he married 'one worse, / And better us'd,' Hermione's offended ghost 'would incense me / To murder her I married' (v.i.61-2). The new wife and the ghostly Hermione become a single image that punishes him by reinforcing his guilt. With his guilt comes his rage, so that he kills again in a cycle of guilt that increases through his efforts to deny it, just as he intensified the image of himself as a child by trying to destroy it. Paulina both identifies herself with the ghostly Hermione and emphasizes her punitive fury when she says that if she were the ghost, she would 'bid you mark / Her eye, and tell me for what dull part in't / You chose her: then I'd shriek, that even your ears / Should rift to hear me; and the words that follow'd / Should be, "Remember mine"'(v.i.63–7). Understandably, Leontes capitulates: 'I'll have no wife, Paulina.'

Having eliminated the homosexual alternative with Mamillius' death, Leontes has left only two versions of the same image – a vision of himself in a childlike celibacy that conceals frightening masochistic impulses, and one of mature sexuality in which women become avenging mothers. To escape these and to retrieve his identity as husband and father, he defines Paulina's maternal power as magically restorative, and calls on the machinery he has kept all along in the wings.

In Paulina he fuses the maternal punitive power, shades of the bad mother, with the beneficent good mother as she stage-manages the return of the lost. When Paulina makes Leontes promise not to remarry until 'Your first queen's again in breath,' Perdita is about to reappear in fulfilment of the oracles' prediction that 'the king shall live without an heir, if that which is lost be not found' (III.ii.134–6). Though we do not as yet know that Hermione will also reappear, the seeming impossibility of her doing so is brought into relationship with the violation of probability already coming to pass in Perdita's reappearance. The images of Perdita and Hermione begin to merge with each other, and both become associated with a semi-magical quality associated with Paulina. A more mature version of Rosalind, Paulina has mysterious power both to spirit Hermione away for sixteen years and to orchestrate her resurrection along with Perdita's. Like her person, Paulina's strategies hover between an inadequately explained naturalistic realm and an incomplete magical one.

Within this uneasy union of naturalistic emotions and magical resolution Leontes clothes the complex incestuous feelings for mothers and daughters in the aura of spiritual redemption. As said earlier, Leontes associates Perdita with the passive and vulnerable self that he rejected in the process of recoiling from the image of woman as mother. At the cost of their sexuality, Lear and Pericles tried to purify their image of the young female by separating her from the fearsome maternal image and from themselves. Leontes reveals the fundamental identity of mother and daughter images in the way the images of Perdita and Hermione overlie each other. Both the interdependence and coincidental timing of their return and verbal associations identify them. The third gentleman tells how Leontes said 'O, thy mother, thy mother!' when he looks on his daughter, and of how 'the majesty of the creature in resemblance of the mother, the affection of nobleness which nature shows above her breeding, and many other evidences proclaim her with all certainty, to be the king's daughter' (v.ii.35–41). To reclaim the daughter is to reclaim the mother, but since Leontes envisions a sexual reunion with the woman as wife, the incestuous basis of his feelings for his daughter are revealed in the identification of the two, which emphasizes Hermione's maternal function.[9] Though Leontes consciously feels that his having submitted to punishment has freed him from the destructive desires that caused him to lose Hermione and Perdita, both the punishment and the restoration show, in greater concealment and in different tones, the same configurations that they were designed to obliterate. Only fairy-tale and magical forms can represent his restoration because there is nothing in the imagery to suggest an inner transformation of his desires, which alone would eliminate his need for both punitive and restorative mothers.

The concluding episodes of *The Winter's Tale* replace the tortured sexuality of the first part with an ideological fairy-tale. Leontes is reunited with Hermione, Florizel and Perdita become the magically ideal heterosexual pair whose flawless but unexplored love will reunite the two divided kingdoms, and by implication the division in Leontes' soul. The suggestion of sexual masochism involved in Leontes' submission to Paulina is replaced by a more or less Christian ideology, for Hermione's 'resurrection' implies that if one accepts one's guilt and embraces punishment, suffering will not only change one's psychic and emotional structure but will also obliterate the consequences of evil. The play recognizes the dream-vision quality of its resolution, but it turns that recognition into another kind of ideology. The comparisons between the stage action and old tales, which increase in frequency as the play draws to its close, suggest that old tales – by implication the play itself – carry into life an ideology of redemption that can compensate for life's failures. Also, the self-reflexive references to the action, particularly in connection with Hermione's revival, as being like that in a play imply that the work of art can come to life and obliterate the distinction between dream-vision and reality. There is a curious double motion. On the one hand the end of the play shows life becoming art – an old tale, a play, a statue – and in so doing obscures the unresolved conflicts depicted on a naturalistic plane. But on the other hand, as though uneasy at that evasion, the play attemps also to assert that art, the statue, can re-enter the realm of life to become flesh.[10]

Shakespeare abandoned that attempt in *The Tempest*. At the same time as he reversed the power relation between man and woman, giving Paulina's magical power to a more than paternal Prospero, he also gave up the effort to envision an unambiguously good and powerful female, and moved fully into the magical realm, abandoning naturalistic causality. However, in *The Tempest* the structure and detail of the fairy-tale resolution still betray both the problems that require such strenuous control and its human cost.

11

Failure in Success:
The Tempest

There are many analogues between Prospero's figure and both major and minor characters in preceding plays, but Prospero's self-definiton as a magician reaches back into obscure corners of the plotting and language of the plays that stretch behind him. His role as magus emerges from and is composed of the various ways in which magic was manifested in the earlier plays. He can be seen as Rosalind's non-existent magical uncle, wise in the ways of love, emerging from his shadowy forest, or as Portia's dead father returned to life. Since he arranges all the circumstances of his play through his magic, he also replaces the benign accidents that bring the comedies to their happy conclusions, and that become the transcendent providence of the romances. Though he has clear relations to some tragic protagonists, particularly King Lear, and though he might be seen as a cleverer version of Friar Lawrence, it would seem at first glance that he has little connection to the passions that move tragic protagonists to their deaths. However, Antony attributes his tragic decline to the magic of Cleopatra's compelling charms, and he also experiences his problematic relation to the paternal values represented by Octavius as an inimical magic; these two versions of bad or black magic merge, are contrasted to, and overcome the good magic of Hercules who leaves Antony. These images that render passion as magic relate to the compelling emotions that seized previous protagonists in their moments of altered consciousness: Macbeth's transfixed state, Hamlet's melancholy, Othello's jealous seizure. These states were not directly related to the magical, but were related to the supernatural elements in the plays: *Macbeth*'s witches, *Hamlet*'s ghost, and the aura of the diabolic in *Othello*. These generally supernatural elements are more specifically related to magic through the bad magic of the depleted figure of Sycorax, whom in the realm of magic Prospero casts as his antagonist. Therefore, the magical powers to which Antony casts himself as victim can be seen as a version of the fears and desires that overcome the protagonists who precede him. Prospero's magic, then, derives from the providential power over time and circumstance of the comedies, but it is infused with the same dark passions, those that led his tragic forebears to their deaths, that he seeks to control by its means.

In so shaping and endowing his magus protagonist, Shakespeare seems to have found what in the other plays he uneasily sought – a means by which all image could become event without creating conflicts between the symbolic and the plausible. The play's economy and obedience to the dramatic unities reflects its protagonist's endowment of himself with commanding powers to control others. Except for the 'accident most strange' by which Fortune brought his enemies to his shore, and which delineates the limits of his powers and the function of his knowledge, Prospero arranges what constitutes reality for the other figures, and places himself beyond the realm of accident while they find themselves subject to the incomprehensible forces that ruled the lives of previous protagonists.[1] In these corrupt but controlled figures Prospero represents his denied desires, which have been drained of the energy he has converted into the magic by which he controls them in the name of a higher reality.[2] In this way he sharply divides his magical powers from the externalized images of his unruly passions. On condition of this self-restraint Prospero allows himself what was denied to other protagonists; he has lost his dukedom, but not his daughter.

Prospero distances himself from and illustrates his supremacy over ordinary political power and its attendant passions in the storm he generates and controls. 'What care these roarers for the name of King' (I.i.16–17), says the Boatswain as he brushes aside Gonzalo and the court party who want to assert their hierarchical authority. In the Boatswain's challenge Prospero shows his contempt for those whose disordered passions have generated the tempest that has no care for the name of king, but has for the name of Prospero. The upheaval of the elements therefore represents social upheaval, its consequences, and the punishment of those responsible, and Prospero's more than political power emerges from a past in which, like Edgar, he cast himself as victim in order to emerge as agent of moral retribution and reformation.

The story Prospero tells Miranda from 'the dark backward and abysm of time' (I.ii.50), reveals the preceding murky emotional level that conditions the present configuration. His past story joins and relates to each other his own struggle with parental forms of power, the sexual implications of both his love of his brother and of Miranda, and the psychic sources of his magic. He focuses first on male power struggles when he tells Miranda that twelve years previously he was 'a prince of power,' that Milan was 'the first' among all the signories, and that 'Prospero the prime duke, being so reputed / In dignity, and for the liberal Arts / Without a parallel' (I.ii.72–4). Prospero equates his dukedom's power with his own reputation for study in the 'liberal arts' and the 'secret studies' for which he withdrew from power. In the image he defines books as a more virtuous means by which to achieve power than arms, at the same time that he disclaims ambition, defining himself as a 'poor man' for whom his library was 'dukedom large enough' (I.ii.109–10). The books prized 'above [his] dukedom' with which Gonzalo kindly equipped his journey are the same books that Caliban knows as the source of his master's power, and that Prospero eventually will drown. In view of that, his past stance as innocent victim of his usurping brother and of King Alonso conceals the ambitions that he represents in the figures over whom in the present he assumes control.[3]

In the configuration he defines as past Prospero has gratified his desire for what he believes to be wrongful power and assuages the attendant guilt by casting himself, Lear-like, as victim of the power of his brother, through whom he expresses his own craving for what he defines as illicit power. His identification with Antonio appears in his love for him, but that love contains a threatening erotic component that appears when Prospero says that Antonio, having turned all hearts in the state against him, became 'The ivy which hid my princely trunk, / And suck'd my verdure out on't' (I.ii.86–7). Prospero images himself as the masculine tree trunk, and Antonio acquires a feminine overtone as the ivy that, like female genitals, deprives the male member of its vitality. But a phallus loses its 'verdure' when it discharges its seed, a suggestion that Prospero develops when he says that his trust, like that of a good parent, in Antonio, 'did beget of him / A falsehood in its contrary, as great / As my trust was' (I.ii.94–6). In the image Prospero's loving trust becomes a seed that impregnates Antonio with evil. That sexual suggestiveness within the spreading evil makes Prospero's passivity to Antonio seem full of a luxuriant desire that, interpreted as evil, generates Antonio's corruption.[4] However, the image of begetting that extends the sexual image is concealed under one of parenting, wherein Prospero becomes not brother but father to Antonio, revealing that the fraternal relations displace parental ones.[5]

The concealed parental forms hinted at in Prospero's image also appear in structural configurations. In resigning his power to Antonio Prospero becomes as a son to Antonio, who now literally represents him as duke-father. His hostility to Antonio then expresses his own hostility towards the paternal. Like Lear, Prospero carries the paternal function in his own image, and thereby identifies himself with other father-figures in the play, most obviously Alonso. His victimization of himself to Antonio, therefore, stands for his desire to victimize Alonso, 'This King of Naples, being an enemy / To me inveterate' (I.ii.121–2). The past implacable enmity goes unexplained, but a clue to it can be found in the gap between the Italian city-states of the play's setting and the symbolism inherent in the Elizabethan hierarchy of power with which it is concerned. Prospero, as duke, should owe allegiance to the king, but concerning Milan prior to Antonio's rise to power, Prospero says, 'Through all the signories it was the first, / And Prospero the prime duke'(I.ii.71–2). This, taken together with the 'inveterate enmity' between Prospero and Alonso, suggests a long-term, unresolved power conflict. Prospero attributes to Alonso his own resentment of Alonso's royal power, once more reversing relationships. He therefore sees Alonso, properly the father in terms of the symbolic hierarchy, joining forces with the bad son against him to regain for Naples its rightful ascendancy, though the ascendancy is interpreted by Prospero as wrongful. Therefore his withdrawal from rule represents a conflicted desire to submit to Alonso's paternal authority in a way that will later ensure his supremacy. But, as with Antonio, the temporary submission carries its own gratification. The enmity between Prospero and Alonso participates in the sexuality implied between Prospero and Antonio, when Prospero describes how Alonso and Antonio,

> A treacherous army levied, one midnight
> Fated to th' purpose, did Antonio open
> The gates of Milan; and, i' th' dead of darkness,
> The ministers for th' purpose hurried thence
> Me and thy crying self.   (I.ii.128–32)

The image of the treacherous army that in the 'dead of darkness' opens the gates of Milan does not suggest sexuality directly, but has the aura of a kind of rape of 'fair Milan.' Prospero, in saying that the midnight was 'Fated to th' purpose,' suggests the compulsive forces that Macbeth and Antony experienced as fate or magic. The 'treacherous army' whose men were 'ministers for th' purpose' acquires significance in relation to the later passage in which Ariel, having removed the illusory banquet from the court party, appears as a harpy to punish them for their past sins and says, 'You fools! I and my fellows / Are ministers of Fate' (III.iii.61–2). The fate of which Ariel proclaims himself a minister becomes a universal moral force that, concealed in seemingly accidental events, awakens the dead past so that forgotten wrongdoing will be re-enacted and punished in the present. In this context those treasonous soldiers become ministers of fate who, from Prospero's moral perspective, inflict on him a punishment for past crimes. The full import of that fateful night appears in the last line. Prospero's reward for his temporary submission is not only the power that derives from it; it is also Miranda, who is imagistically born to him on that 'fated midnight,' and who is the central concern of his enterprise, since he says that he has 'done nothing but in care of thee, / Of thee, my dear one; thee my daughter' (1.ii.16–17).

In Miranda and Sycorax, Prospero more radically than any other of Shakespeare's protagonists has split the images of women. The significance of Miranda's infancy is suggested in the fact that Prospero, like Lear, has eliminated from his world any suitable woman for his wife. We know only that Miranda was 'not quite three years old' when Prospero was banished, and while logically she had to have had a mother, her images of one are all but obliterated. When Prospero asks Miranda what she remembers, she vaguely recalls only 'Four or five women once that tended me'(1.ii.47); later Miranda obliterates even that vague suggestion of a motherliness in telling Ferdinand that she has never seen a woman's face other than her own. Prospero avoids the dangers that Othello or Leontes confronted when they unsuccessfully struggled to wrest from filthy pools of sexuality an image of female virginal purity in an aura of maternal loving comfort. Instead, Prospero reduces Miranda and Ferdinand to a neo-Platonically pure couple, whose union symbolizes and ensures the correct ordering of state and cosmos. As such, they together represent the union of cosmic male and female principles, which, blessed by the fertility represented in the masque, ensures the harmony of human affairs. To win this ideal vision of lust-free fecundity Prospero must rigidly control and almost dehumanize himself and Miranda to prevent sexuality from casting its polluting shadow. However, the denied sexuality appears in his separation of Miranda from a mother whose sexual taint might spoil her, and, more important, in the rigid control in which he holds her figure.[6] He limits the attributes by which he defines her to compassion and wonder. Her first words express compassion for the storm-wracked sailors, and her love for Ferdinand comes forth as compassion for the labours he must suffer at Prospero's command, and as wonder at his beauty. Prospero denies her intelligent curiosity, 'More to know / Did never meddle with my thoughts,' and her wonder at Ferdinand and the brave new world prompts no questions to her lips. Nor does she question Prospero's strange behaviour to Ferdinand, but rather accepts Prospero's absolute power. Prospero seems to fear the action of Miranda's mind when he enforces her strict attention as he narrates past events, and when his tale is told he binds her in sleep, preventing her then, or ever, from witnessing his communication with Ariel. As though worried by this extreme constraint, he allows her the freedom of disobeying, in the service of her love, his commands neither to see Ferdinand nor to reveal her name. But he hedges even that freedom by eavesdropping on them and congratulating either Ariel or himself for how well her seeming rebellion conforms to his plans. And finally she transfers to Ferdinand obedience and self-abnegation that previously she had made to Prospero when she says to Ferdinand, 'Yes, for a score of kingdoms you should wrangle, / And I would call it fair play' (v.i.174–5).[7] Prospero's desire to confine and restrain, visible formally in the dramatic limitations of Miranda's figure, prevents her sexuality, associated with corruption and treason, from becoming manifest. Instead of separating himself from the young woman as Lear, Leontes, and Pericles did, Prospero limits her character and action, reduces her to a child, and casts himself as her schoolmaster so that her femininity will not arouse his sexuality, which in turn would sully her figure in his eyes.[8]

The restraint under which he keeps Miranda is an aspect of his self-restraint, which he expresses also in relation to the play's male figures, all of whom he threatens with imprisonment of various kinds. Caliban has been 'Deservedly confin'd' into a rock, the court party is 'confined together,' Ariel, having been released from the cloven pine, is threatened with imprisonment in an oak. The tension between Prospero's impulse to control and the passions that become the more dangerous for being so controlled appears particularly in relation to Ferdinand, who merges with Caliban when Prospero threatens to 'manacle [his] neck and feet together' and makes him, like Caliban, a 'logman.'[9] Ferdinand represents Prospero's idealized self when he, unlike Caliban, shows his essential virtue by willingly submitting to correct authority when he finds that his 'spirits, as in a dream, are all bound up' (I.ii.489). But the threatening union of sexual passion and illicit ambition appear in the imagistic links between Ferdinand, the usurping court party, and the would-be rapist, Caliban. These links render Ferdinand to Caliban what Posthumus is to Cloten.

Prospero's definition of himself as a magus derives from his power to repress his own passions for Miranda, represented in his confinement of other figures. The passions that would otherwise fill out Miranda's portrait instead inform his image of himself as beneficent magician. His tale of the sea journey, which bridges the gap between the image of himself as powerless in the play's past and his power in the play's present, shows the process of this conversion. When Miranda asks whether foul play or blessed circumstance caused their exile, Prospero attributes the compassion that characterizes Miranda to the random winds and seas, which 'with pity sighing back again' do them 'but loving wrong.' Prospero links Miranda with this beneficent providence that guided him to his island when he says she was 'a cherubin' whose smile, 'infused with a fortitude from heaven' (I.ii.152–5), preserved him.

One aspect of Prospero's magical powers therefore represents a sublimated form of the tender beneficence that he attributes to the positive aspect of maternal femininity. The maternal power of which he deprives Miranda's figure he attributes to the universe and he exercises it himself, while he relegates her sexual power to the images of a dead Sycorax. Just as Goneril and Regan represent a deeper evil than their male counterparts, so Sycorax does for Prospero. Her evil defines his virtue when he is able to release Ariel from the spell she was unable to undo and thereby establish himself as the island's magus. Since she is associated with woman's foul sexuality, his magical powers that derive from women are also designed to contol and limit the female image from which emanates all evil figures. Sycorax is a 'foul witch' who 'with age and envy / Was grown into a hoop' (I.ii.258–9). Her physical ugliness and unspecified envy of all human beauty renders her the other side of the coin to Miranda's beauty and compassion. Her 'mischiefs manifold and sorceries terrible,' are associated with sexuality in that she 'did litter here / A freckled whelp, hag-born, / Caliban' (I.ii.264,282–3). The animal imagery that describes Caliban's birth recalls Leontes' attribution to his child of the bestiality he associates with Hermione's supposed adultery. As well, Caliban's saying to his drunken friends, 'As wicked dew as e'er my mother brush'd / With raven's feather from unwholesome fen / Drop on you both!' (I.ii.323–5) recalls the swamps, fens, and cisterns that were in earlier plays associated with corrupt sexuality. This link suggests that Caliban is born of Prospero's fear of the befouling odour of sexuality, which becomes explicit in his attempted rape of Miranda.

But Prospero has relegated his image of the foully sexual and cruel maternal female to a fairy-tale image of past. Along with her he has relegated Caliban's sexuality to the past. The Caliban of the present has no desire for Miranda, but rather offers her to Stephano: 'Ay, lord; she will become thy bed, I warrant, / And bring thee forth brave brood' (III.ii.102–3). His sexual powers depleted, he is associated instead with infantile sensuous pleasures in food, pleasant sights and sounds, sprigs, berries, and jays' nests, and an infantile consciousness when he describes the island's 'sounds and sweet airs, that give delight, and hurt not,' the humming voices, and his dream of clouds that 'show riches / Ready to drop upon me; that, when I wak'd, / I cried to dream again' (III.ii.133–44). With genital desire sufficiently obliterated, Prospero through Caliban allows himself pre-Oedipal pleasures, immersion in food, sleep, dreamy contemplation of sights and sounds. As long as he can restrict Caliban's range, the food images do not turn to garbage, nor does the sweet music become sound and fury. When Prospero's nerves are, like Ferdinand's, in their infancy, he can allow himself remote visions of sensuous delight.

But those apparently innocent pleasures carry their own dangers. They represent the sottish pleasures of the animalistic body that has natural emnity to the mind, or its head. Prospero expresses fear of these seductive pleasures in the images of animals and foul water that accumulate as Ariel leads them 'calf-like' through filthy mantled pool so that the 'foul lake / O'erstunk their feet' (iv.i.180–4). Like Othello in his 'foul cistern,' Antony in the muddy Nile, or Lear and his smells, Prospero links the body to befouling dirt, while he keeps his own figure cleanly clothed in images of moral authority. In doing so he becomes the agent rather than the victim of the sadistic punishment that Othello and Lear experienced. But images of his suppressed sadistic fury against the body's delights appear when Ariel describes how he led Caliban's party 'through / Tooth'd briars, sharp furzes, pricking goss, and thorns / Which enter'd their frail shins' (iv.i.179–81), and when Prospero tells Ariel to 'charge my goblins that they grind their joints / With dry convulsions; shorten up their sinews / With aged cramps' (iv.i.258–60). Despite the comic reduction of Caliban and his party, they conceal at least as great a danger as the more adult threat of the court party, for the configuration replicates Macbeth's polarity between a swinish drunken passivity and violent sexuality. Their potential danger to Prospero's rational control of conflicting passions surfaces when Caliban, who is disgusted with his friends for being diverted by costumes that are the mere trappings of power, tells them to 'knock a nail into his head,' and says,

> Why, as I told thee, 'tis a custom with him
> I' th' afternoon to sleep: there thou mayst brain him,
> Having first seiz'd his books; or with a log
> Batter his skull, or paunch him with a stake,
> Or cut his wezand with thy knife. Remember
> First to possess his books; for without them
> He's but a sot, as I am, nor hath not
> One spirit to command.   (iii.ii.85–92)

In the threat Caliban poses to his head and to his books, the symbol of his head's potency, Prospero opposes his intelligence to and feels threatened by sottish sensuous pleasures, the scorn for which he expresses in Stephano's and Trinculo's drunken comic impotence.

The potency Prospero denies Caliban he gives instead to his brother. The relation between Ariel and Caliban, which is like that of Edgar to Edmund, Posthumus to Cloten, Prospero to Antonio, Orlando to Oliver, is both obscured and heightened in their association with the elements, the one with air and fire, the other with earth; both are associated with water, Ariel with clear and moving water, Caliban with standing and polluted pools. But all the elements are born of mother nature, and Ariel is imagistically born of Sycorax when Prospero releases him from her cloven pine. His release represents the sexual energy of which Caliban has been deprived when, with Sycorax's defeat, he becomes reluctantly obedient to the controlling intelligence. The images of Prospero's 'princely trunk' depleted by Antonio's ivy and of Ariel's imprisonment in Sycorax's cloven pine both carry phallic suggestions. The first one associates a homosexual encounter with evil, depletion, and impotence, since overtly Antonio sapped Prospero's authority. In the second image Ariel becomes as Prospero's phallus, or more precisely his phallic potency, refusing to yield to woman's pleasure and refusing to release the seed that will propagate more Calibans. She 'in her most unmitigable rage' imprisons the phallus, which will neither yield to orgasm nor lose its erection. In breaking her spell on Ariel, Prospero transforms his phallic power into the potent art that he holds temporarily and uneasily.

Prospero, having separated his phallic potency from his image of the body, Caliban, has converted it into the figure of Ariel. The reason Caliban in the play's present lacks desire for Miranda is that his master has sublimated his sexual potency into the will to power. Ariel's genesis in Prospero's phallic power also accounts for his invisibility to all but Prospero. His invisibility to the court party and to Caliban's party, one can argue, coheres with the therapeutic masks Prospero assumes to cure the one, and the others' unworthiness to see him. But Prospero magically puts Miranda to sleep before calling Ariel to him. He has no overt reason for hiding Ariel from her, since she knows of his 'Art,' but the privacy Prospero thereby ensures is appropriate for an Ariel who represents Prospero's phallic powers, and that he puts Miranda to sleep rather than sending her away shows his uneasy desire for her proximity to those powers.[10] His use of Ariel to punish the others suggests the fusion of sexual and aggressive energies with which Prospero both controls his more immediate impulses and creates a culminating vision of familial and political harmony. In Ariel Prospero has transformed his sexual desires, which he experiences as depleting with men and as evil and deathly with women, into a vision of transcendent magic that can prevent sexuality from turning the world into a waste-land kingdom like Tarsus, or like the one Oberon averted by forcing Titania to give him the changeling child. But the cosmic ideal in the name of which Prospero exercises his power betrays its sources in the desires it suppresses. His denial to himself of immediate pleasures, which for him carry associations on one level of violence and on another of swinish impotence, has become an ideal of self-restraint, and has commandeered to its service the now repudiated erotic force.

But Prospero's phallic powers are not easily held in such restraint. In Ariel they press for freedom, demanding Prospero's cajoling, alternately affectionate and irritable tones to make them 'cleave' to his thought. Sometimes, in wanting premature release, they threaten his continued control over the various forces represented in the figures with whom he has peopled his island. Using his denied sexual energy in order to control others' sexuality, Prospero deviously satisfies the hostile components of his desire under the guise of generating in Miranda the ideal of redeeming femininity, untainted by the world or by the flesh. When he has accomplished her marriage to an equally idealized and desexualized Ferdinand, he acknowledges Caliban, 'this thing of darkness,' as his own. As he merges into Caliban, whose undetermined fate suggests the insoluble nature of the problem, he also releases Ariel, and he feels depleted, with every third thought on the grave. Having desexualized himself, his sexual powers as imaged in Ariel become the means by which he accomplishes his major task, which is to arrange Miranda's marriage without allowing her sexuality to arouse his imagination of incestuous horrors.

Prospero's ambivalent feelings condition the confusing emotions of the Ferdinand-Miranda plot. Ferdinand at first experiences the island as maternally beneficent, the aura of enchantment generated largely through Ariel's songs. Ferdinand's reaction to these songs also pervades Miranda's and Ferdinand's responses to each other, linking Prospero's control of circumstances to the lovers' feelings. Ferdinand, as a pale reflection of Prospero, is both a symbolically pure mate, suitable for Miranda, and at the same time in need of cleansing from the taint of the impure world from which he has emerged. Both his purity, a reflection of Prospero's consciousness of himself, and his taint, a reflection of Prospero's unconscious drives that have been externalized into plot and other figures, are suggested in Ariel's songs:

Come unto these yellow sands,
   And then take hands:
Curtsied when you have and kiss'd
   The wild waves whist:
Foot it featly here and there,
   And sweet sprites bear
The burthen. Hark, hark.
Burden, dispersedly. Bow-wow!
   The watch-dogs bark:
(Burden, dispersedly) Bow-wow!
   Hark, hark! I hear
The strain of strutting chanticleer

Cry cock-a-diddle-dow!   (i.ii.379–89)

The contrast between the ethereal dance and the barking and crowing of dogs
and cocks forms a microcosm of the play. The cock, elsewhere in the plays
associated, as it is traditionally, with comically strutting male sexual assertion,
and the dogs are without further associations in this play. But since so much
in this play relates back to *King Lear*, wherein dogs are associated with fawning
or debased authority, the passage can be seen as having reduced and contained
elements that earlier had loomed larger. In that context, the image foreshadows
the punishment Prospero imposes on Ferdinand for having usurped his father's
title and for wanting his own, even though he 'knows' that false. That is,
Prospero's otherwise unexplained harshness to the overtly guiltless Ferdinand
derives from his concealed identification with him. At one and the same time
he punishes in Ferdinand his own tainted sexuality, and he makes him a
representative of the male purity and self-control by which he defines himself.[11]
    Ferdinand aligns himself with the magically beneficent when he appreciates
the music that 'crept by me upon the waters, / Allaying both their fury and
my passion / With its sweet air' (i.ii.394–6), which told him that,

> Full fadom five thy father lies;
>   Of his bones are coral made;
> Those are pearls that were his eyes:
>   Nothing of him that doth fade,
> But doth suffer a sea-change
>   Into something rich or strange.
>   Sea-nymphs hourly ring his knell.   (i.ii.399–405)

On the one hand, in accordance with the overt ideology, the song places the
seemingly tragic event within a context of cosmic beneficence. The vague
beauty of the images, pearls and coral under the sea, emerging from the remote
but horrible image of rotting eyes and bones, and the softening of death into
a 'sea-change,' obscure the passage's statement, which is that it is good that
Ferdinand's father died. If we take the song as Ferdinand's dream, then the
suffused feeling of sad beauty expresses his pleasurable vision of his father
dead in a way that obscures any associated guilt. He generates Miranda as
the ideally virginal woman, given, as it were, to him by that same universe
that kindly disposed of his father so that he can make her 'The Queen of
Naples.' But as with Pericles, his fears flood back, so that he finds a yet more
powerful father figure in Prospero, who accuses him of the patricide and
usurpation he has covertly imagined. Drawing his sword, Ferdinand resists

succumbing to his guilt, but the overtly violent motion increases his guilt so that he finds himself immobilized, or impotent. On the condition of his impotence his guilt is sufficiently assuaged so that he can have Miranda, just as Posthumus and Leontes submitted to punishment in order to regain their women. Just as Prospero in the story of the past cast himself as victim to Alonso in order to win the right to Miranda, so also does Ferdinand see himself victim to Prospero. But in Ferdinand the process goes a step further, for he internalizes Prospero's authority in as precise an image of introjection as one can desire when he concurs with Prospero that his nerves are 'in their infancy again / And have no vigour in them' (1.ii.487–8). Feeling himself in a dream-like state that, as for other characters, indicates the surge of long-repressed emotions, Ferdinand accepts 'the weakness that I feel' as the condition of once a day beholding Miranda through his prison bars. The image functions simultaneously to prevent one of genital fulfilment and to satisfy the more infantile fantasy of feasting his eyes. His image of Miranda as the wondrously radiant goddess, whom he associates with the island's sweet sounds, links her to the imagery in which Prospero depicts his power magically to embody a maternally beneficent cosmos. Despite the different emotional tenor, Ferdinand's retreat to an infantile state as a strategy to claim the woman parallels that of Lear or Leontes.

Subsuming Ferdinand's experience to Prospero's, we see that Prospero through Ferdinand expresses in a remote way his rich pleasure in the vision of Alonso dead, while in his own person he punishes himself for doing so, in a strained system in which desire and punishment are indistinguishable. But through that identification he manages to transfer overt possession of Miranda from himself to Ferdinand, and in so doing frees himself from the danger of his excited sexuality. In being safe from violating his daughter, he is also safe from symbolically violating his mother, for whose tender lovingness the infant child substitutes. But Prospero's efforts to ease his tensions by satisfying his Oedipal desires in the process of forgoing them are only partially successful. His obsessive interest in the sexuality of Ferdinand and Miranda is expressed voyeuristically in the several scenes in which he, Polonius-like, spies on them, and in his repeated cautions to Ferdinand against lust, which make Ferdinand sound uncomfortably like Angelo when he says, 'The white cold virgin snow upon my heart / Abates the ardour of my liver' (IV.i.55–6). These themes are reiterated in the wedding masque, which centres on the exclusion of Venus and 'her blind Boy's scandalled company.' Since it is Ceres who repudiates Venus and her son, Prospero drives a wedge between natural fertility and sexual passion. But he can entertain no fuller imagination of Miranda's marriage than is generated by Iris' image of the nymphs' 'country footing' before finding his life threatened by 'the beast Caliban and his confederates.' In that configuration he betrays the threat posed to Miranda's wedding by his rebellious passions despite all he has done to make them obedient. Therefore, as he imagines Caliban approaching his cell and books, he must still his 'beating mind,' and for the only time in the play, he feels his control jeopardized, distantly in the image of Caliban and immediately in his 'anger so distempered.'[12]

In the two parties that wander his island, Prospero separates and thereby diminishes the power of the components that, under his strict vigilance, he allows to join in Ferdinand. He obscures beneath his mock accusations of Ferdinand his fear of threats to his own and Alonso's power, and to Miranda's virginity. In Caliban and his party Prospero expresses in more distanced but less controlled ways the threat to his self-image and to Miranda. In contrast, in the court party he gives more dignity to the issues of violated authority in an ordinary political realm, but he separates them from himself and from the issues of sexuality. Alonso is linked to women only in the story of Claribel, which shows Prospero's self-congratulation not to have lost his daughter to Caliban as Alonso lost his to the distant Moorish figure in Tunis.[13]

In stage-managing the Alonso plot, Prospero accomplishes what he would have liked but feared to accomplish in the story of the past. In that story, by falling victim to Alonso's power he justified his escape with Miranda. In the present he both revenges himself upon and gains power over Alonso, but only in the process of giving Miranda to Alonso's son. In the island replay of the past story, Prospero expresses his wish for illegitimate power through Antonio, who seduces Sebastian into an attempt on Alonso's life. Should that attempt have succeeded, Antonio would have accomplished what Prospero wants and eventually does bring to pass: 'One stroke / Shall free thee from the tribute which thou payest; / And I the King shall love thee' (II.i.287–9). Prospero gets double satisfaction from the scenario that he has produced. He expresses his own hostility towards the paternal authority represented by the king, and at the same time demonstrates his own superior power. Prospero's need to protect, even while attacking, the king's power appears in his relative leniency towards his party. Ariel leads them through mazes, and confronts them with the illusory banquet that represents the illusory goals of the 'real' world, in contrast to Prospero's ideal one, and Prospero articulates their punishment as a kind of therapeutic education, and himself as a moral schoolmaster.

Prospero demonstrates his power over those in the court party as he did over Ferdinand, by rendering them impotent, their swords, like Ferdinand's, useless. In the style of Edgar he realizes as fully satisfying a revenge for past wrongs as could be desired. Malvolio, who left the stage crying, 'I'll be revenged on the whole pack of you,' or Lear, who impotently cried, 'I'll have such revenges on you both / I know not what they are' could not be more gratified than is Prospero when Alonso says that he hears, as the 'bass' to his trespass in the winds and waves and thunder's 'deep and dreadful organ-pipe ... the name of Prosper' (III.iii.98–9). In defining his revenge as moral education, Prospero hides a basic confusion of feeling. His diminished desire to punish his enemies appears when Ariel says that his 'affection / Would become tender' at the sight of their sufferings. In the language of high moral purpose Prospero renounces vengeance for the 'high wrongs' that have been done him, and, 'they being penitent,' he espouses his 'nobler reason' (v.i.25–30). The emotional confusion appears in the confusion of fact: Prospero here renounces a desire for vengeance that he has never announced, since his elaborate reassurances to Miranda that 'not a hair perished' in the seeming storm repudiate revenge; though Prospero later renounces his anger, 'they being penitent,' in the action 'they' are not penitent – only Alonso is. This confusion of evidence reveals the personal passions, which have been concealed beneath his self-image, uneasily pressing towards consciousness.

Prospero's unease about his right to his powers lies behind his renunciation of them. That he has accomplished his purpose does not in itself explain why he forgoes his beloved books, since Antonio and Sebastian will still be in Milan. But in his celebration of his 'so potent art,' he betrays his intuition that he can make no further use of it without revealing its shaky foundations. He first associates his 'rough magic' with romantically sensuous images from the tradition of natural magic, the elves that 'with printless foot / So chase the ebbing Neptune, and do fly him / When he comes back,' the demi-puppets 'whose pastime / Is to make midnight mushrooms, that rejoice / To hear the solemn curfew.' From these images of pleasures like those he permitted to Caliban his mind moves to his power over more formidable elements – the sun, waves, and sky – and finally challenges the archetype of paternal power: 'to the dread rattling thunder / Have I given fire, and rifted Jove's stout oak / With his own bolt.' Having taken Jove's bolt, he moves with it downwards, as he describes his powers to shake the earth and uproot trees. He concludes, 'graves at my command / Have wak'd their sleepers, op'd, and let 'em forth / By my so potent Art' (v.i.33–50). Having usurped Jove's power, with it he invades the earth, an image that, particularly in association with Jove, suggests the forbidden maternal realm that he, like Hamlet, associates in his image with death. The power he has generated to suppress images of violation, decay, and death, itself now threatens to elicit them, and he has raised as many spectres of the dead from his psychic past as he can bear to look upon. He has exhausted his capacity to silence their squeaking and gibbering or to keep their foul odour from contaminating his world. He can no longer stand the stress of controlling others, but he also ensures that no one else will assume such powers over him when, as Ariel demands his freedom, he promises to break his staff, 'Bury it certain fadoms in the earth, / And deeper than did ever plummet sound / I'll drown my book' (v.i.55–7).

In abandoning his magic, into which he has channelled all his vitality, Prospero experiences his world as a meaningless void. Hamlet did so when he drained life of significance by seeing it in a vast time perspective that reduces the grandest enterprises to dust and clay. When all Macbeth's ruthlessness would not prevent the spectres of his denied desires from rising against him, he reduced life to the unreality of 'a tale / Told by an idiot, full of sound and fury, / Signifying nothing.' And Antony, defeated by Caesar and thinking Cleopatra dead, experienced a similar though more mellow unreality when he compared the world to shifting clouds. Prospero clothes in his neo-Platonic ideology a similar feeling of emptiness. The void that replaces his denied passions appears first in association with the interrupted masque, when he says that the 'baseless fabric' of the visionary revels is like

> The cloud-capp'd towers, the gorgeous palaces,
> The solemn temples, the great globe itself,
> Yea, all which it inherit, shall dissolve,
> And, like this insubstantial pageant faded,
> Leave not a rack behind. We are such stuff
> As dreams are made on; and our little life
> Is rounded with a sleep.   (iv.i.152–8)

Prospero mutes the despair that protagonists in other plays felt when confronted with the void by asserting a better reality that is to our ordinary world as our waking world is to our dreams. And, since Prospero as magus is the reality behind the 'insubstantial pageant faded,' so, the passage implies, does a similar beneficent power inform the 'baseless fabric' of the great globe itself. But dramatically his sense of unreality derives from his having relinquished Miranda and buried his desires, and just as Lear refused other-worldly compensation for Cordelia's loss, so the neo-Platonic reassurance of meaningfulness does not eliminate Prospero's bad feeling, for after dispersing the masque he must in his vexation take 'a turn or two / To still [his] beating mind' (iv.i.162–3). No ideology can cancel the image of Ferdinand and Miranda in Prospero's cell, outside of which Prospero uneasily paces.

Prospero similarly idealizes his sense of unreality when he assembles the court party inside his magic circle and says,

> The charm dissolves apace;
> And as the morning steals upon the night,

Melting the darkness, so their rising senses
Begin to chase the ignorant fumes that mantle
Their clearer reason.   (v.i.64–8)

Since the 'ignorant fumes' represent the illusory goals Antonio and the others have ruthlessly pursued in the ordinary world, their 'rising senses' do not show them an ordinary world, but would, if Prospero did not change clothes, show them an extraordinary, or magical world, ruled by Prospero, who has associated himself with a transcendent beneficent power. Therefore, the 'clearer reason' to which they will come is not reason in the ordinary sense, but an intuition of a higher reality, represented by Prospero in his magical robes, the ordinary reality having been reduced to 'ignorant fumes.' The same relationships are implied when Prospero adds, 'Their understanding / Begins to swell; and the approaching tide / Will shortly fill the reasonable shore, / That now lies foul and muddy' (v.i.79–82). In the implied ideology, the 'reasonable shore,' fouled with the mire into which Caliban was led or with the rank weeds among which Ophelia died, represents ordinary reason that pursues the ordinary goals of lust and power. It will be transformed into a higher reason when filled with the transforming waters that Prospero controls. These passages are calculated to reverse the normal terms of reality and unreality, so as to seduce the audience into seeing the unseen and sensing the insensible and thereby to awaken them from the dream of life.

In these passages Prospero transforms the despair other protagonists felt as they succumbed to the net of their mutually defeating desires into an ideology of world-denial and transcendence. After the masque, Prospero, still in conflict, begins to experience his world as unreal. Having completed his self-denial by giving Miranda away, he fulfils his desire for power. He has transformed his hostile feelings for the father, as represented by Alonso, into a vision wherein he, having trifled with Alonso's despair to cure it, enjoys being the unseen power behind what appears miraculous to others. Even as the passage articulates an ideal of transcendence that repudiates the desire for illegitimate power manifested by the court party, Prospero enjoys a veritable feast of power. As magus he raises the dead, first himself as duke of Milan, then Miranda who, he tells Alonso, was like Ferdinand lost in the tempest. As the duke of Milan he has the satisfaction of hearing Alsono both resign the dukedom and beg his pardon. Though Prospero denies interest in the dukedom, Miranda as queen of Naples represents Prospero's claim to the king's power, and so both carries his line into royalty and resolves in his own favour the contest between himself and Alonso. Gonzalo, like other ineffectual and mocked father-figures, makes a major point when he emphasizes in his summarizing question the import of Prospero's victory: 'Was Milan thrust from Milan, that his issue / Should become Kings of Naples?'(v.i.205–6).

However, Prospero can allow his self-congratulation only remote satisfaction, for to acknowledge it would involve acknowledging its illegitimacy. Since Alonso functions as Prospero's father, and since in Miranda's youth and innocence are hidden the symbolic components of the mother, Prospero returns the mother to the father, but interprets the restitution not as submission to lawful authority but as a maganimous gift that signifies his victory over Alonso in their ancient feud. His fundamental sense of having won, with the help of his 'tricksy spirit,' a trickster's victory appears, as I suggested before, in the way the politics of Italian duchies translate into the symbolism of Elizabethan rule. In the latter a king has rightful dominion over a duke, making the initial crime Prospero's refusal to submit to Naples. Prospero justifies his supremacy to Naples on the basis of his superior knowledge and wisdom when Ferdinand says that Miranda 'is daughter to this famous Duke of Milan, / Of whom so often I have heard renown' (v.i.192–3). But to base authority on individual achievement violates the principle of inherited hierarchical order that so much of Shakespeare's drama struggles to maintain. Seen in this way, Prospero becomes not a version of Shakespeare's heroes, but of his usurping villains who aspire beyond their station. However, his claim is not based on the martial powers with which other contenders for status fended off the dangerous power of women and proved themselves worthy both of them and of rule. Rather, he is more like Edmund in basing his claim to power on his intelligence. However, the intelligence that makes him so able a trickster, relates him to Hamlet, a protagonist who does not think himself a usurper, and who refuses to the end the martial prowess that would in his own eyes define him as a king. Rather Hamlet goes to his grave studious and thoughtful, shades of the trickster having been submerged. One could say that he rises triumphant on his own rather than his father's terms as Prospero, his death-dealing phallus having been transformed into the now obedient Ariel, who, once free, will join the birds and the bees. The price, however, is to remain unthroned and uncoupled. It is ironic that in Prospero, the figure who most strenuously justifies his power within a traditional ideology, Shakespeare should have allowed to escape some secret celebration of the Faustian rebel.

Prospero has struggled to extricate himself from his passions and to legitimate his power but has succeeded only in temporarily depleting his energies, for Antonio, who at the beginning contains the force of Prospero's rebelliousness, whose usurpation of his power represents his own desire to usurp the king's, is stubbornly unrepentant. Prospero silences him, and secretly protects him, but cannot be rid of him. The consequent feelings of weariness and despair pervade the epilogue, in which the figure of Prospero merges with both the actor who plays him and the author who created him:

> Now my charms are all o'erthrown,
> And what strength I have's mine own,
> Which is most faint: now, 'tis true,
> I must be here confin'd by you,
> Or sent to Naples. Let me not,
> Since I have my dukedom got,
> And pardon'd the deceiver, dwell
> In this bare island by your spell;
> But release me from my bands
> With the help of your good hands:
> Gentle breath of yours my sails
> Must fill, or else my project fails,
> Which was to please. Now I want
> Spirits to enforce, Art to enchant;
> And my ending is despair,
> Unless I be reliev'd by prayer,
> Which pierces so, that it assaults
> Mercy itself, and frees all faults.
>> As you from crimes would pardon'd be,
>> Let your indulgence set me free.

Prospero has extricated himself from the dangers of incest, but has neither redefined sexuality as non-incestuous nor freed sexual desire from associated guilt. Having strenuously converted his sexual drives into power over himself and others, justifying his use of control within the ideology of beneficent magic, he has his 'dukedom got,' but only at the cost of a depleted energy that ensures the containment of 'the deceiver,' pardoned but unrepentant, who remains, without the protection of fatigue, ready to begin again.

In that fatigue, the image of the island transforms into and overlaps with the image of the stage, an image that has hovered previously in the language: 'The great globe itself.' The image of the speaker as actor in London overlies his image as magus on the island when he addresses the audience: 'I must be here confin'd by you, / Or sent to Naples.' With the 'here' he equates the bare stage on which he stands with the bare island on which he exercised his power, and in doing so he equates his power as actor, and by implication the power of the dramatist's words that the actor speaks, to control the audience, with Prospero's power as magus to control the denizens of the island. He feels confined to the barren island unless he can enter into the marriage celebration at Naples, and confined to the stage unless swept into a celebration of the performance. His magical powers are not sufficient to generate in him any joy over the marriage he has worked so arduously to arrange – therefore the relatively bleak tone of 'or sent to Naples.' Nothing on the bare island can alleviate his isolation, and so the emphasis shifts to his isolation on the bare stage, where he can hope to find the release he seeks in the ritual of audience applause. But in the lack of a corresponding term to complete the analogy with the island, he equates the audience's applause with his power to send the others on their way to Naples. This implies that he now gives to the audience the kind of power over him that he on the island exercised over others, and that he deviously identifies himself with the sinners whose reformation or containment he effected. He says that unless he is released by applause, he will end in despair, and 'lingering perdition, / Worse than any death / Can be at once.' It was from this fate that he, through Ariel, saved the court party by confronting them with images of their own evil desires and deeds, which illustrated to them the illusory nature of worldly power and pleasure. His equation of himself with those sinners empowers the audience's acclaim or his fame as actor or playwright to release him from the despair of the barren island stage or from the isolation in which he has left himself as a consequence of the strenuous control he has exercised, a control that leaves his desires unchanged and unfulfilled. But since the desire for applause hovers dangerously close to those worldly goals criminally pursued by Antonio and Sebastian, he changes the image of applause to one of prayer, which 'assaults / Mercy itself, and frees all faults.' In the process he changes his magical powers, which he has now conferred upon the audience, into Christian prayer. But the Christian ideology reinforces the equation between sexuality and guilt from which Lear and Antony fleetingly escaped, and substitutes a vision of other-worldly salvation for the vision of an earthly heterosexual loving union that was briefly glimpsed.[14]

12

Conclusion: The Hidden Hand

This work has been concerned primarily with analysing each of the plays as the dream of its protagonist. However, the significance of kinds of character, structural forms, and images in some plays has been explained and expanded in the light of similar forms in other plays. The links among the plays imply that the dreamer behind the protagonist is neither a person more or less like the protagonist nor a person more or less similarly placed in the world as he. That device helped assimilate the play, seen as dream, to what would be ordinary reality for the dreamer, thereby taking into account the play's mimetic level. It permitted me to assume that, though the protagonist cannot have an unconscious any more than can the figure whom we take to represent ourselves in our dreams, other figures he encounters and the language he uses give clues to what would be an unconscious dimension in the sleeper who dreams. That strategy permitted me to join dream-level analysis to what would constitute the waking experience of such a dreamer, since I assumed that other figures in his dream represented people who in his waking life had their own hard-edged reality. In this way I accommodated the mimetic level of the play, for in the figures, events, and circumstances that surround the protagonist the dreamer expresses the way in which he signifies his experience that he encounters in his waking world.

However, insofar as links among the plays are used to elucidate components of a single play, and are significant in their own right of an underlying continuity throughout the plays, the one who sleeps and dreams is not a 'waking' version of the protagonist, but Shakespeare, who pours his imaginative energy into his protagonists. Stepping back in this way, one can see different stages of Shakespeare's psychological enterprise in the changing kinds of protagonists, the changing attitudes of the protagonists towards the figures and circumstances they meet, the differing levels of their consciousness of their experience, and the changing degrees of control given the protagonists over their world. In order to collect some of what has been implied about the story of Shakespeare's imagination as it appears in the sequence of plays, and to summarize some of the concerns that have shaped this study, in this concluding chapter I will concentrate on two related aspects of the plays – the ways in which women appear in them in connection with an aspect little commented upon, that is, the locus and kind of control manifested in the plays.

This issue can be treated on several different levels. The first, the most obvious, but also the most vague, has to do with the author's control of his play. In one sense the author obviously has full control, since he has created the entirety, but one often feels that some works are more controlled by conscious intention than others. In this area one necessarily relies on a kind of general intuition, so that many people speak of Falstaff 'getting away from' Shakespeare, and many intuitively feel that *King Lear* or *The Winter's Tale*, with their somewhat rambling scenes, are less controlled than, for example, *Othello* or *The Tempest*. Such intuitions, if they have any significance, would indicate in the terms of this study that a character or sequence in a play that seems less controlled drew the author farther into the desires that had initially directed his choice of material than could be integrated into his conscious purposes.

On another level, control has to do with genre form. It is often though not always the case that comedy suggests a stronger authorial hand than tragedy. It is commonplace to observe that comedy, which begins in disorder and ends in restoration, requires a strong hand to bring characters who have started on a downward path back to harmony, and that the more fully realized those characters are, or the deeper the issues involved, the more obvious will be the hand that pulls them back from the brink over which in tragedy they plummet. Generally, in comedy the sense of the author's control is felt in comic time and circumstance, beneficent accident, that can be counted on finally to arrange the necessary coincidences, and in tragedy the sense of authorial control is felt in the sense of fate, or destiny, that participates in the gravity of the downward movement. A third level of control appears in both genres when the author in a sense appoints a character to exercise some or all of that genre control for him. In comedy that character becomes the manipulator, and if the manipulation is too vicious or the other characters too fully realized to keep sympathy at bay, then the genre control is endangered. When tragic control passes to a character that character is likely to become a villain, but for the play to remain within the tragic realm, he too must be overwhelmed. Otherwise, he is likely to turn into a comic character, or, like Richard III and Iago, he may become somthing like a con-artist.

A fourth level of control enters when the nature of control is itself the play's subject matter, so that the way it is exercised or abdicated invites moral commentary, raises moral questions, or is the object of aesthetic contemplation. In this way, especially for Shakespeare, it merges with the problems that appear so regularly in his plays surrounding the justification and right exercise of authority.

These four levels carry the author down into his work. That is, when the author delegates a figure to control events in a play, that figure represents the control that he would otherwise exercise through the shaping force of the genre and, therefore, in a unique way represents him as artist, though he may or may not be the locus of the play's central imaginative focus.

Whether that control is beneficent or malevolent would then reflect the stance the author has taken towards his chosen subject matter, and by implication towards the part of himself that selects and most forcibly shapes his material. When the nature of control is itself the concern of the work, one sees the author reflecting on his power over the figures he has generated, or, on the dream level, over the aspects of himself that have shaped them. One suspects, for example, that Shakespeare's portrayal of Lear abdicating his power and allowing his stage to crumble is related to the substantial admixture of grotesque comedy and farce and the violation of genre decorum upon which many critics of *King Lear* have commented. Of course, all those aspects of the play might have been deliberate, that is, they might express Shakespeare's intention to craft a form that would mirror Lear's loss of control over his inner state. There is no way to know that with certainty, but in view of the many images that break sentence logic and the other discontinuities that have been discussed, I am inclined to believe that Shakespeare's intention to depict the consequences of ill-used authority was directed by the force of forbidden desires, which achieved expression in the broken genre form, and in other ways as well. Sometimes the inner disorder finds expression in ways that harmonize with the author's conscious intention and concerns, and sometimes in ways that threaten to or do violate it.

If we assume that the level and locus of control in a play bear upon the manner in which the dream level of the author's imagination will manifest itself, then the kind of protagonist he chooses, characterized in large measure by the degree of control he has in relation to his world, will reverberate with the author's psychological relation to the material of the play. Since this study has traced the ways in which love and sexuality appear with greater and lesser immediacy, aura of significance, and distance from the protagonist, in association with different value systems, I will now review those changing forms in relation to the locus and kinds of control within which they appear.

Apart from *The Comedy of Errors*, in which Shakespeare instantly lit on plots and characters that were seminal to his later works, the earliest plays show Shakespeare experimenting with many different forms before coming upon, in *The Two Gentlemen of Verona*, the basic romantic plot line to which he would return many times. These plays, until *Hamlet*, are characterized by clever uses of conventionalized forms that have little moral or emotional weight or symbolic significance. Within the overall control of conventional comic circumstance, women, whose goodness and purity is taken for granted, are allowed considerable control, for which they have moral justification to use punitively against men. Such a woman first appears in Antipholus' wife who, without intending to do so, locks her wayward husband out of his house in the night, though she is herself punished by the priestess-cum-wife whose appearance saves her long-lost husband from an unmerited death. The theme of punishment rings in a deeper timbre in *Love's Labour's Lost*, where the women, having playfully mocked the king and his comrades for their denial of them, as a condition for accepting their proposals impose on them a year's penance of abstinence and service to the sick. In most of the romantic comedies, beginning in sketchy ways with *The Two Gentlemen of Verona*, a woman, sometimes assertively, controls the action by virtue of her knowledge of her secret identity. The most powerful figure of this kind is Portia, who interprets her harshness to Shylock as justice in a way that, for many viewers, shakes the containing comic framework. In a softened version, this figure reappears as Rosalind. Though sharply witty, she is more playful and vulnerable than Portia, at the same time as she has less complete control over Orlando and others.

In *Twelfth Night* the two sides of Rosalind separate to form two characters – the witty and manipulative Maria, whose punishment of Malvolio seems to many to exceed comic restraint, and Viola, who though passive retains an overriding, but powerless consciousness of the meaning of the confused events. In this play, having approached the fascinating and fearful punitive power of women, Shakespeare disperses that power and preserves in his universe a beneficent female presence by dividing, or splitting, the image of the female in two. That split between an assertive woman and a passive one has appeared earlier, though in plays that for the most part do not pass control to a woman; an exception is Tamora in *Titus Andronicus*, who arranges the mutilation of the passive Lavinia, though the play's Senecan excess absorbs the reverberation of Tamora's ruthlessness.

The split also appears vaguely in *The Two Gentlemen of Verona*, wherein Sylvia contrasts with Julia, who, like Viola later, combines passivity with the secret knowledge of her own identity. The split is more marked in *The Taming of the Shrew*, *Much Ado about Nothing*, and *A Midsummer Night's Dream*.

In these plays the opposition between an assertive and a passive woman, the assertive one tinged with punitive energy and the passive one bringing about the plot's resolution with the revelation of her identity, remains character-ological. But because of the deep emotions that will attach to them and the range of significance they will acquire in later plays, the patterns suggest that Shakespeare, within the safety of comic conventions and distance, hovered around the edges of, and occasionally dipped into, what later became a night-mare imagination of woman's cruel power to emasculate men, and started to generate a counterbalancing image of the passively virtuous woman.

Later on, when these images of women come laden with psychological, political, and cosmic implications, they combine with a third element scarcely apparent in these plays – that is, her sexuality. A prostitute appears in *The Comedy of Errors*, but little significance or blame attaches to her, and in *Much Ado about Nothing* Hero, who is maligned by Don John, is thought to be corrupt by her father and her lover. This pattern, wherein the false belief of a pure woman's lover introduces powerful images of sexual vice, while her 'true' character maintains an image of a pure redeeming feminine presence, reappears in *Othello*, *Cymbeline*, and *The Winter's Tale*. The only plays in which the image of the sexually corrupt woman, as wife, lover, mother, and daughter has evolved into important characters are *Hamlet*, *Troilus and Cressida*, and *King Lear*. Shakespeare's reluctance to engage his conflicting feelings around women's sexuality shows itself in the infrequency with which the flood of associations of harlotry with disease and death generate characters. Sexuality, which when joined with woman's capacity for self-assertion and control threatens to infect the entire cosmos as it does in those three plays, is contained by the strategy of reducing the sexually impure woman to a thought in the protagonist's head, balanced by the external 'truth' of her purity.

Shakespeare's restraint of threatening female sexuality in these early plays also appears in the relatively flat and undeveloped portrayals of the young male lovers, like Bassanio, Orlando, and even Romeo. More emotional intensity attaches to fathers or paternal figures, so that equal love relationships are deemphasized in favour of the seeming safety of the familial. However, within that seeming safety the sexual, which becomes more threatening for being placed within the incestuous realm, thereby endangering the concept of the family within which safety was sought, also tends to leak out under the guise of power and control. These early paternal figures also fall into two categories that later on accrete depths of emotion and significance as they become more central to the action. These two categories are the irascible father, who wishes for no apparent reason to control his daughter's marriage choice, and a quasi-magical or magical male, who is instrumental in setting things right. The irascible father first appears as the Duke in *The Two Gentlemen of Verona*, who for no reason prefers the foolish Thurio to Valentine, and appears again as Capulet in *Romeo and Juliet*, who has no reason that he knows about so violently to rush Juliet into marriage with Paris. This figure also appears as Egeus, who again for no reason to do with social appropriateness opposes Hermia's choice. In *Much Ado about Nothing* a hazier version of this figure may be seen, as well, in Leonato, Hero's father, who does not oppose her choice, but who expresses most passionate feeling for her in the play's most emotionally resonant language when after the aborted wedding ceremony he is persuaded of her impurity. These figures anticipate their later avatars and suggest the ways in which the father-daughter relationships will express some of the darkest associations with sexuality and the ways in which power relationships can express and substitute for sexual ones.

If these irascible fathers in more and less obvious ways occasion the disorder in which the plays begin, the magical father or beneficent father-figure, again in more and in less obvious ways, helps or tries to help set things right. This figure appears first in *Romeo and Juliet*, in which Friar Lawrence with his secret knowledge of herbs and his desire to resolve the family feud can be seen as a failed Prospero, especially so in combination with the magisterial prince, whose strenuous justice helps hasten the lovers to their death. More immediately, he anticipates Oberon-Puck in *A Midsummer Night's Dream*, a play that can be seen as the comic side of *Romeo and Juliet's* tragic coin. Oberon, whose magical power is less moral than Prospero's, uses it through the agency of the irreverent Puck, and the dominance he thereby achieves over Titania spreads harmony through all the human couples, overshadowing Egeus in the process. In the later comedies this figure retreats into the background. A shade of him appears in the princess's father in *Love's Labour's Lost*, whose death occasions the ladies' withdrawal. He combines with the irascible figure in Portia's dead father whose power passes to Portia once she has submitted to his strategy for choosing a husband. Finally, in this early period, he appears in the 'magical uncle,' whom Rosalind conjures to explain her power, an image that merges with the good Duke Senior, whose forest dwelling is the locus of the nuptial celebration from which issues the harmony that the lovers will restore to the court, and by implication to the commonwealth, to which they return.

The uneasiness in some of the comedies, and the sense most people have of emotional currents getting out of the genre control are the visible sign that underlying emotions that had directed Shakespeare's choice of plots, conventions, and kinds of characters were pressing for greater expansion than was allowed by the forms he had thus far used. The revenge convention, to which he turned next, in its very nature invites concern with emotions from the past that press for acknowledgment in the present, and the sense of tragic fate or destiny, which replaces comic time and circumstance, suggests the force of inner compulsion that overrides the desire for ordinary pleasure.

In tragedies, when control passes from an overarching destiny the figures on whom it falls tend to become villainous counterparts of the comic manipulators of earlier plays. That development is clear in Shakespeare's later tragedies, in which the protagonists are defeated by evil or manipulative characters, but Hamlet confronts a divided antagonistic force, as he fends off the ghost's demands, and deals with Claudius' strategies and Polonius' inept manipulations. A large part of the play's action portrays Hamlet's struggle to evade rather than assume power. He prides himself on not being a pipe on which Fortune or Rosencrantz and Guildenstern can play. More than any other protagonist in Shakespeare's tragedies, he remains unmanipulated by other figures; by the time Claudius arranges the final duel, Hamlet participates in it under the aegis of Providence, rather than that of Claudius. In his death, I have argued, he gains ascendancy over his father, having first overcome all the others. In the midst of the uncertain and shifting locus of control in *Hamlet*, women lose power, but pervade the play with diseased sexuality, treachery, decay, and death, which also come to symbolize male corruption in power relations when Claudius' conscience is like the corrupted flesh beneath the paint on a 'harlot's cheek.' Associations of women with violence and mocking cruelty are only hinted at in the player scene.

In *Hamlet* Shakespeare made his first attempt to confront the Oedipal struggle with which he had toyed in the early plays. In this play he aligns himself with the younger man, and allows his animosity towards the paternal, expressed in those earlier irascible fathers, to blossom fully. The idealized version of paternal authority, in the line of magical fathers, appears as the ghost, whom Hamlet guiltily evades and undermines, while male sexuality generates the figure of Claudius, through whom Hamlet expresses his self-loathing as well. He achieves dominance over the representative of the irascible father by mocking and killing Polonius. Shakespeare disguises Hamlet's victory over the paternal realm by minimizing his desire for power, and by devaluing the other object of the struggle – women. The image of woman as diseased, rotten, death-dealing, and betraying probably expresses several psychic layers. First, it expresses Hamlet's unease with his own and woman's sexuality, with the emphasis shifting from one to the other. But that image, once established, accrues to itself and is increased by all the guilt deriving from the challenge to paternal authority, at the same time as it obscures the nature of that struggle by denying the worthiness of its object.

Shakespeare's disgust with the Oedipal project he had ventured upon in *Hamlet* pervades the atmosphere of *Troilus and Cressida*. Like Gertrude and Ophelia, Helen and Cressida are unworthy, and they debase the wars fought for them. In this play the Oedipal outlines retreat, since there are no parents and children, leaving in the foreground an atmosphere coloured by the 'pestilent vapours' of an imagination like Hamlet's. As conflicts about both love and power are set in a world that is 'weary, stale, flat and unprofitable,' the major characters lack charismatic appeal, and the play lacks any aura of providential significance. As in *Hamlet*, various characters make ineffectual bids for control and manipulative power, but in becoming more evident, the desire for power also becomes less ideological. In the midst of the shifting tides of a now meaningless power struggle, the play pulls back from a fully tragic form, as though the image of corrupt and diseased women and sexuality infects even the shaping principle of the genre.

The plays that follow show Shakespeare retreating from the depths of the tragic realm by reaffirming the value of paternal authority and suppressing the fumes that arise from the love-death grave. But the vision of women's sexuality has started to combine with images of their potential cruelty, creating a force that does not allow Shakespeare to return to a comic form that is easily resolved by the harmonizing powers of a pure female. *All's Well That Ends Well* attempts such a return to a comically ordered world. It does so by giving control to Helena, behind whom lurks, as for Portia, shades of a dead but magical father, whose power is reflected in parental figures who now carry moral authority. Within that control, women remain virtuous, though in a nicely ironic reversal, Helena remains associated with disease by virtue of her quasi-magical power to cure it, anticipating both Cordelia and Marina. Within Helena's orbit, all women are virtuous, but the split image of women is contained in the mind of Bertram, who wants to corrupt Diana, and who evokes images, albeit lying ones, of whorishness, even while he is saved from his own vice by Helena's trickiness.

That pattern, wherein the mind of the protagonist sharply splits between images of a virtuous woman who carries the aura of spiritual redemption and an evil or corrupt woman who, though existing only in his mind, is associated with pervasive cosmic corruption, reappears in many plays. It appears first, though with little symbolic extension, in *Much Ado about Nothing* wherein Hero, libelled by Don John, is thought to be a whore by Claudio and her father, and it becomes the dominant motif of *Othello*. Control in that play passes to Iago, though the impromptu, moment-by-moment quality of his plans, his lack of an overall strategy like that of Don John, leaves room for a sense of tragic destiny to pervade the interstices of the fortuitous events that he turns to his purposes. His relation to tragic destiny parallels Rosalind's relation to comic circumstance. With part of the tragic control passing into Iago's hands, Shakespeare's imagination contrasts the symbolically pure Desdemona with the whorish traitor of Othello's imagination, but he does allow her to show, between these extremities, some straightforwardly sexual and loving impulses.

If we assume *Measure for Measure* to have been written after *Othello*, it represents a second retreat from a tragic brink into comic form. As in *All's Well That Ends Well*, a paternal figure firmly suppresses a young man of corrupt imagination, who might otherwise become a Hamlet figure, or an Edmund. Shakespeare's imagination in these plays divides almost equally between the paternal and filial figures, but, unlike in the earlier comedies, it endows the paternal figure with moral authority.

The control of the play seems close to lighting on Isabella, who at first appears to function as did her counterparts in the earlier plays. But as Angelo's sullying passion forces the issue between sexual purity and slightly tainted but loving fertility, she appears life-denying, and control passes to the Duke. He is a mid-way figure between Oberon and Prospero, in whom the divided aspects of the paternal image begin to merge. He is enigmatic, sometimes irascibly harsh, and arranges test situations for other figures as well as the coupling of appropriate lovers. Also like Prospero, he controls events by manipulating his appearance, but his control, more than Prospero's, depends on fortuitous circumstance, and the ideology from which his authority derives is less clear. He emerges from the tangle he helps to create with a mate whom he has reclaimed from a life of celibacy, even while his resumption of his ducal authority coincides with the closing of the city's brothels. Though without extended significance, these brothels maintain an image of sexual corruption, while the possibility of female cruelty is associated with the pure Isabella. The ambivalence towards sexuality in this play, the desire to affirm it on the one hand and control it on the other, makes the play uneasy, and its intense concern with sexuality lends it a seriousness that strains the comic framework and renders its conclusion abrupt and problematic. The comic control that seems ready to break apart may be so strained because this play, like the tragedies that soon follow it, brings together with almost equal emphasis two concerns that until this time have been kept relatively separate.

For the most part the early comedies concerned themselves centrally with love relationships, relegating political or power relationships to the background, and the history plays, concerned mainly with power relationships, have only minor episodes involving women. The two themes, power and love, approached each other earlier in *The Merchant of Venice* and *Troilus and*

Cressida, in both of which the uneasy tone jars with the love relationships, around which they are plotted. Characters in both plays have much to say about the nature and principle of law and the exercise of authority, but the plays do not fully dramatize those issues. *Hamlet* reverses that relative dominance, giving central dramatic focus to personal power relationships in a way that does justice to the protagonist's thoughtfulness, and leaving the love relationship submerged. In *Macbeth* and *King Lear*, Shakespeare intertwines the themes in a way that allows the two aspects of Oedipal emotions to erupt with full force.

Control in *Macbeth* issues from the compulsive desires of its protagonist more overtly than in other plays. The consequent dreamlike quality of the play renders as his tragic destiny the force of Macbeth's entranced desire to kill the paternal Duncan. In expressing openly the force of that hatred, Shakespeare associates it with the cruel, mocking woman, whose fierceness makes her Macbeth's equal. His destiny is made to derive from the feminine principle that extends from her to the archetypal extension of her in the witches and Hecate. That extension of the realm of the female turns the play as a whole, now seen as Shakespeare's dream, into a rendering of the ways in which evil female powers seduce the male to a self-destructive crime against authority.

Women's cruelty and their power to manipulate, mock, and humiliate men, developed fully in *Macbeth*, had appeared in earlier plays as well – in the characters of Maria in *Twelfth Night* and Beatrice in *Much Ado about Nothing*, and in the player scene of *Hamlet*. The aura of women's corrupt sexuality that had suffused the worlds of *Hamlet* and *Troilus and Cressida*, in *Othello* retreated to the protagonist's mind. The world Othello sees is like that of the two earlier plays, while the audience sees one pervaded by some of the transcendent spirituality that suffuses the late romances. In *King Lear* these threads – women as cruel and mockingly manipulative and women as sexually corrupt – fuse to create Goneril and Regan, while the vision of redemptive female purity, now more emphatically than Desdemona defined by compassion, is contained in Cordelia. This vision of the sexually evil female, having crossed the boundary of the protagonist's imagination, now shapes independent characters who are symbolically extended into a cosmic principle of evil, which is equated with Gloucester's vision of the gods who kill men for their sport. Correspondingly, more intensely than any character before her, Cordelia carries the aura of cosmic redemption, and is correlated to an evocation of heavens that are both just and merciful. This deeply polarized and most symbolically laden, and therefore, dehumanized, rendering of women coincides with Lear's abdication of authority, and the capacity to control action. As Lear becomes Shakespeare's most irascible father, control of events passes first to Edmund, then to Edgar, resting briefly, but most horrendously, with Goneril and Regan. The sense of tragic destiny, or control, is somehow fractured – too overt in the storm, almost comic in the missed timing and confused events at the end. It would seem as though by creating an aged protagonist, Shakespeare gained enough imaginative distance from overt sexuality to allow him to abandon some inner control, so that the monsters might emerge from the depths.

It is difficult not to see *King Lear* in this context as functioning as a kind of catharsis of the imagination that permitted Shakespeare, once he had given form to and looked upon these images, to dream a sweeter and more moderate dream. Cleopatra is neither greatly good, nor greatly evil, even though images suggestive of both ranges surround her. Control in *Antony and Cleopatra* falls principally to the two protagonists; no one manipulates them, no other character expresses a major emotional dynamic that is unknown to them. Though he erotically dies into love, Antony also lives some love, which represents a victory at least of the imagination over its own darker side. That victory is articulated in transcendental images, but the vision generated by both Antony and Cleopatra of their union beyond the grave elevates, rather than transcends, sexuality. However, seen retrospectively, the play contains two elements that foreshadow Shakespeare's retreat from its more generous and more integrated emotions in the face of the nightmare images that threaten to flood back. Cleopatra's images of herself as carrion recall the way in which Ophelia is 'like to conceive,' and the quasi-magical power that, associated with Caesar's power, seems to control the final episodes anticipates the way in which Shakespeare in the last plays suppresses sexuality by converting it into magic.

The two plays that intervene concentrate on male relationships. *Timon of Athens* all but excludes women, and if that exclusion is taken as a retreat from the problems surrounding women and heterosexuality into the realm of the potentially homosexual, still, homosexuality is approached only tentatively and is associated with betrayal and exploitation. *Coriolanus* approaches homosexual suggestiveness much more immediately, in association with battle and battle wounds. Coriolanus can be seen as the other side of Hamlet – the Fortinbras side writ large; he is a figure who would fully satisfy King Hamlet's martial expectations for his son. But as the homosexual implications of the martial stance emerge, control passes to Volumnia. She shares her power with the tribunes and finally with Aufidius, but all of them play upon Coriolanus' stops precisely in the way Hamlet feared for himself. Although the symbolic overtones previously associated with women have subsided, the split image reappears, the many dimensions of Cleopatra splitting apart once more. Virgilia, young, silent, and compassionate, shows Shakespeare again limiting the potentially sexual woman to expressions of compassion. Coriolanus is the only one of Shakespeare's major figures who has a powerful mother. Though Volumnia's manipulative skills and punitive tongue contribute to her son's destruction, and though she functions in ways parallel to Lady Macbeth and the witches, she maintains ordinary human dimensions. Perhaps Shakespeare can allow this powerful mother to emerge in fully human clarity because some of the sexual energy that surrounds other female figures with penumbras of radiant light or of infernal malice has been drained away by the play's more overt homosexuality.

However, these are the last portrayals of ordinary women, not surrounded by language that extends them into cosmic principles, but they are also without sexual suggestiveness. The late plays manifest increasingly rigid control, as Shakespeare tried to wrest from the mire an imagination of lovers who could be both pure and procreative, unsullied by the corruption and destructiveness inherent in his imagination of sexuality. In turning his attention to that project, he experimented with a form in which control rests not so much with a comic but rather with a magically directed fairy-tale ordering. As soon as Pericles has acquired a wife, a daughter, and a throne, he passes quickly from a quest similar to Hamlet's for his mature place in the world to a simulacrum of an aged man like Lear. In emotionally distanced forms he evokes and destroys an incestuous father and daughter as well as a wicked queen. He tries to heal the split in the image of woman when he has Thaisa go to a nunnery and has Marina prove the powers of her purity in a brothel, demonstrating her power to transform the male imagination before he can with safety remove the beard that conceals his vigor and reclaim his wife. In *Cymbeline* once again, as in *Othello*, the dark side of the image of woman becomes internalized. However, this play makes such obvious parallels between Posthumus and Cloten that it seems likely that Shakespeare intended to show that Posthumus' susceptibility to Iachimo's lies arose from his own unacknowledged sexual lewdness. This point is also made when Posthumus blames himself for his anger before he knows Imogen to be guiltless. As Shakespeare portrays the dark image of woman arising from the corrupt male imagination he allows Imogen to assume some measure of control. Though her place in the play is structurally similar to Desdemona's in *Othello*, she has little inclination to die to the wrath of her lover. Tapestries of Cleopatra and Diana adorn her walls to indicate her combination of sexuality with virtue, but the wrathful purity of her actions makes her most like Isabella; also like Isabella, she is desired by an openly lascivious male, though Cloten, on the way to becoming Caliban, shows no trace of Angelo's inner conflict. *Cymbeline* suggests that Shakespeare's conscious intention was to envision correct familial and love relationships and to dramatize the process by which Posthumus' imagination might be cleansed so that he could accept Imogen's sexuality. But the stresses remaining in that project show themselves in the shades of Goneril and Regan that remain in the still externalized Queen. As Sycorax will spawn Caliban, she spawns Cloten, plots against Imogen's life, and is made responsible for Cymbeline's political errors. He reforms after her death, regains his daughter as well as his lost sons, who render his sceptre fruitful, rather than barren like Macbeth's, but he has no mate. That is significant, since the play is prevented from becoming a tragedy by having figures from the political level take charge of the love relationships, subsuming them into the restoration of political order. This process reverses what occurs in the early comedies, in which renewed political order is an implied consequence of correct love relationships; in this it is similar to but more emphatic than *All's Well That Ends Well* and *Measure for Measure*. Though the Duke in *Measure for Measure* takes Isabella to wife, Shakespeare's imaginative attempt to couple his ruling male falters in *Cymbeline* despite Posthumus' dream of his dead family.

In *The Winter's Tale* that attempt is made once more. Leontes is the only one of Shakespeare's major protagonists who at the beginning of his play is married to the woman who is the mother of his children. As with Othello and Posthumus, the image of woman as corrupt and betraying exists only in his imagination, but unlike them, he solely is responsible for turning his initially idealized wife into her opposite. The immediacy of the drama sharply declines when Paulina replaces Hermione as a version of the punishing mother. She functions in a way parallel to Goneril and Regan, but carries the moral authority that earlier fell to Edgar. Something like an older version of Rosalind, she shares her power with the quasi-magical coincidence that ordains events in the Bohemian world. Shakespeare's uneasiness as he endows a woman with controlling and morally defined power appears in the uneasy comic tone that hovers around Paulina, and his uncertainty that there is a way to transform an imagination like that of Leontes appears in the uneasy mixture of naturalism and magic by which Hermione is returned to Leontes.

If the uneasy form of *Pericles, Cymbeline,* and *The Winter's Tale* derives from Shakespeare's strained and probably conscious efforts to envision a mature, fruitful, ruling couple, the confident form of *The Tempest* derives from his having abandoned that attempt and having settled for the disembodied promise expressed in Ferdinand and Miranda. In *The Tempest* control of all events rests with Prospero, except for the time at which the ship approaches his shore, which is attributed to fortune, and except for the narrated events of the 'past' that reveal the process by which he acquired his power. His capacity to manipulate others and to control events carries full moral authority, and by virtue of being defined as magical, is also associated with a principle of cosmic order into which the remnants, still visible, of the irascible controlling father are absorbed. Women are represented by the sharply divided images of Sycorax and Miranda. Sycorax, firmly within Prospero's control and further reduced by being in the play's past rather than present, is the last cardboard descendent of Goneril and Regan who can imprison Ariel and spawn Caliban, a 'thwart disnatured torment,' and the last lustful usurper reduced to comic impotence. Limited to the attributes of compassion and naive wonder, Miranda is all that remains of the virtuous female. Prospero's control of his world and himself, which suggests Shakespeare's control over the emotional dimensions of his characters, permits him, the last of the irascible fathers, uneasily to relinquish Miranda to the flattened figure of Ferdinand. He manages the conflict between his desire to control Miranda and his desire to believe in her instinctive and unsullied virtue, by stage-managing even her rebellion against his authority. But at the end of his play he has neither wife nor daughter, only the pale satisfaction of power over ordinary representatives of authority. He succeeds in bringing about a vision of ideally pure lovers to rule an ideal commonwealth, but the strenuous denial of his sexuality leaves him feeling empty in an ashen world 'signifying nothing.'

Some implications of Prospero's mastery, and perhaps of Shakespeare's from whom he derived it, are suggested by a series of images that foreshadow Prospero's relation to his world. In *The Taming of the Shrew*, Petruchio proves his mastery over Katherina by forcing her to agree to however he describes the shifting cloud shapes he points out to her. Brought about by starvation, her submission to his vision seems to carry no extended significance beyond the conventionally comic. In *Hamlet*, when Polonius reminds Hamlet that his mother expects him, Hamlet similarly mocks Polonius' time-serving by insisting that Polonius agree with his descriptions of shifting clouds. That being Hamlet's last encounter with Polonius before he kills him, the image becomes associated with the complex of feeling surrounding his encounter with Gertrude. Though the emotional tenor differs, the shifting indeterminacy of cloud shapes in the two plays is a means by which one character, by his mockery, proves his mastery over another. The image of shifting clouds takes on more central significance when Antony, feeling his powers wane and himself deprived of all familiar sense of his own identity, compares himself to the insubstantial shifting images of the clouds. The image here signifies Antony's fearful experience of dissolution, of losing the lineaments of his autonomous manhood. Both Petruchio and Hamlet assert their manhood by claiming, in a sense, mastery over those clouds. Psychologically, though this connection is not supported by any specific image in the plays, such an experience relates to fears of losing one's adult ego and succumbing to a state of oral merger. It suggests those feelings that might be experienced by the infant Perdita or the infant at Lady Macbeth's breast, or those that impel Lear to reject Cordelia for whose comfort he also longs. Both Antony and Pericles abandon control long enough to experience a moment of such comfort, but for Prospero there is none. The image of the indeterminate clouds appears for the last time when Prospero compares 'the cloud-capp'd towers' and 'the great globe itself' to the 'insubstantial pageant' that he has created and dispersed. That image expresses the control Prospero assumes over what others see and experience on his island, and symbolically extends his power, acquired through knowledge, over the realm of the indeterminate, which now includes the created universe. What began as an image suggesting comic mastery over a victim now suggests spiritual and transcendent mastery over the shifting forms of human life. Since Prospero controls those shifting forms, he need not fear dissolving into them, but the price he pays for his dream of mastery is the feeling of depletion in an insubstantial world. Except for the 'beating brain' of which Prospero complains after dispersing the marriage masque, *The Tempest* in no way questions Prospero's sanity because of this dream of power, although a living person who thought himself so empowered would be closer to madness, in a modern sense of the term, than were Hamlet in his frantic uncertainty or Lear in his impotence.

The easy analogy between Prospero's 'art,' by which he creates worlds for others on his island, and Shakespeare's art as a dramatist, by which he created worlds for characters on the stage of the Globe, has led many to suppose that Shakespeare intended Prospero as an image of himself, and that in drowning his book and burying his staff Prospero represented Shakespeare's farewell to his life in that theatre. If that is so, then the epilogue, the imagery of which slides from island to stage, expresses not so much a farewell as Shakespeare's consciousness that through his art he had explored as deeply as he was able the conflicts that had informed it, and that his creative energies could not draw on them any longer. Prospero's confused use of the stage image in the epilogue suggests some of the problematic ranges the images of the stage as world and the world as stage had for Shakespeare's imagination. If he consciously expressed through Prospero a concept of himself as artist-magus, then as Prospero separates his role as magus from his sense of himself as man, so Shakespeare would have separated his definition of himself as artist from his ordinary humanity, in analogy to Kantorowicz's conception of the king's two bodies.[1] His task, then, as artist or dramatist, would be through the creation of staged microcosms to reorder and re-educate the minds of his audience, including those of the monarchs who summoned his company to court, by reminding them that they had but 'a little brief authority.' If the world is a stage, then the parts played by kings and queens are no more real than those of the actors who play them, and if the artist's claim is to hold a mirror up to nature in such a way as to show 'the very form and pressure of the time,' then staged monarchs, or the hand of the playwright who stages them, are informed by a higher reality and claim a greater ontological status than the shadowy realm of courts and kings, with their tales of who's in and who's out. It may be that in creating Prospero Shakespeare penetrated to the logical conclusion of his favourite metaphor in a way that confronted him with a perception that the complex network of interacting roles out of which are woven the glorious dramas enacted on the world's stages might signify nothing beyond the ambitions and lusts of the mighty. Irving Goffman, who drew from Shakespeare's plays his metaphors for the role behaviour in which he described the world of everyday life, withdrew in some hesitation from the vision of selves that did not exist apart from a complex enactment of deeply imbibed and inscribed role behaviour.[2] Goffman had no cosmology at stake, while for Shakespeare a world without authentic being and without an authority that defined itself within a hierarchy that claimed its legitimization from a higher realm, threatened to become one in which we devour each other like sea monsters. But he had himself given to Prospero's personal achievements, which he authenticated by their virtue and wisdom, priority over the traditional claims of kings, which were rendered unreal by the kings' failure to incorporate the spiritual values on which their authority rested. If Shakespeare identified with Prospero as master of images, he could logically have concluded that he, who dramatically rendered an ideal vision of authority, could claim a priority over the kings and queens whose failings seemed to create so great a gap between the body politic and the spiritual realm with which they were supposed to infuse it as to erode the distinction between them and Shakespeare's player kings.

While for him to entertain such a conclusion would have undermined the values that he overtly espoused, Shakespeare, like the kings he dramatized, might have failed to maintain the distinction between his body natural and his body theatrical. Though he had secured a coat of arms for his father and himself, and though he had become wealthy, he might have resented that being king of the players did not affect as much as he would have liked his relatively low status as a mere player, a man not far removed from Faustus' peasant stock. Perhaps he had some unacknowledged ambition, not made virtuous by the spirit of service, in portraying almost as or just as effectively as his conceptual antagonist Machiavelli the ways in which authority derives its power from staging itself.[3]

If in creating Prospero as an ideal magus, mastering forces that in the major tragedies had undermined every ideal of ordered authority and love, Shakespeare knew or intuited that the ideal of control itself was infected with the passions over which it sought supremacy, then he might well have felt that the control he exercised over his dramatic creations was similarly infected. 'Your actions are my dream,' says Leontes to Hermione. Shakespeare may have come to know as his own dreams the characters that he created, and may have put down his pen for fear of the dreams that might flow from it if he shook off the ashen world-weariness he had rendered in Prospero. The last plays then would represent his relatively conscious effort to sweeten his imagination and his failure to do so.

Though I presume the psychic journey that these pages trace through the plays is also at least a portion of Shakespeare's personal story, the large outlines of that story would not be his alone but also part of the culture that bred him, informing as well the materials and dramatic conventions that fell to his hand out of which he forged his plays. But regardless of Shakespeare's biography, and regardless of the degree of conscious intention, the plays tell a story of a civilization and its discontents in which our own still participates.

Notes

These notes for the most part are designed to place my work in relation to some recent psychoanalytic criticism of Shakespeare, and in relation to theoretical studies of dreams and of the connections between dream and art, though I apologize for much relevant material that is necessarily omitted. For a full bibliography of psychoanalytic studies of Shakespeare's plays up until 1964, consult Norman Holland's in *Psychoanalysis and Shakespeare* (New York: McGraw-Hill, 1964), and for works up to 1978 consult the bibliography by David Willbern in *Representing Shakespeare: New Psychoanalytic Essays*, ed Murray M. Schwartz and Coppélia Kahn (Baltimore: Johns Hopkins University Press, 1980). All text references are to the Arden editions of Shakespeare's plays.

CHAPTER ONE

1 The importance of the family for Shakespeare has recently come into focus from several quarters. In 'The Family in Shakespeare's Development: Tragedy and Sacredness,' *Representing Shakespeare*, 188–202, C.L. Barber places this issue in a historical perspective, arguing that Shakespeare and others in his time endowed the human family with the sacredness previously associated with the Holy Family. Roger Stilling in *Love and Death in Renaissance Tragedy* (Baton Rouge: University of Louisiana Press, 1976) makes a related point in arguing that the shift from divine to secular concerns sharpened 'the poetic and dramatic tools for representing the texture of human life and its basis in human relationship. It also often meant the refounding of values themselves within an earthly context, often with some dislocation of the old' (292). He sees the issue of love as central to Shakespeare, and as the source of his influence on later dramatists who use love stories for serious purposes (3), but does not note that the inher-

ited Christian misogyny became more intense as the symbolic freighting of love increased. A similar observation is made by Lorie Jerrell Leininger in 'The Miranda Trap: Sexism and Racism in Shakespeare's *Tempest*,' *The Woman's Part: Feminist Criticism of Shakespeare*, ed Carolyn R. Lenz, Gayle Greene, and Carol Thomas Neely (Urbana: University of Illinois Press, 1980), 285–94. She sees the symbolic freighting of heterosexuality rendering diabolic any deviation from so laden an ideal. Meredith Skura in 'Interpreting Posthumus' Dream from Above and Below,' *Representing Shakespeare*, 203–16, also asserts the importance of the family to Shakespeare's imagination in terms of the protagonists' struggles towards maturity (204), and Robert B. Pierce in *Shakespeare's History Plays: The Family and the State* (Columbus: Ohio State University Press, 1971) emphasizes the family's importance as a microcosm of the state for Shakespeare's penetration of the psychology of kingship (242). Arthur Kirsch in *Shakespeare and and the Experience of Love* (Cambridge: Cambridge University Press, 1981) notes the interdependence for Shakespeare of the realms of love and power. In *Coming of Age in Shakespeare* (London: Methuen, 1981), Marjorie Garber discusses the new value placed on love within marriage. See also Lawrence Stone, *The Family, Sex and Marriage in England* 1500–1800 (New York: Harper and Row, 1977), and Ian Maclean, *The Renaissance Notion of Women* (Cambridge: Cambridge University Press, 1984).

2 Freud's complex attitude towards art is discussed comprehensively by Jack J. Spector in *The Aesthetics of Freud* (New York: McGraw-Hill, 1974). While Freud sometimes exalts artists for intuiting what he later systematized, he also says that they narrowly escape neurosis. Although Freud states that by softening the egocentricity of his day-dreams the artist allows us to satisfy our own shameful ones, he also, in *Introductory Lectures to Psychoanalysis*, tr and ed James Strachey (New York: Penguin, 1966), 385, disparages the need for such evasions, in asserting that he would prefer to go down 'if there were a choice ... in an honourable struggle with fate.'

3 Norman Holland, *The Dynamics of Literary Response* (New York: Oxford University Press, 1968)

4 Frederick Crews, 'Anaesthetic Criticism,' *Psychoanalysis and Literary Process* (Cambridge: Winthrop, 1970), 18–24. An example of his inclusiveness is his 'Conrad's Uneasiness – and Ours,' in *Out of My System* (New York: Oxford University Press, 1974), 41–62. Leon Edel in *Stuff of Sleep and Dreams* (New York: Harper and Row, 1981) advances a theory of 'literary psychology' or of how literature expresses its author (12). Using authors' dreams, he traces a project's passage from the realm of dream and fantasy to the public realm of art, in order to read literature for how it reveals particular forms of the general process by which human beings struggle with life's problems. While interesting, his study is unsystematic and dependent on extra-literary evidence.

5 See Norman Holland's *Poems in Persons* (New York: W.W. Norton, 1973) and
Five Readers Reading (New Haven: Yale University Press, 1975). In 'Reductionism and Its Discontents,' in *Out of My System*, Frederick Crews points out how
the movement into subjectivist criticism or reader response avoids the theoretical
problems involved in psychoanalysing either an author or a literary character,
but deplores the consequent loss of a humanistic dialogue. A similar practice is
discussed by Richard Jones, who in *The Dream Poet* (Boston: G.K. Hall, 1979)
develops a strategy of 'dream reflection.' He bases his work on a theory of
dreaming as integrative of past affective schemes into present cognitive structures, which he used in a Dream Reflection Seminar that related dreams to literature, making 'a kind of blending of group therapy, literary criticism, and
creative writing; mixed with the study of psychology and literature' (102). Gail
S. Reed in 'Toward a Methodology for Applying Psychoanalysis to Literature,'
The Psychoanalytic Review 51 (1982) 19–42, tries to rescue the text by arguing
that the literary 'surface elicits the same fantasy in its reader as organizes it'
(21), but on that premise Reed does not account for different responses.
6 Jacques Lacan in 'Desire and the Interpretation of Desire in *Hamlet*,' *Yale
French Studies* 55/56 (1977) 11–52, though he goes outside of the text into theory and uses the text to advance the theory, locates affect in the ebb and flow of
langue.
7 In *The Hidden Order of Art* (London: Weidenfeld and Nicolson, 1967) Anton
Ehrenzweig argues that he, unlike Koestler in *The Act of Creation* (New York:
Macmillan, 1965) or Ernst Kris in *Psychoanalytic Explorations in Art* (New
York: International University Press, 1952), sees surface thought in art not
merely linked but 'wholly immersed in the matrix of the primary process' (262).
In *Fiction and the Unconscious* (Boston: Beacon Press, 1957), Simon Lesser in
emphasizing the ways in which a work satisfies its readers' needs, cognitive as
well as emotional needs, emphasizes the psychoanalytic importance of formal
and aesthetic elements of a work, developing Freud's suggestion that aesthetic
form constitutes the artist's means of making his fantasies acceptable to others.
Before him Ernst Kris explored the ways in which formal and aesthetic aspects
of art function for both the artist and the audience.
8 Arthur F. Marotti, 'Countertransference, the Communication Process and the
Dimension of Psychoanalytic Criticism,' *Critical Inquiry* 4 (1978) 471–89. Marotti reviews the work of the Anglo-American psychoanalytic theorists who re-
vise Freud's polarity between primary process and rational thought, seeing
instead a continuum from infantile to adult structures, and relates their theoretical work to Ehrenzweig's. More recently Alan Roland in 'Imagery and the Self
in Artistic Creativity and Psychoanalytic Literary Criticism,' *The Psychoanalytic
Review* 68 (Fall 1981) 409–20, argues that the artist draws images from the primary processes that unite personal feelings with larger social and cultural issues.

The terminology of this discussion is correlated with Lacan's by Joseph C. Sitterson Jr, 'Psychoanalysis and Literary Theory,' *University of Toronto Quarterly* 51 (Fall 1981) 78–92, though Sitterson is unenthusiastic about psychoanalytic criticism. The theory I here put forward provides means by which the dream strategies of art can be analysed specifically, and it overcomes the objection, repeated by Sitterson, that authors do not provide associations to their works.

9 These studies are anticipated by Eric Erikson's seminal work, 'The Dream Specimen of Psychoanalysis,' *Journal of the American Psychoanalytic Association* 2 (1954) 5–56, in which he argues that the manifest content reveals the dreamer's mode of assimilating the latent content to his waking life. His ideas have been developed in work that integrates dream study with studies of the function of both REM sleep and cognitive psychology. Louis Breger in *Clinical-Cognitive Psychology* (Englewood Cliffs, NJ: Prentice Hall, 1969) sees dreams as a form of 'information processing,' which creates the inner perceptual structures by which infants assimilate experience, analogous to REM sleep, which allows mammals to 'differentiate and structure the central nervous system' (186). See also his 'Play, Fantasy and Dreams,' in *From Instinct to Identity* (Englewood Cliffs, NJ: Prentice Hall, 1974), 161–91. A similar theory informs the work of Richard M. Jones, *The New Psychology of Dreaming* (New York: Grune and Stratton, 1970), who thinks that dream structures indicate habitual thought processes, and represent the way we assimilate and accommodate 'systems of meanings' (166).

10 Jones, 10–14

11 Sitterson, 88

12 The manifest content of dreams is the sole concern of Calvin S. Hall and Robert L. Van de Castle in *The Content Analysis of Dreams* (New York: Appleton Century Crofts, 1966). Arguing that a 'dream is a manifest experience' (20), they establish categories for images, relationships, settings, and actions in dreams, the analysis of which reveals the concerns of the dreamer. David Foulkes in *The Grammar of Dreams* (New York: Basic Books, 1978) proposes a method of analysing the 'sentences' of dreams by eliminating the distinction between associations found within a series of dreams and the material produced by free association. His method, too, tends to dissolve the manifest-latent dichotomy. Other studies that suggest that dreamlike components of literature are responsible for an underlying organic unity, an idea touched upon by Freud when he said that the author's ego ideal appears in the protagonist, appears in the biographically oriented work of Ella Freeman Sharpe, 'From *King Lear* to *The Tempest*,' in *Collected Papers on Psycho-Analysis*, ed Marjorie Brierley (New York: Brunner/Mazel, 1978) 214–41, and the work of Mark Kanzer, 'The Central Theme in Shakespeare's Works,' *The Psychoanalytic Review* (1951) 1–16.

Some criticism employs concepts drawn from dream theory, such as that of Patrick Colm Hogan in 'King Lear: Splitting and Its Epistemic Agon,' American Imago 36 (1979) 32–44. Norman Holland in Psychoanalysis and Shakespeare works towards a conception of literature that roots the intellectual aspects of a work in the unconscious unifying principle. Another study of the relation of dream to literature is Elizabeth Dalton's in Unconscious Structure in The Idiot: A Study in Literature and Psychoanalysis (Princeton: Princeton University Press, 1979), which most closely approaches the theory advanced here. She makes use of associations within a work in a way somewhat like the one I propose here, but not as systematically and without attention to structural and tonal features. Stating that the 'work itself may be said to have an unconscious' (27), she looks for 'impulses suppressed in one character [to] emerge in another' (146), and finds in action 'repressed ideas' that have 'lost their connection with words' (43). Many works, notably Leslie Fiedler's The Stranger in Shakespeare (New York: Stein and Day, 1972) and Robert Rogers' A Psychoanalytic Study of the Double in Literature (Detroit: Wayne State University Press, 1970), use dream concepts without systematically discussing the theoretical issues involved. Rogers, for example, discusses Cassio as Othello's projection, but does not say why Emilia should not also be so considered, or why Othello's own figure is less dreamlike than Iago's.

13 My attention to the topography of dreams, to the dreamer's relation to figures in his dreams, and to different emotional levels in dreams, as well as to some of the ways in which dream theory relates to literature is deeply indebted to Loehrich's work. Some of his published works are Oneirics and Psychosomatics (McHenry, Ill: Compass Press, 1953), The Secret of Ulysses (McHenry, Ill: Compass Press, 1953), and more recently, Thought Operations with Dreams and Reconstructions of Symbolic Systems, volume three of a six-volume work, Exercitium Cogitandi (Oxford: Centre for Medieval and Renaissance Studies, 1978). Loehrich's theory differs from Freud's in that he regards dreams not so much as fulfilments of wishes, but rather as manifestations of the dreamer's existential state. He emphasizes the significance of dreams in sequence, the way the dreamer relates to other dream figures, and the indications of different emotional levels in dreams. Though he does not elaborate a theory of the application of dream theory to literature, he uses one in The Secret of Ulysses. My work differs from his in its emphasis on genre structures and tone in tracing the ways in which conflicts come to or retreat from consciousness. The approach to literature based on this dream theory has some affinity to post-modernist criticism, for to treat the work as a dream structure depersonalizes the text and dissolves figures into a play of linguistic associations that invite an intertextual approach. It differs, however, in taking account of affect in relation to those structures. This

theory clearly shares some common ground with that of Norman Holland in *The Dynamics of Literary Response*, but differs in its emphasis on the protagonist's movements towards, away from, or around what Holland calls the core fantasy. If one limits oneself to statements that arise only from the chains of association, one cannot go beyond or under the mind of the protagonist, so that some works will not reveal the centre around which the action plays. One might never know which drive or desire serves as a defence for which, and often it seems that conflicting drives defend and express each other, and that the protagonist is, like Lear, caught in the 'to-and-fro-conflicting wind and rain.'

14 Roger Scruton in 'Photography and Representation,' *Critical Inquiry* 7 (Spring 1981) 577–603, emphasizes the role of selectivity in the concept of representation. He contrasts painting and photography in a way that implicitly suggests a meeting point for a mimetic and expressive theory of art.

15 I am using the useful distinction Barbara Herrnstein Smith makes in *On the Margins of Discourse* (Chicago: University of Chicago Press, 1978) between natural and fictive discourse, but I am concerned with the space such fictivity opens for 'primary process' thinking when conceptual language is free from the 'linguistic marketplace.'

16 Roy Schafer in 'Narration in the Psychoanalytic Dialogue,' *Critical Inquiry* 6 (Autumn 1980) 29–53, sees the therapeutic process as a dialogue designed to restructure the patient's narration of his story. It coheres with his concept to see dreams as revelatory of the dreamer's strategy of self-narration, and to regard the narrative structures of literature as images of the protagonist's self-creation. This conception also coheres with that of Frederic Jameson, who in *The Political Unconscious: Narrative as a Socially Symbolic Act* (New York: Cornell University Press, 1981) disputes in the Lacanian mode that one can speak in the classical Freudian way of an unconscious apart from the social-cultural nexus within which the individual has been formed. To assume the protagonist as dreamer allows one to see in literature portrayals of the way in which subjects constitute themselves within their worlds, and of the ways in which social and cultural ideals and forms are held within their intense emotions, each level infused with the symbolic resonance of the other.

17 Norman Holland in 'Hermia's Dream,' *Representing Shakespeare*, 1–20, uses a similar strategy in interpreting Hermia's dream from associations found in other parts of the play. In 'Giving New Depth to the Surface,' *The Psychoanalytic Review* 62 (1975) 1–27, Jim Swan takes issue with Holland's analysis of the witch joke that begins *The Dynamics of Literary Response*, to argue that the joke's manifest aspects, the world of business and stock-market, show the joke transforming fears of economic aggression into sexual fantasy, rather than the other way around.

18 Other people have commented on the features of Shakespearean and Jacobean drama that suggest both particular relevance to the dreamlike, and conscious interest in dreams and their relation to art. Among them is Jackson I. Cope, who in *The Theater and the Dream: From Metaphor to Form in Renaissance Drama* (Baltimore: Johns Hopkins University Press, 1973) traces the way in which neo-Platonic conceptions of reality infused first the language and later the form and conception of the drama. While Cope's work touches the periphery of the theory proposed here, my project is different, for I see Shakespeare's use of dream techniques and his characters' reflections on dreams as aspects of the protagonist's dreaming, analogous to a dream within a dream. The same distinction separates my work from that of Marjorie Garber, who in *Dream in Shakespeare: From Metaphor to Metamorphosis* (New Haven: Yale University Press, 1974) traces the ways in which dreams or dreamlike experiences become both the formal principle and the subject of the plays.

19 The self-reflexivity of the stage image expresses the characters' self-reflection. Hamlet, Shakespeare's most self-reflexive character, is suitably in his most self-reflexive play.

20 Janet Adelman in *The Common Liar: An Essay on* Antony and Cleopatra (New Haven: Yale University Press, 1973) makes a related observation when she notes that the metaphors of the tragedies tend to become the action of the late romances (16). Madelon Gohlke in ' "I Wooed Thee with My Sword": Shakespeare's Tragic Paradigms,' *The Woman's Part*, 150–70, argues that Shakespeare's tragic action should be seen as expanded metaphor, and finds the tragic plots shaped by conflict about heterosexual union (152). Since psychoanalytic theorists link literature to dream processes through the relation of image to primary process thought, the argument that action and character can be considered on a continuum with image draws the full structure of a work into the dreamlike orbit. Much earlier, J.I.M. Stewart, in *Character and Motive in Shakespeare* (London: Longmans, Green, 1949) implied such a relationship, saying that the exaggerated situations open gaps that allow the poetry to take us to the depths (36). A related literary strategy is found in Edward A. Armstrong's *Shakespeare's Imagination* (Lincoln: University of Nebraska Press, 1963). Armstrong studies the ways in which images in Shakespeare's plays bring others in their wake, so that similar clusters regularly reappear. Though he is not inclined to psychoanalysis, his method coheres with psychoanaytic theory.

21 Harry Berger suggests a similar approach, saying that villains can be so only with the collaboration of others. They, 'like ethical vacuums, suck the guilt out of their social environments' (350). This technique of displacement keeps the 'dreamer/character from wakening to self-knowledge' (351). Though he does not state his theoretical assumptions, he suggests a similar view of the relation of

figures to one another when he says that the language that surrounds villains and heroes reveals that the 'self-justifying function and scapegoating function' are complementary (350).

22 This discussion coheres with the work on object relations and the concept of the self. See particularly D.W. Winnicott, *Playing and Reality* (New York: Basic Books, 1971). Winnicott's concept of a transitional space between self and others in which children can preserve their autonomy while defining themselves in reference to others, like Lacan's concept of the mirror stage, calls attention to the integral connections between one's sense of self and experience of others.

23 Marion Milner in *The Hands of the Living God* (New York: International University Press, 1969) suggests the psychological significance of dramatic form. She says that 'encompassing ambivalence' such as one finds in the tragedies is more psychologically mature than splitting and projection, which suggest infantile defences (356).

24 On this level one is clearly addressing Shakespeare's psychic life. But this work does not claim to have psychoanalysed Shakespeare; our uniqueness derives from a particular balance of similar components, and Shakespeare did other things than write plays. If the plays speak to many, they do so because we share with one another similar drives, desires, and emotional mechanisms. But it remains the case that one cannot work long with an author's works without formulating some mental image of who he was. And so I will give a hostage to fortune. What emerges for me from Shakespeare's work is the portrait of a man divided between homosexual and heterosexual impulses, each functioning as a defence against the fears and horrors of the other and unable to rest or find gratification in either form, a situation made particularly difficult at a time when love and family relationships were increasingly significant. The writing in which he expressed his desires and the barriers to their fulfilment was also the means by which he sublimated them into an eroticized desire for power. His ambition, however, conflicted with the ideology of hierarchy, which functioned, whatever its other justifications, as a means of restraining his confused desires. As a consequence, he deviously celebrated the power of the stage, by implication his own power, by questioning the ontological distinction between player kings and 'real' ones, between role and reality, though the implications of such an insight were more than he wished to pursue after he wrote *The Tempest*.

My guess is that his emotional dynamic arose from having an intelligent, powerful mother, who was also seductive, but who punished with her mockery the response her seductiveness elicited, and a genial father, who could be intimidated by his wife's higher social status and could in frustration be erratically tyrannical. Shakespeare's tendency to identify with his father would be impeded by scorn for his father's weakness and fear of his outbursts, while hate and fear of his powerful and intelligent mother's untrustworthy sexuality would prevent his identifying with her. I hasten to add that this hypothetical analysis does not purport to explain Shakespeare's genius, nor the form his genius took, for the same psychological portrait might fit great mathematicians, painters, composers, philosophers, or those who make no mark in the world.

25 Although I have made no direct use of the concepts of love that Freud elaborated in *Mourning and Melancholia* and in his *Contributions to the Psychology of Love, Collected Papers*, vol IV, many of my conclusions conform to his theories. An interesting application of Freud's thought to love-death literature, and particularly to *Romeo and Juliet*, appears in an article by Robert C. Bak, 'Being in Love and Object Loss,' *International Journal of Psycho-Analysis* 54 (1973) 1–7.

CHAPTER TWO

1 The opposing views are represented on the one hand by Leslie Fiedler, who in *The Stranger in Shakespeare* (New York: Stein and Day, 1972) says that Shakespeare hates and fears female sexuality (61), and on the other hand by Charles Frey, who in ' "O Sacred, Shadowy, Cold and Constant Queen": Shakespeare's Imperiled and Chastening Daughters of Romance,' in *The Woman's Part*, ed Carolyn R. Lenz, Gayle Greene, and Carol Thomas Neely (Urbana: University of Illinois Press, 1980), 295–313, observes that daughters who oppose their fathers' tyranny represent regenerative forces; he ignores, however, the threats they pose to male dominance.

2 In ' "I Wooed Thee with My Sword": Shakespeare's Tragic Paradigms,' in *The Woman's Part*, 150–70, Madelon Gohlke observes that the 'prospect of heterosexual union arouses emotional conflicts which shape the plot, unleashing a kind of violence, which in the comedies remains imagined rather than enacted' (151). Melvin Goldstein in 'Identity Crises in a Midsummer Nightmare: Comedy as Terror in Disguise,' *The Psychoanalytic Review* 60 (1973) 169–204, argues that tragic themes become comic in this play through the use of dream forms that reach into the realm of nightmare (176).

3 Many interesting discussions of Hermia's dream include those of Melvin D. Faber in 'Hermia's Dream: Royal Road to *A Midsummer Night's Dream*,' *Literature and Psychology* 22 (1972) 179 90, Marjorie Garber in *Dream in Shakespeare: From Metaphor to Metamorphosis* (New Haven: Yale University Press, 1974), and Norman Holland in 'Hermia's Dream,' *Representing Shakespeare*, ed Murray M. Schwartz and Coppélia Kahn (Baltimore: Johns Hopkins University Press, 1980), 1–20. Holland analyses Hermia's dream on the basis of verbal echoes and images she uses elsewhere in the play.

4 Richard Wheeler in *Shakespeare's Development and the Problem Comedies*

(Berkeley: University of California Press, 1981) observes that the heroes of the early comedies move through truncated and disguised Oedipal situations (176). In *Shakespeare and the Ambiguity of Love's Triumph* (The Hague: Mouton, 1971) Charles R. Lyons states that the fairies expose love's cruel irrationality in ways that the shallow human characters cannot embody (43). Goldstein observes that Shakespeare regularly buries tragic themes and motifs in his comic structures (171).

5 In 'The Adolescent Suicides of Romeo and Juliet,' *The Psychoanalytic Review* 59 (1972) 169–81, Melvin D. Faber sees the feud as an image of intrafamilial regressive narcissism that prevents the young lovers from seeking non-incestuous love objects. In 'The Balance of Themes in *Romeo and Juliet*,' *Essays on Shakespeare*, ed Gordon Ross Smith (University Park: Pennsylvania State University Press, 1965) states that fate expresses the lovers' feelings (39).

6 Otto Kernberg in 'Adolescent Sexuality in the Light of Group Processes,' *Psychoanalytic Quarterly* 49 (1980) 24–47, argues interestingly that the love between Romeo and Juliet is intense because it is unconsciously experienced as breaking the Oedipal prohibitions. Fiedler also argues that Romeo and Juliet die to pay for their fathers' incestuous fears, a theme he sees persistent in Shakespeare's plays (129). Norman Rabkin in *Shakespeare and the Common Understanding* (New York: Free Press, 1967) sees this play, as well as *Antony and Cleopatra* and *Venus and Adonis*, as works that link love to the urge for annihilation, or the death-wish (151). A similar point is made by Roger Stilling in *Love and Death in Renaissance Tragedy* (Baton Rouge: Louisiana State University Press, 1976). He argues that in *Romeo and Juliet* and *Antony and Cleopatra* death is made to serve rather than subvert love (286). Harry Levin in 'Form and Formality in *Romeo and Juliet*,' *Twentieth Century Interpretations of Romeo and Juliet*, ed Douglas Cale (Englewood Cliffs, NJ: Prentice Hall, 1970) also sees in the love-death connection the play's shaping principle (90).

7 In 'Portia Revisited: The Influence of Unconscious Factors upon Theme and Characterization in *The Merchant of Venice*,' *Literature and Psychology* 26 (1976) 5–15, Vera M. Jiji sees Portia as a castrating and devouring woman (11). She argues that the casket scene reveals Oedipal fears of the father, while fears of the mother shape the ring episode (14).

8 Many critics see Antonio as latently homosexual. In *Psychoanalysis and Shakespeare* Norman Holland states that latent homosexual feeling accounts for Antonio's melancholy (238–9). Lawrence W. Hyman in 'The Rival Lovers of *The Merchant of Venice*,' *Shakespeare Quarterly* 21 (1970) 109–16, and Marianne Novy in 'Giving, Taking, and the Role of Portia in *The Merchant of Venice*,' *Philological Quarterly* 58 (1979) 137–54, also see the struggle between Portia and Antonio as the play's main action. In '*The Merchant of Venice*: A Reconsi-

deration,' *Essays in Criticism* 10 (1960) 120–33, Graham Midgley sees the play structured on parallels between Shylock, outcast to Venetian society, and Antonio, outcast to the world of marriage (130).

9 Laurence Lerner in *Love and Marriage: Literature and Its Social Context* (London: Edward Arnold, 1979) thinks Beatrice and Benedick give themselves therapy for the dangerous aspects of love by raising the implicit hostility to the surface (246).

10 In 'Sexual Politics and the Social Structure in *As You Like It*,' *Massachusetts Review* 23 (Spring 1982) 65–83, Peter B. Erickson sees the love relation happily concluded by means of Rosalind's submission to patriarchal hierarchy (81), and contrasts the play to *Love's Labour's Lost*, which, he says, fails to contain its feminine energy. He also relates *As You Like It* to *The Winter's Tale*, since he concentrates, as I do, on the more hidden father-daughter relationship (83n).

11 Ruth Nevo in *Comic Transformations in Shakespeare* (London: Methuen, 1980) relates the play's triumph to the fact that Sebastian functions as Viola's disguise taking on an independent identity. In 'Twelfth Night: The Limits of Festivity,' *Studies in English Literature* 22 (1982) 223–38, Thad Jenkins Logan relates Maria's sadism towards Malvolio to Freud's *Wit and Its Relation to the Unconscious*. R. Berry in 'Twelfth Night: The Expectation of the Audience,' *Shakespeare Survey* 34 (1981) 111–19, argues that Malvolio's exclusion threatens to reveal the underlying pain (118).

CHAPTER THREE

1 Marjorie Garber in *Coming of Age in Shakespeare* (London: Methuen, 1981) places *Hamlet* in the paradigm of maturation in which she discusses all of Shakespeare's drama. See also Neil Friedman and Richard M. Jones in 'On the Mutuality of the Oedipus Complex,' *The Design Within*, ed Melvin Faber (New York: Science House, 1970), 123–46, and Joseph Barnett in 'Hamlet and the Family Ideology,' *Journal of the American Academy of Psychoanalysis* 3 (1975) 405–17, who think that other characters prevent Hamlet from maturing.

2 Norman Holland in *Psychoanalysis and Shakespeare* (New York: McGraw-Hill, 1964) states that the spying motif shows the threat Hamlet feels to his separate existence (176).

3 Some recent views of Hamlet's relation to women have been based on the work of D.W. Winnicott, *Playing and Reality* (New York: Basic Books, 1971). Arguing that Hamlet's difficulty resides primarily in his failure to accept his feminine side, David Leverenze in 'The Women in *Hamlet*: An Interpersonal View,' *Signs* 4 (Winter 1978) 291–308, sees Hamlet as being caught in a patriarchy that makes manliness depend on repression of feelings for women (113). Coppélia

Kahn in *Man's Estate* (Berkeley: University of California Press, 1981) argues that because Hamlet identifies with his father's tenderness, he refuses the role of phallic avenger (139), and Theodore Lidz in *Hamlet's Enemy: Madness and Myth in* Hamlet (New York: Basic Books, 1975) argues that Hamlet is torn between his conflicting desires to kill his mother for her betrayal and to restore her chastity (82). Linda Bamber in *Comic Women, Tragic Men: A Study of Gender and Genre in Shakespeare* (Stanford: Stanford University Press, 1982) argues that Hamlet's misogyny arises from confusion about manliness. Madelon Gohlke in ' "I Wooed Thee with My Sword": Shakespeare's Tragic Paradigms,' in *The Woman's Part*, ed Carolyn Lenz, Gayle Greene, and Carol Thomas Neely (Urbana: University of Illinois Press, 1980) 150–70, finds tragic plots shaped by conflict around the prospect of heterosexual union (152). Juliet Dusinberre in *Shakespeare and the Nature of Women* (London: Macmillan, 1975) argues that Shakespeare rejects inherited sexual stereotypes (308), and Carol McKewin in 'Shakespeare Liberata: Shakespeare, the Nature of Women and the New Feminist Criticism,' *Mosaic* 10 (1977) 157–64, agrees that Shakespeare stands outside of the stereotypes even as he dramatizes them (160).

The view against which these critics argue has been most strongly stated by Leslie Fiedler in *The Stranger in Shakespeare* (New York: Stein and Day, 1972). He argues that for Shakespeare women, like strangers, represent projected images of the repressed. My view is that while his plays express criticism of conventional gender relations, Shakespeare was often entangled in a morass from which he tried to extricate himself. This conjecture implies no denigration, for one does not expect even great authors to be free of their own time, but rather to render how our progenitors struggled in the toils of their own ideas and values.

4 There have, of course, been many interpretations of Hamlet's relation to his father, beginning with Freud's. His was carried forward by Ernest Jones, who in *Hamlet and Oedipus* (New York: Doubleday Anchor, 1954) argued that Hamlet delayed his revenge because he identified with Claudius. Some more recent views are those of Avi Erlich, Norman Holland, K.R. Eissler, and Arthur Kirsch. In *Hamlet's Absent Father* (Princeton: Princeton University Press, 1977), Erlich argues that Hamlet's longing for his absent and symbolically castrated father prevents him from maturing (239). In *Psychoanalysis and Shakespeare* Holland argues that the play reveals the mutuality of the Oedipus complex, with Claudius and Polonius as well as the ghost functioning paternally. K.R. Eissler in *Discourse on Hamlet and* Hamlet (New York: International University Press, 1971) sees Hamlet making King Hamlet his ideal among a full spectrum of fathers (63). An approach closer to my own is that of Arthur Kirsch. In 'Hamlet's Grief,' *English Literary History* (Spring 1981) 17–36, he uses Freud's *Mourning*

and Melancholia to show how Hamlet's Oedipal concerns cannot be disentangled from his grief. Together they pervade the whole play and are enacted in the present (21).

5 Among other views of the relation between revenge and Hamlet's love life is that of Roger Stilling, who in *Love and Death in Renaissance Tragedy* (Baton Rouge: Louisiana State University Press, 1976) sees the 'breakdown of love between man and woman in Hamlet' as heralding the dissolution of all social bonds and releasing thereby the darker passions (4). Seeing Hamlet and Ophelia as a version of Romeo and Juliet (103), he argues that Hamlet's love for Ophelia impedes his revenge (109). Also, Richard Flatter in *Hamlet's Father* (New Haven: Yale University Press, 1949) emphasizes the conflation of adultery and murder in the closet scene as central to the play.

6 In 'Desire and the Interpretation of Desire in *Hamlet,' Yale French Studies* 55/ 56 (1977) 11–52, Jacques Lacan works with a similar perception, stating that Hamlet's mourning for his father reopens grief for the lost phallus (38), which projects onto the world around him. John P. Muller in 'Psychosis and Mourning in Lacan's Hamlet,' *New Literary History* 12 (1981) 147–65, sees Hamlet liberated in death from 'narcissistic attachment to the phallus,' which subjects him to others' desires. Lacan and Muller in their way attempt an account of the play's atmosphere, which I think was best accomplished by G. Wilson Knight in *The Wheel of Fire* (New York: Meridian Books, 1957). Arguing from 'imaginative impact' rather than causality, Knight saw Hamlet himself as 'an ambassador of death walking amid life' (32). Marjorie Garber in *Dream in Shakespeare: From Metaphor to Metamorphosis* (New Haven: Yale University Press, 1974) touches on a similar issue when she comments that the figures in the opening scene represent Hamlet's interior world (92), which he holds in balance with a real one.

7 In 'A Heart Cleft in Twain: The Dilemma of Shakespeare's Gertrude,' *The Woman's Part*, 194–210, Rebecca Swift also notes the discrepancy between Gertrude's characterization and Hamlet's language. Bamber sees in the gap between their relatively neutral portraits and Hamlet's language a sign of his 'disintegrating manhood' (78).

8 Bridget Gellert Lyons in 'The Iconography of Ophelia,' *English Literary History* 44 (1977) 60–4, sees Ophelia as a negative Flora image from the mud of whose grave arises Perdita.

9 John F. Danby suggests the link between Gertrude and Lady Macbeth in *Shakespeare's Doctrine of Nature: A Study of* King Lear (London: Faber, 1959), 156.

10 Lidz thinks that in the closet scene Hamlet is torn between conflicting desires to kill his mother for her betrayal and to restore her chastity to preserve his image of the pure female (82).

11 Ella Freeman Sharpe, 'The Impatience of Hamlet,' in *Collected Papers on Psy-*

cho-Analysis, ed Marjorie Brierley (New York: Brunner/Mazel, 1978), 203–13, thinks of the play as Shakespeare's rather than Hamlet's dream, and comments that Ophelia manifests the self-destructiveness concealed in Hamlet's feigned madness.

12 Eissler argues that Hamlet identifies with Yorick as the passive jester (84–5), and Fiedler says that Yorick died with the old king to leave the son to play the Fool (161), a figure that later becomes the devil, ie, Iago. Bamber contrasts Hamlet with Othello and Lear in his failure to reconcile himself to women (72).

13 Other people have seen different links between love and death. Gohlke thinks that Hamlet, like Othello, can love only women who are dead, and Arthur Wormhoudt in *The Demon Lover: A Psychoanalytic Approach to Literature* (Freeport, NY: Books for Libraries, 1968) says that Hamlet's anger represses his fear of being passive to women (8). In 'The Basic Pattern of Psychological Conflict in Shakespeare's Tragic Drama,' *Hartford Studies in Literature* 11 (1979) 58–71, Joan M. Byles thinks that by rejecting love, Hamlet, like Othello and Macbeth, releases eroticized aggression (59).

CHAPTER FOUR

1 In *Romeo and Juliet* the sexual episode that seems assumed is absorbed into the rush of the lovers towards their tomb, and though it is reasonable to assume that one occurs behind the scenes in *Hamlet*, it exists only in slender hints. The confusion of timing in *Othello* obscures the issue, and while sexuality between Antony and Cleopatra pervades the play, it is located in no single scene.

2 Again, Shakespeare approaches a similar situation in *Antony and Cleopatra*, but Cleopatra has serial lovers, and the question of her fidelity to Antony is raised, but not answered.

3 This jaded tone, observed by many, is explained differently by Stephen Reid. In 'A Psychoanalytic Reading of *Troilus and Cressida* and *Measure for Measure*,' *The Psychoanalytic Review* 57 (1970) 263–82, he sees *Troilus and Cressida*, like *Hamlet* and *Othello*, as confirming Freud's comment that 'something in the nature of the sexual instinct is unfavorable to the achievement of absolute gratification' (266). In 'War and Manliness in Shakespeare's *Troilus and Cressida*,' *Comparative Drama* 7–8 (1973–4) 107–20 Emil Roy sees Oedipal concerns in the way both the infantile Trojans and the Greeks vie for and debase Helen as a maternal figure (108).

4 Alasdair MacIntyre in *After Virtue* (Notre Dame: University of Notre Dame Press, 1981) speaks of the figure of the aesthete, Diderot's Rameau, and Kierkegaard's 'A,' 'who lounge so insolently at the entrance to the modern world' (70). I believe Shakespeare's Troilus got his toe in the door first, but Shakespeare in-

carnates the experience of such a figure in the absence of a conceptual frame in which to define him.

5 A reading that assumed the king as dreamer would render this configuration more remote from consciousness, but would emphasize the contrast between the authoritative figure who lacks a wife, and the younger figure who has a wife, but no authority. It would align the obscure figure of the king with Lear, Cymbeline, and Prospero.

6 A contrary view is that of Thomas Cartelli in 'Shakespeare's Rough Magic,' *Centennial Review* 27 (Spring 1983) 117–34, who argues that the contrived end reminds us that fairy-tale endings are not true (133). A view closer to mine is that of Richard Wheeler, who in *Shakespeare's Development and the Problem Comedies* (Berkeley: University of California Press, 1981), argues that the issues in this play strain the 'controlled unity' Shakespeare achieved in the romances.

7 Arthur Kirsch, in *Shakespeare and the Experience of Love* (Cambridge: Cambridge University Press, 1981) who sees Shakespeare exploring the psychology of a Christian conception of love, argues that Angelo inevitably projects onto Isabella his ambivalence 'about his own exalted purity' (83). He obscures the conflict, however, by omitting the Christian ideology itself from the analysis. Robert Rogers in *A Psychoanalytic Study of the Double in Literature* (Detroit: Wayne State University Press, 1970), 78, expresses the view that in the final marriages Eros dissolves the fragmentation represented by the sets of split figures. In 'Oedipal Fantasies in *Measure for Measure*,' *Michigan Academicia*, 9 (1976) 173–84, Marilyn L. Williamson argues that by withdrawing from his paternal role the Duke causes Angelo's regress to infantile sadism (176).

8 Wheeler sees *Measure for Measure* as a play that deals with autonomy and isolation, rather than with the problems of trust and fear of merger, and sees it as leading to *The Tempest*.

9 That Lucio, moving between Isabella and the bawdy-house, should be the one to fetch Isabella and encourage her in her plea for mercy, gives literal truth to Isabella's metaphor when she says that to Claudio mercy would 'prove itself a bawd' (III.i.150).

10 In *The Literary Use of the Psychoanalytic Process* (New Haven: Yale University Press, 1981) Meredith Anne Skura sees in Claudio's survival a softening of the play's anti-sexuality (266). She finds Shakespeare to be more like a therapist than a seer, in that he reorganizes our thinking by playing off conventions against each other.

CHAPTER FIVE

1 A related view is that of Leslie Fiedler in *The Stranger in Shakespeare* (New

York: Stein and Day, 1972). He sees Iago as an aspect of Othello's estrangement that we all may experience; it expresses our deepest resentments against what we most deeply believe (159, 92). In 'The Joker in the Pack,' *The Dyer's Hand* (New York: Random House, 1948), 246–72, W.H. Auden comments that Iago, alienated like Othello from Venetian society, brings to Othello's consciousness the resentment and fear that he has guessed is there.

2 Edward A. Snow in 'Sexual Anxiety and the Male Order of Things in *Othello*,' *English Literary Renaissance* 10 (1980) 384–412, states that the patriarchal Othello readily believes in Desdemona's, or 'Everywoman's' guilt because it expresses the sinfulness of sexuality (388).

3 Arthur Kirsch in *Shakespeare and the Experience of Love* (Cambridge: Cambridge University Press, 1981) argues that Desdemona's maternally unconditional love and Othello's childlike quality are the psychological basis for the spiritual elevation of their love (25).

4 An interesting discussion of cuckoldry as 'psychosocial castration' occurs in Coppélia Kahn's ' "The Savage Yoke": Cuckoldry and Marriage,' in *Man's Estate* (Berkeley: University of California Press, 1981), 132. Kahn concludes that patriarchal marriage weds cuckoldry to jealousy, and makes it Everyman's plight by linking male identity to men's sexual and property rights to women. In ' "I Wooed Thee with My Sword," ' *The Woman's Part*, ed Carolyn R. Lenz, Gayle Green, and Carol Thomas Neely (Urbana: University of Illinois Press, 1980), 1–16, Madelon Gohlke states that men defend against the fear of the castrating dishonour of cuckoldry by anticipating it in the fantasy that women are whores (15).

5 As a figure in Othello's dream, Desdemona in her bid for dominance suggests Othello's unacknowledged and fearful desire to be passive, dimly foreshadowing the relation between Macbeth and Lady Macbeth.

6 In *Coming of Age in Shakespeare* (London: Methuen, 1981) Marjorie Garber links the strawberry-spotted handkerchief to sheets stained with hymeneal blood, and sees the wedding sheets as a sign of Othello's confusion of 'sexual and martial impulses' (136).

7 Fiedler argues that Desdemona is the lie men tell themselves about women. As forgiving victim she derives from the 'exigencies of Shakespeare's dream,' (190) which debases women and castrates men.

8 Richard Dickes in 'Desdemona: An Innocent Victim?' *American Imago* 27 (1970) 279–97 discusses the 'hypnoid state' in which Desdemona expresses Oedipal guilt for her choice of Othello and seeks her own death as punishment (290). In 'Desdemona's Guilt,' *American Imago* 27 (1970) 245–62, Stephen Reid argues that Desdemona seeks violence to punish herself for her father's infidelity (261). Another version of Desdemona's collusion with Othello is offered by Alan B.

Rothenberg in 'Infantile Fantasies in Shakespearean Metaphor: Photophobia, Love of Darkness and Black Complexions,' *The Psychoanalytic Review* 64 (1977) 173–202. Rothenberg argues that the fear of blindness expresses castration anxiety, which can be handled by turning voyeurism into exhibitionism, which is then denied. Though strained, this argument touches upon motifs that carry powerful emotions, subtly in *Hamlet* and *Othello*, and more obviously in *Macbeth* and *King Lear*.

9 In '*Othello*: The Tragedy of Iago,' *The Design Within*, ed Melvin Faber (New York: Science House, 1970), 155–68, Martin Wangh sees Iago's homosexual attraction for Othello in the play's relentless movement towards Cassio's murder (165). Robert Rogers in *A Psychoanalytic Study of the Double in Literature* (Detroit: Wayne State University Press, 1970) argues that Cassio represents Othello's habit of seeing women as either saints or whores (80).

10 The relationship between obsessive jealousy and homosexuality that Freud discussed (*Complete Works*, vol 18, 221–33) has been applied to *Othello*, *Cymbeline*, and *The Winter's Tale* by many critics. One of the earliest among them was J.I.M. Stewart in *Character and Motive in Shakespeare* (London: Longmans, Green, 1949).

11 J.I.M. Stewart takes a similar stand in observing that 'Iago's villainy draws its potency from Othello's own mind' (102), and in seeing the play as an exploration of the 'inner processes of romantic idealism' (104). F.P. Rossiter in *Angel with Horns and Other Shakespeare Lectures*, ed Graham Storey (New York: Theatre Arts Books, 1961), wonders whether Shakespeare or Othello idealize Desdemona. In 'Women and Men in *Othello*,' *Shakespeare Studies* 10 (1977) 133–58, Carol Thomas Neely argues that *Othello* is a 'cankered comedy' rather than a tragedy, because women cannot succeed in mending male fantasy (154). Joan M. Byles in 'The Basic Pattern of Psychological Conflict in Shakespeare's Tragic Drama,' *Hartford Studies in Literature* 11 (1979) 58–71, states that Othello loses his own ideal rather than a real woman (62).

CHAPTER SIX

1 In '*Macbeth*: Drama and Dream,' *Literary Criticism and Psychology*, ed Joseph P. Strelka (University Park: Pennsylvania State University Press, 1976), 150–73, Simon O. Lesser relates the play's dreamlike quality to the murder of the sovereign, the symbol of order in the state and psyche, which touches infantile anarchic desires (172). F.P. Rossiter in *Angel with Horns and Other Shakespeare Lectures*, ed Graham Storey (New York: Theatre Arts Books, 1961), implies an analogy to dreams in saying that the play's meaning resides in its plot, rather than in what characters say about it (229).

2 J.I.M. Stewart states in *Character and Motive in Shakespeare* (London: Long-mans, Green, 1949) that Macbeth is compelled by the 'crime and not the crown' (93).

3 In line with Freud's comment on the poetic justice of the Macbeths' being child-less, Ludwig Jekels in 'The Riddle of Shakespeare's *Macbeth,*' *The Design Within,* ed Melvin Faber (New York: Science House, 1970), thinks the play ad-vocates being a good son in order to be a good father (243).

4 The image also suggests that beneath Macbeth's fair exterior is a self-image like that of Richard III. In *A Psychoanalytic Study of the Double in Literature* (De-troit: Wayne State University Press, 1970) Robert Rogers argues that Lady Macbeth is both a double for Macbeth and a mother-figure, a configuration that represents Macbeth's failure of individuation (51). Wagner sees her as Macbeth's 'phallic prop' (248).

5 Marjorie Garber in *Coming of Age in Shakespeare* (London: Methuen, 1981) relates Lady Macbeth's barrenness to the barren world that Macbeth creates around him (153–4).

6 Despite the general agreement that this scene is not in Shakespeare's 'usual style,' the sequence of the Hecate scenes parallels that of the two witch scenes, and accords with the previous emotional patterns. Here, as elsewhere, it is con-ceivable that the style reflects Shakespeare's drawing back from the images of terror he generates, leaving figures uninformed by language that flows from full imaginative evocation, even allowing for the interpolation of Middleton's songs.

7 Dennis Biggins in 'Sexuality, Witchcraft and Violence in *Macbeth,*' *Shakespeare Studies* 8 (1976) 255–77, widens and deepens the significance of the relation be-tween Lady Macbeth and the witches by pointing out that traditionally witches were presumed to be lustful, sexually perverse, and sexually dominant. He also thinks of the murder as a kind of rape.

8 Jenifoy La Belle in ' "A Strange Infirmity": Lady Macbeth's Amenorrhea,' *Shakespeare Quarterly* 31 (1980) 381–6, on the basis of medical terminology of the time, argues that Lady Macbeth literally wants and gets her menstruation stopped, and later suffers the physiological and emotional consequences in the barren sceptre and blood images that substitute for the natural flow (384–5). In 'Lady Macbeth and Infanticide, or How Many Children Had Lady Macbeth Murdered?' *Journal of the American Psychoanalytic Association* 17 (1969) 528–48, Victor Kalef writes that Lady Macbeth's childlessness both punishes her and is part of the crime (539). Vesny Wagner in '*Macbeth*: "Fair is Foul and Foul is Fair," ' *American Imago* 25 (1968) 242–57, states that Macbeth's hatred of his mother leads to his being pursued by children.

9 In '*Macbeth*: Imagery of Destruction,' *American Imago* 39 (1982) 149–64, Joan M. Byles argues that Macbeth's actions are not only in proportion to his guilt,

as Freud suggested, 'but rather to the threats on his manhood they represent' (155). Coppélia Kahn in *Man's Estate* (Berkeley: University of California Press, 1981) relates images of milking babes in both *Macbeth* and *Coriolanus* to their protagonists' denial of infantile vulnerability that leads to a dehumanized masculinity (154).

10 D.S. Kastan in 'Shakespeare and the Way of Womenkind,' *Daedalus* 11 (1982) 115–30, reads *Macbeth* in terms of the the contemporary ideal of equal partnership in marriage. Lady Macbeth 'champions an ideal of manhood that excludes compassion' (124).

11 In 'The Babe That Milks: An Organic Study of *Macbeth*,' *The Design Within*, 251–80, David B. Barron sees incomplete masculinity rendering Macbeth helpless in a 'nightmare world of women' (265).

12 Richard Wheeler in *Shakespeare's Development and the Problem Comedies* (Berkeley: University of California Press, 1981) says Duncan's dead body becomes a 'new Gorgon,' both male and female, murdered, raped, and castrated (145). Madelon Gohlke in ' "I Wooed Thee with My Sword": Shakespeare's Tragic Paradigms,' *The Woman's Part*, 150–70, says that here as in *Othello* murder is a loving act, and love a murdering one (156).

13 In 'The Naked Babe in the Cloak of Manliness,' *The Well Wrought Urn* (London: Dobson, 1968), 17–39, Cleanth Brooks first called attention to the significance of Macbeth's war with children.

14 Carolyn Asp in ' "Be Bloody, Bold and Resolute": Tragic Action and Sexual Stereotyping in Macbeth,' *Studies in Philology* 78 (1981) 153–69, blames the sexual stereotyping of society for Macbeth's narrow definition of his masculinity, and for his consequent alienation (156).

15 In *The Dynamics of Literary Response* (New York: Oxford University Press, 1968) Norman Holland gives a penetrating reading of the core fantasy of this speech as though it were an independent poem (106–14). I depart from him in that I relate the speech to the past of the text, rather than to the character's hypothetical past.

CHAPTER SEVEN

1 In 'The Great Unwritten Story: Mothers and Daughters in Shakespeare,' *The Lost Tradition: Mothers and Daughters in Literature*, ed Cathy N. Davidson and E.M. Broner (New York: Ungar, 1980), 44–53, Myra Glazer Schotz comments on the relation of Lear's sexuality to the late romances, particularly *Pericles*.

2 Ella Freeman Sharpe in 'From *King Lear* to *The Tempest*,' *Collected Papers on Psycho-Analysis* ed Marjorie Brierley (New York: Brunner/Mazel, 1978), 214–

41, cleverly observes that the old protagonists here and in *The Tempest* suggest old, that is, infantile, problems (218).

3 *King Lear* can be seen as Shakespeare's comment on the inevitability of a king's mistaking his 'body natural' for the 'king's body politic,' as defined by Ernst H. Kantorowicz in *The King's Two Bodies* (Princeton: Princeton University Press, 1957). This is a disturbing thought if one also believes that only an ideal kingship can prevent man from being monstrous.

4 The symbolic importance of the vignette becomes clearer in view of the relative improbability of Goneril's suicide. Her last claim that 'the laws are mine, not thine: / Who can arraign me for't?' (v.iii.157–8) is true, for she is England's monarch, and monarchs, in and out of Shakespeare's plays, have gotten away with worse crimes than those she committed. Her exit line, 'Ask me not what I know' (v.iii.159), like Iago's 'demand me nothing,' seems intended to extend the aura of the diabolical.

5 It is difficult to know the conscious level of the play here. On the one hand Edgar's morality is consonant with the overarching ideology found throughout the plays, Lear chooses him as his 'philosopher' in a way that contributes to the reason-in-madness motif, and Edgar becomes a literal knight in shining armour, all of which suggest that Shakespeare intends him as a morally reliable commentator. On the other hand, one wonders if the clear echoes of Goneril's language in Edgar's can have been unintentional, and his harsh moral judgment ignores Gloucester's unselfish service of Lear. It is possible that Shakespeare intended Edgar as an exemplar of the sadistic uses to which moral certitude can be put. However, I believe that Shakespeare conceived Edgar as a parallel to Cordelia, but he gave him so much stage time that his psychological intuition had opportunity to overpower the moral intention.

6 In 'King Lear: The Lear Family Romance,' *Centennial Review* 23 (1979) 348–76, Harry Berger Jr in a cogent analysis sees Lear's need of dominance arising from feelings of weariness and unworthiness. His 'darker purpose' is by punishing himself to find release from the narrow bounds of his world, but by victimizing himself he avoids knowing his own cruelty to others (319). His sense of unworthiness makes him flee Cordelia, while he wants her to hunt him down (367).

7 Stanley Cavell in 'The Avoidance of Love: A Reading of *King Lear*,' *Must We Mean What We Say?* (New York: Scribner, 1969) suggests that Lear denies Cordelia her marriage dowry in the hope of keeping her for himself (295). In 'Interpreting Posthumus' Dream from Above and Below: Families, Psychoanalysts and Literary Critics,' *Representing Shakespeare*, ed Murray M. Schwartz and Coppélia Kahn (Baltimore: Johns Hopkins University Press, 1981), 203–16, Meredith Skura relates Lear to other fathers who, in their attempts to delay their daughters' weddings, betray incestuous longings (204–5).

8 *King Lear*, 1.i.97–103n

9 In 'The Family in Shakespeare's Development: Tragedy and Sacredness,' *Representing Shakespeare*, 188–202, Barber explains the mythological force of these maternal images by the disappearance from the culture of the Holy Family, which could have helped to deal ritually with psychic residues of infantile ambivalence (198).

10 Freud in 'The Theme of the Three Caskets,' *Collected Papers*, vol IV compares Cordelia to Portia and develops the association of Cordelia to death. He does not consider the death motif in context with the erotic dimensions of the play.

11 In 'In Defense of Goneril and Regan,' *American Imago* 27 (1970) 227–44, Stephen Reid sees the two sisters as free to act out with Edmund their infantile rivalry for their father's love only after they have expressed their justified hatred of Cordelia (238). Judith Cook in *Women in Shakespeare* (London: Harrap, 1980) also finds naturalistic sources for the evil sisters' monstrosity (143), but believes Shakespeare's 'radiant' women testify to his undying love of women (144).

12 Alan B. Rothenberg in 'Infantile Fantasies in Shakespearean Metaphor: II. Scopophilia and Fears of Ocular Rape and Castration,' *The Psychoanalytic Review* 60 (1973–4) 533–56, discusses Shakespeare's portrayal of 'scopophilia' or 'sadism of the eyes,' for which blinding is a symbolic castration (540). The basilisk image, containing both the punitive eye of the Oedipal father and that of the terrible pre-Oedipal mother, expresses these fears (550).

13 In 'Madness in Euripides, Shakespeare and Kafka,' *The Psychoanalytic Review* 65 (1978) 253–79, Ruth Perry concurs with Berger in seeing Lear, like Hamlet, obsessively examining himself in order to escape suffering, but feeling isolated instead (278).

14 Susan Handelman in '*Timon of Athens*: The Rage of Disillusion,' *American Imago* 36 (Spring 1979) 45–68, sees the centaur image as expressing Lear's view that women who give birth are unclean (62).

15 Mark Kanzer in 'Imagery in *King Lear*,' *The Design Within*, ed Melvin D. Faber (New York: Science House, 1970) 221–31, sees beneath the violence of Lear's and Gloucester's rebirths the anguish of a primal scene fantasy (229). He also comments that Edgar replaces the Oedipal father in being the agent of renewed order and law.

16 Berger, noting that Cordelia defines herself in relation to her sisters, argues that by disclaiming any cause against Lear, she ignores her own feelings, which emerge in her vindictive language (372). He ignores, however, the way the play idealizes her.

17 In *Erotic Spirituality: The Integrative Tradition from Leone Ebreo to John Donne* (University: University of Alabama Press, 1980) T. Antony Perry gives a good account of the neo-Platonic tradition that shapes Cordelia's character (99).

18 In *Shakespeare's Development and the Problem Comedies* (Berkeley: University

of California Press, 1981) Richard Wheeler argues that Lear's longing for infantile merger destroys Cordelia in order to recreate her in images of his own need (316).

19 *King Lear*, v.iii.21n

20 Though there is no such woman in Shakespeare's plays, a moment of defiance may have made *Antony and Cleopatra* possible. Manipulative power defines Volumnia, while the idealized virgin, as the redeeming aspect of nature, becomes Miranda, and the sexuality is transformed into the aura of magic.

21 Patrick Colm Hogan in '*King Lear*: Splitting and Its Epistemic Agon,' *American Imago* 36 (1979) 32–44, observing that the splitting of mother and father images is an infantile strategy (43), thinks Lear has purged his images of women and overcome the impulse to split figures.

22 The opposition suggested here between manliness and sexuality will appear full-blown in *Antony and Cleopatra*, to replace the equation between manliness and ruthlessness seen here and in *Macbeth*.

23 Most critics and directors interpret the button to be Lear's, but Lear wants Cordelia's button undone while seeking a sign of her living breath, which he thinks he sees when it is undone.

CHAPTER EIGHT

1 In 'The War in *Antony and Cleopatra*,' *The Design Within*, ed Melvin D. Faber (New York: Science House, 1970) 281–7, Cynthia Kolb Whitney argues that the war between Egypt and Rome represents an internal war between Antony's manhood and sexuality. She sees Cleopatra as a mother-figure, and Caesar as a father, who does not want Antony to have the 'mother-goddess, Cleopatra' (284). Her view of Antony as a kind of Everyman seeking the lost maternal haven of infancy coincides with that of Norman Holland, who in *Psychoanalysis and Shakespeare* (New York: McGraw-Hill, 1964) argues that Antony is trying to 'reach back toward an infant's total union with his nurturing mother' (155). Marjorie Garber in *Coming of Age in Shakespeare* (London: Methuen, 1981) views *Antony and Cleopatra* as Shakespeare's most Oedipal play (207), and emphasizes Octavius' journey to manhood as he replaces Antony. One could see the play that way if one took him as the protagonist.

2 The description of Cleopatra's barge differs from Plutarch's primarily in the magical aura that emanates from Cleopatra.

3 In 'The Mother of the World: A Psychoanalytic Interpretation of Shakespeare's *Antony and Cleopatra*,' *English Literary Renaissance* 7 (1977) 324–57, Constance Brown Kuriyama says Cleopatra is both the idealized and the betraying mother (338). The *liebstod* fantasy simultaneously gratifies and punishes infan-

tile wishes (350). I do not agree that Egyptian love is more or less infantile than the Roman self-assertion, though each may be childlike in the absence of the other. In 'The Painted Breast: A Psychological Study of Melville's *Pierre*,' *The Psychoanalytic Review* 66 (1979) 519–51, Melvin D. Faber falls into Antony's or Shakespeare's trap in seeing Cleopatra as a sphinx-like maternal figure who expresses the 'riddle of life' (519). Marilyn French in *Shakespeare's Division of Experience* (New York, Summit, 1981) notes Cleopatra's uniqueness as Shakespeare's only female incarnation of the 'outlaw principle' that affirms sexuality and is treated sympathetically (335).

4 What Coppélia Kahn says of Leontes in *Man's Estate* (Berkeley: University of California Press, 1981) is more true of Antony – that woman 'is at once the seal of his male identity and the greatest obstacle to it' (225). Madelon Gohlke in ' "I Wooed Thee with My Sword," ' in *The Woman's Part*, ed Carolyn R. Lenz, Gayle Green, and Carol Thomas Neely (Urbana: University of Illinois Press, 1980), 1–16, argues that in this play as in *Romeo and Juliet* love makes men effeminate. However, I think that is more true of Troilus or Coriolanus that it is of Romeo or Antony.

5 In several ways Antony's image of himself suggests that just below the surface there are feelings similar to those expressed in *King Lear*. The empty orbs in Antony's heaven suggest those in Gloucester's blinded face, the 'abysm of hell' into which his stars have fallen suggests the images of hell that Lear uses to describe women's genitals. That Lear's images are relevant to this play seems likely because Antony associates with Cleopatra's corruption his own unjustified violence towards the messenger, Thidias, and towards the bondslave whom he invites Caesar to torture. At the turning point of the relatively daylight play, images suggestive of the nightmarish worlds of Lear and of Macbeth appear in the interstices of consciousness. The grim resonance of Antony's 'I am satisfied' after Cleopatra's lugubrious speech suggests a figure skirting the edge of darker territories.

6 In *The Common Liar: An Essay on* Antony and Cleopatra (New Haven: Yale University Press, 1973) Janet Adelman thinks that Antony's transformation of his fear of dissolution into a desire for it resolves the tension that we all experience in loving (160).

7 Roger Stilling in *Love and Death in Renaissance Tragedy* (Baton Rouge: University of Louisiana Press, 1976) sees Antony as vacillating between a romantic and an anti-romantic conception of love (278), and finally embracing a romantic conception that courts death rather than being subverted by it. Richard Wheeler in *Shakespeare's Development and the Problem Comedies* (Urbana: University of Illinois Press, 1981) sees Antony 'reborn through the fertile womb of [Cleopatra's] imagination' (202). Views closer to mine are those of Norman Rabkin in

Shakespeare and the Common Understanding (New York: Free Press, 1967) and Matthew N. Proser in *The Heroic Image in Five Shakespearean Tragedies* (Princeton: Princeton University Press, 1965). Rabkin sees these protagonists, like Romeo and Juliet, linking love to the death-wish. Proser argues that 'the grave's worm and the worm as phallus' fuse symbolically in a kind of sexual act (238), and that in the final scene Cleopatra does not transcend but rather asserts the amoral passion that defined her all along.

8 In 'Egyptian Queens and Male Reviewers: Sexist Attitudes in *Antony and Cleopatra* Criticism,' *Shakespeare Quarterly* 28 (1977) 297–316, Linda Fitz in a refreshing approach sees Cleopatra as similar to male protagonists in her struggle against her theatricality rather than as essentially enigmatic (314).

9 Leslie Fiedler in *The Stranger in Shakespeare* (New York: Stein and Day, 1972) finds a contradiction in Cleopatra's both renouncing the feminine principle by associating herself with 'air and fire' and defining herself as wife, and then as mother (76).

10 These images of eating monstrously or of being eaten are similar to those in *King Lear*, but taken in conjunction with Cleopatra's 'baby,' and with all the images of food previously discussed, they are softened and reduced to jesting. David Willbern in 'Rape and Revenge in *Titus Andronicus*,' *English Literary Renaissance* 8 (Spring 1978) 159–82, sees in the horrible dinner in *Titus* the first expression of the deepest fear in Shakespeare's plays – not of castration, but of the pre-Oedipal devouring mother (171). He is right that fears from the oral level pervade the plays, but characteristically Shakespeare's protagonists bring these fears to Oedipal situations. The fusion of the two vastly magnifies the horror of both.

11 In 'Shakespeare through Contemporary Psychoanalysis,' *Representing Shakespeare* (Baltimore: Johns Hopkins University Press, 1980), 21–32, Murray M. Schwartz ignores the slime into which the lovers disintegrate, arguing that this play 'transcend[s] the dilemma of the other tragedies' because opposites interpenetrate (30). Charles R. Lyons in *Shakespeare and the Ambiguity of Love's Triumph* (The Hague: Mouton, 1971) sees this play, like the problem plays, as displaying a 'surfeited disgust at sexuality' despite the creative aspects of sexuality shown in the lovers' feeling that their commitment is infinite (162).

12 In 'New Heaven, New Earth: The Escape from Mutability in *Antony and Cleopatra*,' *Shakespeare Quarterly* 33 (Autumn 1982) 328–35, William D. Wolf sees the worm replacing the sword as the symbol of sexual pleasure (335).

13 In '*Coriolanus*: The Anxious Bridegroom,' *American Imago* 25 (1968) 224–41, Emmett Wilson Jr argues that Coriolanus, having joined Aufidius in hatred of his mother, is content to die at the hands of the father (240). Janet Adelman in

' "Anger's My Meat": Feeding, Dependency, and Aggression in *Coriolanus*,' *Representing Shakespeare*, 129–49, argues that Coriolanus' dependency, which he despises, forces him to repress his wish to dominate his mother (143).

14 In a complementary insight into the relation of the two plays, Wheeler sees *Antony and Cleopatra* as the culmination of the plays that centre on the problem of trust and merger. In contrast he sees *Coriolanus* as being the culmination of those that are concerned primarily with the problems of autonomy and isolation (210–11).

CHAPTER NINE

1 Though he reaches a different conclusion, for a discussion of the problems of authorship see F.D. Hoeniger's introduction to the Arden edition of *Pericles* (London: Methuen, 1963), lii–lxiii.

2 Leslie Fiedler in *The Stranger in Shakespeare* (New York: Stein and Day, 1972) states that the riddle represents the incest motif, which, he says, haunts Shakespeare from *1 Henry IV* to *King Lear* (213). Richard P. Wheeler in *Shakespeare's Development and the Problem Comedies* (Urbana: University of Illinois Press, 1981) relates the incestuous paternal love of Antiochus for his daughter to the king in *All's Well That Ends Well*, and in ' "Thou that beget'st him that did thee beget": Transformation in *Pericles* and *The Winter's Tale*,' *Shakespeare Studies* 22 (1969) 59–68, C.L. Barber sees *Pericles* resolving the sexual problems that were phrased in *King Lear* (63). In 'Fathers and Daughters in Shakespeare's Romances,' *Shakespeare's Romances Reconsidered*, ed Carol McGuinnis Kay and Henry E. Jacobs (Lincoln: University of Nebraska Press, 1978), 77–90, Cyrus Hoy agrees that the romances overcome the 'dark possibility' contained in *King Lear* (77), and in 'Death, Incest, and the Triple Bond in the Later Plays of Shakespeare,' *American Imago* 31 (1974) 109–58, R.E. Gajdusek argues that all the last plays manifest incestuous guilt through the pall of death that hangs over their protagonists. Through ritual and art they rescue masculine kingship 'from the womb of the Mother goddess' (135).

3 Marilyn French in *Shakespeare's Division of Experience* (New York: Summit, 1981) argues that Pericles learns to love by excluding sexual desire (337). In 'The Great Unwritten Story: Mothers and Daughters in Shakespeare,' *The Lost Tradition: Mothers and Daughters in Literature*, ed Cathy N. Davidson and E.M. Broner (New York: Ungar, 1980), 44–53, Myra Glazer Schotz says Marina's sexlessness undermines the fertility promised by the final reunion.

4 Charles Frey has most recently discussed the psychomachia of the late romances in ' "O Sacred, Shadowy, Cold and Constant Queen": Shakespeare's Imperiled

and Chastening Daughters of Romance,' *The Woman's Part,* ed Carolyn R. Lenz, Gayle Greene, and Carol Thomas Neely (Urbana: University of Illinois Press, 1980), 295–313.

5 In 'Cloten, Autolycus, and Caliban: Bearers of Parodic Burdens,' *Shakespeare's Romances Reconsidered,* 91–103, Joan Hartwig sees Cloten, Autolycus, and Caliban, all associated with music and with bad smells, as parodic of their respective protagonists. She puts the matter nicely in saying that Posthumus, Leontes, and Prospero 'cannot afford to bear the burden, but ... need a burden to complete their song' (103). In 'Between Fantasy and Imagination: A Psychological Exploration of *Cymbeline,' Psychoanalysis and Literary Process,* ed Frederick Crews (Cambridge: Winthrop, 1970), 219–83, Murray M. Schwartz argues that Cloten's sexual drives must be eliminated before the other figures can come together (226).

6 Schwartz also emphasizes the Queen's importance as a split half of the mother image, the other half represented in Imogen (248).

7 Meredith Skura in 'Interpreting Posthumus' Dream from Above and Below: Families, Psychoanalysts and Literary Critics,' *Representing Shakespeare,* ed Murray M. Schwartz and Coppélia Kahn (Baltimore: Johns Hopkins University Press, 1980), 203–16, discusses the 'family matrix that underlies all experience' (207), and observes that Posthumus cannot be a husband until he defines himself as a son.

8 There are various ways in which critics over time have seen the romances as restorative, from G. Wilson Knight, who in *The Shakespearean Tempest* (London: Methuen, 1953) sees these plays resolving the polarity between discord and harmony in a way that transcends death (292), to Murray M. Schwartz, who in 'Shakespeare through Contemporary Psychoanalysis,' *Representing Shakespeare,* 21–32, sees the romances as showing restored trust in feminine capacity that thereby makes possible both masculine identity and cultural community. These positive views of the plays correctly express aspects of Shakespeare's intention, but they do not recognize the strained ideology that rigidifies rather than resolves the conflicts with which the tragedies struggle. Some critics who turn over the coin are Charles R. Lyons, Walter F. Eggers, and Norman Rabkin. In *Shakespeare and the Ambiguity of Love's Triumph* (The Hague: Mouton, 1971) Lyons states that in the late plays 'love's triumph becomes the reality,' whereas in the problem plays it is a dream (16). Walter F. Eggers in 'Bring Forth a Wonder,' *Texas Studies in Language and Literature* 21 (1979) 455–71 argues that the romances make the audience aware of their own capacity for wonder (474). In *Shakespeare and the Common Understanding* (New York: Free Press, 1967) Rabkin argues that the last plays, by creating illusions in a way that calls attention to and questions their own artifice, make a redemptive vision possible

(211). The view closest to mine is that of Janette Dillon, who in *Shakespeare and the Solitary Man* (London: Macmillan, 1981), finds in the late comedies 'a natural solitude in man acting as a barrier to inhibit full consummation of the social vision' (164–5). The characters, in reaching out, confirm their solitude in a way that denies the social vision and renders their reconciliations stillborn.

CHAPTER TEN

1 Coppélia Kahn in 'The Providential Tempest and the Shakespearean Family,' *Representing Shakespeare*, ed Murray M. Schwartz and Coppélia Kahn (Baltimore: Johns Hopkins University Press, 1981), 217–63, says rightly that the homosexuality implied between Leontes and Polixenes expresses Leontes' unwillingness to trust his manhood to women and sexuality, and accounts for his jealousy (233).
2 Stephen Reid in 'The Winter's Tale,' *American Imago* 27 (1970) 262–77, sees homosexual attachment and Oedipal guilt underlying Leontes' jealousy, the guilt overlying the homosexuality and thereby lending to it the aura of innocence (277).
3 In a related comment Murray M. Schwartz in 'The Winter's Tale: Loss and Transformation,' *American Imago* 32 (1975) 145–99, states that Shakespeare here makes psychic reality a dramatic fact (156).
4 In 'Leontes' Jealousy in *The Winter's Tale*,' *American Imago* 30 (1973) 250–73, Murray M. Schwartz sees the spider expressing Leontes' primary fear of maternal engulfment. One gets a more precise sense of the emotions involved, however, by surveying earlier contexts in which the spider appears. In *2 Henry VI* York, who will become Richard III, says 'My brain more busy than the laboring spider / Weaves tedious snares to trap mine enemies' (III.i.339–40). That first image resembles the last one in *Henry VIII*, when Wolsey is described as attaining his success by creating deceiving illusions'spider-like, / Out of his self-drawing web' (I.i.62–3). In both of these images the spider suggests snares of deceit, drawn from the inward being of one who by means of these snares appears virtuous to others. The Duke in *Measure for Measure* makes Angelo's plot to seduce Isabella an example of how one may use idle spiders' strings to draw others into evil and distort their views of reality.

Women's duplicity is added to these images of male deceit by the spider image in *The Merchant of Venice*; Bassanio says of Portia's portrait that 'the painter plays the spider, and hath woven / A golden mesh to entrap the hearts of men' (III.ii.122–4). Though Portia overtly functions positively, the description of woman's beauty as that which entraps man, turning him into a gnat, suggests the darker ranges that also subtly attach to her character as she weaves a web around Shylock. That female association with the spider's power to entrap and devour is also connected with cruelty, when the Bastard in *King John* says that should Hubert consent to the child's murder in the ensuing despair, 'the smallest thread / That ever spider twisted from her womb / Will serve to strangle thee' (IV.iii.126–9). Women's sexual and generative powers here become the spiderlike snares of deceit that, like Cleopatra's, are both drawn from and are designed to draw men back into the horrible womb that creates them. *A Midsummer Night's Dream* links the spider to creeping things that destroy the beauty of Titania's bower, and *Richard II* associates spiders with toads and with poison, wishing his enemies inflicted with 'spiders that suck up thy venom, / And heavy-gaited toads, lie in their way' (III.ii.14–15).

The association of spiders with other obnoxious insects, as well as with poison, pervades *Richard III*. Anne wishes her husband's murderer more wretched things than she can wish to 'adders, spiders, toads, / Or any creeping venom'd thing that lives!' (I.ii.19–20), and the image acquires more force when Margaret, calling Richard a 'poisonous bunchbacked toad,' asks Elizabeth why 'strew'st thou sugar on that bottled spider? / Whose deadly web ensnareth thee about?'(I.iii.246,242–3). These images are used specifically in connection with Richard's sexual seduction of women into embracing his spider self in order to get revenge for his misshapen body by making them love him. That combination of images to describe a foul sexuality also appears in *Cymbeline* when Guiderius tells Cloten that 'Toad, or Adder, Spider' (IV.ii.90) are less disgusting names than his own. These images bring the spider into the range of Othello's foul cistern in which toads 'knot and gender,' and also suggest the various disgusting toads, blindworms, snakes, and other horrors with which the witches fill their cauldron to entrap Macbeth. They also recall the poisonous asp from Nilus' slime that is both Cleopatra's power to poison Antony's hours, and the baby that lulls her asleep.

When all these associations are taken into account the spider in Leontes' cup can be seen to embody Leontes' fear of woman's sexual charms, which will expose and punish his foul sexuality by reducing him to an insect, and will by devouring him incorporate him into her interior foulness.

5 Roger Stilling in *Love and Death in Renaissance Tragedy* (Baton Rouge: University of Louisiana Press, 1976) sees Leontes re-enacting the death of love occasioned by the misogyny of Hamlet and of Othello, but redeemed by Perdita and Florizel, who are reborn versions of Romeo and Juliet. He argues that in the earlier works the romantic view, and in the later works the anti-romantic view, lead to death.

6 Schwartz, in '*The Winter's Tale*: Loss and Transformation,' says that the play is about fear, represented by the bear (156), and desire for maternal power (158).

7 R.E. Gajdusek in 'Death, Incest, and the Triple Bond in the Later Plays of Shakespeare,' *American Imago*, 31 (1974) 109–58, argues that Paulina as a hag-cum-magician uses rites of renewal and restoration to save Leontes from the living death of incestuous desires (152). In ' "O My Most Sacred Lady": Female Metaphor in *The Winter's Tale*,' *English Literary Renaissance* 5 (1975) 375–95, Patricia Southard Gourlay says that Paulina functions as a female magus, anticipating Prospero in reawakening a lost ideal (394).

8 Charles Frey in *Shakespeare's Vast Romance: A Study of* The Winter's Tale (Columbia: University of Missouri Press, 1980) also sees Leontes as a contracted rendering of the issues involved in Hamlet's and Lear's dark vision of sexuality (79).

9 This argument for the incestuous implication of the reunion scene harmonizes with the play's source, Robert Greene's *Pandosto*, in which the father kills himself after falling in love with his unrecognized daughter. It may have been that the incest motif in the source generates the play, but is itself replaced by the final uneasy merger of naturalistic and magical plotting, and by the penumbra of transcendent value that surrounds Perdita and Hermione.

10 In '*The Winter's Tale, Othello* and *Troilus and Cressida*: Narcissism and Sexual Betrayal,' *American Imago* 36 (Spring 1979) 80–93, Joan M. Byles finds Leontes too emotionally thin to be dramatically related to the miraculous restoration (92).

CHAPTER ELEVEN

1 Many people have seen *The Tempest* as one or another kind of psychomachia. For example, see James E. Phillips, '*The Tempest* and the Renaissance Idea of Man,' *Shakespeare Quarterly* 15 (1964) 147–59, and Frank Davidson, '*The Tempest*: An Interpretation,' *Journal of English and Germanic Philology* 62 (1963) 307–8. In *Dream in Shakespeare: From Metaphor to Metamorphosis* (New Haven: Yale University Press, 1974) Marjorie Garber sees the play as a dream that Shakespeare's 'greatest poet and stage-manager' directs and stage-manages (188). Hers is an odd view, for it would seem that Prospero must be awake to direct his own dream, since she does not consider him as a dream figure.

2 In 'Shakespeare's Miraculous Harp: A Reading of Shakespeare's *Tempest*,' *Shakespeare Studies* 5 (1970) 253–83, Harry Berger Jr sees the island as a play area, analogous to Winnicott's play space, in which Prospero acquires control over what was done to him.

3 Following René Girard's claim that fratricidal myths reaffirm binary social order, Joel Fineman states in 'Fratricide and Cuckoldry: Shakespeare and His Sense of Difference,' *The Psychoanalytic Review* 64 (1978) 409–53, that the established

difference between victor and vanquished wards off the chaos of undifferentiation.

4 David Sundelson in 'So Rare a Wonder'd Father: Prospero's Tempest,' *Representing Shakespeare*, ed Murray M. Schwartz and Coppélia Kahn 33–53, says these images represent Prospero's fear of impotence, from which he is reborn when he is banished from Milan (35).

5 Often in Shakespeare's plays authority conflict is articulated in terms of younger and older brothers, probably because under the law of primogeniture rivalry among brothers reflects and conceals father-son rivalry, an issue discussed by Peter B. Erickson in 'Sexual Politics and the Social Structure in *As You Like It*,' *Massachusetts Review* 23 (Spring 1982) 65–83. The unequal power relations between younger and older brothers conflicts with an ideology of brotherly love that could be maintained only insofar as the notion of a divinely sanctioned and loving hierarchy, in family as well as in the state, was engraved in the heart. *King Lear* particularly shows how such an ideal renders horrendous any minor failing.

6 Linda Bamber in *Comic Women, Tragic Men: A Study of Gender and Genre in Shakespeare* (Stanford: Stanford University Press, 1982) sees Prospero's lack of a wife as the central fact of the play, and relates his wifelessness to his total control; however, she finds the play 'redeemed by its freedom from desire' (178). In 'Shakespeare's *Tempest*,' *American Imago* 39 (Fall 1982) 219–37, Jerry L. McGuire sees Shakespeare dramatizing the process by which in a patriarchal society Prospero replaces Miranda's pre-Oedipal nurturing silence with masculine rhetoric in a necessary but regrettable assertion of authority (237).

7 Bethany Strong Sinnott in 'The Father-Daughter Theme in Shakespeare's Plays,' Diss, University of North Carolina 1972, and Carol Lynn Weisz in 'Shakespeare: Growth or Deterioration,' Diss, Purdue University, 1977, trace the evolution of father-daughter relations to show Shakespeare resolving in the late romances the problems that earlier beset him. However, in 'Shakespeare's *Tempest*: A Psychological Analysis,' *The Design Within*, ed Melvin D. Faber (New York, Science House, 1970) 502–19, K.M. Abenheimer observes that Prospero cannot tolerate women with the aura of motherhood, and Coppélia Kahn in *Man's Estate* (Berkeley: University of California Press, 1980) similarly observes that Prospero's omnipotence depends on suppressing Miranda's sexuality (222).

8 Ella Freeman Sharpe in 'From *King Lear* to *The Tempest*,' *Collected Papers on Psycho-Analysis*, ed Marjorie Brierley (New York: Brunner/Mazel, 1978), 214–41, says that the late play shows variations of the conflicts in the earlier one, rather than 'further psychical evolution' (215).

9 Sundelson notes the parallels between Ferdinand and Caliban, saying that Prospero reduces his 'sexual rival to a child and political heir to a servant' (47).

10 This interpretation of Ariel rests largely on circumstantial rather than on direct verbal evidence, but it gains support from studies of mythology. Norman O. Brown, in his study of Hermes in *Hermes The Thief* (New York: Vintage, 1947) links the various attributes of Hermes – thief, trickster, messenger of the gods, protector of trade, and representative of skills – to herms, ithyphallic carvings topped with a representation of the god's head, which were placed at roadsides and entrances to public and private dwellings. He argues that these carvings or stone piles figured not fertility but the self-rising nature of the phallus, in both its potency and its unreliability, and were represented by and invoked through Hermes' magical protective powers. The various attributes of the phallus, he argues, were expressed in Hermes the trickster, the magician, and the craftsman. In this context Ariel, who is a messenger like Hermes, would represent Prospero's magical powers and their phallic source.

Paul Radin in *The Trickster* (London: Routledge and Kegan Paul, 1969) recounts and discusses the Winnebago Trickster Cycle in connection with other North American Indian trickster tales. Whether hare or spider, the trickster figure in these tales often carries his penis in a box or wrapped around himself. When sent on errands it is sometimes obedient, but sometimes makes all kinds of trouble. In 'The Trickster in Relation to Greek Mythology,' tr R.F.C. Hull, and included in *The Trickster*, Karl Kerenyi, commenting on Radin's material, hypothesizes that the trickster can be represented by his phallus. Though Kerenyi does not, like Brown, regard Hermes or other trickster gods as magical, the trickster's phallus shares with its owner the attributes of skill, sprightliness, and deceptiveness.

This relation of the trickster to his phallus still parallels Prospero's relation to Ariel, or Oberon's to Puck, though it does not account for Ariel's being the agent specifically of Prospero's magic. To see Prospero in this context is to think of him as a kind of trickster god overlain by a strenuous morality, who, unlike Oberon, hides or has lost awareness of the phallic nature of his little messenger. These mythic parallels suggest that Prospero as dreamer draws upon a deep psychological connection.

An interestingly different perspective is offered by E.I. Berry in 'Prosper's Brave Spirit,' *Studies in Philology* 76 (January 1979) 36–48, who sees Ariel as partaking in the ambiguity of the Renaissance notion of 'spirit,' based on Peter Charron's *Of Wisedome* (tr Samson Lennard, 1607–8, facsimile reprint, Amsterdam, 1971) in which the word can partake of the demonic, the elemental, the psychic, or the divine. He relates Prospero's anxiety to control Ariel to his concern with self-control (38).

11 In 'Fantasy of the Family Romance: Shakespeare's *The Tempest*,' *The Unspoken Motive: A Guide to Psychoanalytic Literary Criticism* (New York: Free Press,

1973), 88–104, Morton Kaplan and Robert Kloss compare the play to the Beauty and the Beast fairy-tale motif, and see the play's power residing in its primitive motivations.

12 Leslie Fiedler in *The Stranger in Shakespeare* (New York: Stein and Day, 1972) observes that Prospero's 'residual lust' (250) breaks the masque's spell, and sees this interruption as the first stage of Prospero's learning that Caliban is himself (243). He also sees Caliban as a transformation of Cloten (243), and observes the identity between Ferdinand and Caliban (245). In 'Still Harping on My Daughter,' *English Miscellany*, ed Mario Praz (Rome, 1960), 50–74, Barbara Melchior contrasts Prospero's transcendence of incestuous desires to Lear's failure (73) and sees Caliban as expressive of Prospero's beastly impulses, which interrupt the wedding masque.

13 There is no explanation why Alonso, like a perverse Brabantio, gives his daughter against her will to a Tunisian prince. However, Claribel's story is associated with that of Dido and Aeneas, the mockery of which may suggest Prospero's rejection of passionate or romantic death-bound love.

14 Garber sees in the epilogue the 'vital transforming power' (214) of art and dream, but forgets that all transformations are not desirable, and that some dreams, like Hamlet's, can be bad. Shakespeare, I think, wanted to agree with Garber, but couldn't trust what his words might do if he wrote any more plays.

CHAPTER TWELVE

1 Ernst H. Kantorowicz, *The King's Two Bodies* (Princeton: Princeton University Press, 1957). See note 3 to my chapter 7, p 243.

2 See particularly Irving Goffman, *The Presentation of Self in Everyday Life* (Garden City, NY: Doubleday, 1959) and *Asylums: Essays on the Social Situation of Mental Patients and Other Inmates* (Garden City, NY: Anchor Books, 1961).

3 The issues touched upon here are farther-reaching than can be appropriately explored in this context. Some studies that bear upon them are Julia Briggs, *This Stage Play World: English Literature and Its Background, 1580–1625* (Oxford: Oxford University Press, 1983); Jonathan Goldberg, *James I and the Politics of Literature: Jonson, Shakespeare, Donne, and Their Contemporaries* (Baltimore: Johns Hopkins University Press, 1983), and his 'The Poet's Authority: Spenser, Jonson and James VI and I,' in *The Power of Forms in the English Renaissance,'* ed Stephen Greenblatt (Norman, Oklahoma: Pilgrim Books, 1982), 81–99; in the same volume, Stephen Orgel, 'Familiar Greatness,' 41–8; Jonathan Dollimore, *Radical Tragedy: Religion, Ideology and Power in the Drama of Shakespeare and His Contemporaries* (Brighton: Harvester Press, 1984); and Stephen Green-

blatt, *Renaissance Self-Fashioning: From More to Shakespeare* (Chicago: University of Chicago Press, 1980). Also pertinent are Stephen Orgel's *The Jonsonian Masque* (Cambridge: Harvard University Press, 1965), and Gerald Eades Bentley's *The Profession of Player in Shakespeare's Time, 1590–1642* (Princeton: Princeton University Press, 1984).

Index